D1456199

Praise for *Yanks in Blue Berets*

"The US armed forces are reluctant players in United Nations operations but nonetheless have a long history of supporting these missions both directly and indirectly. They have ranged from strictly supporting roles in the Congo to robust operations in Haiti, Somalia, and Bosnia. We do too little to prepare for these missions and then take little notice of our performance. *Yanks in Blue Berets: American UN Peacekeepers in the Middle East* illuminates the vital role Americans played in working to keep the peace in Lebanon during the 1980s. Lingamfelter examines peace missions in Lebanon through the lens of his own service and considers them in the context of what he learned and what US armed forces can and should learn from these complex operations. *Yanks in Blue Berets* is a story well told of soldiers, sailors, marines, and airmen succeeding in difficult operations and a worthy addition to the historiography of peace operations generally."   —Col. Gregory Fontenot, US Army (Ret.)

"Lingamfelter has written a brilliant book that is a critique of a UN mission largely doomed to failure because of its very nature and inherent constraints. It is also a memoir of his journey of professional development in trying circumstances. Few Americans even know that these peacekeeping missions are taking place. These young American warfighters put aside their weapons in the honorable pursuit of peace in a region where it is virtually unknown. As Lingamfelter recalls, it was dangerous: 'Armed elements may have made our mandate difficult to fulfill, but they never dampened our desire to fulfill it.' This is the soul of this book: committed military officers living the essence of the old African saying 'If you think you are too small to make a difference then you haven't spent the night with a mosquito.' A must for the reading lists of every civilian and military policymaker."
          —David E. Johnson, principal researcher at the RAND Corporation
                    and senior fellow at the Modern War Institute at West Point

"As a career special forces officer, I wish I had been able to read *Yanks in Blue Berets* early in my training. In thirty years in the Army, I was never exposed to the operations chronicled in this very important book in any appreciable detail. Not only is this an important perspective of history in the Middle East, but it also provides lessons in leadership, decision making, intelligence, cultural awareness, and so much more. The Army strives to operate with a 'mission command' philosophy. The peacekeepers in this book were living it, and today we can still learn so much from their experiences. Had a book and studies like this been available sooner for military leaders, how would the invasions of Afghanistan and Iraq have turned out? Yet it is not too late to learn from these experiences."

—Col. David Maxwell, US Army (Ret.), vice president of the Center for Asia Pacific Strategy

YANKS IN BLUE BERETS

AMERICAN WARRIORS

Throughout the nation's history, numerous men and women of all ranks and branches of the US military have served their country with honor and distinction. During times of war and peace, there are individuals whose exemplary achievements embody the highest standards of the US armed forces. The aim of the American Warriors series is to examine the unique historical contributions of these individuals, whose legacies serve as enduring examples for soldiers and citizens alike. The series will promote a deeper and more comprehensive understanding of the US armed forces.

SERIES EDITOR: Joseph Craig

An AUSA Book

L. Scott Lingamfelter

Yanks
in Blue
Berets

American UN
Peacekeepers
in the Middle East

UNIVERSITY PRESS OF KENTUCKY

Scholarly publisher for the Commonwealth,
serving Bellarmine University, Berea College, Centre
College of Kentucky, Eastern Kentucky University,
The Filson Historical Society, Georgetown College,
Kentucky Historical Society, Kentucky State University,
Morehead State University, Murray State University,
Northern Kentucky University, Spalding University,
Transylvania University, University of Kentucky,
University of Louisville, University of Pikeville,
and Western Kentucky University.
All rights reserved.

All maps by Dick Gilbreath.

Editorial and Sales Offices: The University Press of Kentucky
663 South Limestone Street, Lexington, Kentucky 40508-4008
www.kentuckypress.com

Cataloging-in-Publication data available from the Library of Congress

ISBN 978-0-8131-9763-0 (hardcover)
ISBN 978-0-8131-9765-4 (pdf)
ISBN 978-0-8131-9764-7 (epub)

This book is printed on acid-free paper meeting
the requirements of the American National Standard
for Permanence in Paper for Printed Library Materials.

Manufactured in the United States of America.

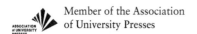

Member of the Association
of University Presses

Dedicated to the Memory and Honor of
All Former United Nations Peacekeeping Forces
1948–1988
Awarded the Nobel Peace Prize in 1988

And to
Isaac, Millie, Abigail, Arthur, and George

Blessed are the peacemakers,
for they shall be called sons of God.
—Matthew 5:9, NKJV

Contents

Abbreviations   ix

Introduction   1

1. Up to Jerusalem   9

2. A Legacy of Conflict   20

3. The UNTSO-US Culture   41

4. The Road to Damascus   59

5. The Bright and Dark Sides of Syria   76

6. UNTSO in the Central Levant   91

7. The Woes of UNIFIL   108

8. UNMO Duty in the "Wild West"   132

9. UNMO Teams in the "Wild West"   164

10. The Gathering Storm Erupts   188

11. Peace for No One   208

12. Sentinels of Peace   223

Epilogue: The Yanks Reflect   236

Notes   247

Bibliography   273

Index   279

Photographs follow page 140

Abbreviations

AMAL	Lebanese political party affiliated with the Shia sect often referred to as "Movement of the Dispossessed"
BG	Brigadier General
CPT	Captain
CDR	Commander
COL	Colonel
COMDT	Commandant
DFF	De Facto Forces–Also see SLA
DFLP	Democratic Front for the Liberation of Palestine
DUTCHBATT	Dutch Battalion
EIMAC	Egyptian-Israel Mixed Armistice Commission
FAO	Foreign Area Officer
FIJIBATT	Fijian Battalion
FRENCHBATT	French Battalion
GHANBATT	Ghanaian Battalion
HKJ-I-MAC	Hashemite Kingdom of Jordan-Israel Mixed Armistice Commission
IAF	Israeli Air Force
IDF	Israel Defense Forces
ILMAC	Israel-Lebanon Mixed Armistice Commission
IRISHBATT	Irish Battalion
ISMAC	Israel-Syria Mixed Armistice Commission
LNM	Lebanese National Movement
LT	Lieutenant
LTCDR	Lieutenant Commander
LTC	Lieutenant Colonel
LTG	Lieutenant General
MAC	Mixed Armistice Commission
MAJ	Major
MG	Major General

MNF I and II	Multinational Force I and II
MSG	Master Sergeant
NEPBATT	Nepalese Battalion
NIBATT	Nigerian Battalion
NORBATT	Norwegian Battalion
ODD	Observer Detachment Damascus
OGB	Observer Group Beirut
OGE	Observer Group Egypt
OGG	Observer Group Golan
OGJ	Observer Group Jerusalem
OGL	Observer Group Lebanon
OP	Observation Post
PFLP	Popular Front for the Liberation of Palestine
PLA	Palestine Liberation Army
PLO	Palestinian Liberation Organization
SENBATT	Senegalese Battalion
SGM	Sergeant Major
SLA	South Lebanese Army (also see DFF)
UNDOF	United Nations Disengagement Observer Force
UNEF I and II	United Nations Emergency Force I and II
UNIFIL	United Nations Interim Force in Lebanon
UNOGIL	United Nations Observation Group in Lebanon
UNLOB	United Nations Liaison Office Beirut
UNMO	United Nations Military Observer
UNOSOM	United Nations Operation in Somalia
UNTSO	United Nations Truce Supervision Organization
USA	United States Army
USAF	United States Air Force
USMC	United States Marine Corps
USN	United States Navy
USSR	Union of Soviet Socialist Republics

Introduction

This is a book about conflict and what people of goodwill tried to do to bring peace. It is not so much a history or academic study as it is my memories of being a combat soldier who—for a season—was dispatched by his nation to participate in a mission to encourage peace in one of the most troubled regions of the world, the Middle East. In 1981, as a young Army captain trained in the arts of combat, I was assigned to the United Nations Truce Supervision Organization (UNTSO) as a military observer along with 35 other American military officers. We observed and supervised peace arrangements between Israel and its Arab neighbors in Egypt, Jordan, Lebanon, and Syria. This region, known as the Levant, was a place where conflict was as ordinary as childbirth. It had been that way for millennia, reaching back to the Judean times of Abraham, Isaac, and Jacob in what some refer to as the "patriarchal age" and reaching forward to the emergence of Christianity and Islam.[1] There, in a region steeped in history and conflict, I would discover that peace was a difficult thing to keep, particularly when the parties to the conflict were bitterly divided over unresolved issues of land, life, and world views. My colleagues from the US Army, Air Force, Navy, Marine Corps, and I found ourselves wedged between contenders and their respective combatant allies who were intent on fighting until one side emerged as the victor and the other as the vanquished. We had been sent to encourage peace in a place where, in some cases, none was desired. How did this peacekeeping mission come about?

From the burnt and barren battlefields of World War I the Allied powers founded the League of Nations to deter and prevent wars after 1920. It was the first international effort to undertake such a noble endeavor. Yet it failed to prevent the onset of World War II and the carnage that followed. The harsh terms of peace that the Allies demanded of Germany set the conditions for Adolph Hitler's dictatorship over the German people. Hitler exploited the odium Germans felt toward the victorious Allied powers, stirring a cauldron of hatred, racism, and disapprobation. World

1

War II boiled over across the globe, resulting in 15 million military casualties and over 45 million civilian deaths, including 6 million innocent Jews brutally slaughtered by Nazi Germany.[2] Sadly, the Allies, having won World War I, lost the peace. The organization they founded, the League of Nations, designed to maintain peace, was hamstrung from its inception.

Following World War II, a more sagacious attempt was undertaken by the Allied powers beneath the foreboding clouds of the nuclear age. The United Nations (UN) was formed in 1945, composed initially of 51 nations with the lofty goal of preventing war.[3] As President Harry Truman put it—now etched in the walls of his presidential library in Independence, Missouri—"Our goal must be—not peace in our time—but peace for all time." That expression of hope, crafted by a man who had personally seen combat in World War I, undergirded the vision of the UN. By 2011, the UN had grown to 193 countries, yet even with a robust membership, the reality of war continued despite the idealism that gave birth to the organization. Nowhere is that disappointment more prevalent and profound than in the region we refer to as the Middle East. Indeed, that was the case for those of us who arrived in UNTSO in 1981. Violence was very much a part of daily life.

The American officers—Yanks in blue berets—who reported for peacekeeping duty with UNTSO 33 years after it was created came from all backgrounds across our four military services. We were for the most part trained combat officers, not peacekeepers. Some of us were also trained as Middle East specialists, having been sent to graduate school by our respective services to become foreign area officers who could render advice and analysis concerning the intricacies of a region like the Middle East. I was fortunate to have earned a master's degree in comparative governments of the Middle East and Soviet foreign policy at the University of Virginia the year prior to my assignment to UNTSO. But most among us were fundamentally combat officers, infantrymen, tankers, field artillerymen, aviators, and sailors. Those skills—especially our survival ones—would be essential, as we encountered much danger. We were young and inexperienced at making peace. Indeed, we were more suited to compelling it with the weapons of war. Those would not be the skills we would be called upon to exert. Our task would be to supervise while encouraging and promoting peace.

Beyond the danger of being unarmed in places where fighting was on-going, most of us had no earthly appreciation for what we would eventually face as peacekeepers. Nonetheless, we embraced the mission and soon would learn that it was one of the most challenging and dangerous things we would ever do aside from armed combat. Moreover, peace-keeping was fraught with frustration as we dealt with warring sides who thought the best way to attain peace was at the end of gun barrels, or with cannons, rocket launchers, land mines, demolition devices, or in the cockpits of combat aircraft. All of these threats were arrayed around us, particularly in southern Lebanon in 1981–1982, where many of us sensed a more immediate conflict over the horizon. We were in a tinderbox wait-ing for a struck match to be tossed in—maybe carelessly, maybe deliber-ately. Nonetheless, we hoped that somehow our efforts would forestall the day when the fires of war would ignite to inflict more death, carnage, and torment on the people of this troubled region.

We were certainly not without authority in pursuing our mission. The UN had given UNTSO officers the imprimatur of its dominion to supervise peace in the Middle East. But the UN's influence in many cases amounted to moral suasion. While the parties to the conflict were mindful of the UN's mandates in the region, for both its military observers in UNTSO and the UN's armed peacekeeping organization, the United Nations Interim Force in Lebanon (UNIFIL), composed of officers, noncommissioned officers, and enlisted soldiers, those formal UN arrangements were sometimes ignored or regarded contemptuously by the belligerents, especially in Lebanon. For-tunately, in 1981 there was peace—albeit a shaky one—along the cease-fire lines with Egypt, Jordan, and Syria. Peace there seemed to be taking hold. But much turmoil and violence troubled southern Lebanon, even as its civil-ians amazingly went about their daily tasks lodged firmly and precariously between contending armed forces who appropriated their fields, farms, and homes as a battleground.

When I arrived in the winter of 1981, the UN was accustomed to the challenges of peacekeeping. UN peacekeeping efforts began shortly after World War II with the best of intentions and represented the spirit of a postwar international community dedicated to avoiding war. So too, UNTSO had a long history in the Middle East when I joined its ranks. The organization's birth followed the creation of the modern state of Israel in 1948 amid significant opposition to Jewish statehood by neigh-boring Arab nations. In November 1947, the UN General Assembly for-mulated a plan to divide Palestine into Arab and Jewish entities. Both would be linked by an economic union, and neither would have a geo-graphical or military advantage over the other. The UN then created the UN Palestine Commission to implement the plan. However, the post–World War II immigration of Jewish refugees from Europe—where they had been brutally persecuted—alarmed Arabs. The influx of more than

100,000 Jewish migrants in 1948 alone threatened their cultural and political future.[4] Unfortunately, fighting—involving guerrilla warfare and terrorism—had already broken out between Arabs and Jews. A complex legacy of conflict would follow and define the region's temperament from that point forward.

That conflict began in earnest when the United Kingdom (UK) decided to abandon its administration of Palestine, a dominion pursuant to a post–World War I colonial arrangement. After World War II, the UK was economically depressed following years of global combat. As a result, the British were anxious to disconnect from the strife and unrest in Palestine and abruptly announced that their mandate would end in May 1948, dropping the issue squarely in the UN's lap. With the departure of the UK, the Jewish authorities promptly announced the formation of the State of Israel. Arabs responded by sending their armies to assist their irregular forces fighting the Jewish population. Major combat ensued in and around Jerusalem. In the wake of those hostilities the UN formed UNTSO. The following June, a cease-fire was agreed to, and the UN dispatched 93 military observers, primarily from the US, France, and Belgium, to supervise the truce as part of the newly formed peacekeeping organization. Eventually combat reignited and, following another cease-fire arrangement, UNTSO's officer corps swelled to 572 United Nations Military Observers (UNMO). UNTSO was officially in business in a significant way.[5]

By July 1949, UNTSO was given an added responsibility by the UN to supervise the cease-fire lines agreed to in armistice agreements that Israel and its Arab neighbors pledged to observe. Among its responsibilities were answering complaints by the contending parties, investigating violations, arranging prisoner exchanges, maintaining the cease-fire utilizing fixed observation posts (OP) and mobile patrols, and reestablishing cease-fires if breaches occurred.

After the initial conflict subsided in 1949, what followed was a series of conflicts that served as a continuum in the struggle over Israel's right to exist in former Arab lands. Arabs and Israelis would fight in major wars in 1956, 1967, and 1973, as well as during invasions of southern Lebanon in 1978 and 1982. After each of those wars, UNTSO would adapt its mission to support additional peacekeeping efforts, including support for UN armed peacekeeping organizations in the Sinai Desert of Egypt, the Golan Heights of Syria, and in southern Lebanon, which had become a haven for Palestinian Arab refugees and its armed fighters opposing Israel. In all of these conflicts, UNTSO supplied unarmed military observers to supervise cease-fires and peace agreements, the latest of which was UNIFIL's effort to stabilize southern Lebanon after the 1978 Israeli invasion.

That was the UNTSO that awaited my arrival to take up duties as an unarmed peacekeeper in one of the most volatile and dangerous regions of the world. At the height of the Cold War, I would find myself initially working alongside one US marine and eighteen Russian officers in Damascus, Syria, overseeing the Golan Heights peace operation. A few months later, I would transition to duty with the UNTSO headquarters operations center in Jerusalem, from which I would deploy to southern Lebanon to perform observation duties from fixed OPs and on mobile patrols. Southern Lebanon was, as we used to say, "the Wild West without a good saloon." Manning OPs and mobile patrols was extremely dangerous business, particularly for unarmed UNMOs wearing sky-blue berets—a mandated requirement for all observers—to say nothing of having to ride around in white vehicles prominently marked with a large black "UN" stenciled on both sides. Together, the headgear we wore and the vehicles we used made us easy targets for those who did not appreciate the UN's presence or its mission to promote peace.

This is a book about what we Yanks did alongside other international military observers sent by nations from around the globe to supervise truces, cease-fires, and other peace agreements that contending nations in the Levant had mutually agreed to observe. The book was written for the general reader who has a curiosity about life and conflict in the Middle East and about what efforts were undertaken to bring peace. My hope is that casual readers will come to appreciate the dynamics of peacekeeping operations. Military historians and practitioners of war and peace can also learn from the stories herein concerning the realities of peacekeeping and the operations related to that noble end. So too, academicians can take a lesson from our experience as UNMOs as they seek to understand and express in their disciplined way the ultimate impact of peacekeeping on those who engaged in the nitty-gritty of it. Scholars will also be informed by this narrative, even as they delve deeper into the art of peacekeeping and what we did to advance it. Indeed, readers from all walks—history buffs, military admirers, and professors—can all benefit from understanding what we did. There is no substitute to better understand the nature of peacekeeping than to appreciate the experiences of those who stood on the firm and troubled soil of conflict to bring about peace.

In all we did, we were not idealists blithely strolling into danger, but rather conscientious and serious-minded warriors who willingly faced danger head-on with a single-minded purpose, to advance peace. This is a story that must be told. Ultimately this is my story of what I saw, heard, and felt as I worked with my American and international colleagues to create and encourage peace in the Levant. The region had been plagued with repetitive rounds of conflict, and that conflict seemed to last forever, spanning from 1948 with the creation of the modern state of Israel to 1981, when peace was hanging by a thread in some places, particularly in southern Lebanon.

The challenges we faced were significant. In 1981, UN peacekeeping in the Middle East was hampered by the scope and limitations of the mission in a region where the parties to the conflict did not have full confidence in the authority of the UN General Assembly. Nor were the belligerents supportive of organizations like UNTSO in general and UNIFIL in particular, as both peacekeeping organizations collaborated to encourage and enforce peace in southern Lebanon. All of this came to a head with the eruption of another conflict in 1982, when Israel invaded Lebanon for a second time, as I was returning to the US to assume a new position as a Middle East intelligence analyst in the Defense Intelligence Agency. For me, that invasion called into question the value of years of peacemaking, peacekeeping, and peace enforcement efforts supported by the US. In 1982, the thin veil of peace was torn asunder—yet again—by war, and that failure left me with many questions about America's role in UN peacekeeping.

In that regard, the status of the US as the most capable and professional entity in UNTSO is scrutinized in this book, including the role and influence of the US contribution to UN peacekeeping and how it benefitted UNTSO. To the extent it was beneficial, was the UN deprived of that advantage when the US eventually withdrew from UNTSO in the years following the brutal murder of one of our number, Colonel (COL) William Richard "Rich" Higgins (USMC), at the hands of radical pro-Iranian terrorists?[6] But notwithstanding America's eventual withdrawal from UNTSO in the years after the Higgins atrocity, was our work until then beneficial to peace? Did our efforts matter? Were they for better or worse? Moreover, was the withdrawal of the US from UNTSO in the best interest of our national policy as it concerns peacekeeping missions? Was something valuable lost? More fundamentally, what did that service mean, both professionally and personally, for the Americans who served in UNTSO? What did we learn about peacekeeping and serving with international officers, and what did we glean about ourselves as individuals? Was that of any value to our nation? And when we left, did our military services foreclose on a vital learning laboratory concerning peace operations and the important insights and lessons that could be learned? This book will examine these fundamental questions, including a suggested framework for policymakers and military strategists to consider when assessing whether to participate in peacekeeping operations in the future.

In telling this story, I relied on my personal notes and direct observations as well as those of colleagues who shared theirs with me. I have woven together the tapestry of our experiences as peacekeepers. Therefore, this is a narrative history and personal memoir of sorts. To that end, it is not designed to be either a comprehensive textbook or a travelogue, but rather the true story about war and peace illustrated by the personal experience—both raw and refined—of young American officers and their international partners who, after donning the blue beret of the UN military observer, went unarmed into the jaws of conflict to be the face and embodiment of peace. I have used the personal vignettes and the input of US colleagues from the Army (USA), Navy (USN), Marine Corps (USMC), and Air Force (USAF) who served before, with, and after me. I also was fortunate to have the valuable insights of some of my international colleagues. All were instrumental in telling this story. They provided me a window into their personal exploits and contributions to the peacekeeping effort.

I owe special thanks to Lieutenant Colonel (LTC) Jack Hammell (USA, Retired), LTC Joe Serviss (USA, Retired), Commander (CDR) Virgil "Virg" Bozeman (USN, Retired), Brigadier General (BG) Dick Vercauteren (USMC, Retired), Colonel (COL) Mike Fallon (USMC, Retired), COL Clay Grubb (USMC, Retired), COL Kevin Kennedy (USMC, Retired), COL Jay Sollis (USMC, Retired), COL Lenny Supko (USMC, Retired), LTC Denny Lindeman (USMC, Retired), COL Steve Cotter (USAF, Retired), and LTC Tommy Cates (USAF, Retired), just to name a few. I also am most grateful to COL Geoff Bell (Australian Army, Retired), LTC Barry Gwyther (Australian Army, Retired), COL Dave Betson (Irish Army, Retired), and COL Des Travers (Irish Army, Retired) for their personal reflections and observations about our service together as military observers. They were very brave men.

I would be remiss, however if I did not highlight the role that COL Mike Fallon played in not only providing input to this work, but for his courage and unique participation in establishing UNIFIL following the Israeli invasion of southern Lebanon in 1978. He provided remarkable details into how UNIFIL came into being. His role then as a young

Marine Corps officer is one I describe in later chapters. He was gallant and determined in the finest traditions of a combat-trained American officer. In many ways his performance of duty was also characteristic of many who served in UNTSO. We were "all in," as the saying goes. But Fallon was "extra all in," regardless of the danger. He was an exemplary Yank in a blue beret.

Finally, to my chief editor, life partner, and wife, Shelley Glick Lingamfelter. As a new bride, she accompanied me to the Middle East to live in Damascus and Jerusalem amid all the turbulence of the region. We both thought it would be something of a holiday. We were wrong. It was more than that, and she too had to live with the daily possibility that things could go very badly quite suddenly. She was a trooper for sure.

So, let us begin by examining the historical record as we delve into the life of a Yank in a blue beret assigned to an organization born amid controversy, intended for peace, wedged between combatants, and not entirely trusted by the parties to the conflict. It would be a fascinating learning experience for me and my fellow American and international colleagues that would affect us both professionally and personally for the rest of our lives. Let us begin by going "up to Jerusalem."

LSL
Upper Sandy Point, Virginia
June 2022

1

Up to Jerusalem

It was a long flight—5,885 miles—from National Airport in Washington, D.C., to Ben Gurion Airport in Tel Aviv, Israel. I slept fitfully most of the flight as we jetted across a dark Atlantic Ocean and over the Mediterranean Sea. Occasionally I awoke to a crying child or a well-intended flight attendant asking if we wanted something to drink, but as we approached Israel's western coast the sun was rising. A ray of sunlight slipped across my face and roused me for good. As we neared our final approach before buckling our seatbelts, I noted three male Hasidic Jews on a pilgrimage to the Holy Land standing in the aisle next to the emergency exit door window praying. Rocking ever so slightly and bowing reverently to the east with prayer books in hand, they observed their sacred daily ritual. From my cultural studies, I knew that faithful Jews prayed three times daily in the morning (*shacharit*), the afternoon (*minchah*), and at nightfall (*arvith* or *maariv*). They were doing what many Jews do regardless of where they are, praying toward Jerusalem, the city that has been the center of Judaism for thousands of years. As they prayed, they must have recounted the words of Psalm 137:5 and its clear admonition for faithful Jews: "If I forget you, O Jerusalem, Let my right hand forget its skill!" These men knew they were going to a very special place. So did I, along with my new bride of seven months, Shelley, who was accompanying me on this great adventure.

I was surprised to learn that all of the US armed services contributing military officers to UNTSO encouraged bringing spouses and family along for the experience. The UN paid a substantial per diem to each UN military observer (UNMO) above and beyond the officer's regular military compensation. That would more than cover the expenses of an accompanying family member. It still sounded strange to me, but I was assured that it was quite safe to bring Shelley along. While UNMOs performed their duties, I was told, wives and children could sightsee, visit historical places, and shop at numerous souks—or bazaars—for every imaginable thing, from fine rugs to Egyptian gold cartouches prized by many tourists. Besides, Shelley was

9

working on her doctorate in education when we met at the University of Virginia and was very keen to visit both Israeli and Arab schools. It seemed like a good opportunity for us both, on the one hand broadening my understanding of the Middle East, and on the other, offering Shelley a practicum in observing how other countries educate their children.

As we prepared to land at Ben Gurion Airport—named for David Ben-Gurion, the preeminent founder and first prime minister of the state of Israel—we were filled with anticipation that Friday, 20 February 1981. Beyond our duties with UNTSO, the Holy Land also held great religious significance for Shelley and me as Christians, and we were excited to be destined for Jerusalem, the Eternal City of Israel. When we emerged from the aircraft and made our way through customs, it was clear that the Israelis took a no-nonsense approach to airport security. Terrorism was not new to Israel, as evidenced by the watchful eyes of armed military scanning our every movement. There were no smiles, just the serious business of meticulous surveillance for threatening situations.

Their posture stood in sharp contrast to that of Master Sergeant (MSG) Bruce Brill (USA), who met us and our UNTSO-bound fellow travelers, Major (MAJ) George Casey (USA), accompanied by his wife, Sheila, and their two sons, and Lieutenant (LT) Virgil Bozeman (USN), who was hobbling on crutches after badly twisting his ankle before leaving Washington, D.C. When we deplaned, Brill greeted us with a hearty "Welcome to the Middle East, gentlemen!" We promptly gathered our baggage as he ushered us through a labyrinth of customs agents to a waiting Volkswagen minibus marked with "UN" on either side. After loading up, we departed for a 66-kilometer trip from Tel Aviv to Jerusalem along the Sderot-Weizmann Highway, named for Chaim Weizmann, the first president of Israel. On our way, all of us were quite eager to begin our work as UNMOs. Bozeman would later admit he was a bit "starry-eyed" over the assignment, a sense I shared with him.[1] But I was particularly impressed with the focused seriousness of George Casey. A graduate of Georgetown University and the University of Denver with a master's degree in international relations, he displayed a notable scope of knowledge and awareness of the Middle East during the several pre-deployment briefings we received from the State Department and the Army staff. His regional knowledge was both thorough and sophisticated.[2]

As we zipped along the highway beholding the landscape, I paused to note in my journal that we were all impressed by the Israeli "economic miracle" that included modern transportation infrastructure, lush orange groves, vineyards, farm fields of all sorts, and the modern construction that dotted the countryside. It was remarkable. But I also could not avoid thinking about the complexities, the struggles, the continuing conflict that sat juxtaposed to this Israeli economic marvel. Brill sped us along the road, "up to Jerusalem," as the biblical expression goes. Later that day I captured my thoughts:

> Yet for me, underlying all of this, despite their tremendous economic effort, was the sense that for every proud Israeli there was one Arab deeply resentful of the Jewish state. Indeed, for all the good that had been accomplished throughout the Jewish struggle for survival, there had also been so much wrong. As we sped eastward along the coastal plain upward to Jerusalem, I had the feeling deep in my stomach that this next year in the Middle East would honestly tax my objectivity. So many rights, so many wrongs, all of which I knew would compete for my conscience and, in the process, further confound the issue of who was right and who was wrong.

"Up" to Jerusalem is an appropriate way to characterize our journey. Making our way eastward, the road wound left and right, rising in altitude. Then approaching the area known as the West Bank—land to the west of the Jordan River—we began to see relics of past wars between Arabs and Jews. The twisted and bullet-ridden hulks of World War II-vintage armored cars used in the wars that had preceded were treated with rust repellant paint by the Israeli government to preserve them. This was to ensure that these combat monuments could resist the corrosive hand of time and serve as a constant reminder to residents and visitors alike. The message was clear. Israelis had fought long and bloody battles along the roads of Judea to Jerusalem to repossess land that had been the Jewish homeland since the time of Moses, almost 1,500 years before the birth of Jesus. Of course, it was not a one-sided affair. Arabs had fought in these bloody battles as well. But the preservation of these monuments to war would herald an Israeli triumph for those headed up to Jerusalem. To that end, they were quite effective as visual reminders that testified to Israel's struggle for survival.

As we crested a rise in the road, I was taken by how quickly we were upon Jerusalem. I made a note in my journal that evening:

> Our first view of Jerusalem was punctuated by the fact the Jewish settlements so often referred to in the western press were in

fact high rise extensions of the city. Ringing the city as they do, they communicate a certain *fait accompli*—a feeling that this once divided city will never be so again. The building colors were just as I had expected; bright sandy shaded buildings punctuated by green patches of gardens and trees. All in all, the city is a pleasant mix of east and west from bread shops many years old to ubiquitous Coke signs found throughout the world.

Jerusalem was an odd mix of two worlds, one of antiquity and another of modernity, blended together in an agreeable fashion, but also mixed with much disagreement. Its climate also sharply differed from Tel Aviv's, which was warm and muggy. High atop the Judean hills where the Old City was situated, the climate was splendid.

After entering the city, "Brill Tours" diverted us to a vantage point atop the Mount of Olives east of the Old City, where we could behold the landscape looking westward, including a spectacular panorama of the Temple Mount, the Al-Aqsa Mosque, and the Dome of the Rock. These impressive structures were regarded by Muslims as their third holiest site, and they dominated our view. The Dome of the Rock's brilliantly golden hemispherical roof rose impressively above the ancient buff-beige stone walls that surrounded the Old City, filling us with amazement. We were awestruck by how the dome shone so brightly in the sun. Yet it sat on terrain that Jews cherished as the center of their faith. It was the site of the former Great Temple, where they made sacrifices to the God of Abraham, Isaac, and Jacob to secure atonement for sins. Frankly, it was a place Jews, Christians, and Muslims all adored from the unique perspectives of their faiths. It, like the tomb of Samuel and others we would visit later, was a place of both religious community and conflict. Likewise, control of the Temple Mount—the Mount Moriah of the Bible—had provoked conflicts stretching from the Christian Crusades of 1095 and 1270 to the 1967 Six-Day War, when Jews took control of the entire city from the Arabs, who had possessed it for the better part of 1,200 years. Yet Jerusalem was also a place of devoted everyday worship, including that of three orthodox Jews praying in its direction at 40,000 feet above the Mediterranean Sea earlier that morning. The Holy City, as Christians referred to it, was the site of contradictions, commonality, and conflict.

As we beheld the wonder of the Eternal City—as Israelis referred to it—Brill pointed out sites we would visit in the coming days, including the UNTSO headquarters perched on a prominent hill south of the Old City. He then loaded us back in his bus and hustled us off along the winding roads to our hotel northeast of the city walls. We took up residence at the Ritz Hotel, an Arab-run facility, not to be confused with anything located in Las Vegas. Modest and clean, our room was exceedingly small and our bed overly soft. However, neither of these disadvantages prevented us from getting the rest Shelley and I both needed after a long flight.

When morning broke on 21 February, I had already arisen, but was charmed nonetheless by the early dawn Muslim call to prayer, called the *Adhan*, and chanted by a *muezzin* whose voice filled the chilly morning air from a nearby minaret associated with a mosque. Muslims pray five times each day: *Fajr* (morning), *Dhuhr* (noon), *Asr* (afternoon), *Maghrib* (evening), and *Isha* (night). Shelley and I then dressed and headed to the breakfast room of the hotel, where we had a light continental meal. Since it was Saturday, or *Shabbat*—the Jewish sabbath—the UNTSO head-quarters was not officially open. So, we took the opportunity to join Brill's standard tour of Jerusalem provided to all newly arrived US per-sonnel. He was quite the expert at orienting people to the Holy City. Not only was he personally knowledgeable, but he had formed an association of friendly local vendors and shopkeepers who doubled as tour guides. On the one hand, they were informed and amicable docents who spoke excellent English, and on the other, they were ready to offer their unique wares found in nearby shops. It was symbiotic and appreciated, even if it was economically beneficial to them.

Initially we traveled to the tomb of Samuel the Prophet, located on a tall hill about five kilometers northwest of the city. The view, despite the haze that day, was remarkable. Samuel's tomb was a monument to con-trast and control. Where else could one find a Jewish tomb with a church built over it and topped by a mosque constructed over both? When we ventured deeper into the prophet's tomb, we entered an underground chamber that also served as a small synagogue. This first stop made us all aware that the relationship between Jews, Christians, and Muslims inter-twined at every turn, creating opportunities for cultural unity as well as revealing the contours of conflict.

From there we departed for the Old City, entering it through Dung Gate—a portal where refuse was deposited in ages past—situated near the southeast corner of Jerusalem, near the Temple Mount. Directly behind the gate was the Western Wall Plaza. There we viewed the Wailing Wall, the foundation on the western side of the original temple that now served as Judaism's most sacred place of pilgrimage and prayer. However, since mosques had been constructed over the site of the First and Second Temples of Jerusalem, Jews were confined to worship at the westmost foundation of the Temple Mount, the only place permitted for them to venerate their former Great Temple. Besides, for a Jew to walk on the Temple Mount—where allegedly the stone tablets with the inscribed Ten Commandments are buried—would be a mortal sin. Consequently, the Israeli authorities put the Temple Mount off-limits to Jews, a prohibition that also accommodated Muslim sentiments.

The potential for conflict in and around this holy place seemed to me to be unavoidable. Indeed, as we approached the Temple Mount, two young Jews wearing their traditional kippah, or yarmulke, were turned away as they attempted to gain entry to the Temple Mount. Later I would observe that they had stashed their headgear and entered the Al-Aqsa Mosque in contravention to Israeli regulations. I thought that was potentially provocative but resisted saying anything to them about their lack of regard for the rules. After all, I was now a peacekeeper, not a provocateur.

When we entered Al-Aqsa Mosque, Shelley and I were immediately taken by its beautiful prayer rugs and stained glass. We also took note of a major restoration effort that was underway in the southern end of the mosque to repair recently inflicted damage. After leaving Al-Aqsa, we walked through the beautiful courtyards about 100 yards northward to the famous Dome of the Rock. According to Muslims, this was the site of Mohammed's ascension to heaven. For Jews, it was also where Abraham was poised to obediently sacrifice his only son, Isaac, until God—moved by Abraham's demonstrable faith—provided a suitable sacrificial lamb ensnared in a nearby thicket, thereby sparing the young boy's life. Likewise for Christians, the Temple Mount was the place where Jesus walked, taught, and righteously expelled the money lenders, whom He said had desecrated a holy place meant for prayer and worship, not commerce. Each of these faiths had a significant claim to this place. That was the case with many sites we would visit that day. The competing affections and loyalties in Jerusalem raised the potential for religious conflict throughout the Holy City.

Departing the Temple Mount, we made our way along the Via Dolorosa that spans the current Muslim and Christian quarters of the Old City. This "Sorrowful Way," as it is translated from Latin, was the path taken by Jesus to His crucifixion after being tortured and condemned to die. We stopped at the place along the way where Simon of Cyrene is said to have taken the cross to bear it himself when Jesus collapsed in utter fatigue. It was a memorable pause in our journey. We then passed a number of shops that sold everything from brass to ceramics until we arrived at the Church of the Holy Sepulchre. There, one of Brill's prearranged tour sherpas met us. He was an exceedingly polite Arab Muslim gentleman who turned out to be quite an expert on the church that conveniently sat only yards from his gift shop. I appreciated his detailed knowledge, but particularly his advice on the reverent protocols to observe when touring the church that housed the tomb that many Christians revere as Jesus's official burial site and the place of His resurrection.

Our guide was very considerate as he carefully led us about the church, which had designated chapels run by the Roman Catholic, Greek Orthodox, and Armenian Churches. Interestingly, priests of one denomination were not permitted to enter the spaces of another. It was then I became aware that differences in the Holy Land were not confined to different faiths. The fault lines were also sectarian, even within Christian denominations. Nonetheless, it struck me as ironic—and encouraging— that an Arab Muslim was escorting American Christians through one of the holiest sites of our faith in a city under Jewish authority.

The Holy City was a remarkable convergence of conflicting sentiments that represented the texture of the Middle East. That was poignantly clear when we paused at a large mural in one of the chapels of the Church of the Holy Sepulchre that had been vandalized by fire. We asked our Arab guide what had happened. Reluctantly, he said, "You will find out in time." In fact, a month before we visited the Church of the Holy Sepulchre, members of the Jewish Temple Mount Faithful, along with other groups, reportedly stormed Al-Aqsa Mosque on 13 January 1981, raising Israeli flags and carrying Torah scrolls.[3] I then recalled the damage we had seen at Al-Aqsa earlier that day. Apparently, vandals respected nothing, regardless of how sacred the place and for whom it was holy.

In a moment that interrupted the seriousness of our visit, the always light-hearted Bozeman gave us a glimpse of his spontaneous wit. He sensed an opportunity to engage some German pilgrims in a mischievous ruse. The tourists had taken note of his temporary need for crutches. In an act of playful absurdity, he took the crutches, held them over his head, tossed them away and declared in a loud voice, "Healed! I've been HEALED!" He then walked away without limping.[4] The incredulous onlookers gasped, thinking they had witnessed a miracle when all they had observed was the theatrical antics of an American naval officer with an irreverent sense of timing. That spontaneity would come in quite handy for the artful Bozeman in the months ahead. If nothing else, he foreshadowed how quick-wittedness would come to one's aid as an unarmed UNTSO observer surrounded by armed militants in southern Lebanon. We all would call on similar wits—both humorous and serious—to survive the months to come.

That evening, and over our six days in Jerusalem, we were wined and dined in excellent fashion by the local US military and UN community. It was wonderful and, frankly, it made it harder to contemplate leaving Jerusalem for Damascus the following week. I had known since October of 1980 that I would be assigned initially to Damascus. I was excited about that, but since I now had my wife with me, I grew concerned about how life would be in Syria. The dictator there, President Hafez al-Assad, was a brutal man and violence could arise from opposition groups without warning. Indeed, there had been running battles and clashes since the fall of 1979 between Assad's forces and the Muslim Brotherhood seeking to overthrow him.[5] Yet, we were encouraged when we met the officer I was designated to replace, Lieutenant Commander (LTCDR) Gary Calnan (USN). He and his wife, Kathy, had lived in Damascus for several months. They loved it. Shelley and I were happy to hear that, and our spirits were lifted. Over dinner, we had light conversation but also delved deeper into life in the Middle East. It was a fascinating discussion, almost a continuation of my graduate history seminars. But that evening my perspective improved across a restaurant table in Jerusalem. Many such conversations occurred in the days that followed, leaving me with a deeper appreciation for the quality and knowledge of the American officers assigned to UNTSO from all branches of our armed services.

Shelley and I attended nearby Saint George's Cathedral for Holy Communion the next morning. The church was quite beautiful, built in a classic gothic style and located about 200 yards from the Garden Tomb, another place many believe to be the actual burial site of Jesus. Afterward, we had a nice chat with one of the priests, informing him we would soon depart for Damascus. He then thoroughly shocked us both by bluntly remarking, "Once you learn the Arab swear words, you'll get along fine." As I noted in my journal, "He was quite British and quite serious about his advice." His remark, however, was yet another revelation about cultural attitudes in the Middle East, even of those in the Holy Orders.

The following Monday morning, Brill arrived to take us to Government House—home to UNTSO's operations—to receive an orientation and begin our official in-processing. Government House was the former headquarters where the British high commissioner resided during the UK's mandate of Palestine from 1920 to 1948. When their administration ended, the mansion briefly served as the headquarters for the International Red Cross. However, in September 1948 the stately facility became UNTSO's headquarters. Situated a short distance south of the Old City wall, the headquarters offered a panoramic view that included Bethlehem further to the south. As we entered the compound and stopped in the circular driveway at the front of the headquarters, we noted the green gardens and olive trees that adorned the grounds. When we entered the main hall of this impressive building, Brill proceeded to give us a tour. That included a stop at the small but pleasant restaurant inside where we had a cup of coffee. Government House was a beautiful octagonal structure built from locally quarried Jerusalem limestone. Since it had also served as the residence for the British high commissioner, it was equipped with a private apartment as well as a lovely fountain and a formal garden. Arches, crossed vaults, and domed ceilings adorned the impressive interior, to say nothing of the remarkably large ceramic fireplace in its expansive reception hall. It was regal. From its second floor, one could see the Old City to the north, Bethlehem to the south, the Mount of Olives to the northeast, and, on a clear day, the distant mountains of Moab in the east toward Jordan. It was a stunning view.

After we toured the headquarters, we headed to Brill's office to complete our required US arrival paperwork, after which our in-processing and training began in earnest. Our first stop was to meet LTC Azad "Al" Husnian (USA), who was serving as the chief operations officer of UNTSO. This position was a key one traditionally filled by a US Army officer, a benefit in four practical ways both for the US and UNTSO. First, we had learned over dinner the previous evening that US officers had acquired a reputation for competency and efficiency and were known to accomplish things quickly and in spite of the fairly bureaucratic framework in UNTSO. Having an American officer in the upper echelons of UNTSO's leadership enhanced our reputation and prerogatives in the operations and planning arenas. Second, Husnian's position served as a counterbalance to a considerably empowered and entrenched UNTSO civilian administrative staff, which paralleled the military staff in structure and authority. In a sense, the UN civilian staff—many of whom were well compensated and protective of their authority—kept watch over the *status quo,* mindful to ensure their interests, longevity, and well-paid tenure were not disrupted by meddlesome military staffers who, at best, would be there for a few years. As my Australian Army colleague Captain (CPT) Barry Gwyther remembered, the UN staff was "very bureaucratic and controlled by longtime civilians who had a vested interest in prolonging the operation and [UNTSO's] mandate."[6] Having an American officer leading UNTSO's operations was a counterbalance to that outsized bureaucracy. It was no secret that the US was a major financial contributor to the UN. Sometimes a polite hint was all that was needed for the civilian guardians to "find a way" to be more cooperative, particularly when it came to providing necessary resources to military operations. Third, having a US officer at the top of the operation served to remind the entire UNTSO organization—civilian and military—that if things turned sour in the region, America's considerable military resources were stationed in Europe and nearby at sea to respond to a crisis. Finally, a US senior officer in the UNTSO hierarchy gave Israeli authorities a degree of comfort that a useful advocate was on hand. It was an open secret that Israel did not trust the UN one bit.

Husnian invited us into his office and gave a brief orientation concerning our duties and the importance of the US reputation in UNTSO. We were expected to be professional at all times and courteous to our UNTSO counterparts, who were more than aware of our prominent role in the operation. Therefore, both humility and diplomacy were important. When our meeting with Husnian ended, we were then ushered to the office of the UNTSO chief of staff, Major General (MG) Emmanuel Alexander Erskine, who had just relinquished command of UNIFIL, the UN's armed peacekeeping force created following the 1978 Israeli invasion of southern Lebanon. It was not Erskine's first time with UNTSO. He had served as chief of staff from January 1976 until March 1978, when UNIFIL was created. Erskine struck an impressive profile. Born in Ghana, he attended the Royal Military Academy at Sandhurst, England, and had a storied career in the Ghanaian Army, including its command. A graduate of the Staff College at Camberley, England, Erskine also had considerable experience in the UN, having commanded the UN's disengagement force, UNEF II, in the Sinai Desert after the 1973 Yom Kippur War.

When Casey, Bozeman, and I entered his office and saluted smartly, Erskine rose, returned our greeting, and offered us a seat. Speaking with a delightfully polished Ghanaian-British accent, he welcomed us and asked where we would initially be assigned. It was light conversation. But we were all impressed with his bearing and professionalism. It was also clear he much appreciated the US contingent and hinted that we had a significant role to play in UNTSO, suggesting that we possessed a level of skill, training, and competence that he regarded as important to the success of the organization. The implication to us was clear.

After we left Erskine's office, we continued our UN in-processing, also obtaining the all-important UN white card that was our official diplomatic identification. Under article 105, section 20, of the UN Charter, the "Privileges and Immunities of the United Nations," military observers were entitled to certain rights necessary while in the territory of a member state in order to operate in an independent manner to accomplish our purpose.[7] In short, we were immune from arrest, detention, seizure of personal baggage, and legal processes of every sort while performing our duties, including protections preventing seizure of our papers and documents. Moreover, white cards were also authorized for immediate family accompanying the UNMOs. Additionally, we were issued an Israeli identification card, written in both French and Hebrew. When asked about our identity we were required to render it to authorities, along with the UN white card.

After completing our in-processing, it was clear that UNTSO had a serious mission and we an important role in it. This was all new to me as a trained artilleryman. The idea of going into hostile regions as an unarmed military observer was quite different from everything I had been trained to do. Was I ready for this? What would be required of me? I sardonically wondered—recalling the Anglican priest's attempt at humor—whether there would be instruction on "Arab swear words" and other essentials for "cultural" survival? That unserious idea along with genuinely earnest questions flooded my mind as we prepared for the next three days of training.

Having traveled "up to Jerusalem," we were now being prepared for duty in less hospitable locations, with just three days to learn what we needed to know. That brevity struck me as insufficient to prepare us for duty in a land of conflicting cultures, complex contradictions, and continuing conflict. Indeed, we were faced with a legacy of Middle East turmoil that would be our ever-present milieu. We would need to grasp the complexity of it to accomplish our mission. So, let us take a closer look at the legacy of conflict that served as a backdrop for those of us tasked with keeping the peace in a place where peace was rare and animosity the dominant condition of everyday life.

2

A Legacy of Conflict

During our initial training session, I was eager to depart for Damascus to assume my new duties, despite my concern that three days was insufficient preparation for new peacekeepers. It is one thing to be a trained Middle East specialist, as I was. It is entirely another to be a trained peacekeeper. Nonetheless, I took comfort in my understanding of the region as one defined by conflict that was involved, perplexing, multilayered, and intertwined. And the immediate Middle Eastern conflict before us that was paramount was the dispute over Palestine, situated at the epicenter of the Levant, that geographic area encompassing Egypt, Israel, Jordan, Lebanon, and Syria. Ancient history scholar Professor Paul L. Maier sums it up accurately: "Palestine is a land rippling with irony. It gave birth to two great religions and nurtured a third, yet it may be the most bitterly contested spot on earth. Jews, Christians, and Muslims all call it the Holy Land, but probably more blood has been spilled there per acre than anywhere else in the world."[1]

A common lament heard by those unfamiliar with the nature of conflict in the Middle East—particularly in the Levant—is "If the Arabs and Jews would just make peace, everything would be fine." This naive framing of the dilemma belies a complexity, not only between Israel and its neighbors, but even in the persistent disputes among subgroups within those contending nationalities, Arabs and Jews alike. At the University of Virginia, my professor Charles G. MacDonald would refer to any simplistic notion of the conflict between Arabs and Jews as the "intolerance of ambiguity." This term described the thinking of people who were unable or unwilling to recognize the multifaceted, multigenerational, and stratified nature of conflict in the Middle East. Confronted with the profundity of a problem, those exhibiting an intolerance of ambiguity think that finding a simple common denominator will uncomplicate the conflict and make it digestible. In fact, to thoroughly understand conflict in the Middle East, one must grasp that the animosity is not merely a one-on-one proposition. To the contrary, the problems are extraordinarily

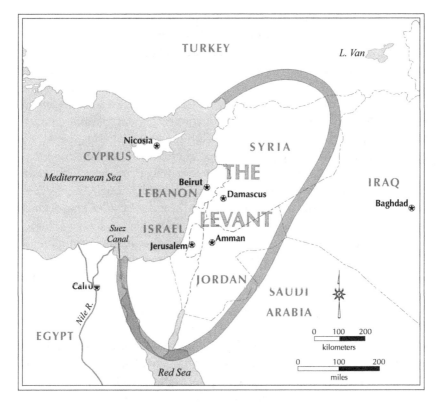

Map 2.1. The Levant

complex and not easily unwound. They are exceedingly knotty. The conflict in the Levant resembles a highly dysfunctional family so profoundly filled with generational and multilayered disagreement that the frequent result is violence and death within the family. Therefore, the solutions to resolve Middle East conflicts resist simplicity. Sometimes solutions must be nuanced and detailed to address the underlying nature of disputes. The peace process is far more complex than simply cutting a square piece of cloth to patch a torn garment. It may require intricate knitting that takes time, patience, persistence, and skill.

The Levant was a very troubled neighborhood in 1981, and the complexity of dissonance there was clear to the trained eye.[2] Take for example the levels of conflict in this region bordering the Mediterranean Sea (see map 2.1).

While the overarching dispute was between Arabs and Israelis, there was also much disagreement within national communities, societies, and states. As we witnessed in Jerusalem from the moment we arrived, religious discord between and within Judaism, Christianity, and Islam—the prominent religions of the Levant—was prevalent. In Israel not every Jew considered himself or herself an orthodox one. Indeed, some Jews placed their ethnicity ahead of religious identity. In Christianity, there is much disagreement about the doctrines of faith, to the point that even in the Church of the Holy Sepulchre—where unity, not conflict, should prevail—a Greek Orthodox priest could provoke a hostile response by entering the Armenian or Roman Catholic portions of that church. Within Islamic communities in neighboring Arab countries, centuries-long tension between Sunni and Shi'a Muslims was prevalent. Disputes festered among Muslims concerning interpretations of their faith. That included smaller and distinct Islamic sects, like the Druze and Alawi communities in Lebanon and Syria, which some Sunni and Shi'a Muslims viewed as doctrinally aberrant. Even among religious groups whose doctrines teach peace, disharmony was endemic in the land of Jesus, Abraham, Isaac, Jacob, Moses, David, and Mohammed.

Take, for example, Syria's leader, Hafez al-Assad, who was an adherent of the minority Alawite sect in a largely Sunni nation. He was—even then—battling against the Sunni-dominated Muslim Brotherhood for the survival of his regime. In neighboring Lebanon, which was suffering a civil war when we arrived, a religious confessional system that allocated proportional political power was flagging badly. Lebanon's system mandated that the presidency—by law—would be held by a Maronite Christian, the prime minister's position would be filled by a Sunni Muslim, while a Shi'a Muslim occupied the speaker of the Parliament's seat. Even before 1975, when civil war broke out between the Palestine Liberation Organization (PLO) and Lebanese Christians in southern Lebanon and Beirut, it was an unsteady triumvirate. By 1981 it was near collapse. After trading violent atrocities in and around Beirut, a sectarian conflict quickly spread across national borders, and within a year Syrian forces had become involved in the fight, primarily in support of Muslim interests in Lebanon. In 1978, this internecine conflict had metastasized to involve Israel, which invaded southern Lebanon to assist the Christian militia there battling PLO forces, their mutual enemy. By 1979, Iran's dominant Shi'a population revolted against and ousted their secular ruler, the shah of Iran, in a revolution that encouraged radicalized Shi'a factions in Lebanon amid that civil war. This was an example of how religious conflict within one country could enflame the conditions in other states. Not only were hostilities fueled in neighboring Israel and Syria, but Iranian-backed militias were introduced into southern Lebanon, a country already swamped by the PLO and its paramilitary forces operating against Israel. The entire region was a cauldron filled with animosity. By 1978 the UN found itself further involved, this time with the deployment of a newly configured and armed UNIFIL that was supported by unarmed UNTSO observers. To say this entire affair was complicated is a profound understatement. Indeed, an intolerance of ambiguity was the last thing that would be helpful in understanding the complexity of conflict in 1981.

Beyond religious strife, major tensions between socioeconomic classes within Arab society were evident. For example, the fault lines between the poor, mercantile, and upper or politically privileged classes were evident in Syria. Notably, the minority Alawite cohort of President Assad dominated Syria's ruling secular Ba'athist Party, which irritated the Sunni majority population, particularly members of the fundamentalist-minded Muslim Brotherhood, with whom Assad had battled for years.[3] That violent contest was in full flower in 1980, and the winner would not only rule the former French protectorate but be in an economically advantageous position, something Assad's Alawites had disproportionally secured for themselves to the exclusion of other Syrians.

Next door in Lebanon, a major influx of impoverished Palestinian refugees occurred after the 1967 and 1973 wars with Israel. Between these years, more Palestinians flowed to Lebanon after the September 1970 conflict between King Hussein bin Talal of Jordan and the PLO leader Yasser Arafat in what is now known as "Black September." Jordan's military forces expelled many Palestinians living there and the PLO to southern Lebanon after they twice attempted to assassinate King Hussein. As a result, the PLO—founded in 1964 and devoted to the "liberation of Palestine" through armed action—took up residence in Lebanon, a development many Lebanese did not warmly embrace. That emigration from Jordan and Syria had not been welcomed by Lebanese Christians who lived in Beirut and in the southern region of the country. The accumulation of impoverished Palestinians there meant more economic competition for indigenous Lebanese, upsetting the balance of economic power in Lebanon. In sum, inter-Arab conflict had major implications for Jordan, Lebanon, and Syria, introducing a form of class warfare that promoted conflict. The economic dislocation within the Levant also created a level of instability that was frequently overlooked by Western observers of the Middle East, particularly those searching for simple explanations to intractable problems.

Competition between traditional life in the Middle East and the forces and influences of modernity from Western civilization also had a profound impact in the Levant. Some traditional Muslim nations, such as Saudi Arabia and nearby Persian Gulf states, elected to minimize or prohibit certain Western cultural influences. However, Western ways had taken hold significantly in the Levant. In Lebanon and Syria, the French influence was pronounced, particularly in Beirut and Damascus, both quite cosmopolitan and home to many fine restaurants that served alcohol. When it came to some Western vices, there was no inhibition in marketing them if there was profit to be made. Lebanon was thoroughly capitalistic, and while some Muslims would not partake of certain goods, such as alcohol or tobacco, the option to buy them was always available. However, for those who lived a life defined by the Koran, the invasion of Western culture and its vices was unbidden and caused tension with those who would tolerate or embrace that lifestyle in Muslim communities. As a result, religiously strident Islamic groups opposed to Western values sprouted. Coupled with an ingrained hatred of Israel, radical groups sought to seize power and "reject foreign and Zionist influences"—a common refrain then—even if the turmoil resulted in civil war within their own countries.

Fortunately, for those of us arriving at UNTSO in 1981, Egypt and Jordan were quite pacified compared to other Arab neighbors bordering the Jewish state. On 17 September 1978, Israel's Prime Minister Menachem Begin and Egypt's President Anwar Sadat signed the Framework for Peace in the Middle East, known as the Camp David Accords.[4] That agreement appeared to be holding up well after two years. Likewise, Jordan's King Hussein—who was not part of the Israeli-Egyptian agreement—had been a fairly reliable US friend, despite having to deal with a rather large, vocal, and occasionally violent Palestinian expatriate population in his country. It was good news that both Egypt and Jordan were cooperative players with Israel in 1981. But that had not always been the case. The legacy of conflict involved them as well and was part of the environment wherein UNTSO was created.

UNTSO took its first breaths amid the violence that followed the partitioning of Palestine and the subsequent creation of the state of Israel. Indeed, it was through the leadership of US president Harry Truman that Israel was recognized as a legitimate state, thereby ensuring that the US would likely have a role to play in mitigating future threats to Israel. When the British seized Palestine in World War I from the Ottoman Empire, they also approved the Balfour Declaration in 1917 that endorsed the idea of a Jewish homeland in Palestine, something supported by then US president Woodrow Wilson.[5] Truman also was sympathetic to the idea of a Jewish homeland and was lobbied consistently by Jewish friends at home to recognize the state of Israel once it was declared. However, he was greeted with significant opposition from his renowned secretary of state, George C. Marshall, at the time one of the most influential men in America and the world. Marshall opposed recognition of Israel, particularly since the Arabs controlled a vital resource—oil—that was necessary to ensure the success of Europe's political and economic recovery after World War II and the viability of the Marshall Plan to achieve that purpose. Nevertheless, Truman was pressed to recognize Israel, even after he was informed that Marshall might not vote for him in the 1948 election if he did.[6] When Truman formally recognized Israel, he was told by the chief rabbi of the British Mandate of Palestine, Isaac Halevi Herzog, that "God put you in your mother's womb so you would be the instrument to bring the rebirth of Israel." Truman was said to have shed a tear at that declaration.[7] Nevertheless, a legacy of conflict was guaranteed to arise from the seed of Israeli statehood. It was in full blossom in 1981.

The 1948 War

The US role in UNTSO began with the arrival of 93 UNMOs, who reported for duty in Palestine to oversee the truce that was declared on 11 June 1948 following an initial outburst of violence that accompanied Israel's recognition as a modern state.[8] Most of the early military observers were officers from America, France, and Belgium, nations that continued to provide observers to UNTSO even as I was receiving my initial orientation. The 1948 war erupted shortly after the British left Palestine. But the conditions were in place by late 1947, when the British put the future of Palestine in the hands of the UN. The United Nations Special Committee on Palestine proceeded to develop a plan to end the violence and settle the status of Jerusalem by creating enclaves for both Palestinians and Jews. On 29 November 1947, the UN announced its Partition Plan that divided Palestine equally into separate Jewish and Arab states, with Jerusalem being administered by the UN as an independent city.[9] The international community was initially sanguine about the agreement, garnering the support of both the US and the USSR. Even the Yishuv, a governing body of Jewish residents in Palestine prior to the creation of Israel, was agreeable. However, Arabs in Palestine, as well as in Egypt,

Iraq, Lebanon, Saudi Arabia, Syria, and Transjordan, now known as Jordan, opposed the plan and advocated for what they believed would be a more palatable arrangement. For Arabs, that better arrangement did not envision a Jewish state, but rather formal recognition of a Jewish minority, which was all the Arabs were willing to accept. They lost that argument in the UN. As a result, Arabs made the decision to combine their forces to attack the Jews and seize territory in Palestine, thereby creating a new reality on the ground that the international community would be compelled to recognize.

Unfortunately for the Arabs, Israel's army, the Haganah, was actually well organized and effective. Initially Israel had 30,000 soldiers, but over the course of the conflict that number grew closer to 90,000. Meanwhile, the Arab League mustered approximately 13,000 that eventually grew to 60,000.[10] Arab forces were simply overmatched in organization and numbers. In short, when offered a partition plan that had broad acceptance in the international community, including the superpowers, the Arabs unwisely rejected it and, in the end, lost badly on the battlefield to a well-armed, well-led, and victorious Israeli Army. As a result of this war, Israel acquired more land than envisioned in the partition arrangement. Arabs were left with the Gaza Strip, a sliver of land bordering the Mediterranean Sea controlled by Egypt, the West Bank of the Jordan River, and a portion of East Jerusalem that would be controlled by Jordan (see map 2.2).

None of this would constitute a Palestinian state. But there would be over 700,000 Palestinian refugees living in camps in Jordan, Lebanon, Syria, the Gaza Strip, and the West Bank at the conclusion of the Arabs' ill-advised effort to create a new reality.[11] In sum, the Arabs failed when they had the chance to recognize and embrace a practical settlement, one that would have had the full support of the international community. Arabs were left with a far less suitable arrangement while Israel gained the clear strategic upper hand territorially and politically. In the eyes of the international community, the Arabs had played their cards badly. Indeed, Israel's position in the international community was affirmed in November 1949 when the Arabs were compelled to sign treaties—known as the General Armistice Agreements—with the new Jewish nation. Nevertheless, even with signed armistice agreements, the table was set for more bloodshed ahead.

In the wake of the 1948 war, UNTSO, with its heavy US presence, assumed a huge role. The UN sent 572 military observers to supervise a cease-fire established on 18 July 1948.[12] The armistice agreements over the

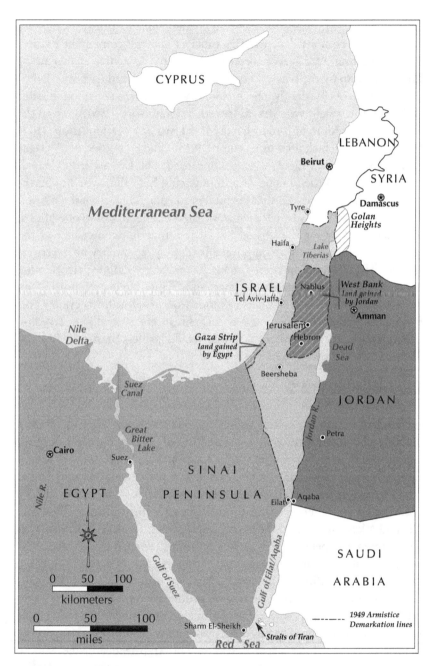

Map 2.2. Post-1948 War Boundaries

next year fixed the cease-fire lines and created Mixed Armistice Commissions (MAC) composed of the UN officials and the combatant parties. There were four MACs that corresponded to the Armistice Demarcation Lines agreed to by the parties. The Egyptian-Israel Mixed Armistice Commission (EIMAC), the Israel-Lebanon Mixed Armistice Commission (ILMAC), the Israel-Syria Mixed Armistice Commission (ISMAC), and the Hashemite Kingdom of Jordan-Israel Mixed Armistice Commission (HKJ-I-MAC) were each chaired by a senior UNMO and composed of a delegation from Israel and the Arab state concerned. The UN Security Council assigned UNTSO the mission of administering both the cease-fire agreements and the four MACs that responded to complaints from the parties, investigated violations by either side, assisted in humanitarian operations, and facilitated prisoner exchanges.[13] The continuing maintenance of the cease-fire operation was accomplished by deploying military observers on OPs positioned along the cease-fire lines, conducting mobile patrols in the areas bordering the demarcation lines, and facilitating negotiations when cease-fires were violated. While violations occurred, calm prevailed following this first major conflict, and cease-fires were generally observed by the warring parties. Unfortunately, that would last less than a decade.

The 1956 Suez Crisis

In October 1956 war erupted again. This time, however, it was the British and French governments who instigated Israeli participation in hostilities against Egypt in response to the latter's nationalization of the Suez Canal. Egypt's president, Gamal Abdel Nasser, seized the canal as part of his effort to restore national sovereignty over a strategic waterway originally constructed by the French, but controlled by the British since 1882. The UK had a keen interest in the Suez Canal, primarily while they were still ruling India and benefiting strategically from shortened trade routes that the canal offered.[14] It also facilitated the movement of Britain's military power throughout its Asian empire. However, after World War II, British concerns shifted to shipping petroleum products via the Suez, particularly oil for a recovering postwar Europe, including France. Nasser's antics threatened everything. The Egyptian president was, in short, a megalomaniac who viewed himself as the preeminent Arab leader in the Middle East and his native Egypt as the dominant power in the Pan-Arab world. In particular Nasser regarded Egypt as superior to the Hashemite Kingdoms of Iraq and Jordan, which had been administered in years past by the British, who retained interests in both countries. Nasser considered Iraq and Jordan as obstacles to enhancing his prominence in the Arab world. Moreover, Nasser was profoundly anti-British. Britain's military influence was widespread throughout the Middle East, including 80,000 soldiers garrisoned at Suez, making it one of the largest military installations in the world. Nasser wanted them gone. His canal provocation was his plan to diminish British control in the Arab world while demonstrating his muscularity to his Arab rivals. It backfired.

On 29 October 1956, Israel, with the encouragement of Britain and France, invaded Egypt's Sinai Peninsula. The invasion, it was thought by Israel and its conspirators, would produce greater security for Israel while offering Britain and France a rationale to retain a military foothold in Egypt to control the canal and facilitate the overthrow of the pesky Nasser. Israeli leaders thought the invasion would be beneficial in two ways. First, the Israelis had suffered attacks from Palestinian militants or guerrillas—the fedayeen or "freedom fighters"—who were based in the Gaza Strip. Nasser routinely encouraged those attacks. Israel wanted to eliminate the Palestinian threat once and for all. Moreover, it was no secret to Israel that Nasser sought to build his anti-Zionist reputation among Arabs, particularly vis-à-vis his rivals in the Hashemite Kingdoms. Therefore, dealing a blow to Nasser's reputation as the preeminent anti-Zionist in the Middle East would diminish him in the eyes of Arab leaders, something Israel saw as a desirable end state. Second, since 1947, Egypt had denied Israel navigation rights via the Straits of Tiran, a narrow sea passage between the Sinai Desert to the east and the Arabian Peninsula to the west (see map 2.3). Israel wanted that denial discontinued since it hampered Israeli economic development.

Meanwhile, Britain and France wanted to use the war as a sound pretext to maintain forces in the region to secure the economic lifeline the canal would provide once Nasser was defeated. London and Paris sought to accomplish their objective initially by calling for an early cease-fire soon after Israel attacked, but only after Jewish forces had attained an acceptable level of initial success. That success was something all three conspirators believed would occur, but they also expected that Nasser would reflexively reject a cease-fire. On 9 October 1956, the European co-conspirators called for a halt in fighting, but Egypt predictably refused it, thereby providing British and French forces with a ready excuse— indeed a planned pretext—to intervene militarily in the conflict.

However, US president Dwight D. Eisenhower was incensed by the recklessness of the British and French in this cabal as well as by Israeli

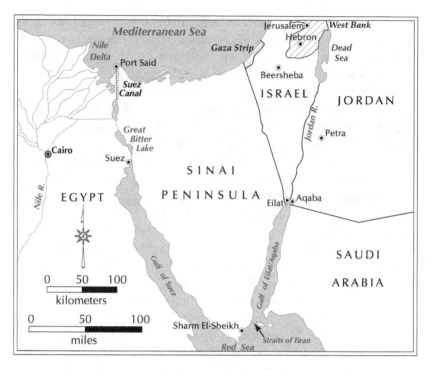

Map 2.3. The Gulf of Aqaba and the Straits of Tiran

participation in it. Eisenhower has been working to co-opt Nasser into an alliance of sorts to oppose the rise of Soviet influence in the Middle East, a major US concern in a region awash with oil needed by Western nations. The entire war was at cross purposes with Eisenhower's strategic concerns. He made clear that if the war were not halted immediately, the US would take consequential action against its own allies, a not-so-subtle threat. Meanwhile, the Soviets looked on with glee as Western allies engaged in an international version of *The Original Amateur Hour*.[15] US pressure prevailed in terminating the conflict. Following that, the UN General Assembly passed a resolution creating an armed observer force, UNEF I, to oversee the withdrawal of forces and maintain quiet along the demarcation line. Since the UN used the Chapter VI conflict resolution process in the UN Charter to create UNEF I, and not its Chapter VII authority to forcefully intervene militarily, both Egypt and Israel had to grant the UN permission to place disengagement forces on their territory.[16] Israel flatly refused and renounced the existing armistice commission, EIMAC, claiming the war had voided the agreement.[17] Moreover, Israel had utterly no interest in returning to the 1949 armistice lines and surrendering their most recent battlefield successes. Egypt, on the other hand, agreed to permit ten countries to occupy its territory on its side of the cease-fire. Shortly thereafter, armed forces from Brazil, Canada, Colombia, Denmark, Finland, India, Indonesia, Norway, Sweden, and Yugoslavia, with support from Italy, Switzerland, and the US, came together to compose a force of 6,073 armed soldiers that took up positions in Egypt in February 1957.[18] The British and French would elect to withdraw, as would Israel from its position in the Gaza Strip. However, Israel stubbornly refused to permit UN forces to occupy land on its side of the 1948 demarcation line (see map 2.4).[19]

Despite Israel's noncooperation from 1957 onward, UNEF I was largely successful for an entire decade.[20] However, it operated solely on the Egyptian side of the border down to Sharm-el Sheikh at the southern tip of the Sinai Peninsula, overlooking the Straits of Tiran that was then open to Israel.[21] Conflict between Israel and its Arab neighbors for the next seven years was characterized by numerous minor border clashes. Over time, tensions would build and eventually explode in a more deadly and dangerous conflict.

The 1967 Six-Day War

That explosion happened on 5 June 1967. The Six-Day War, as it came to be known, erupted following a period of heightened tension between Egypt's Nasser and Israel's Prime Minister Levi Eshkol. Egypt announced that it would no longer allow Israeli shipping to transit the Straits of Tiran, a key concession Israel had won in 1956. Nasser then deployed Egyptian forces along the border with Israel and demanded the withdrawal of UNEF I.[22] In response to the perceived threat of an attack by Egypt, Israel preemptively bombed selected Egyptian airfields.[23] The Egyptians were caught totally by surprise. Their air force was summarily neutralized, giving Israel undisputed air superiority. In conjunction with Israeli Air Force (IAF) airstrikes, the Israel Defense Forces (IDF) simultaneously launched a ground offensive into the Gaza Strip and the Sinai, again surprising Nasser's army and defeating them, even as it hastily retreated toward the Suez Canal. It was a rout that inflicted heavy losses on the Egyptians by a determined IAF and IDF that would not stand by passively as prewar tension mounted on Israel's border.

Similarly, Israeli forces made short work of both the Syrian Army on the Golan Heights and the Jordanian military in East Jerusalem and the

Map 2.4. Post-1956 Sinai War Boundaries

West Bank. Interestingly, even the UN was caught in the fighting between
Israeli and Jordanian forces as combat erupted outside the Government
House in Jerusalem. There, Jordanian forces occupied the compound's
gardens with a machine gun team, and a battle raged between them and
the IDF. At one point the Jordanian machine gun squad attempted to
occupy the second floor of Government House but was forcefully
reproached by UN personnel, including the UNTSO chief of staff, Lieutenant General (LTG) Odd Bull (Norwegian Air Force), who insisted the
occupiers withdraw.[24] In time they did, and IDF forces then swept the UN
building afterward for remaining combatants. At the UN Security Council meeting of 5 June 1967, then United Nations Secretary-General U
Thant noted the incident in what he felt was a "breach of extreme seriousness."[25] Fortunately, there were no UN casualties, but the incident
highlighted the danger that unarmed UNMOs—even the UNTSO chief
of staff—faced then and in the years to come.[26]

A cease-fire was finally agreed to on 9 June after Arab forces were
thoroughly humiliated in a crushing defeat. Arab losses ranged from
10,000 to 15,000 troops, while Israel lost barely 1,000 soldiers.[27] By any
measure, the Arab defeat was devastating. Israel expanded it borders
from the Suez to the Jordan River, including its complete dominion over
Jerusalem. So embarrassing was this defeat that Nasser resigned in dis-
grace, only to return some months later. In the wake of this Arab debacle,
thousands of additional Palestinians fled from the West Bank. Many Syrians also evacuated the Golan Heights. Jews living in Arab countries were
also affected, fleeing to either Israel or other nations throughout the
world. It was a major Israeli victory, but one that would set in motion
more years of war and suffering (see map 2.5).

The UN would again be tasked to restore peace, and the US would be
a major part of that effort. UNTSO personnel redeployed to the new
cease-fire areas and established OPs on the Golan Heights and on each
side of the Suez Canal, the limits to which the Israelis had advanced and
occupied. Jordan's presence in a divided Jerusalem, including its control
of the West Bank, was obviated by the Israeli occupation of these areas.
Israel then renounced the remaining armistice agreements as null and
void as a result of the newly attained reality on the ground.[28] Nevertheless, the UN held that the armistice agreements and armistice commissions contained a provision that each would "remain in force until a
peaceful settlement between the parties is achieved."[29] As such, when I
arrived in UNTSO in 1981 the dormant commissions were still regarded
as valid by the UN.

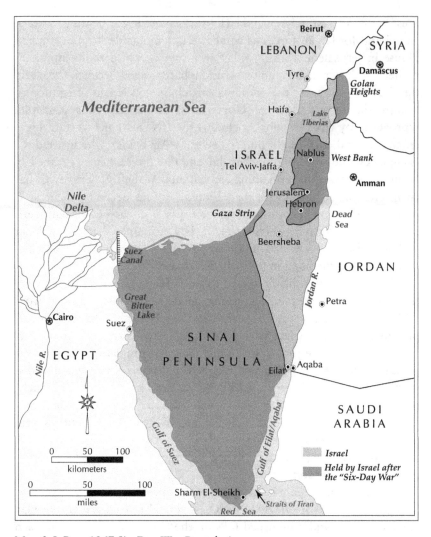

Map 2.5. Post-1967 Six-Day War Boundaries

Military observer duties again entered a period of relative stability between 1967 and 1972. However, violence rebounded, this time in southern Lebanon. The UN found it necessary to establish five OPs north of the Israeli border to address violations of Lebanese territory by the IDF, which was responding to threats from Arab militias occupying southern Lebanon. These new OPs fell under the authority of the ILMAC in Beirut; however, Israel did not sanction or recognize their legitimacy.[30]

As was the case with Israel's earlier renunciation of the armistice agreements and various MACs, by 1973 the UN was less credible and untrustworthy in the eyes of the Israeli government. It seemed that unrelenting conflict was paying off for Israel. The UN and UNTSO, in Israel's view, were of little consequence or benefit to them. By 1973, more conflict would erupt, this time initiated by the Arabs in an effort to finally reverse their record of defeat and humiliation.

The 1973 Yom Kippur War

On 6 October 1973, an Arab coalition chiefly composed of Egypt and Syria launched a surprise attack against Israel. On Yom Kippur—a widely observed holy day of rest, fasting, and prayer in Judaism—the Egyptians advanced across the cease-fire lines at the Suez Canal into the Sinai Peninsula, while the Syrians attacked in the Golan Heights in a coordinated operation to eject Israeli forces occupying both regions. Ominously, both the US and the Soviet Union immediately took sides—the former with Israel, the latter with the Arabs—orchestrating vital logistical and resupply operations to their respective allies, thereby raising the specter of a superpower confrontation, possibly involving nuclear weapons. Unlike previous conflicts, this one had the makings of a world war. Initially both Egypt and Syria made impressive gains, but within three days Israel had blunted both assaults. The IDF then engaged in a dramatic four-day counteroffensive deep into Syria, so deep that its artillery could range the outskirts of Syria's capital city, Damascus. This came as a shock to Egyptian president Anwar Sadat, who, fearing his Arab ally would collapse, commenced a second offensive to regain territory Egypt had initially lost. He sought to bolster Egypt's eventual negotiation stance when the fighting abated. Again, the IDF repulsed Egypt's counterattack, this time crossing the Suez Canal and advancing to the city of Suez during a week of fierce fighting with heavy casualties on both sides. An attempted cease-fire by the UN failed, and by 24 October the IDF had almost surrounded the entire Egyptian 3rd Army, threatening its complete demise in a humiliating defeat.

After much hasty diplomacy, most notably by US Secretary of State Henry Kissinger, a cease-fire went into effect on 28 October. The following December, the parties to the conflict were to assemble in Geneva, Switzerland, for a peace conference jointly held by the US and the USSR. However, the Syrians balked at attending this venue, thinking it would legitimize and enhance Israel's diplomatic position. That provoked Kissinger to seize the initiative and embark on what would come to be known as "shuttle diplomacy," traversing between Israel's capital and those of Arab states to negotiate a peace. The shuttle diplomacy worked with Egypt and Israel. By January 1974 both signed the Sinai Separation of Forces Agreement. Under the agreement, Israel withdrew its forces from the areas west of the Suez Canal that it had seized during the war. Further, the IDF withdrew along the entire Egyptian front to create a 10-kilometer buffer zone in the Sinai between combatants. A second disengagement force, UNEF II, was reinstituted and supported by UNTSO observers.[31] By the fall of 1975, Israel agreed to withdraw an additional 40 kilometers in what would be referred to as the Sinai II Agreement. Both arrangements were important achievements insomuch as they introduced the concept of trading "land for peace," a tactic that would be a vital component in future peace negotiations between Egypt and Israel during the Camp David negotiations four years later.

Meanwhile, Kissinger had to contend with continued artillery exchanges between Israel and Syria that could erupt into full-scale warfare. Four months after the Sinai agreement, Kissinger's shuttling between Israel and Syria resulted in a disengagement agreement on 31 May 1974 that included an Israeli withdrawal back to the Golan Heights, the establishment of a UN buffer zone, and an exchange of prisoners of war (POWs). It was at this point that the United Nations Disengagement Observer Force (UNDOF) was established to oversee the agreement in the Golan Heights between Israel and Syria, again supported by UNTSO observers.[32] In the end, Kissinger's efforts represented the first time since 1948 that Israel and its Arab opponents had engaged in direct negotiations. Without a doubt this most recent war, begun by Arab forces seeking to rectify previous defeats at the hands of Israeli forces, proved to be yet another painfully embarrassing Arab defeat. Conversely, it was another impressive Israeli victory over miscalculating Arabs who once again had been bettered and outmaneuvered in combat by the Jewish state they passionately despised (see map 2.6).

Despite its willingness to establish UNDOF, Israel remained hostile to UN peacekeeping efforts. As Israel had shown in walking away from and renouncing the armistice agreements and commissions, it simply did not trust its security to the UN. In a meeting with President Gerald R. Ford at the White House in June of 1975, Israeli prime minister Yitzhak Rabin made clear his view of UNTSO and other peacekeeping forces that had been deployed to the region in the past: "International guarantees

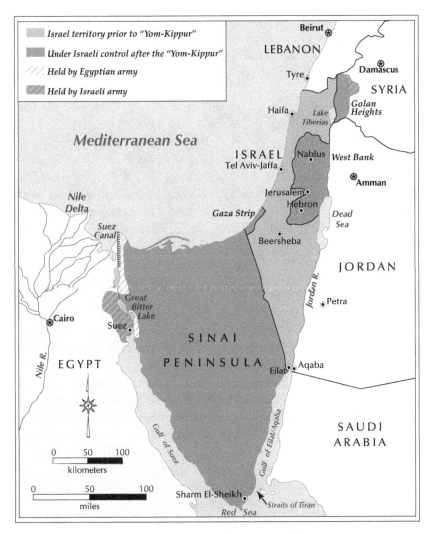

Map 2.6. Post-1973 Yom Kippur War Boundaries

have no meaning whatsoever with us. We have experienced them over many years. We have tried mixed armistice commissions, UNTSO, UNEF. We don't believe in putting our defense in the [their] hands. . . . To drag a major power into a conflict which is local would be a serious mistake. We have never asked for one American soldier to aid in our defense."[33]

Rabin was blunt in his characterization of UN peacekeeping efforts particularly when Israeli security was at stake. However, while he made a point to say Israel had no need of US forces on the ground, he had much need of US armaments, a factor that would come up in private conversations. Israel's attitude concerning the UN would persist in following years. UNTSO faced an uphill battle to gain Israel's confidence in its peacekeeping efforts. But as far as Israel was concerned, UNTSO was useless to their security.

As a postscript to the 1973 conflict, while the Lebanese had not engaged in it *per se*, the war did see minor attacks into Israel by the PLO from bases inside Lebanese territory. However, Israel, already contending with a two-front conflict, did not opt to send forces into Lebanon to confront Palestinian militants there. Nonetheless, PLO aggression would be a harbinger for more conflict ahead. Soon Israel would move aggressively to address the Palestinian threat to Israeli civilians in the Galilee region of northern Israel and, in the process, set the conditions for more conflict in war-torn Lebanon.

The 1978 Lebanese Invasion

When 1978 arrived, it should have been a year of peace in the Middle East. After all, the Camp David Accords were signed between Egypt and Israel on 17 September 1978 and represented the most significant peace initiative in the Middle East since the creation of the state of Israel. The willingness of Egypt's President Anwar Sadat and Israel's Prime Minister Menachem Begin to agree to a peace settlement brokered by US president Jimmy Carter was a stunning and positive development. Egypt in essence would recognize Israel for the first time, and Israel would agree to return the Sinai to Egypt in a "land for peace" agreement. Consequently, both Sadat and Begin would win the Nobel Prize for Peace for their actions. It was an optimistic time. However, that goodwill existed under a cloud of renewed tensions in southern Lebanon involving Israelis and Palestinians only months prior to the signing of the accords.

In March of 1978, Palestinian militants entered Israel and conducted a terrorist attack now referred to as the Coastal Road Massacre of March 1978. That incident saw the cold-blooded murder of 38 Israelis, including 13 children, and the wounding of 71 other civilians.[34] The attack, planned and executed by the PLO faction Fatah, outraged Israel. Israeli authorities decided it was time to push militant Palestinians out of southern Lebanon to positions north of the Litani River, a natural boundary that flowed from the Beqaa Valley in east central Lebanon to the Mediterranean coastline.

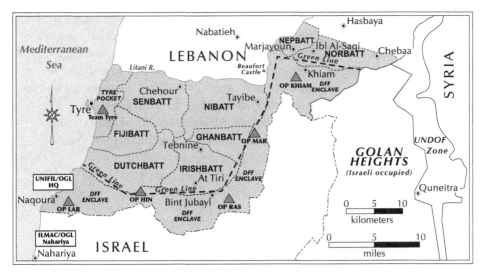

Map 2.7. Post-1978 Israeli Operation Litani Situational Boundaries

Named Operation Litani, the IDF conducted a week-long lightning-fast invasion that resulted in PLO forces retreating northward beyond the Litani River. In the process, an estimated 1,100 to 2,000 Lebanese and Palestinian deaths occurred, with only 11 IDF deaths (possibly as many as 20) and 57 wounded.[35] It was another sweeping Israeli victory. However, the invasion also produced 250,000 refugees in Lebanon, leading to the creation and hasty deployment of UNIFIL (see map 2.7).[36]

That armed force, supported by unarmed UNTSO military observers assigned to the newly formed Observer Group Lebanon (OGL), would have a mission to confirm Israel's withdrawal to its own borders, restore international peace and security, and assist the Lebanese government in reasserting its authority in the southern region.[37] With the imposition of UNIFIL, Israel withdrew most—but not all—of its forces south near their border, but left a remnant and a trusted ally behind as a safeguard. The South Lebanese Army (SLA) remained in the area south of the Litani River and north of the Israeli border as a buffer force friendly toward and armed by Israel but also particularly hostile to the newly arrived UNIFIL force. The SLA, also known as the De Facto Forces (DFF), was a Lebanese Christian militia that had been one of the players in the southern region during the Lebanese Civil War.[38] Originally referred to as the Free Lebanon Army and later the Army of Free Lebanon, it was a militia mainly operating under the direction and authority of MAJ Saad Haddad's Government of Free Lebanon. Backed by Israel, Haddad became Israel's primary surrogate in Lebanon following the 1978 incursion and continued in that role for several years. Both Haddad's forces and the Israelis battled against the PLO and later Hezbollah, an Iranian-backed Shi'a Islamist political party, as well as other militant groups based in Lebanon. Meanwhile, Israeli support for UN peacekeeping forces following the 1978 invasion was nonexistent. And like Israel, the DFF had no amity for UNIFIL.

This was the Lebanon many UNMOs would confront in 1981, with a mere three days of peacekeeping training. Our new neighborhood was one besieged by multilayered conflict and a legacy of violence. My studies had readied me for some of this. But my intellectual understanding about this tumultuous region—one that had witnessed war since the end of World War II—was insufficient. Soon I would see it with my own eyes. The ground that we would occupy as UNMOs—indeed even UNTSO's Government House—had witnessed death and destruction resulting from the animus between Arabs and Israelis. Fortunately, in February of 1981, UNTSO was astride three seemingly stable situations, one in the Sinai Desert, one on the Golan Heights, and one along the Jordan River, a respite of sorts between traditional enemies. But just over the horizon there was a smoldering civil war in southern Lebanon that—given the right accelerant—could quickly erupt in deadly flames. Lebanon had all the markings of further conflict.

The nature of conflict in the Middle East in the winter of 1981 was both dangerous and complex. An intolerance of ambiguity was the wrong frame of mind to comprehend the difficult business of peacekeeping. What was required was a clear-eyed understanding of the multiplicity of conflicts throughout the region. The Army had not taught me much diplomacy, only how to fight in combat. Nor had the UN taught me much about peacekeeping. I would have to rely on all of my tactical skills as a soldier and my untapped ability to deal with conflict diplomatically. In that regard, I was about to get a crash course in the discipline of peacekeeping and the fine art of diplomacy on contested ground.

In the process, I would also learn about not only the culture of the combatants in the Levant, but also the culture within UNTSO and that of US officers assigned to it. Let us examine that a bit closer.

3

The UNTSO-US Culture

Born on 29 May 1948, UNTSO was a well-worn veteran of Middle East peacekeeping by the winter of 1981.[1] It was perhaps well-worn to the point of being staid. Like a sage, slow-moving grandfather, UNTSO's experience—both good and bad—had grayed its temples over the years. With the arrival of military observers in the region after the 1948 war, UNTSO and the US became early collaborators in peacekeeping. Three US Marine Corps officers served as UNTSO chiefs of staff in its nascent years, 1948–1953, 1956–1958, and for six months in 1960.[2] By 1981, the US leadership profile had changed but remained significant with the assignment of two US Army lieutenant colonels to senior positions. One was the UNTSO chief operations officer, the other was one of the senior leaders in the observer group responsible for southern Lebanon. Like US officers before them, both recognized the realities of conflict in the Middle East and the need to move cautiously among contending sides. Both made that clear to every American military observer who arrived in UNTSO. Such a careful posture was part of UNTSO's culture from its beginning.

UNTSO's Cultural Influences

UNTSO was born amid discord and formed its institutional character as it responded to the changing nature of the conflict swirling about. It resisted internal changes that might jeopardize its carefully crafted approach to peacekeeping. Canadian Army LTC Jim Allan, who arrived in UNTSO five months after I did, took a somewhat dim view of the organization and its culture: "In 1981, UNTSO has been in existence as a peacekeeper of one form or another for thirty-three years, and it showed. During the indoctrination, the headquarters in a lovely old mansion of the former British 'Government House' quickly showed itself to be slow-moving, inflexible, hostile to constructive suggestions, and excessively bureaucratic."[3]

Allan's candid observations did not stop there. His impression of UNTSO was that of a "decadent, out-of-the-way garrison, in either the British army in India, or in the Ottoman Empire."[4] There were elements of truth to that description, particularly UNTSO's bureaucratic and procedural tendencies. However, it was hardly "decadent." In fact, Allan understates the delicate highwire balancing act UNTSO walked in its peacekeeping pursuits. While appearing overly cautious and remote to some, UNTSO was assiduously neutral in its early days as it led the mixed armistice commissions—or MACs—with impartiality. However, that was a difficult proposition. When the MAC chairmen proposed resolutions to problems, one side frequently opposed it. Absent unanimity, implementation was unrealized: "Even when the UNTSO chairman of a MAC voted to support a resolution proposed by one of the parties during the meeting, no mechanism existed to enforce outcomes. Thus, the parties used the forum provided by the MAC meeting to attempt to convince the observers of the value of their general cause rather than to clarify the specifics of the investigation at hand."[5]

The MACs were designed to resolve disputes. But the opposing sides were more interested in persuading MAC chairmen to become advocates for their particular view. Frequently when the decision went against one side or the other, the agreed resolution became a dead letter.

The normal routine found each side pressing for UNTSO's support and affirmation for their competing complaints, disputes, and accusations to suit their respective purposes. UNTSO resisted adopting the ancient Semitic proverb "the enemy of my enemy is my friend." Nor did the MACs seek friendship from either side. Consequently, UNTSO acquired the animosity of the more belligerent players on both sides of the conflict who were seeking advocacy, not impartiality. And that animosity could turn deadly. On 17 September 1948, just three months after UNTSO's establishment, UN mediator Count Folke Bernadotte of Sweden and his deputy, COL André Serot of France, were assassinated in Jerusalem by the Zionist group Lehi, also known as the Stern Gang.[6] Bernadotte's assailants viewed him as being preferential toward the Arabs and, therefore, a threat to Israel's future. Hostility toward UN peacekeeping would be part of the organization's future.[7] Neither was the US immune from the animus of the warring factions. On 23 May 1948, the week before UNTSO was established, US consul Thomas C. Wasson, a member of the UN Truce Commission, was assassinated in Jerusalem during what was believed to be an Arab-inspired attack.[8] Chief Petty Officer Herbert M. Walker, who was attached to the US consulate, lost his life in the same attack.[9] Violence and death accompanied both the UN and the US from UNTSO's birth, and sadly continued until 1988, when COL Rich Higgins (USMC) was kidnapped and murdered by Islamic terrorists. That hostility and other deaths served to shape the organizational culture within UNTSO, one that also influenced the US officers who served in it.

UN Profile and Culture

From its inception, UNTSO was overseeing a shaky peace between the parties to the conflict and quickly learned that staying within its designed structure was prudent. UNTSO operated according to Security Council Resolution 50 (1948) calling for a cessation of hostilities in Palestine and the supervision of the peace by the UN's mediator, who was in turn supported by military observers from member nations.[10] UNTSO was that entity, and the MACs were the primary venues used to arbitrate disputes between Israel and its Arab neighbors. Like a good umpire, UNTSO understood that it was best to avoid taking sides. But sometimes the disputing parties interpreted the appearance of neutrality as favoritism for one side over another, particularly when UNTSO resisted sharing one side's outrage at the other's actions. UNTSO's embrace of objectivity was precisely what good umpires do, calling balls and strikes. Unfortunately, UNTSO's inclination to neutrality did not win it much affection among Arabs and Jews in its early years.

From 1948 until the 1956 Suez Crisis, UNTSO dependably pursued its key functions of investigating violations of the armistice agreements, assisting with humanitarian support for displaced populations, facilitating POW exchanges, and fulfilling its observation and reporting duties along the cease-fire lines. Throughout it all, UNTSO was a supplier of unarmed officers who were impartial military observers executing their mission daily not at an "out-of-the way garrison," but firmly planted amid flesh and blood mortal enemies.

In its early years, UNTSO learned much about the parties to the conflict. The Arabs—still bumbling about in the years following their failure to secure the favorable and rational agreement offered them in the 1947 Partition Plan—were regarded in the Western press as somewhat feckless. Meanwhile, Israel's treatment by the press was generally more favorable, particularly given the Holocaust. For UNTSO, however, the story on the ground was more nuanced. Israel, galvanized to bare-knuckled survival from its very beginning, engaged in determined realpolitik to continually advantage itself politically and territorially vis-à-vis the Arabs. It was, after all, an existential motive for them to do so, given Israel's controversial and violent rebirth. Furthermore, in the years following Israel's founding, Egypt's President Nasser—eager to burnish his anti-Israel credentials— encouraged Palestinians to violence toward Jews. That further provoked Israel's defensive aggressiveness. From assassinations to the fomenting of violence, there was abundant blame for both sides of the conflict, UNTSO learned. But in the process, Israel became adroit in maintaining an upper hand both politically and militarily. In that environment, UNTSO slowly became sympathetic to the Arabs, given their history of getting the short end of the stick. That bias was reinforced by the 1956 war that revealed Israel to be the aggressor in the Anglo/Franco-inspired debacle.

UNTSO's creeping favoritism toward Arabs was tempered somewhat following the 1967 Six-Day War, when the Arabs sought to even the scales following the 1956 loss. They failed again and consequently bolstered international sympathy for Israel, which—despite its preemptive strike—was regarded as fighting for its survival. The Arabs attempted a second time during the 1973 Yom Kippur War to settle the score. Israel won decisively, making clear that Israel had no intent to withdraw quietly into the annals of modern Middle Eastern history. Indeed, Israel emerged from the 1973 war as a significant power, one that retained the unambiguous support of the US in resisting annihilation by hostile Arab forces. UNTSO now faced a quite muscular Israel that had not only seized more Arab territory but had occupied the moral high ground as the aggrieved party in yet another Arab-inspired assault. Nevertheless, those within UNTSO remained sympathetic to the Arabs, who were once again thoroughly trounced by Israel.

Following the 1973 war, UNTSO would return to its truce supervising duties while providing observer support to a revived armed disengagement force in the Sinai. UNEF II was deployed to supervise peace in the Sinai six years after Egypt's Nasser demanded the withdrawal of UNEF I during the 1967 war. However, by 1974 there was a new player in the region. UNDOF was positioned atop the militarily significant Golan Heights to keep peace between Israel and Syria. Unarmed UNMOs from UNTSO would support both organizations.

In the autumn of 1978, the Camp David Accords generated much hope, particularly in placating the conflict between Israel and its chief adversary, Egypt. Unfortunately, the previous spring witnessed the infamous coastal road massacre inside Israel by Arab terrorists, provoking

Israel to invade southern Lebanon in March 1978. Arguably Israel's actions were warranted, given the threat posed by hostile Arab forces operating from southern Lebanon to attack the Jewish population. Yet Israel significantly escalated the conflict, literally invading a country that had not attacked them. Regrettably, Lebanon was embroiled in its own civil war and was the unfortunate and reluctant host to militant Arab forces who routinely attacked Israel from Lebanese territory. Something had to give in this struggle of life and death, and Israel was unwilling to wait for the UN, much less UNTSO, to resolve the dispute.

The 1978 Lebanon incursion further stressed relations between the larger UN community and Israel. Following the invasion, Israel regarded UNIFIL as an aggravation. Because UNTSO supported UNIFIL by monitoring and reporting violations of the cease-fire, UNTSO's relations with Israel and its Christian militia allies in southern Lebanon were strained— so badly that in some ways both UNIFIL and UNTSO were viewed as parties to the conflict by Israel and its militia allies. Nor was the PLO supportive of the UN's presence in southern Lebanon, if it meant their paramilitary efforts would be disrupted by peacekeepers. This hostility was worrisome to the UN, and especially to those of us who were unarmed military observers.

So, in 1981 when I formally began my training, accomplishing its mission fairly and impartially was challenging for UNTSO since it encountered persistent hostility from all sides. Much had changed in how UNTSO operated from its early days. Now it was not simply providing unarmed military observers operating from isolated OPs or moving about on local patrols as it did prior to 1956 and between the 1967 and 1973 wars. Now it had military observers positioned amid armed peace enforcers who were precariously wedged between better armed regional belligerents.

Even though that may not have been UNTSO's envisioned purpose, focused as it initially was on maintaining peace between Arabs and Jews in Palestine, its mission had evolved as its operational footprint enlarged. Subsequent wars and expanding territorial conflicts required UNTSO to adapt and augment emerging peacekeeping missions. In a sense, UNTSO's mission changed as it—like a circus trapezist—brachiated from one war to another. UNTSO had evolved into an on-call provider of unarmed UN observers, ready to deploy throughout the Levant as the situation dictated. If anything, in 1981 UNTSO was neither staid nor an "out-of-the-way" garrison, but very much an "in the way" force facing real danger. Moreover, UNTSO's mission to support armed UN forces also had real implications for unarmed peacekeepers, because when the bullets whizzed by, they did not discriminate between armed and unarmed targets.

The US Profile and Culture in UNTSO

From our first day in UNTSO, our US comrades made no secret of the fact that America's military observers were regarded as "go-getters," given our training, the number of combat veterans in our ranks, and our professional stature. Moreover, our English-speaking allies, Australians, Canadians, Irish, and New Zealanders—including the French who spoke English well—were regarded as closely tied to the US in terms of competence. It was hard to ignore this connection in 1981, even among other nationalities in UNTSO whose native language was not English, particularly when it came to planning and executing military operations. American Army officers permanently held both the chief operations officer's position in UNTSO and senior leadership in OGL, the preeminent hotspot in UNTSO's area of operations. Moreover, UNTSO's leadership trusted the US and internationals with close ties to them, even if other nationalities were somewhat put off by that deference. To be sure, our common English tongue was a factor. But English-speaking nations (and the French) also shared much in their military backgrounds, doctrine, and education. In that regard, the "corps'" identity was no accident but quite natural, even if other nationalities had to begrudgingly acknowledge that fact.

To be sure, the US influence in UNTSO was well-established, reaching back to 1948. In 1981 that prominence continued with no less than 35 American officers and one senior noncommissioned officer assigned to influential positions. Indeed, the "corps" of native English-speakers composed 90 of the 293 officers in UNTSO. And the US composed more than a third of that 90 (see table 3.1).

Meanwhile, observers of all nationalities were deployed across the Levant, except those from the USSR. For diplomatic and political reasons, Israel, Jordan, and Lebanon refused to allow Soviet observers on their territory. As a result, the 36 Russians were split evenly between Syria and Egypt, where they had a history of military cooperation apart from the UN. So unwelcomed were the Soviets by Jewish authorities—given Russia's history of prejudice against Jews—that they were not even permitted to enter Israel to visit UN facilities. Beyond our American numbers at the time, events and leadership assignments early in UNTSO's existence had helped shape the US culture and attitudes in the organization.

Table 3.1.   UN Military Observer Personnel, 1981

Country	Military Observers	Comments
Argentina	8	No Assignment Restrictions
Australia	9	No Assignment Restrictions
Austria	13	No Assignment Restrictions
Belgium	7	No Assignment Restrictions
Canada	20	No Assignment Restrictions
Chile	5	No Assignment Restrictions
Denmark	12	No Assignment Restrictions
Finland	21	No Assignment Restrictions
France	25	No Assignment Restrictions
Ireland	21	No Assignment Restrictions
Italy	9	No Assignment Restrictions
Netherlands	15	No Assignment Restrictions
New Zealand	4	No Assignment Restrictions
Norway	16	No Assignment Restrictions
Sweden	36	No Assignment Restrictions
Union of Soviet Socialist Republics	36	Assignments Restricted to Egypt and Syria
United States of America	36	Assigned Position of Chief Operations Officer
Total	**293**	

While not a military observer, the first US peacekeeping casualty, US consul Thomas C. Wasson, was a member of the truce commission. US participants in the early years of UNTSO would recall that tragedy. The US also played a significant part in shaping UNTSO in its early years. LTG William Edward Riley (USMC) took the helm as UNTSO's chief of staff from 1948 to 1953. From 1956 to 1958, COL Byron V. Leary (USMC) served in the top position, and in 1960 COL Robert W. Rickert (USMC) led UNTSO. The US influence was foundational in the organization, and we appreciated our legacy of leadership in UNTSO.

Most US officers arriving in UNTSO had a favorable opinion of Israel, in no small part due to a positive view of Israel in American culture and media. However, once exposed to both sides of the equation, it was not uncommon for US observers to sympathize with the plight of Arabs. After all, Palestinians had been forced from their homes to live in refugee settlements in other lands, a constant reminder that Arabs had consistently fallen short in their struggle with Israel. The Arabs, it seemed to us, made a special effort to be both respectful and tolerant of Americans they encountered, as if there were some well-coordinated *sotto voce* public relations campaign designed to befriend us and enlist our sympathy. I would see this across the region, with the exception of duty in southern Lebanon, where tension caused people to be more reserved. Moreover, the Arabs had become quite adept at using rhetoric to pull at our heartstrings. They would routinely appropriate the rhetoric of the "diaspora," the term used to describe the dispersion of the Jewish people beyond Israel who were scattered throughout a world where they were often mistreated or despised. Now the Arabs would assert they were the ones in search of a homeland, while refusing to acknowledge the huge errors in judgment their leaders had made in not accepting a Partition Plan that would have benefitted them. Having insisted on the whole loaf, they were now stuck with a thin slice. They would entertain no criticism suggesting self-inflicted errors in shaping their condition in the region, not even in casual conversation. As far as some Arabs were concerned, now they were the victims. That view was entrenched and created the overall impression that they were the underdog, even if it was a condition of their own making.

If Arabs were on a charm offensive with UNTSO's observers in general and Americans specifically, the Israelis—particularly the members of their military that we encountered in the course of our duties—were on an offensive to offend. By 1981, UNTSO was thoroughly unwanted by the Israelis, and they made no secret of that in the way they engaged us. In November of 1979, in his first week assigned to UNTSO in southern Lebanon, CPT Lenny Supko (USMC) found the Israelis thoroughly objectionable, noting as his first impression that they were "very aggressive and uncourteous people, pushy and brusque," and did little to disguise their dislike of Americans. On the other hand, Supko found the Arabs "extremely polite, almost fawning."[11] Individual Israelis were considerate enough, like the folks you would routinely encounter in the markets, restaurants, and other places of normal interaction. It was said in popular culture that Israelis were like the sabra plant, prickly on the outside, but having a sweet core. It was a popular myth easily debunked by the impatience Israelis exhibited for any UN vehicle driving anywhere in Jerusalem. With seeming delight, they would blare their automobile horns at us when we took a second longer than necessary to resume travel after a stoplight turned green. The IDF's dislike of the UN—and American observers in particular—was not subtle either. Nor was that hostility a recent occurrence.

In the early 1960s while serving as UNTSO's chief, COL Rickert was subjected to quite disrespectful treatment by no less than the Israeli foreign minister, Golda Meir. In his "In Memoriam" for Rickert, who passed away in 1995, Andrew I. Killgore, who was the publisher of the *Washington Report on Middle East Affairs,* noted that Rickert arrived in Israel "sympathetic to the plight of the Jews and to the State of Israel and tending to skepticism toward things Arab."[12] Rickert's attitude would change over time: "After a few months in Jerusalem, however, those same UNTSO officers, whether from Australia, Britain, Canada, France, Ireland, Italy, New Zealand, Scandinavia, or the U.S., generally became critical of Israeli policies and sympathetic to the plight of the Arabs—especially the Palestinians—who always seemed to get a black eye in the Western media, particularly in America. Nearly all of those Western military officers, like their diplomatic compatriots, saw things in a totally different light after viewing Arab-Israeli relations first hand and at close range."[13]

While leading UNTSO, Israeli hostility toward Rickert was undisguised. He received a series of "summons" to meet with Meir to be dressed down vigorously by the foreign minister, whose lectures seemed a bit contrived. According to Killgore, Meir was perturbed by UNTSO's reporting of firing incidents between Syrians and Israelis in the Golan Heights. Meir would point to coverage by the US press—aligned with Israel's view—that blamed Syria. She would then berate Rickert for UNTSO's investigations that frequently found her army at fault, ultimately leading to UN resolutions blaming Israel.

Colonel Rickert's first meeting with Golda Meir was shocking. Rather than the kindly grandmother he had been led by media reports to expect, he was confronted by a caustic, intimidating figure who seemed to blame him personally not only for the current resolution critical of Israel, but all the previous critical resolutions as well. She more than implied that he and other UNTSO officers were acting from anti-Israel or "anti-Semitic" motives. In fact, the situation on the ground on the Israel-Syria cease-fire line was that a militarily stronger Israel was seizing land, field by field, from a militarily weaker Syria. Colonel Rickert and fellow UNTSO officers realized that in order to cover up this step-by-step territorial aggrandizement, Mrs. Meir's intimidating tirades were aimed solely at effecting changes favorable to Israel in UNTSO's reporting to New York.[14]

A marine, Rickert was not accustomed to such disrespect, but he tolerated it nonetheless. It was humiliating and contributed to the hostility and mistrust between US personnel who came after Rickert and Israeli officials who succeeded Meir. Killgore concludes with this observation: "However, it was demeaning for him and other American officers to be on the receiving end of the foreign minister's tongue-lashings and false personal allegations. Particularly galling was the fact that Ukrainian-born, Milwaukee-raised Golda Meir, who had never relinquished her American citizenship, was making her crude accusations, which she had every reason to know were untrue, in fluent American English."[15]

Meir's causticity to a fellow American was unjustified and influenced attitudes among Americans serving in UNTSO at the time. Unfortunately, that dynamic would continue. A decade and a half later, Prime Minister Rabin had little good to say of either UNTSO or other peacekeeping efforts orchestrated by the UN, calling them "meaningless."[16] While Rabin was not hostile to President Ford in his June 1975 meeting, he was verbally dismissive of the UN and UNTSO. We would experience precisely that sort of attitude from Jewish authorities and their soldiers, several of whom were in fact American expatriates serving in the Israeli Army for a season. I witnessed several incidents of this sort of hostility on the Israeli border with Jordan, crossing Israel's northern border into Lebanon, and at checkpoints manned by the Israeli soldiers in the Jordan Valley traveling north to the Golan Heights region. The treatment was insolent, disdainful, unnecessarily aggravating, and designed to delay and harass UN vehicles carrying US officers, a direct violation of our diplomatic status. It was as if they saw US officers not as international peacekeepers, but as biased and malevolent intruders who were complicit with Israel's enemies. We were not. But it made being impartial difficult.

The toll on US UNMOs gave Israel a black eye in the opinion of many of us, particularly since the military vehicles the Israelis drove and the weapons they carried were likely funded by US taxpayers. In time, I found myself fed up with this contemptuous treatment and on a few occasions took the opportunity to "dress down" a few of the offending expatriate Americans concerning their treatment of fellow Americans. In a few instances, I reminded them that a more honorable military service might be found in the uniform I was wearing, not a foreign one of a "supposed" US ally. I recall exiting my vehicle and bluntly remarking to one smart-alecky Israeli soldier that "I look forward to seeing you back in America," to which he reluctantly motioned me through the checkpoint without further comment. Nothing came of these flareups one way or the other, but attitudes were shaped and misshaped. And in the process, sympathy among Americans for Arabs ascended by default, not design.

US officers formed attitudes about UNTSO that were consistent with those of Canadian Jim Allan. Those attitudes jelled early. During our orientation, we became aware of the paradoxical nature of the UN and its peacekeeping structure. It was a system of old and new, having both direct and indirect lines of authority. That included defunct organizations that continued to appear in UNTSO's structure for legal and diplomatic purposes rather than for any practical reason beyond face-saving. With the ever-changing face of cease-fires—actually fragile periods of attenuated violence—by 1981 UNTSO had become a supplier of military observers to whatever cease-fire arrangement materialized on the heels of the most recent crisis. Now it would be a respondent to the exigencies of the next mission that sprang from the loins of the UN Security Council. In a sense UNTSO became a 9-1-1 emergency call center in the peacekeeping world. "Need an UNMO? Just call 1-911-UNTSO," it seemed.

For the US contingent as well as the other international UNMOs, this approach—essentially reactive—left us pondering whether peacekeeping should be more than dialing up UNMOs as the situation dictated. US officers appreciated proactive organizations with clearly defined missions to achieve fundamental objectives, the very sort of goal definition that would help peacekeeping organizations like UNTSO. Our military training—our culture—equipped us to shape and refine the mission of organizations. That would have begun with a mission evaluation, an understanding of the ends, ways, and means, and a course of action analysis to select the right way to engage that mission. All of that seemed strangely absent in a military organization that had fallen into a rote way of doing business, where innovation and revision took a back seat to doing business as usual. UNTSO's comfort zone was simply supplying observers as required as opposed to improving the way it fulfilled its mission. They seemed blinkered to change. Nevertheless, Americans and our international partners who shared our planning and operating doctrine occasionally managed to exert our skills to help UNTSO execute its mission, despite its ossified procedures and resistance to reform.

UNTSO's organization chart was also rooted in the past. Its construct was at once unified, delegated, and in some instances defunct. The clear line of authority flowed from the UN Headquarters in New York to UNTSO, but through Undersecretary-General in Charge of Peacekeeping Brian Urquhart, who supervised UNTSO's activities as well as UNDOF in the Golan Heights and UNIFIL in southern Lebanon. However, two of UNTSO's main military observer groups were under the operational control of UNDOF and UNIFIL, respectively. Observer Group Golan (OGG) reported directly to UNDOF and Observer Group Lebanon (OGL) to UNIFIL. The other observer groups, one in Jerusalem and another in Egypt, reported directly to UNTSO. Observer Group Jerusalem (OGJ) was based in East Jerusalem and manned the operations center at Government House while also routinely providing military observers to augment OGL in southern Lebanon. Observer Group Egypt (OGE), based in Cairo, was almost entirely without challenge, given the stable situation in the Sinai. UNTSO also maintained liaison offices in Amman, Jordan, and in the Gaza Strip that were obscure in nature. The Jordanian office primarily coordinated border issues along the Jordan River. The Gaza group putatively maintained liaison with the Israeli Army there, but in fact ran the UN recreation center situated on Mediterranean shoreline. Neither did much practical work in peacekeeping per se. Lastly, UNTSO maintained in its structure the two now-defunct armistice commissions that were once the venues UNTSO used to coordinate peacekeeping activities with Israel and its neighboring Arab states (see figure 3.1).

The mixed armistice commissions were significant when first created, but by 1981 were largely defunct. The Israeli-Syrian commission centered on the most precious Middle Eastern commodity—water—and sovereignty in the Israeli-Syrian demilitarized zone in the Golan Heights. Similarly, the commission between Jordan and Israel primarily focused on issues concerning a divided Jerusalem, including the Israeli enclaves throughout and around the city, Arab infiltration across the armistice demarcation line, and refereeing significant Israeli military incursions into Jordanian territory. The commission in Egypt had a focus on the Sinai and Gaza and was all but dissolved after the Camp David Accords were signed. Finally, the Israel-Lebanon commission remained a convenient venue for the Lebanese government to interact with UNTSO, but the Israelis had no interest in it. In 1981, it was little more than a liaison office that coordinated with our observers in southern Lebanon. In essence, these MACs had all become obsolete, only kept alive on paper as a matter of principle and legalese. UNTSO maintained they would "remain in force until a peaceful settlement between the parties is achieved."[17]

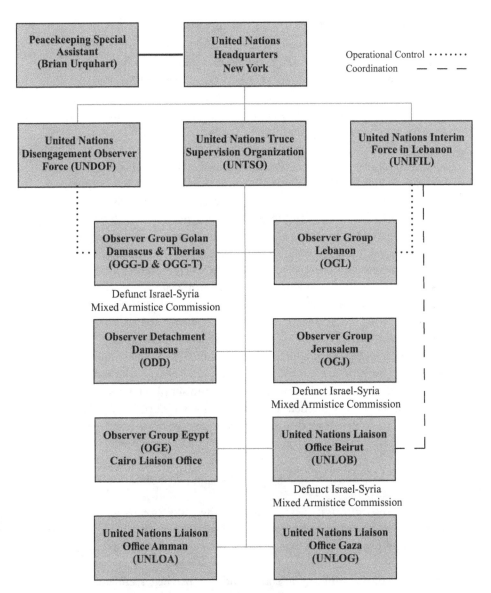

Fig. 3.1. UN Middle East Peacekeeping Organization, 1981

In sum, UNTSO's structure was a patchwork of connections, organizations moribund and active, all differing in significance and concomitant presence on the ground. Nonetheless, it reflected the evolving mission of the organization consistent with UNTSO's disinclination toward functionality. For UNTSO, what the organization lacked in clarity it made up for in consistency, even though it was confusing to newly arriving military observers. Had the competent among us been tasked to make improvements in UNTSO, we could have made some useful changes in mission efficiency, training, and operating effectiveness. However, reform to the well-entrenched UNTSO bureaucracy was akin to swallowing castor oil. It would not go down easily. It was not hard to think of better ways to do business within a military framework. For example, UNTSO's staid approach was evident in our initial training at Government House. The information was trivial and rote, with more emphasis on "thou shalt nots" than the substance of peacekeeping operations and challenges we would encounter.[18] But the message was clear to us. Do it our way, even if there are better ways.

While UNTSO's Byzantine approach to procedures was inflexible, that contrasted sharply with the relaxed and truncated workday. A typical day ended in the early afternoon. That was countercultural to many of us who were conditioned to a full day's work in military units. When asked about my US Army work schedule, I would say, "My workdays are very predictable: 24 hours a day, 7 days a week, not including overtime." All of us who had served in combat units were used to longer hours. Imagine our surprise when we were told the UN workday ran from 8:00 a.m. to 3:00 p.m., consistent with the Middle Eastern practice of curtailing work in the afternoon to escape the heat of the day. In fact, after a long break from the hot sun, many Arab shopkeepers would return to work after sundown when things were cooler. Not so in the UN. When 3:00 p.m. arrived, the workforce departed, except for those deployed on observer duty far from any garrison. Many of us wondered to ourselves and aloud how UNTSO, primarily acting as an outsized peacekeeper replacement detachment, could effectively fulfill its mission with a six-hour workday.

Our preparation as peacekeepers—a new skill for us all—was also underwhelming. Most of our time was devoted to reading volumes of dry history and procedures. It was hard to stay engaged. The topics included a history of UNTSO, its evolving mission over time, the structure of the organization, our diplomatic status and our privileges and immunities, our identification cards and visa requirements, the handling of UN security documents, driver training, restrictions of what merchandise we could carry across borders, and a plethora of regulations including military dress, time off, travel throughout the region, and use of UNTSO aircraft for personal transit. As my Navy colleague Bozeman recalled, after learning how to fill out UN forms, the procedures to start a field power generator, and how to drive a UN jeep, we were left in a distinct state of "boredom."[19] In reality, it was more of an orientation than training. It included virtually nothing on how to actually keep peace or the challenges that would entail. While our Danish trainer, the very affable CPT Paul Hoyer, had experience as an observer, he offered few insights into how to avoid being taken hostage, how to deal with firing incidents, and deescalation techniques we would have found beneficial. My diary entry after our training concluded summed up my view of the experience: "The rest of the week was spent at UNTSO HQ where I and two other fellow travelers, Virg [Bozeman] and George [Casey], endured a series of interminable briefings which were all in all quite useless. Shelley spent the time writing letters and picking up a few things from the local UN store."

Hoyer was also responsible for our driver training in the bulky UN tactical utility vehicles we would use in the mission area. The training also included operating standard Volkswagen Passat station wagons and minibuses like the one MSG Bruce Brill used to retrieve us from the airport in Tel Aviv. Hoyer road tested us on a rocky and unpaved path on the perimeter of Government House, as if that would replicate what we would encounter in the mission area. It did not. What did recreate a realistic setting was when we took our first drive among civilians racing around Jerusalem. Residents in both Israeli and Arab communities in Jerusalem did not drive slowly, but they did generally follow the rules of the road. Impatience characterized the attitudes of native drivers. Any patience on our part was not regarded as a virtue. I recall one of us asking, "Is this the way people drive in Damascus and Cairo?" Hoyer was quite clear, answering us with the question, "Do you know what they call the white lines on the streets there? A waste of perfectly good paint." On a somber note, we were told that if we became involved in a serious accident that resulted in the accidental death of an Arab, particularly desert-dwelling Bedouins, serious retribution could be swift. He related a story where a Scandinavian observer in the Sinai accidently struck and killed a Bedouin child crossing the desert. The father of the deceased child took immediate vengeance on one of the driver's children who accompanied him and his wife. This horrible incident instilled in all of us an added sense of caution. An "eye for an eye" was not simply a saying among some desert nomads. It could materialize right before you.

On a lighter note, we were also advised on how to cook while on observer duty, including menu ideas and the necessary equipment we needed on OP duty. Each OP was manned by four observers for a week at a time. So, there were ample opportunities to cook a meal for the other three during the course of the week. We were instructed to purchase no less than two "OP baskets," which were rectangular wicker baskets with a wooden bottom, to carry dry goods, spices, and cooking utensils. These OP baskets were actually made in Damascus, and observers would make a shopping trip there to acquire them or have them purchased by someone in Damascus and sent back aboard a UN vehicle. We would also need a cooler to take our perishable items, such as meat, dairy products, and eggs. And to our surprise we learned that alcohol was permitted while on OP duty. Enjoying wine, beer, or an aperitif in the evening was quite routine. The exception to the rule was when observers were on shift in the observation tower or conducting local patrols, when they were not permitted to imbibe. Some observers would refer to life on an OP during less active days as "cooking and looking." That, we would come to learn, was much the case on the Golan Heights and the Sinai, where the situation was generally stable. Not so much in southern Lebanon, however, where violence could erupt quickly and without warning. In sum, none of our training at UNTSO was particularly challenging. But Bozeman, Casey, and I all played along, careful to project a studious attitude so as not to betray our contrived interest in learning the ropes to tie a fairly simple knot.

In that regard, we made every effort to cooperate diplomatically. Our senior officers in UNTSO—as well as contacts in the Pentagon who had sent us on this assignment—reminded us that as American officers we had a prominent profile in UNTSO. The US had a reputation of sending competent, well-trained, focused, and no-nonsense officers to UNTSO who would exhibit those traits in the course of their assignment. But that could be misinterpreted as arrogance, something we wanted to avoid. Yet, for most US officers it was hard to resist stepping up, taking charge when the situation warranted, and shaping circumstances and actions to produce the most professional result, whether that involved developing plans and orders or suggesting courses of action when a thoughtful and timely response was required.

US officers were trained to think in a disciplined manner about operations in terms of what we called "troop leading procedures." That contemplated several steps, including receiving the mission, issuing a warning order, making a tentative plan, starting necessary movement to the mission area, conducting a reconnaissance of the area, and completing the plan—all while being careful to use no more than a third of one's available time for planning so as to preserve two-thirds of the time for execution. This was followed by issuing final orders and supervising the execution of them. Add to that our routine use of what we called the "five-paragraph field order" that outlined fundamental areas of planning for any operation. That would include elements like the enemy and friendly situation, our mission, the plan's execution, necessary logistics, and command, control, and communication factors. And when we planned, we also considered what we called "METT-T." That included an analysis of the mission, the enemy we faced, our troops available, the terrain we would occupy, and the time available to conduct an operation, all critical factors in quickly and efficiently evaluating a situation. These processes typified how US officers approached our business. However, such action-oriented behavior could appear heavy-handed to those who were not used to a disciplined and focused framework that, in some cases, required a sense of urgency. Our training instilled in us a bias for action. Standing around wondering what needed be done in any given situation was inconsistent with how we were trained to conduct operations efficiently. Yet as necessary as these skills were, we had to be cautious in employing them as if we knew best and others should simply comply. In truth, our competence in doing our job—quietly, efficiently, and diplomatically—would say more about our skills than demonstrating the hard-charging attitudes we routinely exhibited in the America military, where such a posture is expected and taken without offense. In short, we had to adapt our hard-charging culture to one that relied more on patience and diplomacy than bravado. Some were able to do this as a matter of will. Others among our American cohort were less inclined to rein in their energy and enthusiasm, and sometimes an intervention was needed for those who were harming our ability to work with our international partners.

In sum, the UN and US cultures in UNTSO were shaped by several factors. For the UN it was its identity from its inception, its ability to retain impartiality, and the difficult balance it had to maintain between contending parties who were often hostile and uncooperative. That contributed to a very conservative approach to business. UNTSO resisted change even when change might have been beneficial. So too, UNTSO found little need to reexamine its organizational structure, even as missions changed over time and warranted restructuring. The UNTSO of the past seemed sufficient enough, it thought, even after the situation on the ground changed significantly.

Like UNTSO, the US culture was also influenced by the regional parties to the conflict, and with that a bias resulted. Many of us arrived with an empathy for the Jewish people over history and the challenges they faced from a hostile Arab world in 1981. However, once exposed to the conflict and the perspective of both sides, many of us became more balanced in our view and increasingly sympathetic to the Arabs and their situation across the Levant. In this regard, our shifting sentiments toward the Arabs had the effect of satisfying an Israeli self-fulfilling prophecy: that the UN (and US military observers in particular) favored the Arabs and were fundamentally anti-Israel. That was a false conclusion. It didn't have to be that way. However, Israeli leaders and soldiers bore much responsibility for grooming a resentful attitude among US military observers toward Israel. In reality, Israel did more to alienate American officers than Arabs ever did to effectuate our sympathy for their positions.

Our culture, as very capable military officers, was at odds with our need to be diplomatic and not overbearing toward our international colleagues. We were well-trained and competent hard-chargers used to a full day's work. That could become an impediment if we did not meter our attitudes and avoid being domineering in performing our duties. We had to take upon ourselves a diplomatic restraint in order to work effectively within UNTSO. Regardless of how disjointed, seemingly arcane, slow-paced, and resistant to change UNTSO was, we were compelled to work within that culture. Inside Government House we would learn that the UNTSO heartbeat thumped ever so slowly, yet resolutely. It was not interested in any heart surgery we might be capable of doing.

Yet with the graying temples of a wise old man, maybe UNTSO had a deeper appreciation for the challenges of peacekeeping than we could comprehend, action oriented as we were. More likely, the years resting on a settling foundation of Jerusalem limestone had created a sedentary condition in UNTSO, dimming or blinkering its vision and sapping its vitality to be more productive. In February of 1981, both possibilities alternated in my mind. That said, I had much to learn in the days, weeks, and months to come. My eyes would be opened to things I never imagined. The Levant, a land with a legacy of irreconcilable conflict, held many lessons for those of us willing to understand them. And my assignment in the ancient city of Damascus would be my first stop along the way to grasping some of that wisdom.

4

The Road to Damascus

On Thursday, 26 February 1981, we arose early to depart for Damascus, our new home. Our trip would take us north to the Sea of Galilee and over the Golan Heights and onward to the Syrian capital. MSG Bruce Brill arrived about mid-morning to help us load our luggage into his reliable UN Volkswagen bus. As we took our seats on a chilly and windy morning, Brill informed us that we would have a long trip that day since he had to make a stop at the US embassy in Tel Aviv to drop off and pick up the mail for US observers assigned to UNTSO. We had by then adjusted to Brill's aggressive driving habits as we wound through North Jerusalem to continue our trip down the Weizmann Highway and westward. As we descended toward the coastal plain, a lowering gray sky loomed ahead of us and produced a storm along the way. When we arrived in Tel Aviv, it was more humid, but the weather was clearing. As Brill dealt with his postal duties, Shelley and I visited the US embassy commissary to pick up a few last-minute items we thought we might need in Syria.

By 1:00 p.m. we were back on the road to Tiberias, located on the western shore of the Sea of Galilee. As the day wore on, the sun came out and provided an opportunity to take some superb pictures. We headed through the Valley of Armageddon in central Israel, upward past Nazareth, where Jesus spent his childhood, and then past Mount Tabor, the traditional site of the Messiah's transfiguration. Finally, we arrived in the seaside city of Tiberias to refuel and briefly visit the office of Observer Group Golan-Tiberias (OGG-T) that served as a liaison with the IDF. Tiberias, named for Rome's second emperor, was founded in 18 A.D. by Herod Antipas, the Roman tetrarch of Galilee. From there we beheld the vast Sea of Galilee, the site of so much of Jesus's ministry. It was a beautiful setting, and we were a bit envious of not ending our journey right there. But our destination lay further to the east along that famous road to Damascus.

According to biblical tradition, it was along that road that Saul of Tarsus, or the Apostle Paul, saw Jesus appear before him. In that miraculous encounter, Paul was struck blind and immediately abandoned his brutal persecution of Christians, whom he regarded as heretics, and instead took up their cause. He would go on to become the most celebrated and influential Christian in the early Church period. That event has since been referred to as Paul's "Damascus Road Experience." It struck both Shelley and me that, in a sense, we too were on a journey along the road to Damascus, anticipating less miraculous peacekeeping revelations.

When we finished refueling, it was late afternoon and Brill declared we had exactly 30 minutes to reach the border before it closed at 5:00 p.m. He wasted no time speeding us along the northern shore of the Sea of Galilee. As we transited this historical region, it was impossible to avoid thinking about the contradictions of the place. On the one hand, it was here that people experienced extraordinary teachings of Jesus concerning peace and love. Yet it was a place stained with blood, both ancient and modern. Historically, the Golan also witnessed much strife, especially between the Israelis and the Aramaeans, who lived in the region near Damascus. Later Persia seized the region from the kingdoms of Assyria and Babylon, eventually permitting the Jewish people to return to the area after the Babylonian captivity, 598 to 538 B.C. The Itureans, Arabs of Aramaic descent, then populated the area in the second century B.C. and remained there until the end of the Byzantine period in 1453 A.D. The ancient Jewish city Gamla, the capital of the Jewish Gaulanitis people who had settled east of the Sea of Galilee, was a base of operations for Jews seeking to expel the Romans from Judea from 66 to 135 A.D. But by the sixth century A.D. the remaining Jews there were once again conquered by the Arabs under the powerful caliph Umar ibn al-Khattāb. Following the fall of the Byzantine empire in 1453 A.D., the Ottoman empire controlled the Golan. Then, under their post–World War I mandate in Syria, the French ruled it until 1946, when the modern Syrian Arab Republic was founded. And in 1967 and 1973 Israel seized and consolidated its control over this militarily significant terrain. Indeed, the Golan's history was steeped in conflict. It remained so that day as we approached it in a UN minibus perilously rounding turn after turn—sometimes seemingly on two wheels—with the relentless Brill pressing upward to crest the heights before the border gates promptly closed.

As we transited the northern shore of the Sea of Galilee, we could see the Golan Heights looming before us. Atop it a military force could dominate the land below (see map 4.1).

The Golan is a vast area of about 1,800 square kilometers bordered by the Yarmouk River to the south, the Sea of Galilee and Hula Valley to

Map 4.1. 1981 Golan Heights and UNDOF Area of Operations

the west, the towering Mount Hermon to the north, and Wadi Raqqad (a desert plain) to the east that ran onward to Damascus. As we approached the border, I cautiously put my camera aside, concerned that the IDF would object if I were to photograph their military positions. Brill then turned to me and asked sarcastically, "Now would you please tell me how the hell the Arabs lost those heights? It really says something about how bad their army is, doesn't it?" Having studied tactics, I readily agreed. Approaching the border crossing, we observed many Israeli units. We also saw vehicles belonging to the armed UNDOF, all painted white with a black "UN" stenciled prominently to clearly identify them as peacekeepers. Arriving at an Israeli border checkpoint, we rendered our UN white cards, which allowed us to pass freely. It was 4:55 p.m., just five minutes before the border closed. I later noted in my journal, "Brill had made it, we all had white hair, but we had made it!" When the Israelis motioned us through, we continued to the UN command post in what was called the Area of Separation (AOS). After a brief stop we reached the Syrian sector. As we had with the Israelis, we passed the Syrians without a hitch, leaving me to wonder why some in Jerusalem had made such a fuss about how hard it was to cross the Golan Heights. It was a breeze and very routine. We then immediately were upon the largely decimated Syrian city of Quneitra. This city vividly revealed the destructiveness of war. After the 1973 war, the IDF claimed Syria used the area to stage attacks on Israel. Therefore, Israel destroyed the town to prevent further activity of that sort, leveling almost every building, believing they posed a security risk. That seemed excessive to me, even as a tactical consideration.

As evening approached and the sun set rapidly behind us, we traversed terrain dominated by rocks and small boulders. The exception was Mount Hermon, which was capped with snow and rose impressively to our northwest as we hurtled eastward to Damascus. Soon darkness fell and we were unable to see much except a few shepherds tending their flocks in their fields near the road. When we arrived in the city, we stopped briefly at the UNTSO office of Observer Group Golan-Damascus (OGG-D), housed in the same building that UNDOF used for its headquarters. On entering, I had my first encounter with a Soviet officer. Prior to then, my experience with the Soviets was a faceless one, limited to Russian military units on the border opposite the North Atlantic Treaty Organization (NATO) in Europe. I am sure, as I noted in my journal, that our "curiosity was mutual."

Waiting for us was MAJ Denny Lindeman (USMC) and his wife, Brenda, along with LTCDR Gary Calnan (USN) and his wife, Kathy. Gary and Kathy, whom we were replacing in Damascus, had dined with us our first night in Jerusalem. They escorted us to our lodging at the Hotel Omayyad, an exceptionally fine place despite the traffic noise outside. After we settled in, we joined our American entourage and Brill for a pleasant dinner at the Station restaurant nearby.

Over dinner, as in Jerusalem, we received more sage advice on every aspect of life in Damascus, including where to shop, live, and how to comport ourselves with the 18 Russian officers we would serve beside.

While I cared about how to secure a permanent residence, my particular interest was understanding what it was like working with Russians. Lindeman and Calnan had much wisdom on that matter. A square-jawed marine, Lindeman was dismissive of the Russians, whom he was certain were either KGB agents—the paramount intelligence agency in Russia— or members of the GRU, the Soviet's military intelligence arm. "Don't trust them for a second," I recall him advising. Calnan was a bit less severe, noting that life with them was interesting, if for no other reason than observing their awkward profile in and among the other military observers. "They'll think you are a CIA agent, Scott, no matter if you declare to their face you aren't," Lindeman warned. Calnan added that not only were all of the Russians serving in their nation's intelligence service, but a number of their wives were as well. I turned to Shelley—my schoolteacher wife—as we then both laughed aloud at that idea. Lindeman concluded our soiree by remarking with a slight edge to his voice, "And don't let them push you around just because they're majors and lieutenant colonels who outrank you. Don't take any crap off them."

Once we returned to our hotel to settle in for the evening, I was more curious than ever about how my first meeting with the Russians would go. The USSR had joined UNTSO in November 1973 after the Yom Kippur War, when Moscow and Washington agreed to each provide 36 UNMOs to UNTSO.[1] While US officers would be utilized throughout the UNTSO area of operations in the Levant, Soviet officers would be restricted to Syria and Egypt. Nonetheless, the description my US colleagues provided of the Russians seemed a bit adversarial and contrary to our peacekeeping charge. True enough, it reflected the Cold War superpowers rivalry at that time. Only two years later, President Ronald Reagan would label the USSR the "evil empire," a moniker that certainly characterized US-Soviet tension in 1981.[2] However, beyond my fascination with the Russians, I was eager to learn firsthand about the entire UNTSO organization, including UNDOF, which we supported.

The United Nations Disengagement Observer Force (UNDOF)

While there were no US personnel assigned to UNDOF, it very much had the imprimatur of the US firmly affixed to its pedigree. In 1973, as the Yom Kippur War was winding down—albeit amid continued artillery exchanges in the Golan—the US undertook a diplomatic initiative to end the violence along the strategic heights between Israel and Syria. Following the efforts of Secretary of State Henry Kissinger, both sides signed the "Agreement on Disengagement." Pursuant to that, on 31 May 1974 the UN Security Council adopted Resolution 350 formally constituting UNDOF.[3]

The Kissinger-inspired arrangement provided for a buffer zone to be occupied by UN forces. It also called for two equal areas on both sides of the UN zone, one for Israel, the other for Syria. However, both countries had limitations on the armaments and forces they could deploy on their respective sides. When I arrived in Syria, UNDOF was led by the stately MG Erkki R. Kaira of Finland, who commanded a force of 1,280 from Austria, Canada, Finland, and Poland, augmented by UN civilian staff. Additionally, UNTSO provided UNMOs that UNDOF operationally controlled. UNDOF's mandate required renewal every six months, the most recent having occurred in November 1980.[4] From its beginning, UNDOF appeared to be an effective peacekeeping force. In 1989, John Mackinlay, a senior research fellow at the Centre for Defence Studies, King's College London, noted that from its inception UNDOF was the beneficiary of a well-crafted peace agreement, both militarily and diplomatically: "[I]t could be said that UNDOF was merely fortunate to be the instrument of a most skillfully designed agreement which anticipated the requirements of each party as well as provided a workable *modes operandi* for the peacekeeping force."[5]

Of its diplomatic impact, Mackinlay observed that UNDOF was more than "just the inert arbiter." In its dealing with both the Israelis and Syrians, UNDOF was "extremely careful of the sensibilities of both parties."[6] Moreover, UNDOF's leadership and operational forces had "shrewdly avoided" becoming a politico-military football to be tossed from player to player seeking an advantage. Militarily however, even lightly armed and equipped, UNDOF's forces were very much an "inert arbiter": "The sense of inertness is nevertheless there. It is caused by the feeling that, although there are [tactical] positions, observation posts, and quick reaction forces deployed throughout the AOS [Area of Separation], their presence is largely symbolic, and their real military value minimal."[7]

Mackinlay concluded that UNDOF possessed the right characteristics to achieve overall success. It had gained the trust of both parties to the conflict, was configured "not so powerful as to impinge" on the sovereignty of either nation, was reliably impartial, and was able to alert the world if there was a violation to the agreement. Moreover, UNDOF served as a "limited but important diplomatic link between the Syrians and the Israelis."[8]

LTC Jim Allan (Canadian Army)—who while assigned to UNTSO was serving as the deputy chief of staff for UNDOF—further suggests that UNDOF's success went beyond being a "limited but important diplomatic link" between the contending parties and an "inert arbiter" in the Golan Heights. Of Mackinlay's assessment, Allan observed that UNDOF was fundamentally necessary and a successful organization that did more than simply provide a useful politico-military connection between Israel and Syria: "The fact that both the Syrians and Israelis are demanding the presence of a U.S. intervention force of some type on the Golan as a *sine qua non* for any Syrian-Israeli peace agreement would indicate that there is some useful function to be performed by such a force."[9]

Indeed, Kissinger, in skillfully negotiating the disengagement between Israel and Syria, understood that US advocacy for an intervention force would go a long way in not only legitimizing UNDOF in the years ahead but advancing the hope of peace in the region. In that regard, UNDOF was far more than a static force on the Golan encouraging everyone to get along nicely. Its most important contribution was found in creating a respite from combat in the Golan while serving as a prominent reminder that the US and Russia—both having observers in UNTSO—stood behind UNDOF. In Allan's assessment, UNDOF represented an excellent example of peacekeeping given the legacy of conflict between Israel and Syria: "Since 1974 UNDOF has helped to buy time for peacekeeping diplomacy to be conducted by the UN, by the superpowers, and by both parties to a limited extent. This is a classic role of a peacekeeping force and it is the best that could be expected between two ancient enemies in the Middle East on such a strategically vital piece of ground."[10]

As testimony to its effectiveness, the situation on the Golan Heights was relatively calm in 1981. Indeed, its only recent casualty was the accidental injury of an Austrian soldier wounded by a land mine, an ever-present danger in the AOS.[11] Beyond that, this US-inspired arrangement had all the thoughtful aspects of an effective peacekeeping operation: trustworthiness, reliability, and transparency in reporting violations. In its periodic report from May to November 1980 to the UN Security Council, UNDOF glowingly characterized its relationship with the two parties to the conflict: "UNDOF has continued, with the co-operation of the parties, to fulfil the tasks entreated to it. This has been facilitated by the close contact maintained by the Force Commander and his staff with the military liaison staffs of Israel and the Syrian Arab Republic."[12]

However, there was a cautionary note in the report, one echoed throughout my time in Syria: "Despite the present quiet in the Israeli-Syria sector, the situation in the Middle East as a whole continues to be potentially dangerous and is likely to remain so unless and until a comprehensive settlement covering all aspects of the Middle East problem can be reached."[13]

The quiet in UNDOF's area of operations was encouraging, but in the Middle East violence could erupt at any moment. Just over the horizon from UNDOF and beyond Mount Hermon was UNIFIL, whose situation was vastly different, dangerous, and deteriorating. Any eruption of violence there could portend a collapse of the peace in the Golan, particularly if Israel and Syria found themselves at war in Lebanon.

Nonetheless, UNDOF was succeeding in part because it bore the US seal of approval. That alone enhanced its credibility with Israel and Syria. From a geopolitical perspective, UNDOF could have been labeled "US-DOF," so vital was America's prominence in establishing the organization that gave every evidence of effectiveness and legitimacy. Yet, at the tactical level, the involvement of US personnel in UNDOF was limited. Americans and Russians alike were excluded from serving as observers in the disengagement area by the agreement that constituted UNDOF. So, both superpowers were assigned to a detachment, Observer Detachment Damascus (ODD), that set us apart from international observers who were permitted to serve in the Golan. While in ODD, MAJ Lindeman served as the security coordinator for United Nations Agencies in Syria, traveling throughout Syria to ensure that the UN's humanitarian agencies there had proper security and were prepared for evacuation if the need arose. My duty was primarily as an operations officer with the 18 Russians who worked in the operations center in Damascus. Despite our limited role in Damascus, it was practically the only place on the planet where US and USSR military officers worked together daily, literally side-by-side, and that was of no small consequence. Allan made this observation about the arrangement: "In general, in 1981, neither superpower wanted a return to open fighting on the Golan or elsewhere. In fact, the presence of observers from both superpowers in Damascus, and of US observers in Israel, tended to keep the parties honest. These superpower observers were not allowed to man posts on the Golan or to do patrols, but their presence reminded the parties of what behavior their superpower patrons expected of them."[14]

I knew the US-Russian relationship would be watched closely by many people in and outside of the UN irrespective of the seemingly minor practical role both countries played in keeping peace in the Golan Heights. In reality, our contribution was more strategic than operational. But it was also not without consequence.

Table 4.1. Observer Group Golan-Damascus Military Observers, 1981

Country	Military Observers	Comments
Argentina	1	OGG-D
Australia	1	OGG-D
Austria	2	OGG-D
Belgium	2	OGG-D
Canada	6	OGG-D
Chile	2	OGG-D
Denmark	2	OGG-D
Finland	7	OGG-D
France	2	OGG-D/ODD
Ireland	5	OGG-D
Italy	1	OGG-D
Netherlands	5	OGG-D
New Zealand	1	OGG-D
Norway	3	OGG-D
Sweden	6	OGG-D
Union of Soviet Socialist Republics	18	ODD
United States of America	2	ODD
Total	66	

Observer Group Golan-Damascus (OGG-D) and Observer Detachment Damascus (ODD)

Early on Friday morning, 27 February, MAJ Lindeman arrived at the hotel to transport Shelley and me to the Damascus headquarters for OGG-D, our base of operations. After a short drive through bustling and noisy traffic, we entered a four-story apartment complex that housed the OGG-D operations. The majority of observers who performed duty in the Golan were stationed in Damascus. While there was a smaller liaison team in Tiberias, the Damascus operation formed the backbone of support for UNDOF. There were of 75 UN personnel assigned to it, of which 66 were UNMOs (see table 4.1).

Of those, 21 would be assigned to Observer Detachment Damascus (ODD), which housed US and USSR observers. The rest would be utilized as observers on one of the 11 UNTSO OPs on the Golan Heights in support of UNDOF.[15] Aside from the two-man Lindeman-Lingamfelter "juggernaut" serving with 18 Russian officers, there was also a Frenchman, MAJ Noel Perrin. Perrin was assigned to perform logistical duties, which included serving as the housing officer in Damascus as well as the chief logistician for our barroom located in the basement of the headquarters. He performed those duties admirably, particularly since he was able to negotiate with French-speaking Arab landlords in Damascus as well as the suppliers of alcohol, cigarettes, cigars, and foodstuffs across the border in Lebanon, where he traveled to replenish the basement pub. However, to say that the superpower contingent in ODD engaged in peacekeeping would be a generous characterization. In truth, it seemed that the Soviet officers in Damascus were little more than window dressing since Israel would not consent to their performing duties in the Golan Heights. Therefore, it became obvious to me—almost immediately—that my presence with Lindeman in Damascus was merely to legitimize the presence of 18 otherwise idle Russians with no other place to go except Egypt. In a sense, the US and Russian officers in Damascus were less peacekeepers than "place keepers" in an ongoing regional rivalry where the Soviets would insist on the same number of Russian UNMOs as there were US observers assigned to UNTSO. As such, some US officers, like me, would be assigned to less gainful duties while the majority of Yanks in UNTSO were actually engaged as genuine peacekeepers, primarily in southern Lebanon. Meanwhile, the other 45 officers from other nations in OGG-D had useful employment, even if mostly passive.

From Damascus, two-man teams would be dispatched to OPs on the Golan Heights for a seven-day period to observe and patrol the UNDOF area. There, each team would occupy a concrete block house with an observation tower, kitchen, bath facilities, and a bomb shelter. Their equipment included radios and very basic binocular observation devices mounted on a tripod stand that were suitable for daylight use, but not night observation. A patrol vehicle was also available for the unarmed team. Generally, OP duty in UNDOF was sedate, with observers characterizing their duties as "cooking and looking." Often, preparing meals was the most challenging activity these observers undertook. Nonetheless, they did have a clear mission and took their job seriously. I frequently asked observers about their duties as they were heading out or returning from an OP tour. One of my closest friends then in OGG-D was

Australian CPT Barry Gwyther, a lean, mustachioed infantryman and consummate professional who made no secret that he thought some of the operational activities of UNTSO could use "a bit of refreshing now and then."[16] He would share his OP experiences and, in particular, the horror stories about meals prepared by some of his "OP mates," including the unfortunate gastroenteritis that resulted. A standard joke rose between us concerning the hazards of food preparation in the field when we inquired of one another's health, employing the salutation, "How ya bowels, mate?"

Beyond indigestion, OP duty was dangerous. One misstep by either side could put everyone in serious danger by treading on or driving over a buried land mine or other unexploded ordnance. Nonetheless, I was envious, having only my stories of riding a desk to legitimize the presence of 18 Russians whose utility in peacekeeping was symbolic. In that regard, Gwyther made great sport of my duties. In his delightful accent—typically forming his questions with an upward inflection at the end—he would ask, "Well mate, have you a proper inventory of your Russians today?" Laughing, I would sometimes respond to his humor by reminding him that the reason there were only two Americans to 18 Russians was to "keep things even" so as not to provoke a global conflagration. Nonetheless, it was UNMOs like Gwyther who were doing gainful duty and facing the danger that I would have preferred over desk duty.

In fact, the US-inspired UNDOF did important things prior to and after my arrival. For example, in 1980 three mine-clearing teams of the Polish contingent in UNDOF were busy disposing of unexploded ordnance in the AOS, making it safer for UN forces to operate there.[17] And while there were no deaths in the six months from May to November of 1980, one Austrian had been serious injured by these hidden demons. Following November, those same land mine-clearing teams were even busier, deactivating 12 artillery shells, 2 bombs, 2 mortar shells, and 11 hand grenades and recovering 1,115 rounds of small arms ammunition.[18] Simply walking in the Golan Heights was dangerous duty, even if Israelis and Syrians were not exchanging fire. Throughout the remainder of 1981, mine-clearing teams continued to neutralize unexploded mines after two UNDOF soldiers were injured by one on Mount Hermon.[19] Mines also endangered local civilians, particularly nomadic shepherds tending sheep in the region as their forefathers had done for millennia. In the 18 months from May 1980 until November 1981, UNDOF cleared 116,753 square meters of unexploded ordnance throughout the Golan region.[20] Our UNMOs were not as concerned with dodging bullets in the Golan as they were with driving over or stepping on undetected mines that could blow a vehicle several feet into the air.

The ODD Couple

When I took up my duties in our Damascus operations center, I found them rather rudimentary and above all intensely boring. My primary function at the ODD holding cell was to serve as a watch officer stationed at a small desk in the front area of the headquarters that overlooked the main avenue of Al Jala Street in central Damascus. Around me were phones connecting us to other UNTSO offices in the region. They were undoubtedly wiretapped by both the Syrians and my Russian colleagues. A conversation, I was advised, should be considered monitored and recorded. There were also wireless radios used to communicate with the UNTSO headquarters in Jerusalem, UNDOF in the field, and the OGG-T team in Tiberias on the other side of the Golan Heights. Hourly radio checks occurred to ensure all the parties on the net were in communication. Once all answered, I would note in the duty log that the check was made, that I had participated in it, and nothing significant was reported. That was almost always the entry. Occasionally, I received a call from the UNTSO headquarters in Jerusalem and would note it as well. But aside from these routine and monotonous duties, I spent most of my time writing in my journal or reading books.

My favorite was *The Russians*, by *New York Times* writer Hedrick Smith. Smith had been assigned as that paper's Moscow bureau chief from 1971 until 1974 and had great insight into Russian government and culture. What better book for me—a US officer assigned to a superpower holding pen—to read than Smith's? I am sure that when my Russian colleagues observed me buried in its pages, it must have provoked a sense of both curiosity and a degree of admiration. In truth, Smith had them pegged to a tee. They were dour, humorless, officious, and inclined to rigid orthodoxy in towing the party line. I experienced this personally during my first official office call with the senior Soviet officer in ODD. At first blush, I didn't find the Russians as a group to be very intimidating. In fact, in my early estimate, one I noted in my journal, they did not strike me as an impressive lot: "My impression, initially, of the Soviets has been mixed. Some of them are quite polite and likable. Others are less so, but all in all, [only a] few 'stone-faces.' Generally, their appearance is sloppy, uniforms ill-fitted, shoes un-shined, and posture poor. I must say that these facts were pointed out to me before I arrived by others who had preceded me. Nevertheless, this was borne out as I met them one-by-one. All of them need haircuts badly! In general, they do not impart a soldierly image and hardly seem to carry themselves as leaders."

The Russians were, however, quite punctual in showing up for duty when they relieved me from my shift, a professional courtesy that I reciprocated. Despite their standoffish nature, a few were quite willing to engage in friendly conversation, something I saw as an opportunity to gain a better insight into them and their thinking on topics of the day. This frequently ranged from what they did in the military to world politics and economic theory. This immersed me in a learning laboratory of Soviet foreign policy that provided a practicum for my graduate studies. I wasn't about to miss the opportunity to learn a bit more through direct observation and conversation. Sometimes it would take place in the UN bar at day's end. But just as frequently, it might take place in the hallway of the headquarters during the duty day when we would strike up a conversation on various topics.

Through it all I was keenly aware of my role as a representative of the US government and the need to be on my best behavior diplomatically. I had no interest in confirming any stereotypical notion they might have of loud, pompous Americans. I sought to project a professional and thoughtful—albeit on occasion lighthearted—persona. After all, these Russians would eventually return home, and I wanted to be sure they had a positive image of American officers. If nothing else, it might provoke them to relate to others in Russia, "You know, the Americans are not so bad, and they know their business, too." That seemed to me the right image to advance, but it was not the initial posture I assumed in my first meeting with LTC Yuri Stepanenko.

After reporting for duty in Damascus, I was informed that I needed to make an office call with the senior Soviet officer in ODD. As I entered Stepanenko's office and saluted, I recalled Lindeman's admonition not to let the Russian officers "push me around." Stepanenko invited me to take a seat across from his desk. Deferring to him as the senior officer, I paused until he sat down. But as soon as I sat down, he stood up and began pacing about the room as if he were about to give a lecture or conduct an interrogation of some sort. After rattling through an awkward introduction, he then asked knowingly, "Have you been briefed by your side on the mission of ODD?" His question seemed to imply he knew that the US had briefed me on the likely preoccupation the Soviets had in Damascus, namely one of intelligence gathering. I suspected he was hopeful that I would confirm that suspicion so he could officially refute it. I didn't take the bait, but rather responded that I had a "very clear understanding of my role." Stepanenko—as I noted in my journal—continued "to pace about beating around the bush as to why we were here, so on and so forth" while making references to our "mutual" superpower status, only pausing to finally take the chair beside me. His manner then turned furtive, suggesting that I had a corresponding role in the American intelligence structure beyond peacekeeping that mirrored his. As he was engaging in this line of inquiry, I remembered Lindeman's warning that the Russians were all likely intelligence operatives. In fact, I would later learn that while Stepanenko posed as the senior man, the real ranking officer in the Soviet delegation was MAJ Vladimir Shaida, a KGB agent. When I met Shaida later and engaged him in conversation, he would insist that he was a "combat engineer." In truth, we had reliable information at the time that he was in fact a civilian posing as a military officer. But Stepanenko was the "front man" in the organization. After a few more minutes of patiently listening to Stepanenko wax on, I interrupted the conversation and politely injected that it was "clear to me as to why we were here as I was sure it was clear to him." I then rose, shook his hand, saluted, and left his office.

Stepanenko didn't seem to take offense with my abrupt departure, and in fact may have taken it as a sign that, while I was a junior officer, I would not be easily manipulated. However, later that week, when Shelley and I were officially welcomed by the other international officers and wives stationed in Damascus, the Soviets were a bit standoffish. Altogether, it was a very pleasant event and I made brief remarks about how we were happy to join the team. Afterward, in typical European style, Shelley was presented a bouquet of flowers. Not surprisingly, the Russians there didn't have much to say to me, and they continued to size me up for several days thereafter.

In time a thaw developed. Most of my conversations with the Russians—both on duty and in the basement bar, where we would adjourn for libations after duty—were pleasant. After a few drinks, both sides would engage in a bit of parlor room intrigue, trying to glean from each other what life was like in our native lands as well as service in our respective military organizations. Most of my exchanges with the Russians occurred when I was at my desk on watch, or when I passed through the headquarters on my days off and encountered one of them on duty. Our ad hoc conversations were unofficial and generic in nature yet enlightening. To their credit, the Russians all spoke an acceptable level of English, whereas I spoke no Russian at all. But I was surprised with how little accurate information they possessed about world events. I suppose I should not have been since I was fully aware that most of their news was filtered through the Communist Party state media. Nonetheless, it was revealing to learn how much inaccurate news and information they relied upon.

One day while speaking to an affable MAJ Youri Badyoukov about the world's oil economy, he argued that the only reason the US cared about the Middle East was because we imported 60 percent of our oil from Saudi Arabia. In reality, America was importing about 140,160 barrels per day, of which 1,027 barrels came from Saudi Arabia in March 1981, representing a tiny 0.73 percent.[21] He was correct, of course, that the US then depended on foreign oil, but the accuracy and certitude of his views were wildly incorrect. I gave him the facts, which he promptly and predictably dismissed as propaganda.

On another occasion MAJ Misha Davidenko from Leningrad validated the Soviet tendency toward paranoia and xenophobia. I had taken a liking to Davidenko, as he had to me. So pleasant were our conversations that I began to wonder if he was actually a regular military officer stuck among stodgy and cautious intelligence operatives. One day while we were discussing our respective superpower roles in the world, Misha asserted that the US was attempting to "ring the USSR with military force," an unsurprising declaration. This was an oft expressed idea by the Soviets, and it reinforced in my mind a geo-paranoia that was endemic and ingrained in the Soviet thinking.[22] He viewed the US as encircling the USSR. We viewed ourselves as containing their expansion. I reminded Misha that perceptions are strange things indeed, pointing to the simple example of whether the glass was half full or half empty. I noted my exchange with Davidenko in my journal: "That what is seen as a 'ring' by him is seen as 'expansion' by us. He was also sure that the US and China were going to sign a military pact aimed at the Soviet Union. I fear they may give us more credit than we deserve."

As Misha and I concluded our discussion about the superpower rivalry, Badyoukov—with whom I had had similar exchanges—lingered nearby to absorb this one. He was clearly interested in the back and forth as Misha and I took up another subject, Russia's role in the Afghanistan civil war. I noted Badyoukov's interest:

Badyoukov was most interested in my "lecture." I say lecture because it is not my purpose to debate with them, as our assumptions are so vastly different the exercise would be purely academic.

I do, however, want to educate them to some cold, hard facts. Badyoukov kept coming back for more. He listened carefully and with great interest as I explained to him that the U.S. was "red hot" about Afghanistan and that as long as Soviet policy leaned in this direction, they would find life very unpleasant in dealing with the U.S. He seemed very interested in my genuine knowledge of the USSR and, all in all, did not attempt to debate certain issues I heretofore believed would cause sparks. Indeed, I learned a bit about myself.

My exchanges with the Russians revealed something in me. The Soviets were fed a steady diet of Soviet propaganda. They did not have the benefit of factual information. But I was careful to debate them calmly and pleasantly, mindful that while my peacekeeping duties were mundane and uneventful, I was also a representative of both the US government and UNTSO. That required tamping down my own enthusiasm and not acting like a petulant and argumentative know-it-all. The US was always on parade, and every day we had a duty to exemplify confidence and capability while avoiding the image of an ugly American on a European holiday unhappy with the hotel service or screaming louder to make ourselves understood by a person who didn't speak any English. We had a serious reputation at stake in the UN, particularly as credible peacekeepers. After all, despite our boring desk duty in Damascus, both the US and the USSR lent credibility to UNDOF. Our presence in Damascus was an affirmation that the superpowers agreed that peace on the Golan was a mutually important endeavor. I had to remind myself of that often.

I had other conversations with the Russians in my role as a quasi-goodwill ambassador from the US that involved economic theories. I had suffered through a Marxist-Leninist economic theory seminar in graduate school. At the time I was absolutely convinced that it would be of no future benefit beyond confirming to me that Marxism, socialism, and communism were pure hokum. I was wrong. My studies equipped me to have some fun with my Russian counterparts. One pay day, when all the UNMOs received their UN per diem check, I had some light conversation with MAJ Yuri Voshchinski, allegedly an infantry officer, about how he was about to upend Marx's theory of the surplus value of labor. As he was collecting his check, I said to him that he would have to send his to Soviet leader Leonid Brezhnev. He protested, saying that he could keep his check in full. I responded by saying, "Yes, but if you do, you'll violate Marx's theory."[23] I continued, "Marx says your labor is equal to your value. Now, your value to the Soviet state is 'X' wherever you are because you are a soldier wherever you are. 'X' in your case is equal to the pay the Soviet state pays you for your services as a soldier. But here you receive another 'X' from the UN. Therefore, your labor is equal to '2X.' Therefore, you would violate Marx if you accepted this money."

Of course, my point was pure rubbish and meant as good fun. The surplus value of labor theory is indefensible nonsense anyway. But initially, Voshchinski took my point seriously, responding, "Then why do you keep yours?" I quickly responded, "Because I'm a capitalist and we have no such constraints!" I then advised him that if he liked he could give his per diem to me, and anytime he wanted a drink at the bar I would buy him one. He then, as I argued in jest, "could have the best of both worlds—lots of vodka and a Marxian theory intact!" At that point he knew I was joking, and we had a good laugh. Again, in building relationships, even lighthearted ones, I believed then that I was enhancing the US reputation in the UN. Besides, other nationalities who observed these exchanges between the superpowers must have found them interesting and disarming. In sum, the give and take evidenced that profound differences held by seemingly implacable global opponents could find some commonality in good-natured dialogue.

In the final analysis, while I would have no frontline peacekeeping duties in Damascus, my relationship with the Russians turned out to be beneficial. It demonstrated that avowed adversaries could engage amicably. Nonetheless, I was eager for the day I would leave Syria and have a chance to involve myself in genuine peacekeeping operations in UNTSO, not at the strategic level in Syria, but the tactical boots-on-the-ground level in southern Lebanon. I had learned much in my early days in Damascus about the UNTSO mission and my Russian colleagues. But there was still more to learn in Syria beyond how to debate and coexist with the Russians.

5

The Bright and Dark Sides of Syria

Apart from my desk job debating with Soviet officers assigned to the superpower holding cell in Damascus, much of my time in Syria was very rewarding. I used my days off to tour Syria, shop in Damascus, take excursions to Lebanon, and engage in one-on-one conversations with everyday Syrians living under what amounted to a dictatorship by a repressive minority clique. As in Jerusalem, just about everyone in Syria paused work at 3:00 p.m. until the oppressive heat dissipated, especially during summer months. This was routine and, like UN employees at Government House, everyone in OGG-D vanished or repaired to the bar to enjoy adult beverages. The only exception was when UNMOs were on duty in the operations center or stationed at OPs in the Golan Heights. In the US Army, there was always plenty to occupy officers throughout a duty day, usually to at least 5:00 p.m. or later. But just like my comrades, I departed early each day and used the opportunity to experience Syria and learn as much as I could about Middle Eastern culture.

Lessons in Syrian Life and Culture

Syria was a fascinating place, and like every Middle Eastern nation it was filled with contradictions and revelations for a person like myself whose only understanding of Syria was what I studied in graduate school 5,968 miles away. Our first immersion into the culture occurred when MAJ Lindeman and his wife accompanied Shelley and me to the Al-Hamidiyah Souk, the largest marketplace in Syria located inside the old walled city of Damascus and next to an ancient citadel near the city's center. The souk was quite impressive, running about 2,000 feet in length, 50 feet wide, and covered by a tall, metal, arched roof. There we walked down the "Street Called Straight," the avenue referenced in the New Testament book of Acts that was Saint Paul's first destination after his biblical encounter with the risen Jesus on the road to Damascus.[1] It felt as if we were traveling back in time as we strolled past shops offering brass pots and pans, silk, fine rugs, tapestries, food, and spices. The aroma of curry, sesame, nutmeg, and cinnamon surrounded us as Arab vendors beckoned us in to inspect their wares. We stopped at a shop that sold the famous OP baskets, rectangular wicker ones every UNMO was expected to acquire to transport personal gear and foodstuffs to an OP. I purchased two for the day when I would be assigned to an observer group and would need them.

After entering the small shop, we were invited to sit with the owner and have *chai*, very sweet hot tea. Hospitality was ever-present among the souk vendors, who would have regarded the fast-paced business exchanges of the Western world to be both undignified and rude. When dealing with a merchant in an Arab souk, one was expected to barter politely but earnestly. It would have been unheard of to abruptly ask, "How much is that?" and then agree to the first offer. Short-circuiting the bartering process would amount to an insult. Lindeman prepared me by suggesting that I offer a lower price than expected for an OP basket, allowing the vendor to counteroffer. I did, and the vendor predictably offered me more tea and engaged in pleasantries about what I thought of Damascus, whether this was my first trip, and so forth. We conversed about his family and we both shared our backgrounds, all the while inching toward an accommodation on wicker baskets. As we did, I was cognizant of my role as a US ambassador of sorts and mindful of the impression I was making. After all, our UN duty notwithstanding, we were guests in Syria. As such we were accorded the niceties of Syrian hospitality and were expected to reciprocate. It was simply the way things were done.

Eventually we settled on a price that followed a predictable pattern. I made an initial offer for one basket. The vendor responded with a higher price as he admiringly noted the quality of his baskets. I then asked—as expected—what his "best offer" would be for two baskets instead of one. He agreeably reduced his price for two, and I countered slightly lower. We finally settled on a price, I paid him in Syrian Pounds (£S), and we bid one another a fond farewell. It would not be the last time I would visit this gentleman's shop. When other UNMOs traveled to Damascus, I would escort them there to purchase baskets. And just as Lindeman advised me, I would share the proper protocol to engage merchants in the souk. My new shopkeeper friend was aware that I would eventually bring others to his shop as he warmly shook my hand.

Lindeman then took us to meet his preferred goldsmith, Garo Ostayan. His shop in the El-Sagha souk was in the Harika district inside the walled citadel of the Old City. This establishment was the top choice for both US embassy and UN personnel seeking to purchase gold or exchange currency. Garo was a delightful man and an honest merchant who made splendid gold jewelry. Eventually he would host Shelley and me to a wonderful meal with his family, and in due course we would do business with him. Bartering was more than buying and selling. It was about forming relationships, and Garo was a trustworthy and loyal friend to his UN clientele.

As evening approached, we concluded our first visit to the Old City souk and walked back to our hotel, passing restaurants and cafes along the way populated by older men playing *Tawla*, the Arab word for backgammon. As they smoked their *sheesha* water pipes and sipped *chai* or Turkish coffee, it struck me that I was immersed in a very different culture. Indeed, my bartering experience was a cultural awakening. I had learned how to relate to people in a new way, not only as an Army officer sporting a blue beret, but as an American living everyday life among Syrians. Those relational skills—rooted in a profoundly different culture— would come in handy in the weeks and months ahead.

However, my next engagement with Syrian culture was not without some difficulty. That occurred when we went house hunting that same week. MAJ Perrin, who doubled as the UN housing officer, kept a list of flats or apartments for rent within walking distance to the OGG-D headquarters. The following Saturday, Shelley and I joined the Frenchman to inspect some of the options. Perrin was very helpful but tended to lose patience when his selections did not meet with ready approval. Unfortunately, several were located in very poor neighborhoods, many with several flights of steps. We did locate one across from the US embassy, but after we agreed to take it, the landlord informed us it would not be ready for another two months. In fact, we thought this excuse was contrived since we asked for some upgrades in appliances. At that point, the impatient Perrin made clear to us we were "on our own." So, we sought out a Syrian housing agent and eventually settled on one. Between his French and my poorer version of it, the housing agent connected us to a nearby landlord. When we visited the home of Jamal al-Sabbagh, we were greeted by the owner and his son Bassam, who spoke limited English. They showed us around, but we were very reserved in our comments, being "old hands" at the game by then. Any expressed enthusiasm could make it harder to settle on a good price.

The place was beautiful, at least compared to other places we visited. It had two big bedrooms, a large two-room salon, a single bath, and a nice kitchen. It met our expectations, even if the décor, as Shelley thought, resembled that of "a 1950's Danish funeral parlor." We sat down in that parlor to negotiate a price. They wanted £S3,000 per month. I told them I would pay only £S2,500. We must have haggled in the tradition of the souk for 90 minutes before we agreed on £S2,600, utilities included. After a pleasant back and forth, the negotiation was completed and the fun began. "Baba," as the old man now insisted we call him, broke out a bottle of Johnnie Walker scotch and we all had a drink. This really caught me by surprise since I had not expected a Muslim to offer such a libation. But I took it in stride, happier with that option than a warm cup of overly sweetened tea. When we left Baba and his son, we were quite satisfied with ourselves and promptly reported our success to our Australian friend, Jill Lloyd, whose husband, CPT Trevor Lloyd, was on OP duty at the time.

Unfortunately, the next day found us bartering again. Since I was on duty that morning, Shelley returned alone to the Syrian housing agent who introduced us to the al-Sabbaghs to pay him for his services and finalize the rent arrangement. To her surprise the agent insisted we owed him £S500 for his services. Shelley politely refused his demand. Both of us had been advised by our UN comrades that we should not pay a large fee to an agent who had facilitated no more than an introduction. I borrowed a UN car and accompanied Shelley back to the agent the next day, eager to try out what I thought were my superior negotiating skills. I told him that £S500 was too much, and I'd only pay £S200 at the most since I had done the lion's share of the negotiating with our new landlord. He was plaintive and insisted that £S200 would not cover his expenses, which were next to nothing since he played no role at all in the negotiation. I insisted that he quote me a fair price. He stuck to his guns. I told him that if he insisted on being absurd that I would ensure that no UN person ever crossed his threshold again. He seemed unconcerned with this threat—one I really meant. Our negotiations then became terse and somewhat heated. We argued loudly. Eventually the agent agreed to accept £S300 and we left in an agreeable fashion, but not until the agent asked me kindly not to "make a fuss" with the UN, which I agreed to do. While I may have won the argument with this fellow, I was far too impolite. Afterward, I felt I had provided a perfect example of an overbearing, rude, and ugly American pretending to be a peacemaker. It was not my finest hour, and it caused me to think long and hard about how to properly barter with Arabs in the future.

Feeling somewhat embarrassed by the obnoxious row I caused, I resolved to do better the next day when I encountered the Syrian governmental bureaucracy. The multi-agency approval process for a prospective housing lease was complex. Indeed, it was a legacy of French colonial officialdom. The rental agreement—a stack of papers at least an inch and a half thick—required many approval stamps from layers of Syrian officials. "Baba" met me early in the morning and said in French that he would lead me around that day to ensure I obtained the needed approvals without difficulty. That was fine by me until he abruptly took my hand and locked his arm in mine as if I were his long-lost child. Stepping out briskly, he then proceeded to escort me—in public and in my military uniform—from one office to another. To say it was culturally uncomfortable being dragged in my Army uniform by Baba would be an understatement. But I was not about to cause more offense like that of the previous day.

First, we stopped to make a copy of the massive rental contract using an open-air mini-Xerox machine on the street corner operated by a fellow who charged us about the equivalent of 30 cents, or £S1. Then, with the agreement in hand, we began—locked arm in arm—our *tour de force* through a labyrinth of Syrian bureaucracy. I noted as much in my journal:

> Then we were off to have a copy stamped forty times by the ministry of whatever. Baba got in line—more a crowd pushing relentlessly to stuff their respective papers through the teller's window than a line—and waited to have the copy of my security paper validated. Finally, Baba was able to out push everyone else, and we were done. We then proceeded onward weaving in and out of the traffic as if there was none. On several occasions, I literally pulled Mr. al-Sabbagh out of the path of onrushing cars but each time he turned to me and shrugged as if to say—"so what, if it's my time, it's my time."

When we arrived at the police station, we encountered another mass of humanity all crowded around the one person who provided an all-important stamp and signature. Once again, Baba pushed ahead of others, after which we were dispatched to a high official's office in the same building. After Baba politely bowed to that fellow, the officer smiled and signed our papers. We returned to the first desk we had visited, where once again Baba succeeded in preempting a throng of humanity to obtain yet another signature. I was glad my first encounter with the Syrian bureaucracy was, literally, in the arms of Baba. After we left the last official's office and entered the hall, the police were carrying a woman out the door who appeared to have fainted. It puzzled me. I suspect that she had received some bad news. In time I would better understand what a police state Syria had become.

Eventually, the entire bureaucratic affair was completed, and Shelley and I settled into our new residence. The next evening we met with the al-Sabbaghs again and paid our first month's rent in advance. Then we sealed the deal with a bottle of Johnnie Walker, this time from my cabinet. I also gave the elder al-Sabbagh a US flag patch and a bottle of white wine, German Liebfraumilch 1979. He was grateful. His son protested mildly, but I said disarmingly, "If you'd like, give it away, but I want him to know that he is my friend." Besides, I had asked him for a new stove and oven, which was delivered earlier that very day. After making an utter fool of myself two days earlier arguing with the Syrian housing agent over what amounted to a $100 dispute, I felt somewhat better about my interactions with Baba, his son, and the hundreds of other Syrians I had rubbed elbows with the previous day, all the while smiling mildly throughout the ordeal. I had to remind myself that I was a guest in this county, not its Crusader overlord. I was a peacekeeper, not a conflict instigator, and I was an American soldier on parade in everything I said and did.

Once we were settled in our new home and job, Shelley and I discovered that in addition to being Arab and Islamic, Damascus was very cosmopolitan. This was in large measure due to the influence of the French mandate period after World War I. When Syria obtained independence in 1946, the French influence persisted, including grand boulevards, ornate facades, traffic circles, and several excellent French-style restaurants. Our favorite was the Chevalier in central Damascus, where UN officers and their wives would gather for dinner and socializing well into the night. The place was always packed and served alcohol, including a beer that was something of a paradox. It was actually brewed by an Israeli company, relabeled with an Arab name, exported to Lebanon, then reexported to Damascus. In some ways, the Arab-Israeli dispute could find a way forward when there was a mutually advantageous economic benefit, especially one appropriately disguised. This surreptitious beer "tradesmanship" was indicative of the possibilities for peace when warring sides found a way to accommodate one another.

Most of our free time was spent traveling with our Australian friends, the Gwythers and the Lloyds. We took advantage of our diplomatic status to move about Syria unhampered by the authorities in a borrowed UN car to take in the sights and culture. We toured the impressive Roman ruins at Palmyra and Bosra and the massive Crusader castle, the Crac des Chevaliers, west of the city of Homs in the central coastal region of Syria. We also traveled to Lebanon, where we shopped for food and other goods. While there, we visited the ancient Greco-Roman ruins near Baalbek. Once known as Heliopolis, Baalbek was a city located east of the Litani River in Lebanon's Beqaa Valley, about 67 kilometers northeast of Beirut. A trip to central Lebanon was like visiting a free market paradise. During Lebanon's civil war, tariffs or duties on goods brought into Lebanon were not enforced. One town in Lebanon, Chtaura, was located halfway between Beirut and Damascus. It was a capitalist dream come true for anyone with money to spend. There was a grocery store stocked with American goods—shipped in by the owner's brother, who ran a supermarket in Detroit—as well as a central market plaza dominated by a very large and old gnarled tree where other goods could be acquired. There, just about anything could be ordered. Need a Mercedes convertible? You could place an order, and sure enough one would appear in a week under "the tree" in Chtaura, likely acquired illegally but conveniently bearing new plates and serial numbers. From radios to Raisin Bran cereal to cigarettes and alcohol brands of all kinds, Chtaura was the place to go. In a sense, it was—like the relabeled Israeli beer available in Syria via Lebanon—a seeming contradiction. Here in the middle of the Lebanese Civil War—to say nothing of the Israeli-Palestinian conflict lurking in the south—people of all sorts engaged in friendly commerce under "the tree," asking no questions of allegiance but devoted exclusively to free enterprise. Like most UNMOs, I found the place fascinating and also inspiring. If there could be peace under the tree in Chtaura, why not elsewhere?

There were also plenty of opportunities to shop in Damascus for daily sustenance and different commodities. There was a souk for everything. The bread souk served up fresh government-subsidized pita bread every morning. The aroma from the bakery would entice you to simply follow your nose. There was also a meat souk, and soon we found our favorite butcher. The downside to meat purchased in the Middle East was that after being butchered, it was fully bled in accordance with religious law. That removed any flavor in might have had. As a result, Westerners resorted to spicing the meat significantly and refrigerating it for a week to cure and age it further. There was also a fruit and vegetable souk, but one needed to exercise great care in consuming these products. The use of human waste as a fertilizer on Syrian farms was widespread, and it was not uncommon to see local farmers washing their products in the water-filled sewage ditches next to their fields. Therefore, meticulous cleaning of fruits and vegetables was necessary. We used a sterilizing agent called Milton to ensure any contaminants were thoroughly dealt with before we consumed anything fresh. We also used bottled water, as recommended by our UN comrades.

One of my American colleagues who arrived in Damascus after us, MAJ Jack Hammell (USA), had the unfortunate experience of becoming quite ill after consuming the local water. Hammell actually replaced Lindeman and lived in the marine's apartment for a while. Lindeman was an avid weightlifter and drank lots of local water that he sterilized and kept refrigerated until he consumed it. Hammell took up Lindeman's practice of drinking much water, primarily to stay cool in the Damarcus summer heat. But shortly thereafter he became very ill and had to travel to the UNTSO physician at Government House in Jerusalem to seek treatment. There the doctor told him that over consumption of the bleach-laced Syrian water was the problem. Hammell recalled the ordeal: "I went to the UNTSO store and bought some bottled water. Within 24 hours, my system had recovered, and I never had any digestive problems again during my tours in the Middle East."[2]

While I would playfully trade jokes with my Aussie buddy Gwyther over threats to our bowels, it was indeed very easy to get deathly ill in Syria doing the simplest thing, from OP duty to consuming tap water.

Notwithstanding the perils of food and water, our lives in Syria were enriched by our experiences, including our travel, shopping, and sightseeing among the Syrian and Lebanese people. We also learned much about the culture as we perfected our bartering skills in various souks. Bartering shaped how we would engage people, especially Arabs. To that end, for those of us who represented the US, we made a special effort to be dignified, friendly, and accommodating as we engaged the locals in commerce. My poor performance with the housing agent would, thankfully, not be repeated. Rather, in interacting with merchants, I learned lessons that would be of great value when I wound up in a far less hospitable environment in southern Lebanon. When facing danger as an unarmed military observer, having negotiating skills in one's rhetorical holster was essential, given the threat of violence to UNMOs, particularly those serving in the middle of civil wars. What I learned in the souk eventually would be applied in far more difficult situations.

Syria's Secret Civil War

Like its neighbor Lebanon, Syria was engaged in a civil war of its own, even as Shelley and I took up residence there. Indeed, during out first night there, rebels bombed a nearby residence just a few blocks from where we slept peacefully. When the jarring noise of the blast reverberated through our bedroom, I reached to turn on a light and looked at Shelley, whose puzzled expression seemed to say, "Where have you brought me?" The next morning I was told the attack had targeted a Ministry of Defense official. We noticed as we walked around neighborhoods in Damascus that it was not uncommon to see armed guards and blockades in front of houses, presumably those housing Syrian officials. Our new ground floor apartment, however, had no such guards, and neither did our OGG-D headquarters just a short walk from where we now lived. The bomb that night served as a thunderous exclamation mark that there was profound danger in Syria, even in the neighborhood where we resided.

Syrian violence was on the upswing since 1976 when Sunni Islamists—primarily those from the Muslim Brotherhood—undertook a series of revolts and armed uprisings against President Hafez al-Assad's secular Syrian Ba'ath Party. Referred to as the "long campaign of terror," the Brotherhood and their allies routinely attacked both Syrian civilians and military personnel, both on and off duty.[3] Syria's president had not stood by idly. He dispatched security forces under his maniacal brother to exact, in some cases, gruesome revenge. Rifaat al-Assad, who commanded those forces, conducted retaliatory strikes against the insurgents, sparing no effort to brutally suppress them.

Indeed, eight months before we arrived, the elder Assad had survived a machine gun and hand grenade assassination attempt, causing heightened security throughout Damascus.[4] The Sunni Muslim Brotherhood, and their fundamentalist Islamic co-insurgents, were implacable enemies of the Syrian dictator's secular Ba'athist regime, one dominated by members of Assad's Alawite clan, a minority Muslim sect inclined to Shi'ism. The Brotherhood despised Assad and was determined to overthrow his regime and replace it with a majority Sunni version. There was some justification in that desire. If a Syrian citizen was not an Alawite clan member and a supporter of the Ba'athist Party, his prospects for power and influence in Syria was next to nothing. As long as Assad was in charge, Sunnis would be relegated to second-class status in Syria. In their estimate, Assad had to be deposed. Conversely, Assad wanted the Muslim Brotherhood and its co-conspirators to be crushed, and his brother Rifaat would wield the bloody hammer.

The watershed moment in this civil war occurred in the northwestern city of Aleppo when insurgents slaughtered 32 cadets at the artillery school there in June 1979. Some reports placed the death toll as high as 83.[5] This attack was conducted by a group known as Tali'a Muqatila, or the Fighting Vanguard, a Sunni Islamist guerrilla organization that derived from the Muslim Brotherhood. The massacre of these cadets, mostly Alawites, was the first of many directed toward the Assad clan, including targets like police posts, military vehicles, barracks, factories, and businesses susceptible to guerrilla assaults. In the city of Aleppo, Sunni terrorists killed many people between 1979 and 1981, primarily Ba'athists and Alawites.

By the spring of 1980, Syria was beset by fighting, yet the Assad government covered it up. Assad was determined to suppress the Muslim Brotherhood and used his murderous brother Rifaat to put a target squarely on the Brotherhood's chest. Rifaat pursued a systematic and bloody crackdown in Aleppo by employing overwhelming military force, involving tens of thousands of soldiers supported by tanks and helicopters. In Aleppo and the surrounding area, hundreds of demonstrators and civilians were killed and thousands more arrested. By April the uprising was crushed. However, more violence was on the horizon. Within two months the attempt on President Assad's life occurred. Retaliation was swift. On 27 June 1980, Rifaat's security forces summarily executed an estimated 600 to 1,000 Islamist inmates at the Tadmor prison in Palmyra.[6] A month later, Assad proclaimed that even membership in the Muslim Brotherhood would be punishable by death.[7] Retaliation by both sides continued throughout 1980.

The Syrian civil war—while secretive in nature—served as a muffled but bloody backdrop to life in Damascus and throughout the country. Assad was quite adroit at covering up deaths, particularly large-scale killings. Indeed, UNTSO did not seem to notice since its mandate did not encompass Syrian civil strife. UNTSO viewed the civil war going on behind the scenes as a problem for Syria to deal with. At least that was the case up until the wee hours of 25 April 1981, when I received a call to report to the OGG-D headquarters "ASAP" for an important mission. I hastily dressed and headed out in the cool night air toward the operations center. When I arrived, I was met by my American colleague MAJ Denny Lindeman, who informed me that a massacre was reported in the Syrian city of Hama, north of Damascus. UNTSO headquarters wanted Lindeman to lead a team to immediately assess the situation, particularly since he was the official security coordinator for UN agencies in Syria and could move freely throughout the countryside. He decided it was wise to bring me along, knowing that our intelligence community would be very interested in our findings and that two sets of US eyes were better in this case.

We departed for Hama in Lindeman's UN vehicle immediately and under the cover of darkness, not knowing what and where we would investigate the situation. The only information available to us were the reports that the UN had received stating that a large housing area in Hama had been attacked by security forces. Our charge was to assess what occurred, including whether there were any signs of violence or casualties that resulted from the attack. We followed the Syrian highway northward for about 210 kilometers for nearly two-plus hours, unsure of what we would discover. When we arrived in Hama a few hours before dawn, the place was a ghost town. We detected little to no movement except for a mobile Syrian security patrol keeping a watchful eye on our movements. Lindeman and I drove about carefully in our prominently marked white UN vehicle, not wanting to provoke our onlookers into an overreaction. In time we came upon a large apartment complex that was riddled with bullets. Virtually every window was blown out. The place was deadly silent and badly damaged. The bullet scars on the building's walls were larger in size than those that would have been caused by a .50 caliber machine gun, a weapon used by both the US Army and Marine Corps. Lindeman thought the Syrians had used a ZSU-23, a Soviet-made towed 23 mm twin-barreled antiaircraft autocannon. If that had been their weapon of choice, it was capable of producing the destruction we observed as the sun rose on Hama that morning. Not a living thing was in sight. We grimly came upon a large, mounded area that had recently been bulldozed. It was at that point we both knew what had transpired. There were no witnesses whose testimony we could gather, as survivors were likely cowering in what was left of their homes. What was clear to us was that the Syrian authorities, who monitored us closely, had been remarkably efficient and orderly in removing any obvious evidence of a massacre except for the telltale and deadly bullet damage to the exterior walls of buildings.

Unable to inspect as thoroughly as we would have liked, we resigned ourselves to the fact that the Syrians had surgically covered up this deadly event. Only later we would learn through savvy news reporting the additional facts taken from victim testimony unavailable to us that morning. On 25 June 1981, the *Washington Post* reported the deadly details: "In the sweep through several Hama neighborhoods in late April, adult and teen-age males were jerked from their homes in the middle of the night, lined up against walls and machine-gunned with bullets large enough to have torn up their bodies, a witness reported. Reports on the number killed vary, with the most reliable estimating between 150 and 'several

hundred.' According to a Hama resident who later fled, municipal gar-
bage trucks picked up bodies from the streets and police buried them in
holes scooped out by ditch-diggers."[8]

Lindeman was right. That description of the remains was consistent
with what a 23 mm antiaircraft gun—twice as large as a .50-caliber—
would do to a human body. Moreover, the disturbed ground we found
was in fact a mass grave containing between 150 and several hundred
Syrian men and boys, murdered on the early morning of 24 April. According to the *Washington Post*, Assad's security forces were retaliating for "a
machine-gunning of participants in a spring festival in fields near a village
inhabited by members of Assad's minority Alawite Moslem sect"[9]:

> According to the former Hama resident, the sweep began with a
> helicopter landing about 1 a.m. April 24. Soldiers burst into
> apartments at random and took out teen-age boys and men, he
> said. There was no resistance, he added, because people thought
> it was a raid such as those carried out earlier in which the men
> arrested would be questioned about antigovernment activities
> and released. This time, however, the soldiers had different
> orders, he said, and gunfire rattled through the neighborhood
> until 9 a.m.[10]

One of the witnesses described the brutality of the Assad response,
saying there were 15 piles of bodies, each variously containing 15, 25, or
30 slain Syrians whose faces were so torn apart by gunfire that they were
unrecognizable. "I think the bursts were shot at head level because I saw
bits of brains on the ground and on the walls. And then, when I saw the
bullet holes, it couldn't have been anything but 50-caliber machine guns,
not Kalashnikovs (AK47 assault rifles, the standard Syrian Army issue). I
don't think a Kalashnikov could tear up bodies like that. Mush. There
were bodies of all ages, 14 and up, in pajamas, gallabiyahs, in sandals or
barefoot."[11]

After reading subsequent reports, I was certain that these descrip-
tions were accurate and sadly comported with what we had seen in Hama
early on the morning of 25 April 1981. As Lindeman and I rode back to
Damascus, we collected our thoughts and made notes that we would
report up the chain. Beyond that, there was nothing for us to do as peacekeepers. But I was glad that both of us were called on to participate in the
grizzly task. As US officers, our observations would be credible. We knew
that. And we would be able to confirm the early suspicions that an evil

butchery had taken place in Hama by the Syrian dictator in Damascus. If it became public, undoubtedly the Assad regime would assert that the slaughter was justified retaliation for equally deadly atrocities by insurgents. But this act was the wholesale murder of men and teenage boys, not directly targeting known insurgents.

I had arrived in Damascus in February as a peacekeeper assigned to rather mundane duties with my Russian colleagues. But on the early dawn of an April morning, MAJ Denny Lindeman and I were truth tellers, and the truth we would relate was that a massacre had taken place in a remote corner of the world. It was all so secretive then. Who else would care? That dismal morning, a US Army captain and his US Marine Corps colleague cared. We cared a lot.

Back to Jerusalem

In early May, I learned that I would be reassigned to Jerusalem, where I would serve as an operations officer in the UNTSO headquarters while also participating in observer duty in southern Lebanon. I was thrilled to be moving on, even though I had only been in Damascus for four months. I knew that this new assignment would put me at the forefront of peacekeeping duties, which was why I came to UNTSO in the first place. Shelley and I eagerly made plans for our transition, including a trip to Jerusalem where we secured a wonderful set of quarters soon to be vacated by a departing UNTSO member. But before we left Damascus we had occasion to visit our favorite butcher in the meat souk where we shopped.

We were planning a farewell cookout for our fellow UNMOs at our apartment, where we had a pleasant patio next to and above the two-way residential street we faced. Since we would need a few days to season the meat before the cookout, I visited our friendly meat vendor and made my way to his counter at the back of a long and narrow shop displaying fresh meat of all varieties. As he was filling my order, I mentioned to him in my broken French that I would be headed for Jerusalem soon. He seemed sad to see me go as he handed me the meat he had carefully wrapped. As I made my way to exit his shop, he rushed from the back of the store to intercept me before I stepped out onto the main street. Grabbing me by the back of my arm, he spun me around and repeatedly poked his outstretched finger in the air while emphatically declaring out loud in English, "We hate the Russians, we love the Americans!" Shocked, I acknowledged his earnest confession, with a quiet "Yes, I know you do." Then I thanked him for his kindness to us over the past several months and departed.

Honestly, it surprised me that this fellow used that very public moment to make such an unambiguous declaration. However, it did not surprise me one iota that he held those sentiments. I was certain many Syrians agreed with him, particularly the 70 percent who were Sunni Muslims and resented their subjugation by a minority of Alawites. Sunnis, of which this butcher was likely one, despised Assad and knew full well that the USSR was his most steadfast ally. They thought one was as bad as the other, particularly among the religiously observant Sunnis who detested the Syrian regime. That day, I was this butcher's convenient "father confessor" and I was glad—indeed honored—that he had made his views known to me in such a demonstrative manner. This common Syrian citizen, relegated to second-class status, chose that day to express his defiance to an American he hardly knew. That moment has stayed with me for years.

In a cruel and somber irony, months later Sunni terrorists struck a blow directly against the Russians in Damascus, including those with whom I had served. In the late summer and autumn of that year, just months after I left Syria, terrorists retaliated against the Assad regime for its brutality against fellow Syrians, particularly those in the Muslim Brotherhood. In October 1981, a car bomb exploded in front of an apartment complex that housed many Soviet officials.[12] Among the dead were wives and children of Soviet officers serving in our UNTSO detachment in Damascus.[13] Canadian LTC Jim Allan, serving with UNDOF at the time, later recalled the Soviets dispassionately going about their work the next day as if nothing had happened: "They all reported to work the next day, gave no indication anything abnormal had occurred, and within days had taken the bodies of their dead home to the Soviet Union and replaced them with new personnel. They never gave the bombers the satisfaction of knowing that they had been hit, let alone hurt. The stoic performance impressed me with the dedication and courage of our Soviet comrades."[14]

By the time this tragedy had occurred, I was performing observer duty in southern Lebanon. Yet it left a hole in my heart about my tour in Damascus. Yes, the Russians were our arch opponents, but I had nonetheless grown fond of them as fellow peacekeepers. Regrettably, Middle Eastern strife had struck those who were there to foster peace. It was a sad note to punctuate my memories of conversing with the Russians.

They, like us, were there to contribute to the credibility of peacekeeping, even if superficially. Unfortunately, their government's unqualified support for the vicious Assad dictatorship had dragged them into the civil war, making those Russian officers and their innocent families prominent targets for anti-Assad terrorists.

The road to Damascus led to many lessons. But the one revelation I least expected was to find myself saddened by the death of Russian officers. While we were in the middle of the Cold War and very much rivals for influence in the Middle East, the senseless deaths of those officers and their families was tragic, even if Russia's staunch support for the Assad autocracy contributed to their vulnerability. I never learned the identities of the Russians who had perished in Syria's secret war. Those deaths were surgically covered up too. In the end, it was something I would put out of my mind as I soldiered on. But I have wondered since and earnestly hoped that those with whom I had shared both light and serious conversations were spared. We had connected at the basic level of our humanity. Besides, isn't that the goal when peace reigns?

On a spring day in May 1981, Shelley and I left Damascus driving westward in our UN car across the rocky Golan Heights toward Jerusalem. I felt more ready than ever—particularly given my limited duties in Damascus—to engage in genuine peacekeeping where it was vitally needed in southern Lebanon. I would soon learn that was not easy. Not one bit. As we raced westward, dark clouds were gathering in southern Lebanon. Sometimes clouds like those brought rain to a parched region of the world. But just then those clouds were also symbolic of the tears of war-weary Lebanese men, women, and children who deserved far better than the misery besetting them. And I was headed there, a Yank—as my Aussie colleagues would call me—in a blue beret.

6

UNTSO in the Central Levant

As we passed through the Syrian checkpoint after leaving Damascus and transiting the rocky plains of the Golan, we crossed the UNDOF occupied zone and arrived at the IDF checkpoint on the western side of the Syrian border with Israel. After rendering our UN and Israeli identification cards, we continued down the winding road taking us from the heights above to a valley road below that skirted the eastern side of the Sea of Galilee. Looking westward across the blue water, we detected in the distance the skyline of the city of Tiberias, where we had stopped for fuel and refreshments as we made our first journey into Syria. But now we were headed southward into the distinctly hotter and more humid Jordan River valley that led to the ancient city of Jericho. Jordan means "the descender" or "flowing downward," which was certainly an accurate description of the 600-foot descent we made while paralleling the riverbed leading to Jericho. An oasis, Jericho is aptly described in the Bible as "the city of palm trees." Indeed, as we came under the influence of its massive palm limbs, the temperature discernibly moderated. When we stopped at a fruit market filled with oranges, apples, dates, grapefruit, and fresh vegetables, we imagined how people of biblical times would likewise have found Jericho an inviting and pleasant respite from the unforgiving heat and humidity that blanketed the Jordan Valley.

Rested and stocked with market delights, we continued our 46-kilometer journey to Jerusalem. Driving south from Jericho, we approached the northern limits of the Dead Sea, a vast and very salty inland lake 50 kilometers long and 15 kilometers wide. Its location is the lowest dry land point on earth, 1,280 feet below sea level. Turning westward on the Jericho Road, the highway rose and wound impressively before us. On either side of us were rocky hills and valleys that composed what the Bible refers to as "the wilderness." Indeed, it was inhospitable terrain, as in the parable of the Good Samaritan who showed mercy to an unknown victim left to die on that road. Occasionally we would encounter small villages, but the landscape rising toward Jerusalem was bleak compared to Jericho. As we approached Jerusalem, 3,754 feet above the Dead Sea, the heat and humidity dissipated. Cresting the hills just east of the Holy City, we beheld the breathtaking panorama we had first experienced with MSG Bruce Brill four months earlier. We paused briefly to take it in before continuing on our way to Government House.

Minutes later, we entered UNTSO's headquarters, signed in, and took a brief tour of the operations center, where I would report for duty to monitor activities across the UNTSO area of operations. After lunch at the UNTSO café, we departed on a 20-minute drive to our new residence in the community of Shu'afat in northeastern Jerusalem, an area populated by Arabs and known as the West Bank. There we met out new landlord, Yosef Adawin, a very successful Arab soft drink vendor who did an amicable and lucrative business with Arabs and Jews alike. Our new home was in a large and impressive three-story limestone building. Taking up half of the entire second floor, our apartment offered two bedrooms, a large living room, kitchen, bath, and a delightful sunroom that occupied the southwest corner of the terrazzo-floored apartment. Compared to our flat in Damascus, it was modern and full of sunlight, something Shelley found most pleasing. Yosef, a jovial Palestinian, was a very kind man with a large, welcoming family of six children spanning ages three to 16 years. He took an immediate liking to us, and we to his family, including his youngest son, a delightfully sweet boy with Down syndrome.

We were not the first UN personnel to occupy one of the six apartments in this massive home. Both military and civilian UN employees had lived with the Adawins. Yosef and his family respected the UN and its peacekeeping mission. Often I would converse with him on the issues of the day, sometimes casually, but always honestly, including when he invited us to late-night dinners to break the fast during the Muslim holy month of Ramadan. Arrayed around a sumptuous table of Arab cuisine, Yosef shared with me his love of their land and his broken heartedness over the conflict in the Middle East. His perspective was important to me as a peacekeeper, particularly a US one. And he was genuinely interested in mine as an American military officer. He knew that the US was very supportive of Israel and recognized that I likely arrived in the Middle East with a similar positive view. He was right. However, he did not use our conversations to embitter me toward Israel, but rather as an opportunity to simply share his views.

For Yosef, the divide between Arabs and Jews was tragic. Not only were they both Semitic people, but each had a tie to the land. Yosef thought that Palestinians had been horribly wronged by the creation of the modern state of Israel. That was to be expected. He was also pragmatic about the situation. Israel, he readily acknowledged, was not going away. In fact, he had very agreeable commercial relationships with Jewish businesses in West Jerusalem as well as Arab customers living in their quarter of the ancient city. In a sense, he was both a lamenter and a celebrant of the cultural and political divide in Jerusalem. He understood that while peace was an unlikely hope amid festering conflict, there was also an opportunity for reconciliation to take root under the right circumstances. For that to happen, however, Yosef was clear. The Israelis must cease being occupiers of Arab lands and become good neighbors who recognized the legitimate property rights of Palestinians. That meant that Israel would have to take the initiative to set the relationship right, since all of the high cards were in Israeli hands.

I vividly recall Yosef relating to me a persistent nightmare. Every day he drove to work on streets controlled by Israeli checkpoints, conducted business with Jewish merchants, and benefited financially from that exchange. But when night fell, his movements on the very same street adjacent to his home in Shu'afat would be severely restricted and controlled by the same authorities who made them readily available to him by day. His fear, as he expressed it then, was that one evening his oldest son, Bassam, would awaken from his innocence as a second-class citizen in lands controlled by Israelis and revolt openly against them. It was that possible act of resistance that haunted Yosef's dreams, creating in him the profound fear that one evening Israeli police would knock on his door to tell him his son had been killed in a confrontation throwing rocks at an IDF checkpoint. It was a realistic fear and opened my eyes. My conversations with Yosef helped to prepare me for my UNMO duties in southern Lebanon, where conflict was part of everything. Like Jerusalem, in southern Lebanon peaceful commerce intermingled with the potential for deadly conflict. Yosef Adawin was not a bitter man. But Yosef was a keen observer of reality and understood that if there were to be peace, there would need to be open-minded people to bring it about. He made me think. He made me think a lot.

The UNTSO Operations Center and Observer Group Jerusalem (OGJ)

The day after arriving in Jerusalem, I headed to UNTSO's operations center, leaving Shelley to unpack and arrange our new home. Technically I was assigned to OGJ, which was formed from the remnant of the largely defunct Hashemite Kingdom of Jordan-Israel Mixed Armistice Commission (HKJ-I-MAC) that refereed disputes concerning a divided Jerusalem after the British mandate ended. But once the Israelis withdrew from that commission, OGJ took up residence in the MAC headquarters, now housing a small staff, a bar, and a sauna, a luxury especially appreciated by our Scandinavian UNMOs. The "MAC House," as we called it, was an impressive building constructed of the familiar stone found throughout the Old City. However, as a center of activity, it had practically no value except offering a venue for a regular ceremony where UNMOs were awarded their United Nations Medal after six months of service. Indeed, one Irish Army UNMO and a skilled artilleryman, Commandant (COMDT) Dave Betson, recalls that he didn't give OGJ "much consideration" when he was assigned to duty in Government House. As he put it, most UNMOs stationed for duty with OGJ thought of themselves as UNTSO "staff officers" and the MAC House as "simply a place for recreational use."[1] Nonetheless, it was a beautiful relic. There were 32 UNMOs assigned to OGJ, not including the two most senior members in UNTSO, the chief of staff, MG Emmanuel Erskine, and his Swedish deputy, COL Carl Forssberg (see table 6.1).

Forssberg, unlike his boss, regarded US officers as somewhat haughty. Despite his view, a collegial disposition imbued OGJ, Americans and our international partners alike. Indeed, as Betson would later observe, he and UNMOs from foreign lands worked "seamlessly with U.S. UNMOs."[2]

Over time, OGJ's mission had transmuted from earlier MAC duties. Now it was simply a place where UNMOs were assigned on paper. In reality, OGJ personnel performed duty at Government House, where they also constituted UNTSO's reserve stock of observers ready for dispatch anywhere that a situation required. Normally that was in southern Lebanon augmenting Observer Group Lebanon (OGL). However, in the past OGJ assisted newly established observer groups in the Sinai and the Golan Heights. Indeed, Betson, who worked in the UNTSO planning office in Jerusalem, recalls developing plans of this nature, including one that envisioned UNMOs deploying from the Middle East to the South Atlantic when the Falklands War between the UK and Argentina erupted in April 1982.

Then Betson, along with MAJ Jack Hammell (USA), "hurriedly researched, prepared and produced a contingency plan for a possible deployment of UN observers to the Falklands." That included OGJ personnel who would deploy to supervise a cease-fire and armistice agreement in the Falklands.[3] However, that UN contingency never materialized

Table 6.1.   Observer Group Jerusalem Military Observers, 1981

Country	Military Observers	Comments
Argentina	1	
Australia	1	
Austria	2	
Canada	3	
Denmark	4	
Finland	2	
France	2	
Ghana	1	UNTSO Chief of Staff
Ireland	2	
Italy	1	
Netherlands	1	
New Zealand	1	
Norway	1	
Sweden	4	Deputy Chief of Staff
Thailand	1	Civilian Field Support Officer (FSO)
United States of America	5	Chief Operations Officer
Total	32	

and UNTSO's leadership elected to "store the plans" away for future reference.[4] Notwithstanding unusual situations like the Falklands, when I joined OGJ in 1981 one's duties were essentially binary: either assignment as a staff officer at Government House or performing observer duty in southern Lebanon. Otherwise, as a unique and discrete organization apart from the UNTSO headquarters, OGJ had essentially no impact on me or my colleagues as we went about our daily jobs. We were ready to serve in Jerusalem or swing into action in southern Lebanon as we were directed.

Arriving at UNTSO headquarters on the second day of my new assignment in Jerusalem, the chief operations officer, LTC Al Husnian (USA), welcomed me. After a brief discussion, he escorted me to the operations center for an orientation. There I reconnected with LTCDR Gary Calnan (USN), who was approaching the end of his year-long tour with UNTSO. Calnan—as he had in Damascus five months earlier—showed me the operational ropes and helped me settle in. I also reconnected with Brill, who showed me how to reserve the UN minibus from UNTSO's motor pool to make the daily mail run to the US embassy in Tel Aviv, a duty I would share with him and other UNMOs. Brill was also preparing to redeploy to the US, and I would assume responsibility for welcoming incoming US replacements to UNTSO, including meeting new arrivals at Ben Gurion Airport, arranging for lodging, and orienting them to the Old City before they deployed to their respective observer groups. It was a lot to grasp from Brill in one sitting, but when I began to execute those duties, I found them agreeable, particularly leading new American UNMOs on tours of Jerusalem, where I continued to learn more about the Old City and its historical sites.

In that regard, my best instructor was Father Jerome Murphy-O'Connor, a resident Dominican priest at the École Biblique in East Jerusalem.[5] "Father Jerry," as we all knew him, was both a scholar and an archaeologist. His books on the life and ministry of Saint Paul, *Paul the Letter-Writer: His World, His Options, His Skills* and *Paul: A Critical Life,* would both become significant contributions to modern biblical scholarship. But for those of us in UNTSO, his primary contribution was conducting "Father Jerry Tours." UNTSO offered up a large, white school bus marked with "UN" on the sides and a driver who would transport Father Jerry and a load of UNTSO personnel and family members to retrace the historical ground once trod by the prophets, Jesus, and others of biblical fame. Father Jerry regaled us with facts while debunking the fiction surrounding some religious lore. He brought the past alive before our eyes, whether along the Sea of Galilee, where Jesus taught and ministered, or high atop the plateau at Masada overlooking the Dead Sea, the fortification where recalcitrant Jewish rebels resisted the legions of Imperial Rome in 66 B.C. I was particularly interested in the tours he conducted in and around Jerusalem. They provided me with a sound factual basis for conducting my own orientation tours for newly assigned officers.

Father Jerry had a wonderful delivery style, a mixture of profound knowledge and endearing humor that he leveraged to dispel myths, all with a delightful Irish lilt. On one occasion he clarified a point of history concerning a large commemorative stone that Crusaders placed at a site in East Jerusalem. A stone block, easily a full cubic meter large, was positioned where the Crusaders were told that Jesus had mounted a donkey to make a triumphant entry into Jerusalem a week before the crucifixion. Father Jerry observed that had Jesus actually used the tall stone to mount a much shorter donkey, "He might well have tumbled to the ground in the process, no doubt protected by the angels." "Of course," he added, "for any of us, we'd have broken our neck!" But Father Jerry was understanding of the Crusaders, who must have reckoned that if *they* needed a stone *that* size to mount *their* horses 15 hands high, so too did their Lord, even for a donkey one-fourth the size of a knight's steed. It was a matter of perspective after all. And that was certainly the case with so much in the Middle East in 1981, where distortive and divergent perspectives resulted in dangerous actions by opposing sides to a conflict.

Father Jerry's informative tours, beyond emphasizing the importance of perspective, reminded us that context was important, both in history and in relationships. The people of antiquity were complex creatures. So too are those of the present. Indeed, the stories people tell and the events they experience contribute to that complexity. Those stories and experiences must be understood and unpacked to get at the truth, which is why the intolerance of ambiguity—the phenomena of over-simplifying the genuine complexity of a thing to understand it—is completely inadequate in grasping the challenges of peacemaking in the Middle East. As a US peacekeeper, I was becoming keenly aware that clear-eyed reasoning, facts, and well-shaped policies and proposals to pursue peace were needed if we—particularly the American contingent—were to contribute to UNTSO in any meaningful way. But there was more to it than that. Much more. Father Jerry's lessons were all about nuances and perspective as he explained the truth about events and people in a proper context. I went on Father Jerry's outings to learn something of history and archaeology. I came away with increased understanding, courtesy of an amicable Irish priest with a dry, mischievous sense of religious humor.

In time Brill left for the US and was replaced Sergeant Major (SGM) Ralph B. Stockbridge (USA), who hailed from Spokane, Washington. Ralph was a quintessential reliable soldier and was accompanied by his friendly, warm-hearted wife, Harriet. I recall picking them up at the airport in Tel Aviv. By then I had mastered all the skills to seamlessly usher new arrivals quickly and efficiently through the Israeli security labyrinth and onto my minibus to transport them to Jerusalem. Both Ralph and Harriet were delightful people who would eventually rent the apartment above ours in Yosef Adawin's UN residential complex. After Harriet and Ralph had settled in, I frequently rode to work with him in the morning and we became quite good friends. He quickly relieved me of duties Brill had placed in my care, permitting me to turn my focus toward operational matters, including preparing for UNMO duties in southern Lebanon.

Typically, my duty day at Government House was spent in the operations center. Located on the second floor, UNTSO's nerve center consisted of a single large room with windows facing eastward to the West Bank and Jordan. It was neat and well-organized, comparable to most operations centers I was familiar with in previous US assignments. The American influence was clearly evident in its layout, organization, and procedures. That was unsurprising since it sat across from UNTSO's senior operator, a US Army lieutenant colonel. One wall was covered with maps of our operational area. Appearing prominently above them was the title "UN Peace-Keeping Mission Middle East." The map array included the Suez Canal in the west spanning eastward across the Sinai Desert, the Gaza Strip, Israel, Lebanon, the Golan Heights in Syria, the West Bank, and then across the Jordan River to Amman, the capital of Jordan. On the wall next to the maps hung several clipboards where teletyped reports were placed when they arrived from our communications center just down the hall. Adjacent to the reports were standard situational awareness boards, where unit strengths, recently reported incidents, weather, and related information was updated hourly. A few desks and tables were arranged throughout the operations center, and reference books—including UNTSO policies and procedures—and office supplies were neatly shelved nearby. Additionally, there was a radio room directly accessible to the operations center that was equipped with tactical radios that could range all of UNTSO's observer groups. Also on our desk were telephones for official calls and—most importantly—an AM/FM commercial radio that we kept tuned to the British Broadcasting Corporation (BBC). Frequently, the BBC was the most reliable source of information beyond our official UNTSO communications when it came to regional politics or military incidents in the Middle East, not to be confused with another essential "BBC," Bernie's Bottle Club in Tel Aviv. That establishment was a standard lunch stop for us when we made the daily mail run. While the BBC in Tel Aviv had the best cheeseburger in all of Israel, the BBC in London had the best and most reliable news.

Much of our time in the operations center was devoted to cataloging tactical reports from southern Lebanon, where both UNTSO and UNIFIL personnel were engaged in ongoing situations, many quite dangerous. Our job was to record any incident that occurred and, when serious, immediately inform Erskine and Husnian. Over the course of a 12-hour duty shift, we would also be responsible to assemble a hand-off briefing for the shift that relieved us. If that relief occurred in the early morning, the duty officer also had to prepare a morning update for Erskine and

Husnian including all activities during the previous 24 hours. Personally, it was great training for a junior officer like me, and in short order I learned much about the myriad of possible events that might occur across UNTSO's area of operations. When I was not in the operations center, my administrative duties occupied my time, including assisting SGM Stockbridge in processing and orienting new arrivals. That also included arranging a welcome dinner where we would properly greet new American UNMOs while "dispensing wisdom"[6] about life in UNTSO and the Middle East. In the summer of 1981 there was a robust turnover of new US personnel arriving in country that kept both Stockbridge and me busy getting them in-processed, trained, and dispatched to their respective observer groups.

One of those who arrived in Jerusalem the same month I transferred there from Damascus was MAJ Joseph A. Serviss (USA), who would be joined the following month by his wife, Carolyn, and son, Emory. Serviss was an easy-going but very focused and competent armored cavalryman. He was also a Vietnam veteran and brought that experience to his new duties. Possessing a delightful Alabama drawl—one our Irish comrade Betson jokingly thought was a distant cousin of proper English—Serviss quickly got to work. He was sent to UNTSO based on his operational experience, a genuine benefit to any UNMO. Like me, however, he spent most of his time in the UNTSO operations center or deploying for observer duty in southern Lebanon. We struck up an early friendship, as did our wives. Serviss and I found our duties quite different from the fast-paced life in US Army combat units. Indeed, Serviss—having just arrived from a unit that maintained what we called a "high operational tempo"—thought duty in UNTSO was a bit "laid back." He also felt the officers who were assigned to the headquarters "varied in ability."[7] I didn't disagree. In particular, he was surprised to learn that the duty day ran from 8:00 a.m. to 3:00 p.m., as was the very leisurely case in Damascus. Yet we both realized that to have a positive impact in UNTSO, we needed to project a measured élan that enhanced our credibility among other nationalities serving with us, particularly given the relaxed environment in UNTSO.

The "laid back" inclination of the UN generally—as opposed to the American military's affinity for hard-charging leaders, up-tempo operations, and longer duty days—was very apparent. That contributed to some tension between different nationalities. To illustrate the challenge, Serviss experienced firsthand some of that underlying hostility while on his first OP tour in southern Lebanon. While serving with three UNMOs from other nations, Serviss's teammates gave him the unmistakable cold shoulder in the initial hours on the OP. He was flatly surprised that his three colleagues had virtually nothing to say to him, not a single word. It was as if they were giving him the silent treatment for some unarticulated offense. He found it curious, and after a full day of complete quiet, he asked them at dinner, "Hey fellows, what did I say to offend all of you? If I said something, I'm sorry. I simply want to contribute my share to this tour of duty. Let me know what I did so I won't do it again." After a short pause, one of the UNMOs declared that they all "despised" the US contingent in UNTSO because they were "arrogant know-it-alls." Serviss quickly explained that he was not of that persuasion and just wanted to be part of the team.[8] Serviss was wise. He was aware that there were some American UNMOs—mostly "hard chargers" with a high degree of self-confidence—who were inclined to be braggadocious or demanding. But Serviss quickly set the right example after detecting the hostility. His comrades were appreciative, and in no time all were working amiably. I was also warned that this was a problem, and while I was fortunate not to have encountered such anti-American sentiments in my interaction with other nationalities, Serviss's experience clearly exposed the potential for underlying resentment. US UNMOs had to deal conscientiously with it up front by setting the right example to promote comradery. Serviss tackled it head-on and was well-respected among his peers for doing so.

Shortly after Brill left, Husnian also departed and was replaced by LTC Robert H. Sholly (USA) as the chief of operations. A very level-leaded and even-tempered officer, Sholly had considerable experience in Iran as a foreign area expert as well as a combat infantry officer in Vietnam. He was every bit the right example for us on how US Army officers properly and professionally engage others within an international organization. In short order, he also won the trust and confidence of UNTSO's leadership.

Sholly took a distinct interest in the leadership development of all of his subordinate officers and wanted to deploy me to southern Lebanon soon to broaden my expertise in the region. A Middle East specialist himself, he wanted me to be in the field gaining experience and not spending time riding a desk in Jerusalem as I had in Damascus. In short order, Sholly dispatched me to OGL, based in Naqoura in southern Lebanon, for my initial orientation to the area. At last, I would be doing what I had sought to do from the first day I arrived in UNTSO. It was exciting and I was full of anticipation. I was also a bit wary because I knew that I had much to learn quickly. And I knew that soon after this orientation I would be dispatched to OP duty, and I wanted to be at the top of my game when I showed up. Southern Lebanon would offer all the challenges and toughness anyone could imagine, going unarmed into a hostile fire situation under the protection of a woolen blue beret.

Observer Group Lebanon (OGL)

Just as UNMOs assigned to OGG-D supported UNDOF in the Golan Heights, those of us in Jerusalem would find ourselves in southern Lebanon augmenting OGL, the primary observer force in southern Lebanon that supported and was operationally controlled by UNIFIL. The substantial difference was that OGL had 22 US officers assigned to it who—unlike the 18 Russians and 2 Americans in Damascus—were by no means window dressing.[9] Americans assigned to OGL were full-fledged observers on the ground and in harm's way in southern Lebanon. Now I would join them. The initial cadre of OGL observers was hastily assembled in the aftermath of the Israeli invasion of southern Lebanon in 1978, and by 1980 it had grown to 74 UNMOs.[10] Its roots were in earlier UN organizations that supervised peace in southern Lebanon. The first was the United Nations Observation Group in Lebanon (UNOGIL), formed in June 1958 pursuant to UN Security Council Resolution 128.[11] Conceived to prevent troops and weapons from entering Lebanon during civil upheavals, UNOGIL was short-lived. Tensions eased, and it was disbanded the following December. The second observer mission was undertaken in 1972 to address renewed Israeli and Arab hostilities in southern Lebanon. It employed 42 UNTSO military observers—including eight Americans—who were assigned to the Israel-Lebanon Mixed Armistice Commission (ILMAC) in Beirut to supervise disengagement activities along the Israeli and Lebanese border.[12] While Israel no longer recognized ILMAC, UNTSO was within its mandate to assign observers to it to perform duty in southern Lebanon. Five observation points were established on Lebanon's side of the border, taking their names from nearby Lebanese towns. Initially, each OP was manned by two UNTSO observers. Arrayed west to east, OP LAB was sited near the coastal town Labbuna, OP HIN next to Marwahin, OP RAS close to Maroun al-Ras, OP MAR situated near Markaba, and OP KHIAM south of the town of Khiam (see map 6.1).

Following the 1978 Israeli invasion of southern Lebanon, OGL drew its initial members from other UNTSO observer groups in the region, including those in Egypt and Jerusalem. It also wisely absorbed the

Map 6.1. UNTSO Observation Posts in Southern Lebanon, 1972

observers who had been assigned to ILMAC in Beirut, all of whom were very familiar with duty in southern Lebanon. The newly configured OGL would eventually occupy all five OPs—four of which were increased to four-man teams—to observe and report border violations, overflights, and small arms or artillery firing incidents.[13] However, for a time follow-ing the 1978 Israeli invasion, four of the OPs were temporarily manned by two-soldier UNIFIL teams since the IDF forced UNTSO observers to abandon them. It was not until the first half of April of 1980 that UNTSO began to reoccupy all five posts after OGL had been reinforced with addi-tional manpower.[14] Additionally, OGL made the decision to always include one US member among the four-man teams that served on these OPs, putatively because the IDF might be more cooperative if they knew a US member was nearby.[15] When I arrived in UNTSO, those same OPs were in operation, and soon I would occupy one of them to do my part as a US peacekeeper. As of September 1981, OGL had grown to 88 UNMOs, of which 22 were Americans, a quarter of the entire observer group (see table 6.2).[16]

All of OGL's observers—and any family members who accompanied them—lived in the northernmost Israeli coastal city of Nahariya just south of the Lebanese border. From there, UNMOs would deploy north-ward about 15 kilometers across the Lebanese border to the village of Naqoura, where the headquarters for OGL and UNIFIL were co-located.

Table 6.2.   Observer Group Lebanon Military Observers, 1981

Country	Military Observers	Comments
Argentina	2	
Australia	6	Alternated with US as Chief OGL every 6 months
Austria	3	
Belgium	3	
Canada	6	
Chile	2	
Denmark	3	
Finland	5	
France	14	
Ireland	4	
Netherlands	5	
New Zealand	1	
Norway	4	
Sweden	8	
United States of America	22	Alternated with Australia as Chief OGL every 6 months
Total	88	

Nahariya was a thoroughly modern Israeli coastal city by the Mediterranean Sea. Settled by German Jewish immigrants fleeing Nazi persecution, it had all the conveniences of a European setting: cafés, restaurants, parks, beaches, and other recreational activities. My first journey to OGL was to familiarize myself with the duties I would have in southern Lebanon. After arriving in Nahariya, I stayed with my Australian friends, CPT Barry Gwyther, his wife, Jo, and their one-year-old daughter, Kylie, who had moved from Damascus for duty with OGL.

The next day, I traveled across the border to OGL's headquarters in Naqoura for my orientation. There I met with LTC John Wilson (USA), the senior US military observer. Wilson was my primary boss and, at the time, was also the chief of OGL, a duty that rotated semiannually between the senior US and Australian officers in the observer group. He quickly handed me off to his team for orientation. Wilson, like Husnian, would soon redeploy to the US to be replaced by LTC Al Baker (USA). Meanwhile, he was our boss in southern Lebanon. The US members of the operations team in OGL were very competent and mission-focused. At the time, the operations chief was MAJ James "Digger" Byrnes (USMC), who the recently promoted LTCDR Virg Bozeman (USN) considered "a consummate professional."[17] While he was somewhat braggadocious, I can attest that Byrnes was a focused and professional operator. Nevertheless, he had a penchant for ruffling feathers among other international UNMOs with his forthright persona. Bozeman also regarded MAJ Joe Moynihan (USAF) as "another class act who was a powerful force" in the planning section of the OGL headquarters.[18] To be sure, Wilson had a strong and assertive team of Americans at OGL, many like Byrnes with combat experience from Vietnam. I was privileged to learn from them. Indeed, Erskine also had high praise for all of the UNMOs assigned throughout the Middle East: "UNMOs are seasoned, well-trained and mature officers. Some of them come to UNTSO with varied combat experience and senior staff appointments behind them, which are the best preparation for their field duties in the mission area. Their professional qualities . . . make their services invaluable to UNEF, UNDOF, and UNIFIL. Thus, they provide the force with a necessary continuity and provide the experience which is so vital in areas such as Sinai, Golan, and South Lebanon."[19]

My American colleagues, however, did not hesitate to point out to me that, in fact, the US and other officers who were fluent in English and shared our degree of military training composed the core group—the "corps of competence"—that accomplished most of the planning in the organization. Many of those who shared English as their native tongue—or spoke it as fluently as the French did—were also active duty officers, while other UNMOs, particularly those from the Scandinavian countries who also spoke English well, tended to be reserve officers with less operational experience. MAJ Jay Sollis (USMC) recalls a Swedish colleague's candid admission: "He freely admitted that most Scandinavian UNMO's were reservists, 'weekend warriors, and uniformed bureaucrats,' not full-up professional soldiers. Most of them had served multiple UN tours, as he had. They did not fancy themselves professional soldiers."[20]

Nonetheless, it was easy to see how a gung-ho attitude—particularly among some Americans—could offend other nationalities. My OGJ colleague Serviss observed that some Americans who were combat veterans from Vietnam "wanted all to know that they had been in combat and as a result were much more knowledgeable in military tactics than those who did not have that experience."[21] Unfortunately, the "I'm better than you are" attitude did not sit well with officers from other countries. The trick was to get work done without walking all over others in the process. However, if you happened to be a hard-charger unworried about offending someone else in the process of *getting* "work done," you risked *getting* the "silent treatment" when isolated on an OP with an offended lot of fellow international UNMOs.

OGL's mission was straightforward. It supported UNIFIL with military observers who were stationed on the OPs arrayed along the border between Lebanon and Israel. OGL observers also manned mobile patrols to resolve disputes throughout the region occupied by UNIFIL. As Serviss put it, "there was a greater sense of urgency at OGL" than we witnessed in OGJ.[22] Australian Gwyther concurred in that view, finding OGL "far more interesting and dynamic" than what he had experienced as an UNMO assigned to OGG-D and supporting UNDOF in the Golan Heights.[23] In his estimation, operations in OGL were more military-like. A regular Army infantryman, Gwyther also found that serving alongside other career officers from Canada, France, Ireland, New Zealand, and the US contributed to an environment in OGL that was "more focused, professional, and worthwhile."[24] Irishman Betson held a similar view. His experience included tours of duty in both OGJ at Government House and OGG-D on the Golan Heights. In Betson's estimation, the difference between OGG-D and OGL was as stark as "chalk and cheese."[25] In contrast to OGL, Betson considered OGG-D to be classic "cooking and looking." It was a "totally static situation with virtually nothing happening between Israeli and Syrian forces deployed on the Golan Heights." However, OGL was "more tense and volatile with the constant threat of incursions" into Lebanon by the IDF—supported by their Christian militia allies—as well as armed element cross-border attacks into Israel.[26]

OGL's mission was a high-profile, "boots on the ground" situation. That was clear to Bozeman, who was very impressed with OGL and felt all of its UNMOs were performing both "noble" and "honorable service." He also had high praise for his fellow US officers, who, in his estimate, "set the bar for professionalism."[27] In truth, both Serviss and Bozeman were right in their differing assessments of US officers. They were quite good, but sometimes that competence showed up as arrogance in the eyes of others. One thing was true for certain: the Americans in OGL took their jobs very seriously, even if they occasionally ruffled international feathers.

The members of OGL, augmented by some of us from Jerusalem, manned the five stationary OPs and were primarily responsible for noting and reporting activity within sight of their positions. That also included conducting limited mobile patrols by two of the four OP team members to scout out and report violations and other incidents in their immediate area of responsibility. Unrelated to the fixed OP sites, OGL and OGJ personnel also manned dedicated mobile teams, which included Team Metula, Team Romeo, Team Sierra, Team Tyre, Team X-Ray, and Team Zulu. These teams frequently found themselves tasked to resolve difficult situations between the UN and parties to the conflict.[28] That included the IDF and their Christian militia allies—the South Lebanese Army (SLA) or the De Facto Forces (DFF), commanded by MAJ Saad Haddad.[29] OGL's mobile teams also had to contend with conflicts that arose and involved the "armed elements," a term encompassing (1) the Palestine Liberation Organization (PLO), (2) its army (PLA), (3) the secular-Marxist Popular Front for the Liberation of Palestine (PFLP), (4) the Democratic Front for the Liberation of Palestine (DFLP), (5) the leftist pan-Arabist Lebanese National Movement (LNM), and (6) the Shi'a Muslim group AMAL, an Iranian-leaning religious and political organization. The mobile teams also worked to build positive relations between UNIFIL and local government leaders and civilians.

When initially formed, the two most significant of these teams were Team Tyre and Team Zulu. Team Tyre was positioned in the western area of southern Lebanon and focused primarily on the PLO forces under or allied with Yasser Arafat, while Team Zulu was oriented to the central and western areas and interacted with the IDF and the DFF. By 1980, Team X-Ray was formed as the new liaison with the DFF, while a refocused Team Zulu and the other teams would have broader liaison missions in various sectors throughout the UNIFIL area of operations.

Frequently teams dealt with conflicts involving blood feuds between opposing sides that sometimes resulted in hostage-taking and deadly conflicts with UNIFIL. However, in all of this, UNTSO observers—whether serving on fixed sites or patrolling with mobile teams—were there to assist UNIFIL in their armed peacekeeping mission. In that regard, activities in OGL were far more influenced by and focused on UNIFIL's support requirements than on any guidance or requirements originating from UNTSO's headquarters in Jerusalem. UNIFIL was on the ground and armed doing the work of peace enforcement, while UNTSO was in the background unarmed and facilitating that work while observing and reporting violations from the field as they occurred.

OGL's relationship with UNIFIL was distinctly different from that of OGG-D with UNDOF. While "cooking and looking" was the routine in the Golan, danger in southern Lebanon far exceeded stepping on land mines. Working with UNIFIL, OGL's unarmed observers could be subjected to armed violence at a moment's notice. OGL was amid an active, constantly smoldering conflict between the Israelis and their DFF pawns on the one hand, and the PLO and other militant armed elements on the other. OGL observers found themselves attempting to keep a peace that none of the combatants seemed to want. Everywhere OGL turned there was the potential for deadly trouble. In that regard, OGL's US-led command group of Wilson and Byrnes was clear that UNMOs who supported UNIFIL needed to follow the protocols of unarmed observers and not become involved in conflict. Rather, they would report and—to the extent possible—resolve issues peacefully. As Erskine maintained, the concept of peacekeeping was to "talk and negotiate and not to fight if you can avoid it."[30] Serviss recalled this point being driven home in our initial training concerning observer duties: "We were briefed on what to do if we were hijacked or kidnapped. The bottom line was to give them everything they wanted and do not put up a fight. If any personal gear was stolen, you would be reimbursed."[31]

Consequently, for US officers in OGL and OGJ, it was important to create an air of steadiness that highlighted both the discipline and focus needed to assist UNIFIL's mission to keep the peace. The key, therefore, was to solve problems, not create them—and certainly not to overreact.

In that regard, UNTSO observers attempted to have a very close and cooperative relationship with UNIFIL forces spread across southern Lebanon. However, whereas UNTSO had very professional leaders, including a robust US representation, the eight international combat battalions that composed UNIFIL were not all equally capable. Some, like the Dutch, Fijians, French, and Irish, were quite good and well led. Others, like the Senegalese and others from Africa, were less so. The varying abilities of those battalions, along with a lack of standardized procedures, made it difficult for OGL to adequately support UNIFIL. But OGL made every effort to assist UNIFIL wherever and whenever it could.

Nevertheless, it was UNIFIL that had the weapons. We in UNTSO had only the protection of our blue berets and our wits, the former useless in deflecting bullets, the latter vital in avoiding them. Did being armed result in UNIFIL being more effective in keeping peace? Indeed, was it enough? To understand fully UNIFIL's capabilities and limits requires a better understanding of UNIFIL itself, its inception, deployment, operations, and efficacy. To do that in a comprehensive manner that sets the stage for understanding UNIFIL, one needs to turn the clock back to the organization's beginnings and consider the circumstances that brought it into being.

7

The Woes of UNIFIL

It was the Israeli sabbath—Shabbat—on Saturday, 11 March 1978. Two days earlier 13 Palestinian fighters from the PLO's Fatah element departed southward from Lebanon's coast. Equipped with Soviet-made AK-47 Kalashnikov rifles, rocket-propelled grenades, and indirect fire weapons including mortars, Fatah's objective was to assault a beachfront hotel in Tel Aviv hosting tourists and foreign dignitaries. Their plan—one developed by Khalil Ibrahim al-Wazir, also known by his *nom de guerre* "Abu Jihad" and one of PLO chairman Yasser Arafat's top aides—was to take hostages and exchange them for PLO prisoners held by Israel. Implicit in that objective, however, was the PLO's desire to disrupt the emerging peace initiatives between Israel's Menachem Begin and Egypt's Anwar Sadat. Much was on the line.

On that Saturday, when Jews would be enjoying a day of rest, the terror squad transferred into two rigid-hulled inflatable highspeed Zodiac boats and set out for their beachhead. Losing two of their fighters in a capsize episode and having steered off course, the remaining terrorists landed at a kibbutz north of Tel Aviv. There they encountered American photographer Gail Rubin taking nature pictures. The PLO promptly killed her after learning from her where they had mistakenly landed. They were unaware that they had just murdered the niece of a sitting US senator, Abraham A. Ribicoff.[1] The terrorists quickly adjusted their plans and proceeded south on the coastal road headed for Tel Aviv. In the process they hijacked a taxi, killed the occupants, and then seized a busload of civilians out for a holiday tour. After commandeering the bus, they continued southward, attacking other passersby with gunfire and hand grenades. The bus was eventually intercepted by Israeli police and military personnel in a northern suburb of Tel Aviv. A major firefight ensued. Many other civilians died amid the hail of bullets, with terrorists killing civilians trying to escape the bus. Eventually the bus exploded in a fireball. In the end, a total of 37 Israelis and 1 American were massacred, including 13 innocent children. Of the 11 perpetrators who made it ashore that awful day, nine were killed, but not until 71 other civilians were wounded. Israelis were outraged. On 13 March 1978, Prime Minister Begin expressed the collective view of Israelis that mournful day: "Gone forever are the days when Jewish blood could be shed with impunity. . . . We shall do what has to be done."[2]

The Israeli response to this despicable attack on innocent civilians would reverberate from the halls of the Knesset, north to Lebanon, across the Atlantic to the United Nations headquartered in New York, and throughout capitals around the world.

That same day, Vietnam War combat veteran CPT Mike Fallon (USMC) was preparing for a week-long tour manning an UNTSO OP in southern Lebanon. One of 42 observers assigned to the ILMAC in Beirut, Fallon expected this rotation on OP RAS to be similar to others he had experienced. Occasional truce violations, firing incidents, hijackings, and systematic harassment of observers were normal occurrences. But soon a huge surge in violence and mayhem between Israel and the PLO would erupt. It was a confrontation that had been smoldering, and the PLO had just tossed a lit match into the tinderbox. If the Israelis needed an excuse to attack the PLO in southern Lebanon, the brutal slaughter of innocent Israeli civilians served one up on a bloody platter.

While Prime Minister Begin sounded the war tocsin in Jerusalem, Fallon and his fellow UNMOs were busy "cooking and looking" and patrolling in southern Lebanon, even as the IDF was making plans to launch Operation Litani. Its design was simple: push the PLO's 5,000 soldiers in southern Lebanon and their allies north of the Litani River, making it difficult for Palestinian 122 mm rockets and artillery to range Israeli communities in northern Galilee.[3] While the coastal road attack was a suitable justification for retaliation, MAJ Dick Vercauteren (USMC), assigned as an UNMO to OGJ, recalls that it was an "open secret" that the IDF had been mustering troops for an invasion of Lebanon. Vercauteren had been privy to UN reporting that the Israelis would likely attack on a four-axis approach and were massing the necessary forces south of the border.[4] Yet UNTSO's reports conflicted. On the one hand, they reported that "ground activity was at a moderate level." On the other hand, they noted that Israeli forces were very busy building tactical roads and conducting related preparatory activities, including minefield breaching and marking the locations of those mines, well ahead of the 11 March coastal road attack.[5] There were other indications. Across southern Lebanon—just in February 1978 alone—Israel's DFF allies and armed elements associated with the PLO had been harassing UNTSO's ILMAC observers with 14 vehicle hijackings, 33 forced entries into OPs, 17 thefts of UNMO personal equipment, and six shootings in the immediate area of OPs or firing incidents directed at supply operations.[6] Of those specific violations in February, most of them were committed by the Israeli-sponsored DFF near the border, including 12 hijackings, 30 forced entries, and four shooting incidents, all undoubtedly designed to disrupt UNTSO's operations.[7]

Deploying from Beirut on 13 March, Fallon and another UNMO from Belgium occupied OP RAS just prior to the IDF's armored and infantry assault into southern Lebanon that would begin in earnest on 15 March. OP RAS had originally been constructed by the French during the mandate period, and in 1972 it was turned over to UNTSO. Overlooking the Israeli border from Lebanon, its observation deck provided a 270-degree view toward Israel.[8] There, sitting on a hillcrest of 900 meters, UNMOs could easily observe activity from the south where the IDF was positioned. Along the border frontage, the IDF had made other improvements, including parallel chain-link fence barriers with a manicured sand path between them to detect the foot traffic of infiltrators. Additionally, the roads south of and adjacent to the Israeli border were upgraded with asphalt and culverts to accommodate heavy transport vehicles rapidly repositioning tanks from one area to another. So close was Fallon to the border that he could "see and smell cooking fires from the small town of Yir'on two kilometers further south" in Israel.[9] Fallon suspected something was about to happen and was in the perfect place to observe all of it.

For some weeks, the Israelis had been preparing artillery positions on both sides of and adjacent to the Lebanon border, something that ILMAC observers had reported to UNTSO for weeks. While the Lebanese government did not support the IDF's encroachment on their territory, they were powerless to stop it. Fallon recalls the IDF's diligence in readying for future combat north and south of the border. On the southern side, the IDF had improved artillery revetments stocked with ammunition for its 155 mm self-propelled howitzers. Additionally, artillery positions were constructed on the north side in Lebanon that could be quickly occupied through gates installed in the border fence. These forward positions enhanced the IDF's ability to range deeper into Lebanon to destroy PLO artillery and rocket units.[10]

From OP RAS, Fallon could observe the small village of Maroun al-Ras that sat just south of the key crossroads town of Bint Jubayl, a Lebanese farming community. This strategic intersection was controlled by multiple Palestinian factions, each with its own headquarters and checkpoints. In total, about 1,000 PLO soldiers operated in Bint Jubayl, a certain IDF target in any future invasion.[11] And on Monday evening, 13 March, the IDF took advantage of their preplanned artillery positions to initiate a barrage, removing all doubt concerning their immediate intentions near and around OP RAS.

The weather was cold and wet with little to no visibility. But the dismal conditions did not deter the IDF as its artillery erupted to bombard targets in southern Lebanon. Initially, the IDF lobbed 155 mm artillery shells near OP RAS to drive Fallon and his Belgian comrade into the OP's protective bunker and disrupt their ability to directly observe IDF military movements and report them to ILMAC. But the stouthearted marine was not shaken and continued to make reports from his position atop the OP's roof, even in low visibility. When he returned to the OP's observation deck below, he reported the bombardment to ILMAC's radio relay station in Naqoura. He confirmed that the IDF's preplanned and precisely targeted fires had indeed originated from the prepared artillery positions on both sides of the Lebanese border.[12] Artillery would continue to fall throughout the following day, and while the IDF would later issue a statement to the UN in the wee hours of 15 March announcing it had "begun a short . . . mopping-up operation along the Lebanese frontier," nothing could be further from the truth.[13] There were no "mops" of any sort being employed by the IDF, but rather the full force of its artillery and tanks to sweep away the PLO.

The battle against the PLO was intense and relentless, but the two UNMOs on OP RAS made the best of their situation. Fallon's Belgian colleague was a reserve officer from Brussels and, by trade, a professional baker. During the IDF shelling, the two repositioned the OP's butagaz cook oven to the bomb shelter. Fallon then volunteered to remain on the observation deck making reports while the Belgian baker made fresh bread and pastries in the bunker below. Fallon recalls the arrangement: "We lowered a rope and a basket from the roof to the bunker. For the next 26 or 28 hours, every hour on the hour, I hauled up fresh pastries, bread, and hot coffee. As I manned the OP, he manned the stove. We had a great relationship."[14]

Indeed, it was international "cooking and looking" in the most intense fashion imaginable. The Belgian officer contributed his culinary expertise while Fallon contributed his observation abilities, even as artillery and tank fire exploded all around.

Sporadic artillery fire continued throughout daylight hours on 14 March, growing much heavier in the evening as the ground invasion approached. On the morning of 15 March, the full force of the IDF's artillery and tank firepower erupted. Fallon observed their tactics. Israeli

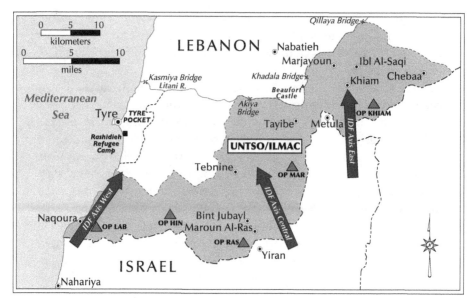

Map 7.1. Israeli Operation Litani Invasion, 15 March 1978

tank, mechanized infantry, and artillery units moved in columns across the border to drive the PLO north of the Litani River. Each column was led by a tank formation, followed by 155 mm self-propelled howitzers, and then infantry soldiers in armored vehicles.[15] What Fallon did not know then, but later learned, was that IDF columns were attacking simultaneously all across southern Lebanon. One was to the west, moving north along the coastal road, seizing ILMAC's radio relay base in Naqoura before continuing onward to the ancient port of Tyre. There the IDF would attempt to seize the strategic Kasmiya Bridge north of Tyre that spanned the Litani River. However, the IDF met determined resistance from the PLO and was thwarted in capturing the bridge. In the east, the IDF moved north en route to the Khadala Bridge west of Marjayoun and a smaller span near and west of the village of Qillaya at the mouth of the Beqaa Valley. Meanwhile, Fallon witnessed the attack in the central sector moving northward toward the strategic Akiya Bridge spanning the Litani River. The IDF chose those bridges to impede future access by the PLO into southern Lebanon once its forces had been pushed north of the Litani. Unquestionably, this was far more than a "mopping up" operation. It was a full-scale invasion involving 25,000 IDF soldiers with important tactical objectives (see map 7.1).[16]

On 15 March, Fallon continued reporting IDF movements near OP RAS while noting practically no resistance by the PLO. It was then that IDF soldiers approached OP RAS and ordered Fallon to "shut down the radio." He diplomatically—albeit disingenuously—agreed, but when they departed he resumed his transmissions. Fallon's reports to ILMAC in Beirut throughout this saga mattered. ILMAC's spot reports from Fallon and other observers were forwarded to UNTSO, who then consolidated and forwarded them to the UN in New York: "On 14 March 1978, between 2240 and 2340, United Nations military observers reported Israeli air activity in the vicinity of OP Khiam (AMR 2071-3025), OP Ras (AMR 1920-2785), Tyre, Nabatiye and Ras El Baiyada (AMR 1660-2852). Additionally, mortar fire initiated from Israeli territory was reported impacting in Naqoura and tank fire in Maroun Er [al-] Ras."[17]

The tank fire reported in Maroun al-Ras originated from the same units that had just passed Fallon situated at OP RAS. But shortly thereafter, the IDF jammed Fallon's communications. Neither UNTSO nor UNIFIL communications were encrypted. No doubt the IDF chaffed at Fallon's unencrypted reports of Israeli movements that could also be easily intercepted by the PLO. Later that morning, the IDF terminated those reports by detaining Fallon and his OP mate and escorting them to the jailhouse in the Israeli town of Metula. Beyond the IDF's aggravation over unsecure UN radio transmissions of their maneuvers, they also did not want UNMOs observing their systematic and on-going demolition of facilities occupied by the PLO and their factions in the town of Bint Jubayl next to OP RAS. Nevertheless, Fallon managed to photograph some of that activity before he was escorted to the Metula jail. In the wake of this, UNTSO reported that the IDF was concerned, putatively, for the protection of UNTSO observers.[18] However, Israeli actions were more likely designed to obstruct Fallon's ability to make the very observations he—and others—dutifully made, even while under fire. Fallon and his Belgian baker were detained for the night at the jail but allowed to remain on the jailhouse porch and not confined to one of the cells. Indeed, they were not treated like prisoners, but rather were provided good food and even wine. It turned out to be a very tolerable captivity.

On the morning of 16 March, both were released. Immediately Fallon and his Belgian comrade made their way west to the Israeli town of Nahariya in their UN vehicle that the IDF permitted them to keep. Upon arriving, his Belgian colleague dropped Fallon off and continued onward to the Belgian embassy in Tel Aviv, unsure he could make it back to Beirut safely. Fallon remained in the Israeli coastal town to rest, after which he took a civilian cab along the seaside road to the Lebanese border. From there he hiked the remaining 5 kilometers to Naqoura, where he secured another UN vehicle and resumed his duties to further report on the fighting near Tyre. The IDF may have thought they had cowed this marine. They had not. He was undeterred.[19]

Fallon, then joined by a Finnish UNMO, managed to get to the outskirts of Tyre. There they observed a raging battle between the IDF and the PLO, the latter fighting to blunt the Israeli assault of the coastal city. Fallon and his comrade drove inland from the coastal road and then north on dirt trails between orange groves just east of Tyre, into an area known as the "Tyre Pocket," a major concentration of PLO forces as well as 5,000 Palestinians living nearby in the Rashidieh refugee camp. Both UNMOs took up a position on a hill overlooking Tyre and its prominent round-about traffic circle to watch and record the battle. This time they maintained radio silence to prevent compromising their presence. In the process, they observed Israeli tanks engaging PLO fighters, who were responding with two- and three-man teams firing Soviet-made guided antitank Sagger missiles, famed for their destructive employment by the Egyptian Army against Israeli tanks and armored vehicles in 1973. The PLO teams took a page out of the Egyptian Army's handbook, firing Saggers in a coordinated manner, massing them against Israeli tank formations. In doing so, the PLO denied the IDF the opportunity to seize the strategic Kasmiya Bridge spanning the Litani River north of Tyre.[20]

After observing about ten hours of the Battle for Tyre, Fallon with his Finnish comrade returned to Naqoura on 18 March to recover from his nonstop, five-day ordeal. Eventually he returned to the ILMAC headquarters in Beirut after the fighting abated for less stressful debriefings. First, he reported to the ILMAC chairman, LTC Jean Espinassy (French Army), who debriefed him and his Finnish partner over coffee and cognac. That same evening—over dinner at an Italian restaurant overlooking Beirut—Fallon was debriefed by LTC Ed Badolato (USMC), the naval attaché assigned to the US embassy in Lebanon. Altogether, it was much safer than "cooking and looking" at OP RAS the previous week.

In the days following, the IDF would continue its attacks on PLO positions across southern Lebanon, seizing three of the four strategic bridges, Akiya in the central sector, Khadala on the western approach, and the smaller one near Qillaya. In the process, the Israeli invasion created a huge humanitarian crisis with the displacement of 150,000 to

250,000 Lebanese noncombatant civilians and PLO fighters, all fleeing northward across the Litani River to avoid the death and mayhem brought by the invasion.[21] Yet, as Fallon observed from the hill overlooking Tyre, the PLO resistance there was doggedly determined, and its forces were difficult to expel. Overall, Israel was successful in pushing the vast majority of the PLO's 5,000 fighters from southern Lebanon to north of the Litani River.[22] For the meantime, Arafat's cannons and rockets would be nudged out of range to easily attack communities in northern Israel. At that point, the PLO realized their best option was to agree to a cease-fire. They remarkably managed to hold on to the Tyre Pocket and the bridge north of Sidon that gave them access to that Mediterranean enclave. It was no small victory in the face of overwhelming military might involving no less than 25,000 IDF soldiers. In the end, 1,100 to 2,000 Lebanese and Palestinians died in Operation Litani, while the IDF recorded only 11 deaths (possibly as many as 20) and 57 wounded.[23]

Operation Litani was a clear tactical victory for the IDF, but the invasion may have worked more to the PLO's favor strategically than Israel intended. While the PLO were forced north of the Litani River—Israel's tactical goal—the use of US-made air-delivered cluster bombs by Israel proved very controversial. The IAF deployed them against PLO soldiers as well as targets in or near Lebanese towns and Palestinian refugee camps, resulting in civilian casualties. It made them appear to have engaged in the sort of terror they had vehemently condemned only a week earlier following the coastal road massacre. President Jimmy Carter was unhappy with Israel's employment of American-made and -provided cluster bombs, asserting the use by Israel violated US legal requirements, namely that the munitions be used only defensively against armed combatants. Moreover, Israel had provided American tactical weapons—including tanks—to Saad Haddad's DFF militia. That too violated American law. An agitated Carter—concerned with the negative repercussions Operation Litani might have on peace initiatives between Israel and Egypt—was prepared to notify Congress that American weapons were being used illegally. That notification would have resulted in denying further aid to Israel's military. Prime Minister Begin understood the potential embarrassment and immediately announced that the war was over.[24] Israel may have achieved tactical successes on the ground, but they badly lost the political and diplomatic fight. A shaky cease-fire did eventually occur, but fighting between the IDF and the PLO would continue up until 28 March.

The Birth of the United Nations Interim Force in Lebanon

When the dust settled, Fallon returned to his role as an ILMAC observer. Yet much activity swirled about UNTSO. MG Erskine and his staff in Jerusalem quickly shifted into high gear to deploy a new peacekeeping operation formed by the UN Security Council. In due time, Fallon would find himself serving as the UNIFIL "reconnaissance and deployments officer" conducting the preliminary ground reconnaissance to position arriving peacekeeping units. The entire effort would be quite a challenge.

UNIFIL had a troubled birth. Its mandate, organization, deployment, and rules for engaging other armed forces failed to resemble anything that the US military or any other well-trained national army would develop. It was, in the vernacular of a down-home American southerner, a "y'all come" invitation. Unfortunately, UNIFIL was not ready. No serious-minded national military command authority would have contemplated developing, organizing, and deploying a major international peacekeeping force like UNIFIL on such a truncated time line with any hope of success. Moreover, it was poorly equipped. While it had a fairly robust small arms capability, crew-served machine guns, antitank weapons, and armored personnel carriers (APCs), it had no field artillery and only a limited mortar capability to respond to attacks from hostile forces should the need arise. In the spring of 1978, while the IDF, DFF, and the PLO had tanks and heavy weapons, UNIFIL was lightly armed. Erskine would later explain that problem.

> From time to time, we would have had a serious confrontation with the Christian militias. On 9 May, we faced over 20 Israeli tanks. The PLO and other leftist armed groups have their heavy weapons too. Under this concept of self-defence [*sic*], I have had some difficulty in opening up my 120mm [mortars] even in self-defence. We managed to convince UN HQ that APCs are defensive and hence we have them. It is only logical to fight tanks with tanks, but this is viewed from the offensive perspective and [the] Security Council may have to invoke Chapter 7 of the UN Charter to equip any UN force with tanks.[25]

Indeed, UNIFIL was never a true peace enforcement operation as envisioned under Chapter VII of the UN Charter. That provision would have allowed the UN to "determine the existence of any threat to the peace, breach of the peace, or act of aggression" and to take military action to "restore international peace and security," without the approval of the parties to the conflict.[26] For UNIFIL, the UN relied on the restoration of peace provisions of Chapter VI whereby parties to a conflict consented to the peaceful settlement of disputes and the presence of peacekeeping forces.[27] That was fine for those established in the Sinai and the Golan Heights, where peace had taken hold well. However, in southern Lebanon, where violence was still ongoing, UNIFIL would be far less militarily capable against combatant forces. This and other factors—including a weakly worded mandate and terms of reference, a hasty deployment time line, inadequately trained units, and insufficient numbers of heavy weaponry to repel aggression—almost guaranteed that UNIFIL would be disadvantaged in handling hostile situations in southern Lebanon. Succinctly put, in failing to plan adequately for a militarily capable force, the UN was unwittingly planning for failure. In the end, UNIFIL was somewhat anemic, forced to rely more on light arms and moral suasion rather than the application of unambiguous military capability that would have been more useful in enforcing its mandate in a very hostile southern Lebanon.

Following Operation Litani, the UN Security Council held a number of urgent meetings that culminated in the adoption of UN Resolution 425 on 19 March 1978 calling for "strict respect for the territorial integrity, sovereignty, and political independence of Lebanon within its internationally recognized boundaries." It also called on Israel to withdraw its forces while authorizing "immediately" the establishment of a "United Nations Interim Force" for southern Lebanon.[28] UNIFIL's mission included (1) "determine cessation of hostilities" by the IDF, (2) "confirming the withdrawal of Israeli forces," (3) "restoring international peace and security," and (4) "assisting the Government of Lebanon in ensuring the return of its effective authority in the area."[29] None of these goals were likely to be realized by deploying an ill-prepared and limited force, particularly the goal of "restoring" international peace and security. Moreover, what does it mean to restore a condition, if not to return something to its former or original state? Just what sort of restoration was UNIFIL tasked to achieve? Was it the condition prior to Operation Litani? Was it a return to conditions existing prior to the outbreak of the Lebanese Civil War in 1975? Should it have been to demilitarize southern Lebanon altogether? To be sure, that would have required peace enforcers with the ability and authority to compel adherence to the cease-fire. It would also have required a judicial system to punish violators. But UNIFIL was not chartered to be a peace enforcer, nor was there a functional law enforcement system in southern Lebanon to compel civil and criminal justice, a requirement if the

Lebanese were to impose their "authority in the area." Nonetheless, UNI-
FIL was formally established by the accompanying UN Resolution 426. It
would consist of military units provided by member states with a mandate
that, like UNDOF's, would require renewal every six months.[30]

On 19 March, Erskine—who was in his first tour as UNTSO chief of
staff—was tapped by the secretary-general to organize and command
UNIFIL. He was a logical choice, given his familiarity with the region and
current leadership of UNTSO. From the beginning, the establishment of
UNIFIL was a challenge. While UNIFIL's mandate was seemingly clear—
to supervise the withdrawal of the Israelis, restore order, and reestablish
Lebanese control—deploying the force was a challenge. Hastily assembled by an ad hoc staff formed from across UNTSO and driven by the
exigencies of international politics, UNIFIL's top-level planning lacked
the needed depth and detail to implement a major military force capable
of establishing peace in turbulent southern Lebanon. Had this been
strictly an American effort, it would have been subjected to a detailed
planning process. That would have involved a Military Decision-Making
Process (MDMP) and a multistep process that included (1) the receipt of
the mission, (2) a mission analysis, (3) an in-depth course of action assessment (COA), (4) the development of a comprehensive plan, (5) a formal
COA analysis and war-gaming, (6) a critical COA comparison, (7) a preferred COA selection, and (8) the production, dissemination, and transition of detailed and written orders to execute the plan. That is an involved
but necessary process in establishing an organization like UNIFIL. There
is precious little evidence that any effort resembling this sort of discipline
was undertaken by Erskine or his adjunct UNTSO staff. In fact, in the
UN's first formal report on December 1978 concerning UNIFIL, there
was *no* description—not a word—of any formalized planning process
that preceded UNIFIL's arrival and deployment in southern Lebanon, a
remarkable omission for any official account of this nature.[31] Possibly
that was an oversight in the report. However, Erskine's planning staff was
constituted quickly from UNTSO's existing staff and its observers across
the region. They had inadequate time to plan at the level required for
such a complex mission. Indeed, the UNTSO-cum-UNIFIL staff did not
arrive in southern Lebanon until April of 1978 and was not fully func-
tioning until 10 May.[32] By then, UNIFIL troops were already in sector
and, sadly, had already experienced their first death. Master Warrant
Officer Karl Oskar Johansson was killed by a land mine on 29 March
while serving with a Swedish medical company that had redeployed from
Egypt to serve in UNIFIL.[33]

In all fairness, Erskine's planning staff had to be quickly assembled following the Israeli invasion and his appointment as the UNIFIL commanding general. Indeed, on the day of the invasion Erskine had just returned from Egypt, where he was conducting a routine inspection of UNTSO forces.[34] His planning staff would have been hard pressed to leverage the capabilities and resources found in a major military planning headquarters of a force UNIFIL's size. For example, there was little evidence that Erskine directed a formal intelligence preparation of the battlefield (IPB), a systematic process employed to analyze the mission variables of enemy, terrain, weather, and civil considerations that could impact a military operation. A proper IPB would have been thoroughly studied and updated routinely by planners to ensure that when the force entered the area, it would be on a sound footing designed to achieve success then and later. This analysis appears to have been completely absent as UNIFIL cobbled together an interim staff that deployed piecemeal into southern Lebanon. Nevertheless, the people that Erskine did have available were professionals who put their hearts, hands, and minds into a difficult planning mission facing a truncated time line. What is puzzling is that Erskine was a well-trained officer, having attended Staff College in England. He fully knew the elements of a proper campaign plan. Unfortunately, he appears to have been caught up in the urgency the UN insisted upon in deploying UNIFIL, a hastiness that made planning difficult.

On the night of 19 March 1978, after Erskine took command of UNIFIL, he began to form his initial UNIFIL staff, drawing on UNTSO personnel. That nascent team included UNTSO's chief operations officer, LTC J. Potter (USA). Erskine also drafted his senior UNMO in OGE, LTC Thomas E. Leverette (USA), to be the officer in charge at Naqoura, where Erskine would eventually position his UNIFIL staff.[35] Potter brought with him the very capable MAJ Gerald J. Oberndorfer (USMC) to serve as the operations officer. About two days later, Erskine dispatched Potter, Leverette, and others to Naqoura in southern Lebanon, where they had planned to occupy an old Lebanese customs truck inspection station on the compound that would be UNIFIL's new headquarters. Erskine's team was eager to get to work and arrived in Naqoura on 23 and 24 March with a group of nine UNMOs diverted from Egypt to southern Lebanon. Leverette, Oberndorfer, and two other UNMOs immediately proceeded to the central sector of UNIFIL's projected area of operations to conduct an assessment of the situation. However, without adequate communications and logistical support, in a few days they returned to Jerusalem. The IDF—a party to the conflict—previously had occupied the truck station at Naqoura, making UNIFIL's use of that facility as a planning location problematic. As a result, from 24 March to 10 May 1978, UNIFIL's planning staff worked out of Government House in Jerusalem, 180 kilometers from the area of operations. Despite being unable to locate in the forward area, Erskine had a complement of skilled and professional US officers to staff his initial efforts. The question was whether that same staff would be sufficient and robust enough to tackle the enormous task of forming and deploying a force of 6,000 UNIFIL soldiers, and doing so with limited time. As it was, his small UNIFIL staff amounted to an advance party in a normal deployment of this nature, not one designed to fully plan, operate, and sustain such an organization.

Implementing Challenges to UNIFIL

Erskine had his hands full bringing UNIFIL to life. His first challenge was defining UNIFIL's specific area of operations beyond a generalized swath of territory that the IDF, the DFF, and PLO forces had occupied during the invasion. Nor were Israel, Lebanon, the Palestinians, and UNIFIL able to agree on that point. Israel was unenthusiastic about the UN plan. It wanted UNIFIL to be a security buffer force between the Litani River and the northern edge of a narrow enclave that stretched along the northern side of Israel's border that the IDF and DFF would control. Unstated by Israel, however, was their full intent to continue to overwatch and control that enclave with their DFF allies despite UNIFIL's presence. From the beginning, Israel did not trust that UNTSO, UNIFIL, or any other organization with the letters "UN" in front of it would be sufficient to keep the PLO from advancing near the Israeli border to conduct the very raids Operation Litani sought to end. Israel simply was not willing to outsource its security to organizations they contended were openly hostile to Israeli political and security concerns.[36] No amount of good intent in creating UNIFIL, including US support for it, would mitigate Israeli concerns. Therefore, they sought to undermine UNIFIL. Israel made a point of insisting that UNIFIL clear southern Lebanon of the PLO. They knew full well that UNIFIL would not take that bait since doing so would serve to compromise UNIFIL's impartiality with the PLO and their allies. But the Israelis were clever. Once UNIFIL declined to remove the PLO from the Tyre Pocket, Israel could then insist on maintaining the DFF's presence in the larger enclave that ran from the Mediterranean coast to the Syrian border just north of the Israeli border inside

Lebanon.[37] Israel was sly to call on UNIFIL to banish the PLO, something both parties to the conflict knew would never occur. And when it did not, the Israelis could demand that the DFF remain in the enclave as a reliable satrap in southern Lebanon.

The PLO was nearly as clever. Publicly, Chairman Arafat supported UNIFIL's deployment. But there was a condition. The PLO had to remain in southern Lebanon. From the beginning Erskine recalls that Arafat was "negative toward" UN Resolution 425, which established UNIFIL's mandate, contending that it "served the interests of Israel."[38] In fact, Arafat would also undermine UNIFIL's mission by not evacuating the Tyre Pocket. While Resolution 425 required Israel to depart Lebanon, Arafat made clear to Erskine that he was certain the IDF would not completely withdraw. Therefore, Arafat insisted on remaining in the Tyre Pocket. He reasoned that if he left, not only would the PLO be disadvantaged, but the Israelis would not reciprocate in evacuating themselves. Therefore, why should Arafat embrace that requirement if he was sure Israel would not fully withdraw? The PLO chairman was adamant that his forces would stay put, specifically further asserting that the PLO had a right to movement in the UNIFIL area, especially in Tyre and other PLO settlements in the south.[39] As his rationale, Arafat cited the Cairo Accord of 2 November 1969 between the PLO and Lebanon. That unpublished agreement recognized the PLO's "right" to remain as refugees in Lebanon residing in 16 large camps under the auspices of the United Nations Relief and Works Agency (UNRWA).[40] The text was never officially released, yet the UN agreed that it was nonetheless germane with respect to the PLO's presence in the Tyre region. Moreover, Arafat demanded that his forces would not relinquish control of Kasmiya Bridge across the Litani River, which the PLO had successfully defended. Yet retention of that bridge by the PLO also meant that UNIFIL would be denied the ability to control entry of a key crossing point into the area it was mandated to control.[41] Therefore, before the ink was dry on UNIFIL's mandate, the UN acquiesced to PLO demands to retain the Tyre Pocket, including control of the key bridge into the area. In other words, no sooner had the UN mandate been passed by the Security Council than it was undermined by concessions to the PLO, which Israel parlayed into maintaining the DFF enclave, a further disability for UNIFIL.

Like the PLO, the IDF also was keen to maintain access into southern Lebanon. After all, Israel undertook Operation Litani to drive the PLO north of the river. It was not willing to see them return easily. To ensure they did not, the DFF would continue the conflict against the PLO near the Israeli border. The presence of UN troops from the Litani River to the border with Israel, including inside the enclave, would obviously complicate Israel's efforts to sustain the DFF mission. Therefore, the IDF also insisted on controlling the gates they had installed in the border fence. Control by UNIFIL was flatly unacceptable since it would deny Israel the ability to readily enter southern Lebanon unimpeded, either to assist the DFF or to undertake their own military activities.[42]

As a consequence, the parties successfully denied the hastily assembled UNIFIL access to critical territory it would need to enter, occupy, and traverse in order to execute its mandate. Erskine seemed resigned, particularly so with respect to Israel, to his no-win position: "For UNIFIL to fully execute its mandate, we need to deploy fully to the international borders bringing along with us the Lebanese authority. For the time being, this seems unacceptable to Israel and hence the stalemate in our progress. . . . Our mandate is in conflict with their [Israel's] military and political interests in Lebanon and so their cooperation with UNIFIL to make progress is out, for the time being."[43]

In essence, UNIFIL was snake-bitten from its birth by uncooperative combatants, with the notable exception of the government of Lebanon, which maintained UNIFIL had the freedom to move anywhere it required.[44] Not so the PLO or Israel, who did not want UNIFIL to succeed and made it impossible for Erskine to occupy critical territory to keep the peace. Indeed, peace then between Israel and the PLO was seemingly not a goal for either Jews or Palestinians. They were at war, and as far as both sides were concerned, UNIFIL was there to witness a brief break in the action. From its inception UNIFIL had its area of operations defined not by UN authority with the blessing of the sovereign nation of Lebanon, but rather by the parties to the conflict who sought to undermine the organization. Clearly, the combatant tail was wagging the UNIFIL dog.

Erskine was bedeviled by other challenges. He was determined to halt the transport of military arms and uniformed military personnel into southern Lebanon, except for the Lebanese Army or police forces. Left unanswered was how UNIFIL would distinguish local Lebanese citizens, who were armed for their own protection, from armed infiltrators. Was UNIFIL to disarm everyone? How would UNIFIL handle PLO fighters traveling about when dressed in civilian clothes? The PLO had easy access to numerous arms and uniform caches prepositioned across southern Lebanon. This left Erskine to allow all unarmed, un-uniformed personnel in possession of Lebanese identification cards to enter the area.[45] In other words, UNIFIL's interception standards were set very low from the start.

Therefore, the rules against bringing arms into the region could easily be skirted by infiltrators simply donning civilian garb and obtaining an ID, forged or otherwise. Once PLO infiltrators entered the UNIFIL area, they could easily travel to established caches and covertly retrieve uniforms and equipment.

Erskine's next major challenge was deploying forces to the region, which was piecemeal from the beginning. On 19 March, he assembled his staff to discuss UNIFIL's deployment, even while troops were preparing to move into a nebulous situation in southern Lebanon. Simultaneously, he directed additional UNMOs from Egypt and Jerusalem to be prepared to move "on-order" into southern Lebanon to assist in deploying UNIFIL. Erskine then instructed UNTSO's civilian staff to evaluate what administrative and logistical support could be provided from UN storehouses in the region. He then ordered his newly assembled UNIFIL staff to begin planning for arriving forces. Erskine was certainly decisive in issuing these initial directives. After all, contributing nations were already urgently making plans to send their troops to the region. Nevertheless, the approach Erskine took did not embrace a sufficient decision-making process including an intelligence preparation of the battlefield, a mission analysis, and a detailed consideration of courses of action to implement the plan. Erskine was rather cavalier in characterizing the need to understand the factors of weather and terrain as things that were "good to know" before units arrived in the field, a profound understatement.[46] He would have been wise to slow the train and make clear to the UN's leadership that while it was critical to get troops in place, proper planning was necessary before troops cascaded into a hostile fire zone, which southern Lebanon surely was at the time. He did not. Even UNTSO's observers saw that planning for UNIFIL was problematic. MAJ Dick Vercauteren observed from his vantage point in OGJ that planning for UNIFIL's arrival and deployment was done "on the fly" or in an "ad hoc" manner.[47] As a matter of course early in UNIFIL's deployment, many of Erskine's orders took the form of "verbal orders of the commander." In time, the VOCO orders process would improve with the use of abbreviated yet written fragmentary orders (FRAGO) that were accompanied with map overlays depicting the area that operational forces were expected to occupy. Some of those FRAGOs were literally handed to units as they disembarked in Beirut or otherwise arrived in UNIFIL's area of operation.[48] But FRAGOs often lack the level of detail needed for units to properly execute their mission. It was a catch-as-catch-can process by Erskine and his limited staff that constituted UNIFIL's hastily assembled headquarters.

Simply put, their abbreviated planning was inadequate to prepare a force of this size to occupy a combat zone. Fully developed plans available to deploying units before they left their homeland would have been far preferable, particularly in properly training and equipping forces for the rigors of southern Lebanon. Thoughtful planners, like those among US and Western nations, would have insisted on sufficient time to plan, whereas the UN authorities in New York seemed to think Erskine could work miracles. But despite being in the Holy Land, miracles in this case were not readily available to Erskine. What was needed was a disciplined planning process and sufficient time to establish forces on the ground in good order, ideally inside a workable mandate and a clearly articulated area of operations uncompromised by stubborn demands of hostile forces. In truth, Erskine needed to employ evaluative criteria that the US Army and its allies refer to as METT-T (Mission, Enemy, Terrain, Troops, and Time Available), all necessary elements of an effective deployment and transition to mission execution. In his analysis of the UNIFIL deployment, military scholar John Mackinlay noted the disadvantageous conditions Erskine faced: "The General had not had the opportunity to meet and impress his concept of operations upon the individual commanders as they arrived with their embryo units from all points on the compass. Nor could he have had much idea what they would find when they reached their appointed locations. The terms of reference had failed to define the area of operations over which the force should establish its authority."[49]

The hastily assembled operation lacked preparedness, situational awareness, and the specific tactical details addressing the who, what, when, why, and how normally found in a properly developed tactical mission statement and accompanying analysis. Moreover, the broad strategic mandate characterized in UN Resolution 425 was insufficient for that purpose. In fact, that mandate amounted to what the military terms "the commander's intent." But that mandate was not a clear tactical mission statement addressing the nitty-gritty of what UNIFIL's officers and soldiers needed to accomplish to be effective. Most well-trained and well-staffed planning headquarters in the US Army would have found this entire concept of operations utterly deficient.

Deploying UNIFIL

On 21 March, 22 UNTSO observers arrived in southern Lebanon to support the operation. The following day an Iranian unit of approximately

200 soldiers arrived from UNDOF along with a 250-man Swedish outfit from UNEF II based in Egypt.[50] This was UNIFIL's nucleus, a less-than-impressive one that frankly was incapable of having any meaningful military effect. However, UNTSO observers, particularly those from ILMAC, had a very useful and immediate impact in orienting the arriving units. While it hardly constituted a proper IPB for arriving units, at least the Beirut-based ILMAC observers were familiar with the situation on the ground.[51] Both the Iranians (then under the old government of the shah) and the Swedes were completely new to southern Lebanon, unfamiliar with the challenges of the area, and hardly capable of supporting themselves sufficiently, much less doing anything to advance the UNIFIL mandate. They had insufficient liaison with anyone when they arrived, only the limited supplies they brought with them, and sketchy operational direction beyond the specific positions they would occupy. In essence, the first units to arrive were completely unprepared for the mission.

On 23 March, a French commando company was traveling south on the coastal road from Beirut to the Tyre Pocket. Three days later a Norwegian force would arrive in Tele Aviv and make its way north along Israel's coastal highway to the Lebanese border. Other forces continued to arrive throughout the spring and summer of 1978. However, from 24 March to about 3 May of that year, who controlled what in southern Lebanon remained unclear. When May arrived, UNIFIL had only 1,100 soldiers available, including the staff still operating out of Government House in Jerusalem. The small number of available troops was a problem in establishing UNIFIL's control of the area. For example, as the IDF withdrew early on 11 April, there were insufficient UNIFIL forces on the ground to fill the vacuum. The task of filling the gap initially fell on elements of a recently arrived Nepalese Battalion (NEPBATT), but its strength was insufficient to fill the entire void created by rapidly withdrawing IDF units. Erskine would also need an inbound Senegalese Battalion (SENBATT) that was deploying via Damascus to fill in behind the Nepalese as the latter attempted to occupy yet more territory the Israelis were evacuating on 30 April.[52] John Mackinlay notes the challenge even as UNIFIL strength increased:

> As the Israeli forces withdrew, UNIFIL's strength increased to its planned ceiling of 4000. The newly arrived contingents occupied the positions vacated by the retiring Israelis. However, it was not long before the UN ran out of troops to take over the abandoned areas. On 3 May the Security Council agreed to increase the

strength of UNIFIL from 4000 to 6000 but even with the benefit of this swiftly executed increase there were still not enough troops to man all the key positions vacated and in some areas these became points of dispute between UNIFIL and whichever local force occupied them.[53]

A properly developed plan would certainly have anticipated the number of troops necessary to occupy territory that Israel would eventually relinquish. But no such plan was seemingly contemplated so that UN troops could take charge in good order. Instead, both UNTSO and UNIFIL were forced to improvise in a challenging environment where improvisation would never be as effective as a disciplined plan would have been.

With the approval of additional UNIFIL forces, Erskine's team found themselves very busy. By 10 May, the ad hoc UNIFIL staff finally occupied its headquarters in Naqoura and began planning the arrival of more forces. Now UNIFIL was supported by the newly formed OGL, which incorporated ILMAC observers along with other UNMOs from Egypt and Jerusalem. Once again, CPT Mike Fallon was in the middle of the action, this time as the UNIFIL "reconnaissance and deployments officer." Since March of 1978, he had been working alongside a fellow marine, MAJ Jerry Oberndorfer, preparing to emplace UNIFIL's troops in tactical positions. Since the cease-fire had gone into effect, Fallon and his Finnish partner, MAJ Timo Bockman, were routinely dispatched by Oberndorfer to scout for good locations to deploy newly arriving units. Working in the field, they spent their days developing tactical unit boundaries based on a standard 1:50,000-scale military map and spent their nights sleeping on the ground beside their vehicle. Their work included selecting map coordinates for every UNIFIL battalion down to the platoon level, even the specific locations at which to establish machine gun positions. It was a multifaceted reconnaissance that considered not only lines of communication and logistics at the battalion level, but north and south infiltration routes through the locations where platoons would be emplaced, even as UNIFIL was arriving. Fallon and Bockman were very diligent in executing their detailed reconnaissance, which turned out to be as close to an IPB assessment of the terrain as the UNTSO staff-turned-UNIFIL planners could have conducted in a short amount of time.

Indeed, so devoted was Fallon in trying to understand the terrain and the eventual implications for UNIFIL units that he actually conducted a reconnaissance down the Litani River that June in a makeshift raft. His objective was to discover potential infiltration routes into the sectors where UNIFIL battalions were positioned or would be located. With the help of soldiers from UNIFIL's NEPBATT, whom he had guided into position two months earlier, Fallon constructed a raft from scrap wood and poles, bound together with black field telephone wire. With his partner Bockman paralleling him from ashore, Fallon then floated down the Litani in the jerry-rigged contraption, beginning in UNIFIL's central sector at dawn. When he reached the Mediterranean coast, Bockman was there at dusk waiting to pick him up. In the end, Fallon had an enjoyable time but found no discernable infiltration routes across the river. It may have been the most creative waterborne operation in UN history.

Additionally, Fallon and Bockman had to consider how to address positions formerly held by the IDF and PLO as they negotiated with Lebanese farmers and villagers. The locals wanted to return to some semblance of normalcy, including repossessing land that had previously been held by combatants. Unfortunately, some of those positions were necessary from a tactical viewpoint and needed to be occupied by UNIFIL troops. Fallon and Bockman had to work through those details that sometimes disappointed local Lebanese civilians. The new UNIFIL area of operations would cover a vast area from Naqoura on the coast to the Lebanese and Syrian border in the east. Then, when units arrived, Fallon and Bockman would link up with them and guide their units into position.

From March onward, after major fighting had ebbed, Fallon and Bockman were a busy pair. The first full battalion to arrive in Beirut on 23 March was a French one that moved south to Zahrani, north of the Tyre Pocket, where they remained until May. They would proceed no further south, not desiring a combat confrontation with PLO factions who controlled both the road and the bridge Arafat said he would not relinquish. Beyond a simple courtesy call by the French commander to the ILMAC chairman in Beirut, the French did not require any assistance from Fallon and his colleagues. The French commander and his staff preferred to rely on their institutional knowledge of Lebanon from the mandate period decades earlier. Fallon recalled their hubris, noting, "you couldn't tell them anything."[54] Indeed, the French had insisted their forces would remain near the coastline, wary of being positioned further inland, where they could encounter potential violence from armed elements. Ironically, on 2 May the French Battalion (FRENCHBATT) commander, COL Jean Salvan, was seriously wounded, receiving 14 AK-47 rounds from Palestinian armed elements operating on the coast.[55] Remarkably he survived.

A day earlier, on 22 March, the Iranian company, previously deployed on the Golan Heights with UNDOF, arrived escorted by UNMOs from Damascus and Tiberias. The Iranians were to deploy to the bridge at Akiya in the central sector. However, as they entered southern Lebanon through Israel's "Good Gate," they were stopped by Haddad's DFF and held in place for nearly a week. Ironically, that gate derived its name from the goodwill Israel showed to Lebanese Maronite Christians seeking medical care at the Galilee Medical Center in Nahariya. Additionally, it provided a pathway to market the goods of Maronite Christians via the Israeli port of Haifa during the Lebanese Civil War. But in March 1982, UNIFIL units seeking to enter southern Lebanon through the "Good Gate" found it to be a "Wait Gate." Besides, Israel was still busy destroying PLO structures near OP RAS that Fallon had observed a week earlier. The IDF did not want more witnesses to that activity. Eventually the Iranians were allowed to move a short distance inside Lebanon to positions south of Marjayoun, where they were further delayed until the IDF had completed its work destroying nearby facilities it deemed a threat. Clearly, mission interference and obstruction by the IDF and their allies were present from the first day that UNIFIL forces arrived in southern Lebanon. That would not change over time.

The same day the Iranians were delayed, a Swedish medical company assigned to UNEF II made its way north from the Sinai. However, when it arrived at the Israeli border with Lebanon, its commander decided to delay movement forward into Lebanon until the UN changed the unit's deployment status from what it had been in Egypt. In Egypt, the Swedish unit's presence was authorized under Chapter VI of the UN Charter, whereby parties to a conflict consented to the peaceful settlement of disputes and the presence of peacekeeping forces.[56] In the case of Sinai, the status of the Egyptian and Israeli confrontation under UNEF II satisfied that requirement under the UN Charter. However, UNIFIL was not organized under the UNEF II mandate per se, and the Swedes wanted to ensure they were legally included in the UNIFIL structure before moving into southern Lebanon under the correct framework. That was prudent. Fortunately for the Fallon-Bockman welcoming committee, neither the French, the Iranians, nor the Swedes required their assistance.

Not until the Nepalese and Senegalese battalions arrived in early and mid-April would the Fallon-Bockman team serve as ground guides. They would do the same with other UNIFIL battalions as they arrived in sector, following a predictable pattern. Once the incoming units landed at the Beirut International Airport, they were ceremonially welcomed by

UNIFIL officials and their country's embassy team. Afterward, they were provided a deployment FRAGO, instructing them where and how they would be employed. The troops then immediately boarded buses or other contract vehicles to be transported south along the coastal highway, where they were guided to their new positions. Afterward, Fallon and Bockman would check in with the newly positioned battalion for the first five days after they were in place to ensure they were in good order.[57]

Fallon and Bockman's welcome wagon continued to operate throughout the summer, guiding new battalions into position, about one per week. By 13 September eight combat battalions were on the ground. These included units from Fiji (500 soldiers), France (644 soldiers), Iran (599 soldiers), Ireland (661 soldiers), Nepal (642 soldiers), Nigeria (673 soldiers), Norway (706 soldiers), Senegal (634 soldiers), and three logistics units from Canada (117 soldiers), France (537 soldiers), and Norway (218 soldiers), producing a total of 5,931 UNIFIL troops.[58] The problem with this deployment process became evident quickly. While these forces dribbled into the area of operations and took up positions, the resident hostile forces—particularly the DFF and the PLO—had established well-manned checkpoints and enclaves throughout the UNIFIL sector. In fact, parts of the eastern sector near Marjayoun were declared a restricted zone to UN troops by both the PLO and the DFF. Hostile forces would not be easily dislodged, displaced, or dissuaded by the UNIFIL battalions trickling into the region to take up peacekeeping.

Misbegotten Strategic and Operational Planning

In sum, UNIFIL was faced with many problems related to its creation, deployment, and daily operations. From siting their headquarters in Naqoura, where they were easily harassed and obstructed by the DFF, to the challenges of logistics, UNIFIL had much to overcome. To say that UNIFIL was off to a rough start would wildly understate its condition in the dangerous place called southern Lebanon. Unfortunately, in its first six months of operations UNIFIL suffered eight deaths and 52 injuries as a result of firing incidents and mine explosions.[59] Despite UNIFIL's tenuous creation, deployment, and transition to engage hostile forces, the UN secretary-general tried to put the best possible face on the situation in characterizing the first six months of its operations. His description of UNIFIL's initial deployment across southern Lebanon suggested an orderly occupation of the area by the first units arriving in the region.

That was an overly optimistic assessment. In reality, UNIFIL's arrival in the area of operations was significantly uncoordinated, disjointed, and ill-prepared, both operationally and logistically. The UN authorities in New York were also quite sanguine about UNIFIL's actions following the IDF's precipitous withdrawal from southern Lebanon, which was in part due to US pressure on Prime Minister Begin to leave Lebanon quickly.[60] The report from the secretary-general asserts that when the Israelis withdrew from southern Lebanon in April and May, UN forces quickly occupied the void. Erskine's account is different. In fact, he maintained that when Israel withdrew "we did not have troops to fill the vacuum."[61] To say the least, the lack of prior planning for this sort of operation hindered UNIFIL's deployment and eventual operations in southern Lebanon. Mackinlay was sympathetic to Erskine's dilemma: "General Erskine needed to overcome problems of time, leadership and politics. He required more time to organize his staff, assemble his force before it deployed and reconnoiter and plan his tasks."[62]

Despite the professionalism of very excellent staff members composed of both UNTSO and ILMAC military observers, many of whom were extraordinarily competent American officers like the doggedly determined Fallon, the truncated planning and deployment of UNIFIL was an almost incomprehensible task. Like the overextended Operation Market Garden during World War II, the deployment of UNIFIL was simply a "bridge too far." In a moment of candor, even the secretary-general's initial report of UNIFIL's first 180 days notes the difficulty it faced. It speaks loudly to the misbegotten strategic and operational planning in UNIFIL's deployment and utilization, even while failing to acknowledge the UN's own lack of foresight and preparation in assembling the force.

> [W]e must face the fact that the present situation, through no fault of UNIFIL, is unacceptable. The resistance of certain armed groups to its full deployment and the support from outside which these groups are known to enjoy, combined with the resulting difficulties experienced by the Lebanese Government in exerting its authority in the UNIFIL area of operation, constitute formidable obstacles to the implementation of the mandate of UNIFIL. The fact that the Israel Defence [*sic*] Force handed over control of the border area to de facto armed groups, rather than to UNIFIL, has continued to make impossible the full deployment of UNIFIL and the restoration of the authority of the Lebanese Government in the whole area of operation. In this connection it is important to

stress that one of the main tasks of UNIFIL is to protect the rights and security of all of the inhabitants of its area of operation. To do this it requires full freedom of movement and deployment throughout the area.[63]

Curiously, the secretary-general seemed to have completely absolved himself and other UN authorities who, in the wee hours of UNIFIL's existence, agreed to the PLO's demands to exclude UNIFIL from the Tyre Pocket, an act that reinforced Israel's determination in keeping the DFF enclave. UNIFIL needed control of both areas to fulfill its mandate. Indeed, a responsible national command authority would never have dispatched troops to a war zone while undermining that force's ability to complete its mission. But that is precisely what the UN did with UNIFIL in its early days. Is it any wonder that UNIFIL—with insufficient troops—was unable to fill the void of withdrawing Israelis or contend effectively with PLO forces in Tyre when it was denied the ability to occupy the very terrain the UN said was necessary for it to accomplish the mission?

For better or worse, the UNIFIL we found in 1981 was the one we had to support. And despite its inherent difficulties, we threw ourselves into that mission. With that in mind, what was it like for a Yank to serve in southern Lebanon armed with only a blue beret? Let's take a closer look.

8

UNMO Duty in the "Wild West"

In 1981 southern Lebanon was a wild and wooly place. There, I joined international professional soldiers like Argentine MAJ Edwardo Laciar, Australians LTC Pat Marshall-Cormack, CPT Trevor Lloyd, and CPT Barry Gwyther, Belgian COMDT Jean Lichtenberger, Canadian CPT Jean Lefebvre, Irish COMDT Dave Betson and COMDT Des Travers, and many other UNMOs from other nations striving to keep the peace in a place where it was in very short supply. And of course, we had a robust cadre of Americans in southern Lebanon, including Army officers LTC Al Baker, LTC John Wilson, MAJ Hal Carswell, MAJ Al Ingalls, MAJ Jim Judkins, MAJ Steve Justice, MAJ Herman Kafura, MAJ Joe Serviss, MAJ Steve Strom, MAJ Bob Thomas, MAJ Johnny Woolshlager, CPT Ed Anderson, and CPT Todd Wilson. Our Navy contingent included LTCDR Virg Bozeman, LT Jim Carlson, LT Mike Imhoff, and LT Paul Rollins. From the Marines Corps were MAJ Wallace "Chip" Gregson, MAJ James "Digger" Byrnes, MAJ Kevin Kennedy, MAJ Denny Lindeman, MAJ Stuart Lynn, MAJ Jay Sollis, CPT Anthony "Drew" Blice, CPT Dan Holstein, and CPT John Reardon. The Air Force officers included MAJ Terry Brady, MAJ John Deutsch, and MAJ Joe Moynihan. We were the most recent links in a dedicated chain of Yank officers who had preceded us, including US Army officers MAJ Charlie Bauman and MAJ Harry Klein, US Marines MAJ Steve Berkheiser, MAJ Dick Vercauteren, CPT Clay Grubb, CPT Mike Fallon, and CPT Lenny Supko, and Air Force officer MAJ Gordy Breault, just to name a very few.

UNMOs along with the armed battalions of UNIFIL that we supported were in danger every day from recalcitrant and violent combatants, including the IDF and their DFF surrogates on the one hand, and the PLO and their radical armed element allies on the other. None of them trusted the UN, UNTSO, or UNIFIL or respected the legal mandates of any of those organizations. Those who were committed to violence seemingly had no interest in supporting anyone associated with UN peacekeeping. Simply put, southern Lebanon was the "Wild West" without a good saloon. Moreover, the UN "sheriff" was neither welcomed nor well regarded. Nonetheless, as I readied myself for my first tour of duty on an OP in southern Lebanon, I was eager, having learned a lot during my orientation trip a week earlier.

Before leaving Jerusalem, I purchased foodstuffs for my week-long tour with three other UNMOs, enough for myself as well as a sufficient amount to prepare two dinners for all of us in the course of a week. Wanting to make a good impression, I chose spaghetti and meatballs, tossed salad, and garlic bread for one meal. My mom, Marguerite Lingamfelter, had a wonderful meatloaf recipe that I selected for the other. I knew I would face stiff competition from others on the OP. Moreover, I wanted to avoid the experience my friend LTCDR Virg Bozeman (USN) had when he displayed his undeveloped culinary skills on his first OP outing. On his first night on OP MAR, Bozeman's French partners served up rack of lamb, asparagus, and a berry tarte for dessert. The next evening, his Swedish comrade produced a delightful hors d'oeuvre followed by a succulent dish of fish and broccoli. The third evening, Bozeman chose to prepare hotdogs with potato chips. In stark contrast, for the next three nights Bozeman's teammates prepared fabulous gourmet meals with the skill of Parisian chefs. Then it was Bozeman's second turn at bat. He served hamburgers and more potato chips. When he returned to Nahariya the following week, his performance as a culinarian had preceded him. Our senior officer, LTC Wilson, sat "Chef" Bozeman down and bluntly reminded him that while "cooking and looking" was what UNMOs did on OP duty, the "cooking" should be more sophisticated than the menu board at an American little league baseball park. Wilson was succinct, ordering him to get a proper cookbook and to "blow the doors off the OP the next time he fixed a meal."[1] The next day Bozeman hitched a ride to the US embassy commissary in Tel Aviv to purchase a copy of *60 Minute Gourmet* by French chef Pierre Franey, containing gourmet recipes that could be prepared for four diners in less than an hour. The US reputation was then salvaged. To be fair to Bozeman, he was not alone in creating low expectations for meal preparation.

MAJ Denny Lindeman (USMC) recalls that our foreign colleagues could readily detect the warning signs of gastronomical disappointment before they occurred. "The joke was that you knew it was the American's turn when you heard the sound of cans being opened in the galley, and you knew it was the French when there was champagne brunch and shortly thereafter the aroma of sauces being prepared for the evening banquet or *fête, festin régal grand plaisir* as it may occur. For the Dutch it always included black bread, Havarti, and Heineken for breakfast."[2]

But nowhere was the sound of a can opener more terrifying and dreaded than when CPT Mike Fallon (USMC) would prepare his favorite *repas*, Tuna Wiggle, a concoction of cream of mushroom soup, two cans of canned tuna fish, noodles, and one can of peas blended into a stew. The mere threat that Tuna Wiggle would appear on the menu was enough to guarantee that Fallon's OP mates would fix all the meals that week if the marine simply consented to provide the wine at dinner. In his defense, Fallon would joke that, as a former long-range patrol leader during the Vietnam War, he went from "snooping and pooping" in North Vietnam to "cooking and looking" in southern Lebanon. Nevertheless, his partners felt compelled to limit his contribution to the OP to providing the alcohol, meaning he was confined to "uncorking and looking." Bozeman, as it turns out, did all of us a great service in clarifying the expectations for what should *not* be on the American *table d'hôte*, namely ballpark cuisine, and certainly not Fallon's Tuna Wiggle.

As I prepared to depart Jerusalem, I carefully packed my foodstuffs, including table wine and a bottle of Baileys Irish Cream, into the two OP baskets that I purchased in Damascus four months earlier. I also packed my exercise gear for physical training while not on watch or patrol duty, a sleeping bag, and other items to make life comfortable, including writing materials and a book I was reading. On Thursday morning, 11 June 1981, I stowed my equipment in a UN vehicle and began the two-and-a-half-hour, 140-kilometer trip from Jerusalem north to the seaside town of Nahariya. There I linked up with three other UNMOs, including Australian LTC Pat Marshall-Cormack, who, like me, was an artilleryman, Canadian infantryman CPT Jean Lefebvre, and our designated team leader, MAJ Edwardo Laciar, an Argentine Army signal corps officer. After brief introductions, and recalling the Bozeman culinary exposé, I assured everyone that we would not be eating hotdogs, nor were there any "cans in my kit." All were relieved. We then transferred our gear to the UN Jeep Wagoneer that would transport us to OGL's headquarters in Naqoura across the border in southern Lebanon.

After a 14-kilometer trip, we arrived at the border checkpoint, where the IDF scrupulously searched our vehicle as if we were smuggling contraband to their enemies. We had heard that on 15 June 1979 LTC Alfred Gom, a Nigerian officer serving with UNIFIL, was apprehended smuggling weapons from Lebanon to PLO operatives in Israel.[3] As a result, the IDF distrusted UN personnel and wanted to thoroughly search us, looking inside our bags, but our diplomatic immunity prevented that intrusion. The IDF did not like the UN. Not at all. We had grown to expect that, given the strained historical relationship that had built up over the years. Yet I found the hostility toward US observers particularly bothersome. I expected that the IDF would at least show some courtesy toward Americans, who were their best allies on the planet. But the border guards, who bore weapons and equipment in part paid for by American taxpayers, glared at us resentfully. Evidently, US officers serving in UNTSO were now part of "those people." For many in the IDF, "UN" stood for "useless nobodies," and they made no effort to disguise their hostility. Other US officers warned me to be prepared for this. I had hoped it was hyperbole. It wasn't. Our icy treatment at the Rosh Hanikra border crossing north of Nahariya portended a similar hostility from the IDF and their allies in southern Lebanon.

Continuing another five kilometers to Naqoura, we arrived at a large seaside compound that housed both the OGL and UNIFIL headquarters, above which a light blue flag imprinted with the UN wreath flapped steadily in the warm Mediterranean breeze. Entering the compound gate, we passed the Golden Chicken Restaurant, the source of much insight concerning the situation in southern Lebanon at any given time. The 18-year-old maître d', Yousef Yousef, interacted with many of the OGL and UNIFIL staff who frequented the establishment. CPT Clay Grubb (USMC) recalls that the young man, whose native tongue was Arabic, also spoke a fair amount of "English, Swedish, Italian, French and could convincingly curse in Gaelic."[4] His linguistic virtuosity was quite useful in gathering the latest gossip in the UNIFIL area of operations, information he likely passed to others. Parking our vehicle in the UN compound, I noticed white buildings stenciled with "UN," several of which were trailer-like facilities that housed different functions for operations, logistics, and sundry activities. I anticipated a detailed operations briefing prior to our departure to the field, but there was none beyond being warned to be careful and to inform the headquarters when we had arrived safely at our destination near the village of Khiam.

After our cursory check-in, we departed for OP KHIAM, 70 kilometers from Naqoura in the easternmost sector of UNIFIL's area of operations. Our route was along some of the worst roads I had seen, rivaling the rough and narrow byways I traveled near the demilitarized zone in South Korea in 1978. But these roads, unlike South Korea's, were also under constant observation by hostile forces, in this case the DFF, who I was sure was tracking our movements eastward throughout the enclave they controlled. The DFF's buffer zone—stretching from Naqoura eastward to the Syrian border—was about 100 kilometers long, averaged

about 10 kilometers wide, and occupied a space between the Israeli border and a line north of it in southern Lebanon, which we referred to as
the Green Line. As we made our way through the enclave, we passed villages nestled in green valleys and surrounded by rocky hills. There was
widespread destruction and damage to structures—homes and shops—
that had fallen prey to years of conflict. As we passed DFF checkpoints,
MAJ Saad Haddad's personnel looked us over suspiciously, but we were
not impeded. Haddad had been a Lebanese Army officer until that force
began to break apart during Lebanon's civil war. Eventually declared an
outlaw by the Lebanese Army, he assumed the leadership of the DFF and
did the IDF's bidding in southern Lebanon. Haddad operated with impunity in the enclave. Ironically, he had received part of his training at the
US Army Infantry School at Fort Benning, Georgia. Indeed, one of his
instructors at the time was MAJ Harry Klein (USA), who in 1980 was
assigned to OGL, where he liaised with Haddad's DFF. Unfortunately,
Klein's relationship with the DFF took a terrible turn in April of 1980 following the murder of two Irish UNIFIL soldiers who were accompanying
him on a mission in the enclave. The tension persisted, even as we traveled a year later to OP KHIAM.

Just 14 months earlier, DFF and UNIFIL forces had engaged in a violent
week-long clash near the village of At Tiri in the central region controlled by
UNIFIL's Irish Battalion (IRISHBATT). The battle began on 6 April 1980
when DFF tanks ventured north of the Green Line and into UNIFIL territory in an effort to seize higher ground to better observe activities in the
area. When the DFF attacked Hill 880 near At Tiri, soldiers of IRISHBATT,
who occupied the very strategic and dominant terrain, held their ground.
But soon they would call for reinforcements from the nearby battalions—
Senegalese (SENBATT), Dutch (DUTCHBATT), and Fijian (FIJIBATT)—
that constituted UNIFIL's Force Mobile Reserve (FMR). After the FMR
arrived, the confrontation continued over the next six days, alternating
between periods of armed conflict and an unsteady peace.

On 7 April, UNIFIL's commander, MG Erskine, dispatched his deputy
force commander, BG Ole Nielsen (Norwegian Armed Forces) to negotiate
with the DFF. BG Nielsen's efforts failed. Haddad escalated things, threatening to execute nine captive Irish soldiers "one by one."[5] UNIFIL stood
its ground, and a day later three of the Irish soldiers were released after a
diplomatic offensive pressured the Israelis and Haddad to deescalate the
standoff. However, fighting continued throughout 8 April until Israel
became more involved. Initially, it appeared that Israel seemed unwilling
to intervene to restrain Haddad's assault on Hill 880. To be sure, the day

prior to the attack, Israel was preoccupied responding to a PLO raid on their Misgav Am community in northern Galilee that killed two civilians and a soldier and wounded 11 other soldiers and four children. After receiving additional pressure from US ambassador Sam Lewis, Israel instructed Haddad to release the remaining Irish soldiers. Calm resulted the next day. But by 10 April, the DFF renewed their push toward At Tiri, as Haddad personally tried to barge his way into the town. On 11 April, violence surged again when the DFF attacked with machine gun fire. UNIFIL forces responded and blunted that assault. The DFF then pressed civilians to go forward to burn tires in the streets and throw rocks at UNIFIL soldiers. Shortly thereafter, a Fijian UNIFIL soldier was shot in the head by DFF forces. That provoked the Dutch contingent to respond with an antitank missile fired at a DFF armored vehicle, completely destroying it. The DFF was driven back and UNIFIL took complete control of At Tiri. In the process, two UNIFIL soldiers died, one Irishman and one Fijian. Also killed was a DFF militiaman. Haddad was furious and demanded reparations, or *sulha*, for the dead militiaman's family. But none was forthcoming, and the tension was palpable after the battle.[6]

Having been thoroughly humiliated by his defeat at At Tiri, Haddad was steamed. On 12 April 1980, his forces unleashed a punishing mortar attack accompanied by machine gun fire on the very vulnerable UNIFIL headquarters at Naqoura. The OGL operations officer, MAJ Gordie Breault (USAF), reported that 94 mortar rounds, a mix of 120 mm high explosive and white phosphorus projectiles, rained down on UNIFIL's headquarters. Breault later wrote about the attack: "Several landed directly on the UNIFIL HQ building and almost all of the portable work buildings and living quarters in the camp were damaged. Several were demolished by blast and fire. . . . On scouting the area after the attack when the smoke had cleared, several UNMOs assessed the damage done and reported, surprisingly enough, that no UN casualties had been caused."[7]

Breault quickly assembled available UNMOs to man the operations center and report the attacks to UN authorities. That included MAJ Charlie Bauman (USA) and MAJ Steve Berkheiser (USMC), who endured the shelling while facilitating communications with the IDF and Government House in Jerusalem to bring pressure on Haddad to cease the attack.[8] It was a highly dangerous situation. In the aftermath of the shelling, Grubb learned details from Berkheiser concerning an UNMO who had grabbed a platter of food from the mess hall before running to a nearby bunker. Berkheiser told how a mortar round detonated near himself and the UNMO. "Blown off his feet by concussion and stunned, he [the UNMO] hit the ground near the bunker. In the dark, Berkheiser was trying to feel [the UNMO] for wounds, finding thick warm liquid, chunks of flesh and other soft tissues. Turns out that Yankee Pot Roast strips with thick gravy and cooked diced vegetables can be misleading in the dark. Other than a knot from hitting his head when he fell, the guy was unhurt (although gooey)."[9]

Indeed, the shelling continued from 4:00 p.m. that afternoon to 8:40 p.m. that evening. There was extensive damage to buildings, vehicles, and helicopters. Erskine recalls that UNIFIL soldiers—including a Ghanaian defensive platoon and the French logistics battalion—fought back fiercely. However, when the French forces prepared to mount a counterattack, Erskine called them back.[10] The French were stunned by this decision. They would remember this incident several months later when they insisted on formally constituting an independent reaction force to better secure their own units stationed at the very vulnerable Naqoura head-quarters. Erskine and his staff would come to support that decision, and later in September of 1980 a French defense detachment took up posi-tions on high ground east of Naqoura.[11] Fortunately, on 12 April, after Haddad's forces had pummeled UNIFIL's headquarters, French LTC A. de la Forge was the single casualty, wounded in the chin by a sniper bul-let. Of the good fortune that others were not hurt, Erskine would note that "God was definitely with us" in surviving the "extreme danger."[12] Yet his hesitancy to permit the French to counterattack—which they were prepared to do—did not impress them. Later the newly established French reaction force in Naqoura would deal with any "extreme danger" to their logistics unit there. Grubb recalls the French motivation to bring in reinforcements and the false bravado Haddad signaled in advance of their arrival: "The French were so mad that they brought in a wheeled unit via Beirut and drove down to French Log. They made it abundantly clear that this unit would not be under UN command and would respond to any future attacks regardless of UN orders to the contrary. Haddad repeatedly stated that if they came south he would meet them 'with an appropriate military response.' All the UNMOs couldn't wait to observe this. The French unit came south in prepared tactical order. Haddad's 'Appropriate Military Response' was a band playing military music."[13]

Even Haddad knew it was unwise to challenge the French. When nec-essary, French forces were ready to address enemy threats and unwilling to allow their forces to be endangered through UNIFIL's hesitation to go on the offensive when provoked.

As we continued our journey to OP KHIAM, I was struck by the beauty of southern Lebanon, the scars of war notwithstanding. I was

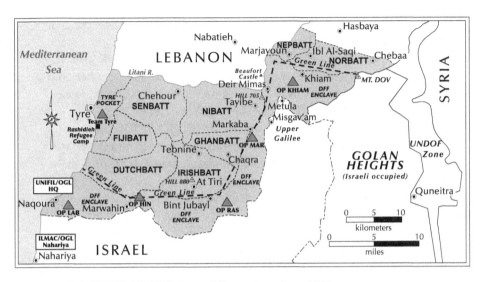

Map 8.1. UNIFIL/UNTSO Area of Operations, June 1981

happy to be with my international colleagues as we bumped and jostled our way toward the outpost where we would "cook and look" and, in the process, contribute to peace in a war-torn corner of the world. Soon we passed the other UNTSO OPs, LAB, HIN, RAS, and finally MAR along the way. Unfortunately, all of the OPs sat inside the DFF enclave and were subject to harassment from both the IDF and the DFF, who restricted our movements in the enclave to Mondays and Thursdays (see map 8.1).

Eventually we rounded the most northern portion of Israel's border with Lebanon. There we entered the large and verdant Marjayoun Valley just north of the Israeli town of Metula and very close to the town of Khiam, the OP's namesake. Minutes later we slipped past the town's southern end. Widespread destruction in and around it was evident. The PLO had occupied it after the 1973 Yom Kippur War. In 1977 they battled the IDF and DFF for control of the town. Eventually PLO forces were driven off, but Khiam was left in shambles. To make matters worse, Haddad refused to allow the 12,000 former residents to return.[14] My OP mates shared with me that the Israelis eventually "cleaned Khiam out" during the 1978 invasion. As with Quneitra in the Golan Heights, the IDF was concerned with Khiam's proximity to the Israeli border and the possibility that PLO fighters would reoccupy it. So, it suffered the same fate for the same reason. It occurred to me then—as it did when I first saw Quneitra—that the destruction of an entire village was disproportionate military action, particularly when that included expelling Lebanese civilians from their homes. One of my OP mates then noted that after reducing Khiam to rubble and banishing its residents, the DFF and IDF appropriated it as an urban training area for their soldiers, further completing its desolation. Khiam's use for urban training was evident as early as January 1980 when CPT Lenny Supko (USMC) and CPT Clay Grubb patrolled the area and stumbled across "a bunch" of IDF commandos operating and training in the area. Supko noted in his journal that he had "never seen so many IDF soldiers and equipment in the El Khiam–Marjayoun area."[15]

After skirting the town, we turned south and proceeded a short distance and up a hill to occupy OP KHIAM, towering 740 meters above the valley floor. When we arrived, the on-duty shift opened the chain-link gate to the outpost and gladly welcomed us. As we unpacked our gear and proceeded to occupy our living quarters, I could see we were on excellent terrain to observe activity for a full 360 degrees. The OP was a large, white cement blockhouse with a prominent black "UN" stenciled on the sides of the building. Next to it was a large, freestanding UN sign easily viewed from both ground and air. The bottom floor of the blockhouse, which contained our living area, was topped with a slightly smaller second-floor observation center with windows on three sides. Beside the blockhouse was a tall radio tower used to communicate with UNTSO, OGL, and UNIFIL. Additionally, there was an interior ladder in the observation center leading to a roof-top deck that offered a completely unobstructed view of the area.

At the center of the residential area was a sitting room and dinner table where we ate and conversed. Below the ground floor was a bomb shelter that we hoped would go unused. Adjacent was the residential area with a kitchen, bathroom, shower facility, and a small bedroom with two bunk beds. As the junior officer on the team, I took one of the top bunks as a courtesy. We then received a short orientation from the departing team on activities that had occurred the week prior. They were as glad to be on their way as we were ready to begin our tour.

"Cooking and Looking" in the Valley of Springs

After we settled in, LTC Marshall-Cormack occupied the observation center, which was manned by us over three shifts, day and night. Meanwhile, our team leader, MAJ Laciar, began preparing the evening meal.

COL Robert H. Sholly (USA), UNTSO chief operations officer (1981–1983). Author's collection.

SGM Ralph B. Stockbridge (USA), UNTSO senior noncommissioned officer (1981–1982). Author's collection.

Father Jerome "Jerry" Murphy-O'Connor, who shared with UNMOs much knowledge concerning the history and culture of the Middle East (1981). Author's collection.

CPT Mike Fallon (USMC) and a youthful PFLP fighter who served as a translator when Fallon was resolving hijacking incidents (1970). Courtesy COL Mike Fallon.

UNTSO military observers (*left to right*) CPT Clay Grubb (USMC), an unidentified Swedish Army officer, LT Carl Lammers (USN), and CPT Merv Griffin (Australian Army) on duty at OP KHIAM (1980). Courtesy COL Clay Grubb.

MAJ Harry Klein (USA) in sunglasses (*second from right*) and CPT Patrick Vincent (French Army) (*second from left*) assist others with wounded UNIFIL Irish Battalion soldier PVT John O'Mahony, who was shot by DFF militiaman Mahmoud Bazzi, who also murdered Irish soldiers PVT Thomas Barrett and PVT Derek Smallhorne (18 April 1980). Homer Sykes / Alamy Stock Photo.

LTCDR Virg Bozeman (USN) (right) and MAJ Jean Paul Morizet (French Army) on duty at OP KHIAM (13 April 1981). Courtesy CDR Virg Bozeman.

MAJ Joe Serviss (USA) doing "light" duty in the UNTSO operations center in Government House, Jerusalem (1981). Author's collection.

(Left to right) CPT John Reardon (USMC), MAJ Randy Young (USA), and MAJ Jay Sollis (USMC) at an Observer Group Lebanon (OGL) United Nations Medals presentation in Nahariya, Israel (May 1982). Author's collection.

MAJ Denny Lindeman (USMC) receiving his United Nations Medal (May 1981). Author's collection.

CPT Scott Lingamfelter (USA) receiving his United Nations Medal in September 1981 and being congratulated by COL Bob Sholly (USA). Author's collection.

COMDT Des Travers (Irish Army), who assembled much experience in both UNTSO and UNIFIL in southern Lebanon (1981). Courtesy COL Des Travers.

UNTSO headquarters at Government House in Jerusalem (1981). Author's collection.

Headquarters of Observer Group Golan-Damascus (OGG-D) and Observer Detachment Damascus (ODD), where the author was assigned along with 18 Soviet officers (1981). Author's collection.

UNIFIL and Observer Group Lebanon (OGL) headquarters in Naqoura, Lebanon (1981). Author's collection.

OP MAR (1978). OP HIN and OP LAB were built on near-identical models.

OP RAS was the oldest of the OPs and one of the most rustic. CPT Mike Fallon and his Belgian "baker" comrade occupied this OP during Israel's Operation Litani invasion of southern Lebanon (March 1978). Courtesy COL Mike Fallon.

OP KHIAM in 1980, where the author performed his first tour of duty in southern Lebanon (June 1981). Courtesy COL Clay Grubb.

OP KHIAM was destroyed on 25 July 2006 by an Israeli artillery shelling and aerial bombs, killing four officers: MAJ Hans-Peter Lang (Austria), MAJ Paeta Derek Hess-von Kruedener (Canada), LT Senior Grade Jarno Mäkinen (Finland), and LTC Du Zhaoyu (China). OP KHIAM was positioned prominently on a hill north of the Israeli border, painted white, and marked with large black UN markers. It was impossible to mistake it for anything but a UN OP. Courtesy N McQ via Wikimedia. CC BY-SA 2.0. https://creativecommons.org/licenses/by-sa/2.0 /legalcode.

The north face of Chateau Beaufort on the high ground next to the Litani River. CPT Mike Fallon's UN vehicle and flag are in the foreground (1978). Courtesy COL Mike Fallon.

The IDF demolishing a PLO building in Bint Jubayl next to OP RAS on 15 March 1978. CPT Mike Fallon was able to photograph this event as he and his OP comrade were being forced by the IDF to evacuate OP RAS. Courtesy COL Mike Fallon.

UNTSO Military Observers (UNMOs) assigned to the Israel-Lebanon Mixed Armistice Commission (ILMAC) in Beirut in 1978. (Left to right) French UNMO LT McNeese (USN), CPT Condon (USA), CPT Lane (Irish Army), CPT Mike Fallon (USMC), and two unidentified officers. Courtesy COL Mike Fallon.

The view of artillery rounds (background) falling on Tyre as seen from Tyre Barracks, where Team Tyre was stationed (1980). Such shelling was almost a daily experience and occurred when the author performed duty there in the fall of 1981. Courtesy COL Clay Grubb.

Two 105 mm "up-gunned" Sherman tanks of MAJ Saad Haddad's De Facto Force (DFF) (1978). These tanks were provided to the DFF by Israel. Courtesy COL Mike Fallon.

A Palestine Liberation Army (PLA) soldier manning an unauthorized checkpoint in southern Lebanon (1978). Checkpoints were frequently manned by older and younger PLA members. Courtesy COL Mike Fallon.

This UNTSO vehicle in southern Lebanon was riddled with bullets by combatant forces (1978). Courtesy COL Mike Fallon.

(*Right to left*) CPT Scott Lingamfelter (USA), Shelley Lingamfelter, CPT Barry Gwyther (Australian Army), and Jo Gwyther holding infant Kylie while touring Roman ruins at Bosra, Syria, in May 1981. Author's collection.

Laciar was selected as the team leader since he was the most experienced UNMO among us. As he did, he dispatched CPT Lefebvre and me on a mobile patrol of the area. Our mission was to inspect four UNIFIL OPs in our sector to verify what could actually be observed or detected from those positions. OGL was suspicious that some UNIFIL reporting in the area of OP KHIAM was unreliable and wanted us to check what observers could credibly see or hear from the four OPs. UNIFIL OPs were dispersed within each battalion's sector and frequently manned by very young and inexperienced soldiers from around the world whose training standards, including map reading, were suspect. The most inexperienced soldiers would report shooting incidents that were not observed but could be heard at a distance. Reporting the echoes of gunfire reverberating around hills, above cliffs, and across valleys was not an accurate and reliable way to pinpoint a firing incident. That difficulty, however, did not dampen the enthusiasm of inexperienced soldiers submitting unsubstantiated reports. When hearing rifle or artillery fire, regardless of how suspect, some of the young observers would eagerly report not only where the munitions impacted, but the presumed location from which they were fired! Our mission was to better understand what could reasonably be assessed from those positions.

Lefebvre and I climbed into a white CJ-5 Jeep with "UN" boldly painted on the sides and loaded with our maps, binoculars, extra fuel, and lots of water. After departing, we immediately observed two IDF ground violations, one jeep and a pickup truck operating nearby. We reported our sighting back to Marshall-Cormack and continued north to inspect our first UNIFIL OP near Ibl al-Saqi. The OP was manned by soldiers assigned to the Norwegian Battalion (NORBATT), based six kilometers northwest of OP KHIAM. Arriving at the OP, we were both unimpressed by what we saw. The position was poorly maintained and not in good military order. Discipline was lax, as clearly evident by off-duty soldiers lounging around in shorts and bathing suits, including the officer in charge! Nevertheless, we went about our business assessing what could actually be seen from the position. As we did, we observed a platoon of DFF tanks on a nearby hill. They were old World War II Sherman models that had been upgraded by the Israelis with an improved 105 mm main cannon, an enlarged turret, and redesignated as the M-51 Super Sherman. We made a note to report the location. But before departing the OP, we offered some avuncular—albeit friendly—suggestions concerning proper military discipline to the young Norwegian lieutenant in charge of his gaggle of sunbathers.

Lefebvre and I then proceeded to the second OP on the list. As we paralleled the Litani River south from Marjayoun, we had a chance to cruise past the infamous Chateau Beaufort—also referred to as Beaufort Castle—home of the PLO and often the target of Israeli jets and artillery. Towering 400 meters above us, it was truly impressive perched on a cliff overlooking the narrow Litani. I made this note in my journal: "For all its years of bombardment by whatever force, it was in remarkable condition. It reminded me of the sandcastles I built at the beach as a child, having received an initial blow from the sea, which would eventually claim it back. I wondered how long the old girl on the Litani would resist the assault of time and machine. From all indications, it would take much more than a surf to wash Beaufort away."

While Beaufort was then occupied by the PLO, that wasn't always the case. In 1978, ILMAC observers established a temporary OP in the castle since it had a commanding view of the Valley of Springs and Marjayoun below. Soon enough the PLO would take up positions there for the same purpose. However, once Haddad realized that both the UN and the PLO were occupying the fort at the same time and looking down on his native Marjayoun, he shelled the castle routinely, forcing UN observers out and leaving the PLO behind to endure artillery fire from both the IDF and the DFF. Interestingly, in 1978 Fallon experienced shelling at Beaufort, while Supko had a similarly unpleasant encounter while visiting the PLO there in 1980.[16] Frankly, Lefebvre and I were glad to view the fortress from afar.

As we traveled onward we encountered our first challenge, a flat tire. We stopped to inspect the damage. Having had similar mishaps frequently in Germany and South Korea while in the field, I took the initiative to change the tire as my Canadian colleague, quite agreeably, stood by watching me labor in the Lebanese sun. Lefebvre characterized our efforts later that evening: "We changed the tire without dispute—an amazing thing when you consider that we were two officers! Yes, we had no argument. I sat back and Scott changed the tire!"

Having recalled what MAJ Joe Serviss (USA) experienced on his first OP tour, including the initial hostility from his international OP mates, I figured that getting my hands dirty changing a tire was a small price to pay for world peace. It worked, and we all had a good laugh at dinner that night. With the tire repaired, we continued to the second OP approximately five kilometers southwest of OP KHIAM. That OP sat next to the village of Deir Mimas, which took its name from the nearby St. Mema Monastery, built by Christian monks around 1404 A.D. Nearby we observed a second IDF patrol and reported its location to our OP. They were clearly busy that day violating Lebanese sovereignty. Returning to our primary focus, we found the second UNIFIL OP team better positioned to observe and report incidents.

We then ventured on to a third OP located near Hill 705, south of Deir Mimas. However, along the way we managed to make a wrong turn and found ourselves winding up the narrow road of a steep hill. When we crested the summit, we immediately found our windshield was just inches from the main gun barrel of a 105 mm Super Sherman belonging to the DFF! Lefebvre wasted no time dealing with the situation.

> Before you could shake a stick, Jean [Lefebvre], a French Canadian, whipped our jeep around and left in a cloud of dust. Haddad doesn't like UN observers bouncing into his positions and has a nasty habit of hijacking those who do. Strange as it may be, we were not allowed to report Haddad's forces as violations because he was Lebanese, albeit an Israeli surrogate. The incident was, nevertheless, a real find and left us with that certain feeling of "getting away with murder" because we were not pursued by Haddad's men who, we later surmised, were partaking of the old and tried Middle East pastime of sleeping on the job.

We were very lucky. Had the driver of the tank been alert, he could have put a single round through the front window of our vehicle, blowing us into the annals of UN history. While the DFF tank could not be reported by us as an actual violation—because the DFF was composed of Lebanese residents and not considered belligerents—we nonetheless reported its location once we regained our senses after hurtling back down Hill 705.

Skidding to a stop at the bottom, we thought we were out of danger, only to encounter an armed DFF soldier—hardly 16 years of age—toting a loaded pistol that he brandished menacingly while holding us hostage. Motioning for us to exit our vehicle, I asked him what was the problem? He replied in broken English that we were violating his territory. To be sure, we were near the enclave bordering the Green Line that the DFF claimed was not open to the UN, but we told him we were right to be there. Not wanting to argue too much with an armed cowboy acting out a Lebanese version of the "showdown at OK Corral," we endured another few minutes being "under arrest" while calmly suggesting to him that, if he put his gun away, we would be on our way. That unfortunately did not deter him, until I said, "You know, you seem like a nice young man, but if you harm us, the US and Canada will be very angry. We are really big countries—really big—with big armies. Now you wouldn't want to make two very big countries like ours who have many guns, tanks, and jets mad at you and your friends, would you?" Reflecting on that idea, he finally decided to allow us to leave.

Having pushed our luck as far as we felt we could, we decided to forgo inspecting the last OP to return to NORBATT headquarters to report the new DFF tank positions we had observed that afternoon, one too close for comfort. The NORBATT operations center appreciated the information and thanked us for our work that day. However, our bad luck was not completely exhausted. We had the misfortune of another flat tire. Unfortunately, we had already used the lone spare we had with us. Our salvation was assured, however, when another UN vehicle happened upon us and offered us their spare tire. I swung into action and changed my second flat tire that day. When we finally arrived at OP KHIAM, we were met by my fellow artilleryman Marshall-Cormack, standing at the compound gate. Grinning, he said with a bit of glee, "Well, I see you've got another flat, mate." As I exited the vehicle brushing off the dust, I thought he was kidding us since he had monitored our difficulties while on patrol. But when I looked down at the tire, I realized he was right! Indeed, we had a third one, a new OP record and quite an initiation for me as a new observer. However, I did not volunteer to change this last one.

Later that evening after a pleasant meal, I ventured up into the observation center to take a look at the surrounding terrain in the valley below as the sun set slowly in the west. Across from us, about seven kilometers due west, was the imposing Beaufort Castle. Approximately five kilometers to the south was the Israeli town of Metula, whose neighborhoods slowly became less discernible as the sun set, save the telltale evening lights ringing its several kibbutzim. To the east was Mount Dov, seven kilometers away and towering 1,170 meters, also on the Israeli side of the border. From its summit a viewer would have a clear line of sight to our position. And to the north, just a few hundred meters from us, was the dark and empty town of Khiam, in the grip of a destructive war that drove all life from a once thriving community. High atop OP KHIAM, for the moment, it was peaceful as dusk descended. That was not always the case in the Valley or Meadow of Springs, as it was alternatively known. That calm could be shattered by the report and flash of artillery impacting in and around Beaufort Castle whenever the IDF chose to do so. It was not uncommon to hear the sounds of war booming and rumbling across the valley. Israeli artillery units to our southwest routinely and relentlessly bombarded the fortress in an effort to destroy PLO fighters residing behind the walls and deep within the dungeons of a seemingly impenetrable and imperishable structure. When those bombardments happened, there was no peace for anyone in southern Lebanon.

War is an awful thing, particularly for the noncombatants and their children. When the IDF chose to fire its artillery, either at Beaufort or at nearby targets, it must have terrorized innocent civilians. I imagined how hard it would be to deal with the violence, particularly at night when parents were doing their best to comfort their children as they tucked them into bed, no doubt hoping the staccato of gunfire or impacting artillery rounds would mercifully miss them. Likewise, Israeli children to our south must have also heard the drumming sounds of battle. Neither Jewish nor Arab mothers wanted the wailing sound of a banshee portending death to drown out the sweet lullabies sung to little ones on either side of the war-torn border. These thoughts ran through my mind as I imagined the worried eyes of innocent Lebanese civilians who wondered if they would make it through another night of hell. It left me thinking how powerless I really was to stop any of it. I had arrived to "cook and look," and as I looked, the face of violence looked back. "Welcome to southern Lebanon," I thought as I descended the stairs to a waiting bunk.

I arose the next morning, 12 June, secured a fresh cup of coffee, and climbed to the top of OP KHIAM to take in the sights before breakfast. The sun shone brilliantly upon the Valley of Springs as it swept slowly westward across the placid, fertile plain. It was a peaceful scene as I sipped my morning joe and contemplated what the day ahead would hold. Despite the calm, I reminded myself that the region below was not new to war. In June of 1179 A.D., Crusader knights under the king of Jerusalem, Baldwin IV, fought the Ayyubid armies commanded by Yusuf ibn Ayyub ibn Shadi (Saladin) on the banks of the Litani River to our west. That battle ended with a decisive victory for Saladin, the first of many that led to an eventual Muslim victory over Christians occupying Beaufort Castle. Yet in recent years, the Muslims of the present—lately the PLO—were the ones sheltering deep within Beaufort and enduring a storm of punishing Israeli artillery. It was incomprehensible how this chateau could have survived Israeli artillery and air assaults, even after resisting centuries of violent punishment. To be sure, it remained an imposing thing to behold in the early morning light. But that morning it stood silent—like the Great Sphinx of Egypt—patiently overlooking the Litani and the Valley of Springs, where another conflict could shatter the peace in an instant. Danger was an ever-present fact of life for the people living in that valley, as well as for the UNMOs who patrolled it.

The close calls that Lefebvre and I confronted the previous day were sufficient reminders that operating in and near the DFF-controlled enclave was dangerous for unarmed observers. In his initial assignment with OGL, Bozeman experienced a taste of profound danger in March of 1981. Assigned to OP MAR—about 10 kilometers southwest of OP KHIAM—Bozeman and his OP partner, Major Jacques Huet (French Army), embarked on a local patrol. While on the way to visit the Ghanaian Battalion (GHANBATT), Huet suggested they stop at an ancient Crusader ruin near the village of Chaqra, roughly five kilometers west southwest of OP MAR. The ruin, known as Qalaat Doubiye, was a fortress built in the twelfth century. Huet was a student of history with a degree in archeology, and he persuaded Bozeman that they should stop and inspect it, hoping to find artifacts like pottery. With Huet at the wheel of their jeep, they turned off the main road onto a dirt path. Bozeman reminded his comrade that they were not to stray from the main routes, given the danger posed by land mines. Huet was unconcerned. Pointing to a house ahead that had several cars parked around it, he assumed their path was safe. Unconvinced, Bozeman suggested they call OGL and let them know they were taking a diversion. Huet insisted "we shouldn't bother them, and we'd only be there for five or ten minutes max." When they arrived at the fortress, Huet quickly exited the vehicle and scrambled up one side of the ruin's wall that had tumbled down over time. He then disappeared into the structure to explore. Bozeman chose to wait outside, uncomfortable with the whole idea. But about five minutes later a PLO soldier draped with a traditional red and white keffiyeh headdress emerged from the fortress carrying an AK-47 rifle and yelling angrily at Bozeman in Arabic. Bozeman thought it best to retreat calmly to his UN vehicle to radio for help. The PLO fighter was having none of that and continued to aggressively gesture for Bozeman to come with him. Bozeman continued to back down toward the jeep. The now very angry PLO fighter proceeded to squeeze off six or seven rounds from his rifle at Bozeman. The bullets zipped passed Bozeman's left ear, producing a cracking, finger-snapping sound that removed all doubt about cooperating. He submitted and the PLO fighter led him to the opening of an underground room and motioned for him to enter.

When Bozeman resisted, the PLO soldier forced him through the entrance with the barrel of his Kalashnikov firmly tucked in Bozeman's chest. Tumbling down and into a subterranean room, he found Huet held captive and profusely apologetic for creating the life-threatening situation. Both were certain that the PLO would not let them go and risk betraying their covert hideaway near the enclave controlled by their enemies, the IDF and the DFF. Bozeman and Huet sat there for four hours as the PLO fighters chatted away on their walkie-talkies with their superiors about what to do with the two UN interlopers. After a seemingly interminable amount of time, another PLO fighter poked his head through the small entrance to the cavern and motioned to Bozeman and Huet to come with him. Bozeman feared that they both would be knocked out, deposited in their vehicle, and then pushed over a cliff to make it appear as if they had died in a careless accident. But the PLO had another plan. The fighter escorted them to their UN jeep, shouldered his weapon, and offered a handshake, saying, "Sorry, Sorry."[17] Apparently the PLO leadership concluded it unwise to kill two unarmed UNMOs, possibly because in recent months it had been their enemies, the DFF, who had cornered the market on killing UN soldiers.

After this ordeal, Bozeman surmised that since GHANBATT had responsibility for the area where the fortress was located, they must have known full well that the PLO occupied it. Bozeman would soon discover that was not the case. Because the Ghanaian government policy was friendly to the PLO, GHANBATT reflected that national attitude and simply ignored the presence of these fighters in what may have been a PLO cache or temporary hideout in preparation for combat against Israel or the DFF nearby. Bozeman found the entire affair quite unsettling:

> We drove off to the GHANBATT village where we found ALL of the officers from that battalion in a giant room at maybe twenty tables, four guys per table, playing Yahtzee for real money all day, every day. They had no idea about the fort and didn't seem to care. We radioed back to OGL HQ and got chewed out big time by Major Cote, a Canadian, who was in OGL Ops. I had quit smoking a year before because I wanted to live longer. . . . I started up again that night at OP MAR because I doubted I'd make it through my first week![18]

Bozeman would not only survive, but also do a tour with the UN Liaison Office in Beirut (UNLOB) before he returned to OGL later that year. But this incident was not forgotten by other US officers. We were assuredly in the Wild West, unarmed and, most of all, unwanted by the parties to the conflict. It was wise to beware of danger and not contribute to it by engaging in scavenger hunts in Crusader fortresses where deadly gunman lurked in the darkness. The Frenchman Huet should have listened to the Yank Bozeman. Better to stay on the roads.

Bozeman was not the only US officer to experience some close calls. When serving on OP MAR weeks later, Serviss received some unwanted attention from the PLO:

> While on OP duty one week, it was my time to sit in the glassed-in observation booth which was located on top of the OP. I heard a thud and could not figure out what it was. I heard a second thud and still could not figure out where the noise was coming from. I was looking to my right facing the border when I saw the earth kick up. I knew immediately that this was from a rocket, probably a Katyusha rocket. I immediately yelled to my mates below that we were taking incoming rockets and that we should move to the bunker.[19]

Serviss determined that the rockets originated from southern Lebanon and, while aimed at Israeli targets, managed to fall just 200 to 300 meters away but at a "perfect range to hit the OP."[20] When the shelling ceased, Serviss and his comrades calmly returned to their observation duties. It was just another day in the Wild West, or as LTC Jim Allan put it, the place where "Each party did what it wanted when it wanted and where it wanted, despite the UN."[21] No truer words have ever been penned about southern Lebanon in the summer of 1981.

Neither the IDF nor the DFF hesitated to disrupt the activities of UNMOs. Grubb recalls that while he and his OP mates were on duty on OP MAR in 1980, they were subjected to harassment by the DFF, even to the point where DFF troops—in this case armed teenagers from the nearby village of Markaba—intruded on OP business. In addition to painting the OP windows black, the invaders played loud music and pilfered UNMO rations. Moreover, Grubb and his OP comrades were prevented by the intruders from using their OP radio to report violations. However, the DFF did permit them to sunbathe on the top of the OP, where Grubb and company made notes of violations and later reported them from their patrol vehicle radio, which the intruders had overlooked. In time, Grubb informed a village elder, or mukhtar, of this harassment. The mukhtar was very unhappy about the intrusion and physically beat the offending teenagers, exiling them to a shed outside the OP fence.[22] Nothing else was done officially to address the situation, the corporal punishment having been sufficient.

In another act of lawless and violent intrusion, the IDF and the DFF attempted to seize OP HIN while Grubb was there on 18 April 1980, the same day when two Irish soldiers were murdered by the DFF a week after the At Tiri battle. That morning Grubb and his teammates were in the process of replacing a UNIFIL team from DUTCHBATT who were manning the OP. Later that day a group of 10 to 15 armed DFF militiamen commanded by one of Haddad's subordinates, Abu Emil, drove up to the OP in an armored halftrack. Accompanied by an Israeli officer identified as "Major Chaim," both demanded that Grubb and his team evacuate the OP so "they could blow the place up."[23] Grubb found that idea absurd and challenged them to show him the explosives they would use. None were produced, and the marine assumed he had called their bluff. A lull in the action ensued and Grubb continued to negotiate from behind the locked gate. That gave Grubb's OP mates time to report the situation to OGL. In turn, OGL notified UNTSO headquarters, who then contacted the UN in New York, who immediately notified American authorities in Washington, D.C. The "showdown" at OP HIN continued for about an hour until the DFF officer's patience ran out. Grubb recalls what happened next: "Abu Emil got frustrated and pulled a Galil [Israeli-made automatic rifle] from his jeep and put it in my chest, through the wire, ordering that I unlock the gate. Next thing I knew, he stepped aside as the half-track smashed through the gate. I jumped over the blast wall of our vehicle park to avoid being run over, but we were now occupied."[24]

Once inside, invaders tore the place apart, seized all the duty logs with observation reports and radio logs that contained a record of the activities Grubb monitored when the DFF killed two Irish soldiers that day. By late afternoon, the UNMO team was herded at gunpoint to their vehicle and ordered to leave. After more argument, Grubb and his team left and returned to OGL in Naqoura. There, the team was told to secure supplies and reoccupy OP HIN. Apparently the US authorities in Washington had confronted Prime Minister Begin on a visit to the US and informed him of this kerfuffle at OP HIN. Begin then promptly issued orders for the DFF and the IDF to withdraw and permit reoccupation of OP HIN by Grubb and his team. That day, a strong-willed American marine had the Israeli prime minister crying "uncle."

As a postscript to the seizing of the duty and radio logs, Grubb was certain that the DFF and the IDF were trying to cover up the murder of the Irish soldiers by destroying the evidence.[25] Interestingly, when a UN investigation team arrived from New York to scrutinize that incident, Grubb was assigned to an OP where he was "unavailable" to investigators to tell what he had heard. Amazingly, the DFF and the IDF kept watch over the OP where Grubb was sequestered, ensuring no one visited the location to speak with him. That OGL assigned him to this duty is all the more concerning, possibly suggesting that OGL officials were anxious to see the incident closed without further ado. To this day Grubb believes there was a coordinated cover-up of the affair, which would have been enormously embarrassing to Israel, their militia surrogates, and possibly OGL and UNTSO.[26]

When UNMOs were not busy being hijacked, kidnapped, shelled, or having their OPs occupied, they were being robbed. On one tour of duty on OP RAS, my Australian friend CPT Barry Gwyther was about to take his turn in the observation center just after midnight. Going outside to visit the latrine, he came across two local villagers with AK-47 rifles. They were in the process of stealing two 20-liter jerricans of gasoline. As Gwyther remembers it, the incident had all the makings for a bad result: "[T]hey both had AKs and threatened me as they commenced to leave. Then an on-duty UNMO had heard the noise and shone a light onto us which caused much anger, yelling, and threats. Luckily, he turned the light off when I politely asked him to, and the locals and fuel disappeared under the fence."[27]

Gwyther wisely deescalated the situation by keeping his wits about him, likely sparing himself and his fellow UNMOs deadly rifle fire, a far worse result than losing two fuel cans. UNMOs didn't have guns to defend themselves, only their cool heads.

As I sipped my coffee the morning of 12 June at OP KHIAM, it occurred to me that it was a Friday, the Muslim sabbath and possibly a quieter day. I was wrong. Shortly thereafter, an Israeli artillery battery opened up with a mission to fire smoke rounds in support of DFF tanks operating in the Valley of Springs west of us. Haddad's forces were clearly maneuvering against a likely PLO position, and the Israelis were attempting to mask his maneuvers by firing artillery rounds that produced a thick, white smoke on impact. The rounds landed precisely between Haddad's tanks and the PLO observers occupying Beaufort Castle. I noted the fire mission in my journal: "The wind blew the smoke southeasterly, perfectly masking any movement in Marjayoun from observation from Beaufort which sits to the southwest. I must say it was textbook in execution regardless of the fact that the IDF battery was a blatant and illegal violation of Lebanese territory."

As an artilleryman, I found myself impressed by the IDF's gunnery skills, thinking back to my days adjusting artillery fire as a forward observer at Fort Sill, Oklahoma. Many Israeli field artillery officers also were trained at Fort Sill, where I had honed my skills. In a way, it was like "old home week" on OP KHIAM for me.

After the shooting ceased, I left the tower and my "looking" duties to head below to begin my "cooking" mission for the day. It was my turn to prepare dinner, and "the heat was on." I chose my mother's favorite: meatloaf, rice, corn on the cob, salad, wine, fresh bread, and Jell-O for desert (*avec* fruit). It proved to be a "target hit" with my colleagues as we enjoyed sips of Baileys Irish Cream along with some original Reagan Jelly Beans, a favorite treat of our president. "After dinner, I went up and joined PM-C [Marshall-Cormack] on the upper deck of the observation tower where we marveled at the sights of Israeli kibbutzim to the south. Each was ringed in light designed as a security measure. They were quite a sight and served as a reminder to us that security for Israel was a 24-hour a day concern. Somehow, though, I sensed that the quiet vigilance of those lights was deceiving. How much longer can Lebanon stand their [IDF] thundering noise."

I then headed to bed, glad my day was slightly less eventful, including not running headlong into 105 mm tank barrels or being taken hostage by gun-slinging teenagers with elevated testosterone.

In fact, kidnapping UNMOs—even US ones—seemed to be a pastime with both the DFF and the PLO in the Valley of Springs, where both contended for dominance. The preceding April, Bozeman, having recovered from his harrowing experience with the PLO, once again found himself taken hostage by them near OP KHIAM. This time he and another Frenchman, MAJ Jean Paul Morizet, were on a local patrol—not unlike the one Lefebvre and I had just completed—when a PLO fighter in a beat-up Mercedes intercepted them. The soldier pulled up, quickly extracted Morizet from the passenger side of the UN vehicle, and stuffed him in the Mercedes. Then a second PLO fighter jumped into the UN vehicle with Bozeman at the wheel and instructed him to follow the lead car. They drove north for an hour into the Beqaa Valley. After about 30 to 40 kilometers, they arrived at a PLO headquarters in a town well outside of the UNIFIL area of operations. Both UNMOs were then escorted to a room where several tabletops were strewn with maps. There they were introduced to a PLO officer who was referred to as "the colonel." Pointing to one of the maps, the colonel asserted that Bozeman and Morizet had strayed "outside the UNIFIL area of operations." Bozeman knew that was false. It was then that the resourceful naval officer showed his wits and moxie. His father had known President Ronald Reagan when both were young men in Illinois, and Bozeman saw an opportunity to appropriate his father's past association with Reagan. Bozeman—who shared his father's first name—proceeded to suggest that "the colonel" might be on very shaky ground in kidnapping the younger Bozeman. Virg then piped up, "Your intelligence people have let you down; you don't know who I am?" Unimpressed, the PLO colonel said that it was perfectly clear who he was because "Bozeman" was stitched on a name tag over one pocket of his uniform and "U.S. Navy" above the other. Bozeman then tightened the noose and disabused "the colonel" of his nonchalant attitude with this clarification:

> "Not me . . . you don't know who my dad is, do you? My dad is also named Virgil Bozeman, but he is a lawyer in Illinois who has been one of President Reagan's closest friends and confidants for almost fifty years since our President was a sportscaster at a local radio station. I know that Chairman Arafat would do just about anything to get the administration in Washington to give him just a little legitimacy. If you attempt to restrict UNTSO officers in the performance of their official duties, when I get back to a telephone, I will call my dad and ask him to call his old pal, the President, and urge him to refrain from taking any steps to recognize the PLO and I'll tell him to make sure that the Chairman finds out that it was you, colonel, who screwed the whole thing up. We're unarmed. We aren't stepping on the PLO's toes here. You should probably just let the two of us go on back home."[28]

Bozeman's exaggerated tale was a brilliant maneuver and a prime example of how quick wits and some creative storytelling could go a long way in extricating an UNMO from a tense situation. "The colonel" promptly let them go, and both returned safely to OP KHIAM, leaving behind a flustered Arafat subordinate hoping that nothing more would come of the matter. Bozeman demonstrated what many of us knew was the best weapon an unarmed UNMO could depend on: blarney. I would draw on a similar strategy with a gun-wielding teenage soldier two months later. When the other guy is holding a gun at your head and you are unarmed, you have to depend on other skills. Well-deployed bovine scatology was one of them.

The next four days on OP KHIAM were surprisingly calm. I arose at 4:00 a.m. on Sunday, 14 June, to take my turn at watch. The sunrise was beautiful and gave the valley and mountains to the west of us a wonderful contrast of blue, green, tan, brown, and rust. I scanned the area with my binoculars and noted nothing unusual. All was tranquil. At 5:00 a.m., UNIFIL conducted their morning radio check. It was very interesting to hear each of the different nationalities answer the call. DUTCHBATT, FIJIBATT, GHANBATT, IRISHBATT, NEPBATT, NIBATT (Nigerians), NORBATT, and SENBATT all responded in English, the official language of UNIFIL, yet each with distinct accents. Unfortunately, our radio transmissions were all in the clear, meaning unencrypted. As such, English speakers among the IDF, DFF, PLO, and other armed elements could monitor every report we rendered. Ironically, the IDF and DFF might have preferred that UNTSO and UNIFIL transmissions be encoded so that when UN reports were broadcast the PLO would not easily learn what the Israelis and their militia partners were doing. Besides, if necessary, intercepting and decoding transmissions was well within the IDF's ability. Israeli military intelligence had linguists for each nationality in UNIFIL and UNTSO. When UN personnel spoke in their native tongue, it would be translated immediately. Interestingly, we later learned that the IDF had a difficult time with Fijian, an Austronesian derivative from Malayo-Polynesian, and whenever the Irish spoke Gaelic, an early Celtic language. It took them about 20 to 40 minutes to translate the latter, while the former proved to be even harder to break.[29] Yet, hearing all the different English dialects made for an interesting morning that gave me a good feeling about being part of this international endeavor. However, I noted this impediment in my journal: "If only UNIFIL could fulfill its mandate."

It was clear to me after a few short days in southern Lebanon that the UNIFIL mandate was weakened after UN authorities had remarkably and unbelievably compromised UNIFIL's mission by giving the PLO control in certain areas, while allowing Israel to justify the presence of its armed puppet in the enclave to roam menacingly and act with ill-will, even to the point of killing and threatening UNIFIL soldiers and UNTSO observers at gunpoint. Denied the ability to occupy the area it needed to keep the peace, on the whole UNIFIL was simply ineffective. As Supko squarely put it, while UNIFIL was armed, it was also "feckless" and not truly "peacekeepers," and certainly not "peacemakers," but rather "somewhat more an impediment to the separated parties."[30] In reality, a boxing referee possessed more authority and freedom to act than UNIFIL had under its anemic and weakened mandate. UNIFIL was no more than a speed bump in the path of the next invasion by the IDF.

After lunch that day, Lefebvre and I decided to conduct a foot patrol of the desolate village of Khiam. We walked down the hill from our OP and into the town. Right away we saw that the village had been subjected to a great deal of local looting, as evident from the total absence of window and door frames, plumbing fixtures, and other household items. Everywhere we turned, clothes were scattered along with children's shoes, more evidence of looting followed by hasty departure. Schools that were once centers of learning and knowledge stood empty and gutted, now monuments to a senseless conflict. We also came upon destroyed and horribly damaged churches and mosques. No longer were they gathering places for the faithful. Now they stood silent, cold, and desecrated—a grim reminder that in war there is little regard for anything held sacred. By far the most appalling display was the sight we came upon in a Christian cemetery. There we found tombs broken into and bodies lying about in open coffins, obviously the work of grave robbers. I recorded this scene in my journal:

> The numbness which descended over both Jean and me at this spectacle removed any fear we might normally have had as we moved from tomb to tomb. We came upon one in which we found several bodies stacked one upon another. This tomb we were able to close. Shortly thereafter we left. A Bible I had found in a nearby Church served to remind me of the fact that in even this place, God was present. I asked a prayer of forgiveness for those who had done this act and set the Bible on a wall near one of the tombs. The thought had occurred to me as well that if I had been observed carrying it out of the cemetery by whomever, I might have been accused of stealing it.

Supko had a similar reaction when he and his OP KHIAM teammate, Major Noel Perrin (French Army), came upon the same cemetery just a year earlier. Supko and Perrin—whom I had served with in Damascus the previous spring—found the scene as tragically disgusting and profane as Jean and I did: "We snooped around El Khiam [and] I showed Noel a Christian cemetery that has been desecrated. The tombs have been opened, caskets opened, and remains pilfered. It looks like whomever did this was looking for valuables, even the little children's caskets were opened; the civil war and [the] Litani Operation have really f——ed up this country. Sad thing is that after having been here 7 months, I would put my money on the Israelis for desecrating the graves."[31]

Of course, there was no way to confirm who had violated the sanctity of that church graveyard in Khiam. But like most crimes—and this would have definitely been a war crime—the three elements needed to convince a jury of guilt were painfully present. And like it or not, both the

IDF and the DFF possessed all three, including the means, the motive, and the opportunity to further defile Khiam. Of course, no one would admit to such a thing. But I had eyes also, and the only organizations present in Khiam in 1980 and 1981 were the IDF, the DFF, UNIFIL, and UNTSO. I was confident that the latter two had no grudge with the people of Khiam. And I was equally certain that the PLO was not the culprit since Khiam had become an IDF urban training area.

When Lefebvre and I returned to the OP, I reflected on a number of things. All the parties of the conflict, the Israelis, the DFF militia, and the PLO, claimed the right to be in southern Lebanon. Yet I was left wondering whatever had become of the rights of the people of Khiam? In a sense, I was glad Lefebvre and I saw the destruction with our own eyes. But I could sense my shifting views concerning Israel's role in southern Lebanon as I transcribed my thoughts that night:

> The U.S. should stand by Israel's right to exist. But to the extent that we stand by her every action simply because it is done in the name of defense, belies the nature of the situation here and does a disservice to the US. America must be able to stand on its record. We must be what we say we are. If we support injustice for the sake of friendship, then we set ourselves up for justified ridicule from our enemies and discredit among our friends. Furthermore, we make a mockery of the very things we stand by. In this way, we do ourselves a disservice. Now it is clearer to me than ever we must put our case strongly to Israel. "We stand firm in our support for your existence as a state. However, to the extent that your actions bring discredit upon the United States, calling into question the extent to which we are committed to justice and peace, we will not support you." I'm not certain whether or not our government will have the courage to act in this manner. If we do, I am certain we will be respected. Time will tell.

My unhappiness did not end there. For the first time since I had arrived in the Middle East, I was beginning to reassess my feeling about Israel's larger policy and military actions. In my mind, Israel was acting more like a "spoiled brat," the actual description I wrote in my journal, while the US was responding like a parent enabling bad behavior: "Israel's actions here in Southern Lebanon, its haughty disregard for the authority of the UN here, its settlements policy in the Golan and the West Bank, its intransigence about Jerusalem, and its 'preemptive' military raids on whomever, are the unreasonable actions of a child who is more wrapped up in paranoia than the responsible pursuit of objectives."

In a sense, I was reaching the same conclusion that some of my US colleagues serving in OGJ and OGL had reached, along with many other international UNMOs who served with us. Yet, what I saw in Khiam rendered by the IDF and DFF did not produce any corresponding sympathy on my part for the PLO and other violent Arab factions. Not in the least. It was not a zero-sum game in my mind, where my flagging feelings for Israel would be replaced by growing sympathy for the PLO and their violent ilk.

To be sure, I would learn and experience much over my military career as both an artilleryman and a Middle East specialist, causing me to continually reevaluate my feeling about the Arab-Israeli conflict. My sympathy for Israel would be bolstered dramatically following the First Gulf War in 1991 after Iraq's Saddam Hussein, having invaded Kuwait, also attacked Israel. That year the US would deploy Patriot antimissile batteries to Israel to intercept Iraqi Scud missiles fired at the Jewish state during a war I would both fight in and write about in great detail.[32] But on 11 September 2001—after Islamic terrorists from Al-Qaeda attacked the World Trade Center towers in New York and the Pentagon in Virginia—I clearly saw our national interest intersecting with Israel's. Our strategic relationship and my personal support for Israel became stronger than ever, and justifiably so. But in the summer of 1981, at a place called OP KHIAM, my attitude toward the PLO and the IDF was like that of the fictitious Mercutio in Shakespeare's *Romeo and Juliet:* "A plague o' both your houses!" Israel and its Arab enemies had made life miserable for the people of southern Lebanon. That said, I knew fully that with my newfound balance between the contending sides, I risked getting the same reception that past US officers had gotten from both Arabs and Jews who sought advocacy from the UN, not the unvarnished truth concerning their mutual transgressions. The credo of Arabs and Jews alike was simple: "If you are not for us, you are against us." And that attitude was very much alive in southern Lebanon.

Indeed, MAJ Lindeman experienced this biased sentiment firsthand the previous year while on duty at OP KHIAM when he found himself accused of being a spy by Israel's marionette, the DFF. In August of 1980, UNIFIL requested that the senior officer at OP KHIAM, Canadian Major Jim Waldron, conduct a reconnaissance of Israeli movements and positions in the Valley of Springs. From his OP position using his binoculars, Waldron spotted several IDF violations and reported them to UNIFIL. Later in the week, UNIFIL sought more details on Israeli movements. Lindeman and a Dutch UNMO serving with Waldron on OP KHIAM volunteered to conduct a further ground reconnaissance to obtain better details to confirm Waldron's visual surveillance. During their inspection, they accurately noted road improvements, Israeli checkpoints, prepositioned ammo dumps, and tactical radio antennas that had been erected in the area. Lindeman and his Dutch partner applied their tactical skills, analyzing what they had observed, making their own assessment of what the likely IDF avenues of approach might be in future incursions into southern Lebanon. They also made an estimate of the likely combat formations and unit strengths that would compose such an invasion force. But in the process of their reconnaissance, they were unexpectedly stopped by an Israeli patrol and held at gunpoint until UNIFIL and UNTSO authorities arrived. Lindeman recalls that the UN authorities "apologized for the incident, professing befuddlement as to our presence and purpose."[33] In other words, the same people who *sought* the information denied ever *asking* for it, as opposed to professing their right to have it consistent with UNIFIL's mandate. Nonetheless, Lindeman eventually delivered his report to UNIFIL, which was not surprised to receive it.

Later that month, and much to Lindeman's surprise, Haddad obtained a copy of the assessment and eagerly waved it in the face of the press, claiming that "two observers, Major Lindeman and Major Waldron, were ordered to report on the militia and IDF movements."[34] Haddad then held up the map that Lindeman provided to UNIFIL. This, Haddad bellowed, was further "evidence of spying" by UNTSO that would justify his decision to limit UN movements in the Valley of Springs in complete violation of our mandate. In point of fact, it was an UNMOs *job* to report the activities of combatants in southern Lebanon as well as their numerous violations, despite the DFF leader's animated theatrics as he protested, "Why do they want to harm us and spy on us?"[35] His rhetorical question was absurd. The only motivation Lindeman and his OP comrade had was to assess the state of combatant activity in the UNIFIL area and the potential for future hostile operations. It was their duty.

After the press had the story, Lindeman was sure that a double agent in UNIFIL provided the DFF with the information, which was plausible. Just as likely, however, was the possibility that the compromise could have been the result of very poor operational security by UNIFIL personnel. They were not the most disciplined practitioners of information security, nor were any of their tactical radio communications encoded. The good news was that Lindeman and his Dutch partner were unharmed, the former being reassigned to Damascus and the latter to Amman more for their own protection from retaliation by the IDF and DFF than to avoid trumped-up espionage charges. Haddad had effectively used the "obtained" map as "proof" that the UN could not be trusted. In fact, Haddad's real gripe was that OGL observers could not be co-opted. His dramatic media *tour de force* before the Israeli press was a contrivance—likely in conjunction with IDF intelligence operatives—to discredit the UN as honest agents, including UNIFIL. This was a tactic that would reappear a year later when I was serving on that same OP.

On Monday, 15 June, my tour on OP KHIAM was nearly half accomplished. That day and the next, we heard gunfire, but all in all it was mostly peaceful. The following day, however, we observed an Israeli artillery survey team emplacing survey markers less than 200 meters to our north atop the southwest corner of an old citadel south of Khiam. These survey points would be used by artillery units to precisely position both firing batteries and their forward observers (who adjusted where the rounds were targeted) to ensure accuracy when those units fired their cannons. It was clear to me that this particular survey team was making preparations for future operations. They knew we were observing them, but they acted as if we were not there. I could not help but note—sitting in the enclave as we were—that we were nonetheless powerless to remove them. It was another clear example of how UNIFIL's mandate to expand to the Israeli border was never fulfilled. Consequently, UN forces were handicapped in accomplishing their mission. Observing yet another blatant violation by the IDF, it was difficult to avoid the conclusion that of all the parties to the conflict, Israel had excelled in making a mockery of the UN. And for US officers serving in UNTSO, this was a particularly uncomfortable reality since American policy was decidedly pro-Israel. Among Americans who witnessed the IDF actions in southern Lebanon, sympathy for Israel was on the decline. I noted this in my journal: "The UN is made a mockery of here. . . . I must say, I know not a single U.S. officer who is what may be grossly termed as 'pro-Israel.' They [US UNMOs] are decidedly 'anti-wrong.' It's a good thing."

Clearly the Israelis wanted no part of the UN or its mandate. They had been hostile toward the UN for decades as a matter of policy. At the time, the IDF maintained 25 permanent ground violations in contravention to Lebanese sovereignty and an unmistakable affront to UNIFIL's and UNTSO's mandates.[36] True enough, the PLO was a continuing and aggressive threat to Israel, firing rockets at and conducting raids on innocent civilian communities in northern Galilee. But that did not justify Israel's treatment of the UN and it's US officers, as if we were the problem. The IDF's hostility toward American UNMOs in particular chaffed us.

Notwithstanding our view of Israeli aggression, US UNMOs remained scrupulously even-handed in our unhappiness with all the parties to the conflict. As Supko recalled, even-handedness was important when dealing with the malevolent armed combatants in southern Lebanon: "You have to understand one important truth. Everybody lies."[37] Sollis recalls how the IDF boldly denied activities, even as they were ongoing in a nearby town: "I recall one evening on OP HIN, as we were listening to the BBC at the dinner table, the news reporter was saying there were unconfirmed reports of Israeli forces conducting night live firing exercises near the Lebanese village of Marwahin. According to the report, IDF spokesmen vehemently denied any such thing. Meanwhile, we were right then observing the night firing in close proximity to our OP. The following morning there was no brass [ordnance residue] to be found anywhere in the area. The IDF had covered their tracks."[38]

Nevertheless, it was important that UNTSO officers be even-handed, particularly when dealing with hostile forces, who would distort the truth for their own benefit. Yet even UNTSO had transgressors. According to Supko, one French UNMO was very open about his affinity for the leftist Lebanese National Movement (LNM) and regularly attended its meetings in Tyre.[39]

However, many UNIFIL officers were particularly open about their criticism and feelings toward the parties to the conflict. When Canadian Jim Allan made his first trip from UNDOF to UNIFIL headquarters in 1981, he noted the almost total lack of "impartiality" on the part of many UNIFIL officers, who "seemed to have a strong bias" for one side or the other.[40] After all, attitudes of UNIFIL officers often reflected their nation's policies. Several contributing forces to UNIFIL recognized the PLO diplomatically, whereas others did not. But UNIFIL's biases were certainly more pronounced than UNTSO's. UNIFIL resented the way its officers and soldiers were treated by all quarters, including the kidnapping, harassment, wounding, and killing of their soldiers by the IDF's DFF allies on the one hand and the PLO and their armed elements compadres on the other. Indeed, the UNIFIL area of operations, including the Valley of Springs, where I was positioned on 16 June, was a deadly place regardless of one's attitude toward either Israelis or Arabs. Unfortunately, in southern Lebanon, not only UN personnel faced the potential for a deadly end.

That Tuesday on OP KHIAM, we would learn how sinister the Israelis could be in carrying out their designs against civilian authorities in southern Lebanon. While conducting our business with NORBATT, we learned that one of OGL's mobile units, Team Sierra, had uncovered an assassination plot to murder the local mukhtar (mayor) of Ibl al-Saqi, located just two kilometers north of Khiam. On 15 June, a local shopkeeper was approached by a DFF operative and told to report to the DFF headquarters. After arriving that morning, no DFF personnel were present, only IDF personnel. The shopkeeper reported that the IDF asserted that the mukhtar was "not good for the village" and should be eliminated. I captured the details in my journal verbatim as the report was related to me:

> The IDF proposed to supply him with 30 kilos of HE [high explosive] in 2 satchels with a 1-minute delay fuze and a detonator. The IDF said the shopkeeper would be paid $6,000 (US). If he failed to participate, the IDF threatened that they had been "watching him" and would "put him in jail" if he didn't cooperate. The IDF proposed arrangement would be to preposition the items near Ibl al-Saqi. The vehicle to be used to position the explosives would not be one that could be checked and in fact would be an IDF vehicle because IDF vehicles could get into southern Lebanon without being searched. The explosives would then be picked up and moved by donkey under the cover of darkness. The shopkeeper would then take the explosives to the village and on 15 June, plant them on the south side of the Mukhtar's house where 12 members of his family sleeps.

Somewhat shocked after his meeting with the IDF, the shopkeeper returned to the village very troubled and decided not to pick up the explosives that evening and carry out the plot. On the morning of 16 June, he went to the targeted mukhtar and informed him of the plot. In turn, both went to NORBATT's headquarters to share the details of the planned assassination. Almost immediately, NORBATT went on alert and later that same day, we were told, they located the explosives. In the wake of this revelation, unsurprisingly, the shaken mukhtar began carrying a shotgun.

This appeared to us, as we thought about it, to be yet another move by the Israelis to discredit UNIFIL and NORBATT particularly in the Marjayoun region, just as the IDF and the DFF had attempted to do with Lindeman a year earlier. We reckoned that had the Israeli plot been successful, together the IDF and the DFF would promptly advance a propaganda line asserting that UNIFIL was "incapable of protecting the local people as evidenced by the assassination of the Mukhtar," a conclusion I noted in my journal. That would, as I noted then, further create an opportunity for Haddad to propose establishment of new and effective "defensive measures in the region" to "protect innocent Lebanese with upgraded tank and mortar positions" by the DFF, yet another scheme to expand Haddad's regional influence. Given the reports to us and the discovered explosives, we had reason to believe that the IDF was behind this malevolent plan. Acts of this nature consistent with the kind of activities other players perpetrated in southern Lebanon—murders, kidnappings, hostage-takings—that threatened everyone, military and civilian alike. To be sure, the violent actors in southern Lebanon did "what they wanted, when they wanted, and where they wanted"[41] regardless of the UN's presence, and certainly without regard for US UNMOs like me who saw what they were doing all the time.

The following day was spent quietly "cooking and looking" on OP KHIAM. When morning arrived on 18 June, my teammates and I were on our final day of duty overlooking the Valley of Springs. That day, Marshall-Cormack and I were dispatched by our team leader to inspect IDF activities that we had detected in the village of Khiam. In order to appear less obvious, we decided we would go for a jog through the village. On our run we paused at a DFF position and spoke with them for a while in an effort to appear nonthreatening. I engaged one of the DFF militiamen in a conversation in broken French for a minute or two while Marshall-Cormack looked for signs of activity. We then said our good-byes and were off. On our way back to OP KHIAM, as we jogged on the east side of the village, we ran past a US-made M113 APC manned by the IDF. We then paused at a cliff to get a better view of any IDF activity in the valley east and below Khiam. As we did, an older DFF soldier intercepted us in a beat-up Mercedes Benz. We immediately noticed that he was armed with a snub-nosed .38-caliber pistol and spoke only in Arabic. That's all he needed to speak because we knew why he had been sent. As he spoke, he made clear by his hand gestures that we were to stay only on the main roads of the town when jogging and that if we didn't we could be shot, making that clearer yet by brandishing his weapon at us. It was a pretty convincing performance, I thought to myself, albeit friendly and firm. That evening I noted both our "looking" and later our "cooking" in my journal:

Pat and I were the picture of cooperation unaccustomed as we are to arguing with a man with a gun. We then retreated to the OP. Before departing, though, the old Lebanese, capitalist to the end, offered to "swap" a ball point pen for Pat's 17-year-old watch. We convinced him it wasn't very good, and he drove off, less one prospective watch to resell and two UN observers to worry about. I took a nap this afternoon. We had chicken for a third time this week. All four of us are sure if the truck breaks down tomorrow, we'll be able to fly home.

Over that chicken dinner, which was delicious, we reflected on the week we had spent "cooking and looking" in the Valley of Springs and laughed out loud about the chicken comment! The comradery was marvelous among our group. There was lots of laughter about our encounters— now that they were safely behind us—coupled with serious reflections about the situations we had witnessed over the past week. After the main course and a nice dessert, we broke out the bottle of Baileys Irish Cream and sipped our way into the evening, although I was cautious to watch my intake. As the junior officer on the team, I would have the final midnight shift in the observation tower.

As we wound up our dinner conversation, our senior officer, Marshall-Cormack, regaled us with a story that—once again—showed not only the peril UNMOs faced every day, but the effort to discredit and intimidate both UNTSO and UNIFIL by the DFF. The story involved Australian CPT Damien Healy. Healy, along with Lefebvre, was on duty with UNTSO's Team X-Ray—one of OGL's conflict resolution teams—on 3 June 1981. Healy decided to go for a jog accompanied by a stray dog named Digger who liked to shadow UN observers. While running, an unidentified person shot at Healy, but actually wounded the dog. Healy heard the shot but didn't realize the dog had been wounded. He noted momentarily that the animal had to limp back to where the team was staying. Lefebvre called OGL in Naqoura for medical assistance for the animal. Shortly thereafter, a civilian jeep arrived with a Swedish medical corpsman, who treated the dog that the UNMOs had befriended. Two days later, the Australian ambassador in Tel Aviv inquired into the incident. As the senior Australian, Marshall-Cormack received a query on 5 June seeking to confirm if— according to news reports—Healy, who was reported to be a Royal Army Aviator (RAA), had been shot and killed in southern Lebanon. The embassy wanted confirmation of this as soon as possible. Marshall-Cormack's first priority was to contact Healy and verify that he was unhurt. When he and Healy conferred later that morning, the unharmed Healy explained that it was the dog that had been wounded on 3 June, not him. Marshall-Cormack promptly called the embassy to advise them that Healy was very much alive and well.

As Marshall-Cormack and Healy attempted to unwind the confusion, they determined that there were three possibilities. First, an air force officer with the same name may have been killed in a crash somewhere, but they quickly dismissed that idea as unlikely. Second, it may have been a case of mistaken identity, since Australians are sometimes referred to as "diggers" and the report assumed that it was Healy that had been shot and not Digger the dog. This seemed more likely, but improbable. Third, a more sinister theory involved an earlier incident where Healy and a teammate from Team X-Ray had been dispatched by OGL to resolve a delicate situation the previous week involving the DFF. It was a particularly sensitive time since there had been ten prior shootings in the area. While Healy was resolving the dispute, he was photographed, something not usually done or encouraged. It was possible that the DFF disapproved of Team X-Ray's intervention in that incident. As a result, whoever shot at Healy—only to wound Digger, who survived—may have intended it to be a warning to Team X-Ray members not to interfere with DFF matters. After much thought, Marshall-Cormack and Healy finally concluded that the shooting had been designed to deter Healy and Team X-Ray's work to resolve shooting investigations.[42]

This story comported with what we had heard from other UNMOs as well as our own experience. Hostile forces—on all sides of the conflict—were notorious for discrediting, deterring, diminishing, and endangering UN officers and soldiers. We were simply the unwanted sheriff trying to keep the peace in the "Wild West" disguised as southern Lebanon. Marshall-Cormack's elaborate story that evening left us all to conclude that while our efforts may be noble, opposition to us was profoundly ignoble. As Supko concluded early in his assignment to OGL, the combatants, whether the IDF, DFF, or PLO, "were all gangsters."[43] Later that evening in the observation tower, I composed my thoughts about the distinct contrast that I had witnessed that week in southern Lebanon, where I had had my baptism as a military peacekeeper: "I came on duty at midnight tonight. The lights ringing the Kibbutzim to the south of OP KHIAM glow securely around their sleeping population. The cold darkness which drapes Khiam village to the north gives peace and comfort to no one. All is quiet."

The next morning, 19 June 1981, I arose and helped my teammates clean the OP for the next shift, pack our equipment, and load our vehicle for the return trip to Naqoura, from where I would travel onward to Jerusalem. When we were relieved by the incoming team, I took my place in the back seat of our UN vehicle and, with my comrades, bumped along the primitive roads of southern Lebanon westward to the OGL headquarters. There was much to think about. But in short order I was back with Shelley in our apartment at "Chez Adawin" for a time of rest and recuperation. I would return to the "Wild West" soon enough.

9

UNMO Teams in the "Wild West"

In addition to performing duty on observation posts, OGL's American and international UNMOs also manned mobile teams in support of UNI-FIL. As we did, we knew that the danger we faced in 1981 was as perilous as that confronting the UNMOs who preceded us. On 18 April 1980, Team Zulu—an OGL mobile liaison team led by MAJ Harry Klein (USA) and CPT Patrick Vincent (French Army)—was ordered to escort a relief and reprovision mission to OP RAS south of At Tiri. Unfortunately, debris from the At Tiri clash—as well as that caused by MAJ Haddad's subsequent mortar attack of the UNIFIL headquarters at Naqoura—was still smoldering. Klein would discover firsthand how the embers of conflict could quickly reignite to cause more death without warning.

OGL had a specific—albeit risky—mission for Klein. Irish UNIFIL soldiers manning OP RAS had been shut off from resupply by Haddad's forces for two weeks. Accompanying Klein's Team Zulu were three IRISHBATT replacements, UNIFIL press information officer Timur Gök-sel, AP reporter Steve Hindy, and his photographer, Zaven Vartan. Prior to the At Tiri confrontation, Team Zulu had maintained routine contact with Haddad's forces to mitigate problems and prevent misunderstandings between the DFF and UN personnel. When Klein and company departed the IRISHBATT headquarters with the replacements for OP RAS, he believed the operation had been approved by both Haddad and the IDF, particularly since OGL ordered Klein to conduct the mission and likely would have made that coordination.

Outside of the village of Beit Yahoun north of At Tiri, Klein had expected to meet Abu Iskandar, one of Haddad's lieutenants, who was to escort Team Zulu onward to OP RAS. But Iskandar did not appear.[1] Meanwhile, as that situation unfolded, CPT Clay Grubb (USMC) was in the process of occupying nearby OP HIN, which was not part of the Klein mission. From OP HIN, Grubb was able to monitor all of the radio traffic between Klein and OGL's leadership.[2] When Abu Iskandar failed to show, Klein—who was both an Arabic linguist and a very experienced

164

Middle East specialist—thought it wise to await the arrival of a DFF liaison officer as a safety precaution and recommended that course of action to his OGL superiors. However, they ordered him to continue on. According to Grubb, Klein "reiterated his concern but was overruled."[3]

Shortly thereafter, the team was stopped and was held hostage in a schoolyard by none other than Mahmoud Bazzi, the older brother of the deceased DFF combatant from the previous week's fighting with UNIFIL and for whom Haddad was demanding blood money. At that point, the situation rapidly spun out of control. Bazzi seized the three Irishmen from Klein's party and—in the process—shot and severely wounded one of them. Klein then hustled the wounded soldier away, put him in his vehicle, and evacuated him to receive emergency medical care. Had he not, that soldier surely would have died. The two remaining Irishmen then attempted to escape, but were apprehended by the DFF, tortured, and then savagely murdered by Bazzi.[4] Fortunately, Göksel, Hindy, and the photographer were unharmed. However, this was a despicable atrocity that amounted to a gruesome blood feud. Such was the case in southern Lebanon between hostile parties, but on that day it also ended tragically for one wounded and two murdered Irishmen.

Fortunately, Klein's quick and decisive action saved one of the Irish soldiers from bleeding to death. Justice for the senior Bazzi would not occur until 35 years later, when he was apprehended in the US, where he had been granted asylum, inexplicably, in 1994. In 2014 he was arrested in the US and deported to Lebanon, where he was tried and convicted by a Lebanese military court in 2015 for his heinous crimes.[5] In hindsight, the mission that day went horribly wrong. There was still much emotion and anger following At Tiri. Sending an unarmed OGL mobile team with UNIFIL soldiers on this mission through this volatile area without an approved DFF escort was a grave mistake. It would have been preferable for OGL to heed Klein's instincts to await the DFF liaison officer or to abort the mission. OGL's leadership did neither. Unfortunately, the situation turned deadly.

This incident was a reminder of the danger UN observers and soldiers faced every day, even during routine relief and resupply efforts. Nevertheless, a year later UNTSO appeared to ignore that exact lesson when they dispatched Irishman COMDT Dave Betson and a civilian Finnish field service officer (FSO) on a similar mission inside the volatile DFF enclave, even as tensions remained elevated. Betson questioned the logic of assigning him that task, but nonetheless followed his orders while wisely removing the Irish patch and officer epaulettes from his combat jacket in case they were stopped by DFF militiamen. Betson's wisdom paid off: "As we drove from Naqoura, I was mentally rehearsing my Canadian accent! As luck would have it we were stopped a couple of miles up the road by a lone SLA [Southern Lebanese Army or DFF] man brandishing a handgun. It was Mahmoud Bazzi! We didn't try to negotiate too hard, and I left the talking to the Finnish FSO. There was no way we were being allowed to proceed so we did a three point turn on the road and high-tailed it (with much relief) back to Naqoura!"[6]

Betson's actions—both in removing his epaulettes and disguising his accent—proved sagacious after encountering Bazzi, who was unaware of the Irish officer's nationality. The murderer of two of his countrymen was still roaming free a year later.

This was not the first time an Irishman would take such a reasonable precaution passing through the enclave, where blood feuds were a reality, particularly after the At Tiri battle. COMDT Des Travers (Irish Army) was also detained by the DFF, until an OGL "rescue" mobile team led by MAJ Johnny Woolshlager (USA) came to his assistance. Woolshlager advised Travers to remove his Irish national patch and don Woolshlager's US patch and brassard for the remainder of their journey back to Naqoura. Travers did and was grateful for his brief "induction" into the US Army that day.[7] To be sure, the battle of At Tiri and its aftermath were prime examples of the dangers we continued to face, especially on mobile teams and certainly to Irishmen at the time.

The Threat of Building Tensions in Southern Lebanon

After my tour at OP KHIAM that June, I was more keenly aware of the job that OGL and UNIFIL were doing, particularly in implementing their mandates in a very hostile and lawless place. Shortly after returning to Jerusalem, I could see that LTC Sholly was quickly involving himself in our operations. Soon OGL's chief, LTC Wilson, would depart and be replaced by LTC Al Baker (USA) in July. Sholly wanted to take advantage of the leadership shift to reset the relationship between the UNTSO headquarters and OGL that had been strained for months over "turf" issues. As part of that effort, he decided to create a UNTSO liaison officer position in OGL to facilitate cooperation. On 10 August, he dispatched me to perform a week's duty with OGL as his liaison. I was to engage in reporting events while hitting the road to attend coordination meetings in the UNIFIL area of operations. I was delighted to be deployed again, particu-

larly if I could contribute to better relations between the two headquarters. Besides, I still had much to learn about the conflict in southern
Lebanon and another week with OGL would be a great experience. Since
I would be staying in Nahariya overnight with Australian UNMO friends
CPT Barry Gwyther and his wife, Jo, Shelley also came along. When I
reported to the OGL operations center in Naqoura, I went right to work
recording events of the day. In short order, our observers at OP HIN saw
that the IDF was continuing to fortify their tactical positions on the Lebanese side of the border, as they had prior to the 1978 invasion. That
included the deployment of an anti-personnel detection radar array position that IDF soldiers would occupy each night to locate and intercept
potential infiltrators. Never mind that the IDF's occupation of this site—
regardless of the defensive military advantage they would derive from
it—was a violation of Lebanese sovereignty.

The previous month, the span between 12 and 24 July had been an
intense period of combat that saw Israeli air strikes against PLO positions, as well as major exchanges of artillery and rocket fire by both sides.
That August we were all very concerned that hostilities would erupt
again. But for Israel, the continuing Palestinian military buildup in southern Lebanon prior to July was intolerable. Therefore, Israel justified preemptive attacks against the PLO forces. Israel's view was simple. They
opposed the flow of arms to the PLO supplied by Arab countries and the
Soviet Union, viewing it as a "grand design for an all-out war against
Israel." On 17 July, Israeli ambassador to the UN Yehuda Z. Blum asserted
as much, saying that "Arab states regard Lebanon as one of the most
important bridgeheads for launching what they call the 'next round'
against Israel."[8] Yet Israel's preemptive strikes against PLO targets on
12 July were a dangerous escalation that provoked an intense response
by Palestinian forces. The fighting that exploded then—known later as
"the storm"—raged on for several days. When Israel attacked, the PLO
immediately retaliated. On 15 July, the PLO unleashed a "heavy barrage"
of rockets fired from "guerrilla positions" in southern Lebanon, killing
three and wounding 13 in the town of Kiryat Shmona.[9] Even the Israeli
town of Nahariya—where many UNTSO observers lived with their family members—came under fire. In the process, three Israelis there were
killed as they headed home from work.[10] Between 12 and 23 July, the IAF
responded with airstrikes targeting PLO positions in Beirut, Damour,
Sidon, Saadiyat, and Tyre along the coastal road. The IDF's artillery then
struck PLO positions in Nabatieh, north of Beaufort Castle, and Hasbaya, northeast of Khiam in the NORBATT sector of operations. Israel

also sought to destroy bridges leading into the UNIFIL area along the coastal road and in the central and eastern area of southern Lebanon to inhibit the resupply of PLO forces and strongholds.[11] Then, on 17 July, the conflict reached an intense stage. Israel bombed the PLO headquarters in West Beirut, killing more than 300 civilians.[12] LTCDR Virg Bozeman (USN), by then assigned to the UNLOB office in Beirut, recalls the intensity of Israeli air strikes: "I was in Beirut—and on duty at the ILMAC/UNLOB offices—when the IDF bombed the Sabra refugee camp across a street and a soccer field away from our offices. I think they had intelligence that put Arafat's offices on one of the upper floors of this building, maybe an eight or nine story building. . . . The IDF put one smart bomb through a window on that floor to minimize damage to the rest of the structure."[13] As it turned out, PLO chairman Yasser Arafat escaped death from the precisely targeted weapon, but the incident revealed how dangerous the fighting had become.

The heat was also turned up on UNIFIL and OGL during "the storm." OGL saw the situation developing. On 13 July, infiltration by the PLO into the FIJIBATT and DUTCHBATT sectors was on the rise. When armed elements were intercepted by UNIFIL, they refused to return to the Tyre Pocket, even after orders from their PLO superiors were purportedly issued for them to withdraw. That tipped off OGL that something serious was afoot. The next day, IAF airstrikes on PLO positions north of UNIFIL increased. By 15 July, tension across southern Lebanon was palpable. IDF artillery rounds targeting PLO forces that had infiltrated UNIFIL's sector impacted near SENBATT and DUTCHBATT in the west and near NEPBATT and NORBATT in the east. In short order, the PLO responded with artillery fire that landed in Nahariya, near UNTSO observers and their families. According to OGL, 623 rounds of artillery and mortars were fired by the IDF and the DFF, with 319 originating from the PLO between 12 and 15 July.[14]

On 16 July, the IAF dropped 36 bombs on the Kasmiya bridge spanning the Litani River north of Tyre while artillery fire increased from both sides and even from IDF patrol boats at sea. On 17 July there was heavy shelling across UNIFIL's area of operations, 500 rounds from the IDF and their DFF allies and 306 by the PLO, the same day the IAF bombed Beirut. On 18 July, the PLO fired on Nahariya, a move that provoked many civilians and UNTSO families to evacuate the town. The next day saw a huge increase in artillery fire, with over 1,800 rounds coming from the IDF and their militia allies and 620 from the PLO. Heavy artillery exchanges continued from 20 to 23 July but began to abate as talk of a cease-fire brokered by the US gained momentum. On 24 July the cease-fire went into effect, but artillery violations continued.[15]

Following the US-negotiated cease-fire, relative calm descended, but peace was more brittle than before "the storm." Tension was as high as it had been when the Israelis invaded in 1978. Southern Lebanon remained a tinderbox drenched in gasoline and just a spark away from a conflagration. Arafat's death surely would have ignited a firestorm had Israel's 17 July attack killed him. On the other side of the ledger, the PLO actually launched Katyusha rockets from inside UNIFIL positions toward Israel. That reinforced the Israeli view that UNIFIL was feckless, proving to them the UN force was unable to stop attacks originating from territory it putatively controlled.[16] By the time the cease-fire went into effect, it was clear that while Israel could significantly harm the PLO with airstrikes, they could not completely eliminate those forces from the battlefield without the introduction of ground units in direct combat.[17] Therefore, in the wake of "the storm," the IDF continued improving its positions across southern Lebanon on both sides of the border into August. It was evident to many of us then—certainly to me—that the next time the Israelis decided to return to southern Lebanon in force, it would be a full ground invasion, and a big one at that.

As my liaison week at OGL progressed, it was clear that the violence had ebbed a bit since the running artillery duels of July. On 12 August—just 17 days after the cease-fire went into effect, a large number of IDF artillery units actually evacuated southern Lebanon. That was good news. One OGL mobile team patrolling west of Khiam reported that two batteries of a M109 155 mm self-propelled howitzer battalion and one battalion of M107 175 mm self-propelled long-range guns departed the area. However, one battery of 155 mm howitzers remained behind and in place, ready to fire. Indeed, the dug-in positions that had been occupied by 175 mm gun batteries—able to shoot 147-pound projectiles almost 40 kilometers—were still in very good condition, including both the gun revetments and the washing and shower facilities the IDF used.[18] Those positions could be reoccupied quickly, providing more evidence that the IDF had not foreclosed on returning in greater numbers in the future. Otherwise, with the exception of the hijacking of a UNIFIL water resupply truck by the DFF, the rest of the week was sedate. However, on 14 August I gained a real insight into the activities of UNIFIL operations when I attended a military intelligence conference with 24 other officers representing all of UNIFIL's battalions and OGL's mobile liaison teams that supported them.

I represented the OGL operations team along with a Swedish colleague, MAJ Olle Fagerstrøm, who accompanied me. At the conference we received updates from the senior military intelligence officer (SMIO), LTC Leo G. Dijkstra (Dutch Army), on several topics, including the current period of calm after "the storm" passed. Both the UNIFIL battalions and OGL's mobile teams weighed in with their opinions on recent activities in the UNIFIL sector, all of which made the conference truly beneficial and educational. But I was somewhat surprised by the rather sanguine assessment the SMIO gave concerning the recent violence. He was quite sure that the July upheaval had ended in a "stalemate," since the PLO had managed to successfully resist the IDF in the Tyre Pocket. He properly noted that the US had not been pleased with Israel's most recent foray into southern Lebanon, concluding that the PLO had achieved a "political victory" since Israel had been regarded as the instigator that July. That part of his observation was accurate. Then he made a rather interesting statement concerning what the recent fighting meant to Israel. He speculated unsurprisingly that Israel would do well to seek a political solution to the entire Lebanese situation. No one could disagree with that particular observation. But then he opined thus: "[I]srael may be willing to hand over the enclave to UNIFIL because recent events proved it had ceased to be an effective security belt, because the PLO can still hit targets in Israel."[19]

Even as a young captain with minor experience in southern Lebanon, I found such optimism to be stunningly naive. Nothing any of us had witnessed—not me on OP KHIAM nor any other competent observer in southern Lebanon—could be interpreted as a willingness on the part of Israel to give up its DFF-manned enclave in southern Lebanon. Indeed, the entire period of "the storm" should have made clear that Israel was willing and ready to reenter southern Lebanon and engage in more bloody combat if attacked by PLO artillery and rockets, as it was in the summer of 1981. Besides, why would Israel leave Lebanon and abandon the enclave to UNIFIL? Even from its current positions, UNIFIL battalions were not able to prevent the PLO from firing into Israel from the very locations the UN controlled. Israel had no hope UNIFIL could do any better in the enclave. As I sat quietly taking notes, I was left thinking that the SMIO must be from another planet if he thought the Israelis were ready to leave southern Lebanon, absent a complete removal of the PLO threat to Israeli towns and village. The SMIO's assessment was unjustifiable and Pollyannaish. In my view he ignored the war clouds gathering on the horizon. I was sure we would see more "storms" ahead.

And that violence would continue to threaten not only southern Lebanon but UN personnel as well.

Indeed, during the fighting on 18 July, even Nahariya was shelled, causing the senior US UNMO to evacuate UNTSO families to Jerusalem. Australian CPT Barry Gwyther was actually on duty in the OGL's headquarters in Nahariya when the bombardment began. He quickly grabbed a UN vehicle to alert UN families to seek shelter in a school used by the children of UNMOs and UN civilians. As he made his rounds dodging incoming rockets, an Israeli police officer stopped him and sarcastically remarked, "Who do you think you are, Superman?" The very mission-focused Gwyther quickly responded, "No, but neither are they," pointing to a nearby apartment housing UNTSO families. He then abruptly sped off to finish his task. On 19 July, when he returned to the OGL administrative headquarters in Nahariya, that facility came under attack, as did many targets in Nahariya. Gwyther could observe incoming rounds through an open window near the lintel of an interior doorway under which he had taken cover. The shell fragments kicked up columns of dirt outside the building near a large fig tree. Afterward, Gwyther went outside and collected a piece of one of the rockets. A few weeks later, while serving on one of OGL's mobile teams, Team Tyre, which dealt with the PLO, the audacious Gwyther showed that he could give as well as he got. While meeting with one of their local army commanders, he handed over the rocket fragment, "thanking him for his gift but that it would be better if he kept it" next time. Gwyther recalls of his sardonic encounter, "He did not appreciate my sense of humor."[20]

OGL's Mobile Teams

To be sure, the mobile teams were an important component of OGL's support to UNIFIL. Even when the DFF and other armed elements restricted UNIFIL's movements in the enclave to Mondays, Wednesdays, Thursdays, and Fridays and UNTSO's observers stationed on OPs to Mondays and Thursdays, the mobile teams were generally allowed to roam about.[21] Ironically, all the parties to the conflict would come to learn that the teams could on occasion be useful to them. In that regard, Grubb recalls that sometimes our teams were regarded with the same respect accorded to the indigenous "clan" negotiators who would intervene in serious local situations to diffuse potential violence. As a result, the UNTSO teams served as a "necessary" and "credible" asset to local leaders.[22] But there was a caution that CPT Lenny Supko (USMC) would share with new American UNMOs: "The American flag on your shoulder will give you instant credibility—far more credibility and attention than any of us deserve. Some people, some Americans, become a bit too enamored of themselves. They run their mouths entirely too much. They call inordinate attention to themselves. I encourage you to avoid that at all costs."[23] Teams did their best work when they heeded advice like this to remain credible.

During the SMIO conference I gained a better appreciation of not only how the teams interacted with combatants, but the insights they obtained. There were six such teams operating in the UNIFIL and OGL sectors. Team Tyre, located at Tyre Barracks in that city 18 kilometers north of Naqoura, engaged in routine tasks, including negotiating prisoner exchanges, incident investigations, and dealing with hijacking cases and other forms of kidnapping. In that regard it spent much time with the PLO and its army, the PLA, as well as other PLO-associated armed elements, including the PFLP, DFLP, LNM, the Shi'a Muslim group AMAL. They also dealt with the Lebanese government and the International Red Cross as needed. Team Metula was co-located with the IDF and the DFF in that northern Israeli town with the mission of communicating directly with those parties. Team Zulu—originally focused on liaison with the DFF—was located in Qana in SENBATT's area of operations. It had a broader mission after the At Tiri incident to be a special liaison team for the UNIFIL force commander and the UNTSO chief operations officer to settle disputes and encourage peace throughout UNIFIL's sector. It also worked on special tasks like dealing with power line disputes between armed groups in the UNIFIL area. Team X-Ray was based at the OGL headquarters in Naqoura. It replaced Team Zulu in patrolling the DFF enclave after the Klein affair.[24] And like its predecessor, Team X-Ray stayed in contact with Haddad to resolve issues that might arise, as they often did, as well interfacing with the PLO when the situation warranted. Team Romeo, situated in Kafr Dunin near NIBATT and GHANBATT, was formed to be a liaison between UNIFIL, the local leaders, and mukhtars. Finally, Team Sierra worked from Ibl al-Saqi in NORBATT's area. It was created to deal with the easternmost sector (OP KHIAM, NEPBATT, NORBATT, the Valley of Springs) because there was so much activity there in 1980 to 1982 (see map 9.1).[25]

While Teams Tyre and Metula had a more fundamental liaison mission, the others were quite mobile and moved about their areas of responsibility as the situation demanded. Teams X-Ray, Zulu, Romeo, and Sierra were "ready reaction teams" given frequently unexpected tasks that would

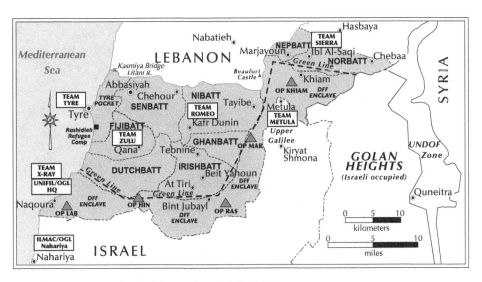

Map 9.1. OGL Area of Operations, 1980–1981

come their way at all times of the day and night (see figure 9.1). They were quite busy in the summer of 1981, and during the SMIO conference we heard their perspective on the current situation. Team Sierra, based in the Valley of Springs, observed much activity by the IDF and the DFF in the eastern portion of UNIFIL's area of operations. While the IDF appeared to be temporarily reducing its forces on the ground that August, it was also posturing for future operations and gave no indication, contrary to the optimistic estimates of the SMIO, that Israel was ready to relinquish control of the enclave occupied by its DFF allies. To the contrary, there was every evidence that the Israelis were poised to return, and quickly if necessary. Team Sierra also observed that after "the storm" the PLO presence had diminished in the area, and in some towns was completely absent. So, for better or worse, the IDF had in fact changed the situation on the ground in the Valley of Springs during the previous month's hostilities.

Cooperation among the teams and with UNIFIL was also ongoing. For example, when Team Sierra observed that the DFF's Haddad had been interfering with electrical utility work between two villages in the Valley of Springs, Team Zulu stepped in as the UNIFIL force commander's liaison to encourage Haddad to cease his disruptive interference. He did, and for a time the tension subsided. Team Zulu also made the conference aware of internal issues that reduced UNIFIL's effectiveness in resolving disputes and conflicts in its area of operations. Specifically, UNIFIL was

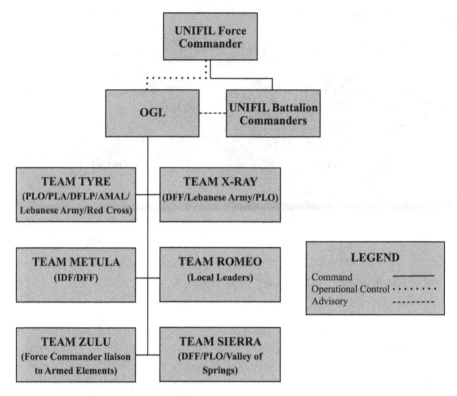

Fig. 9.1. OGL Mobile Liaison Teams, 1980–1981

not providing enough background information on disputes that the teams were dispatched to resolve. In particular, some of the points of contact that the teams were instructed to work with were the very elements instigating the problems! Moreover, Team Zulu made the embarrassing observation that UNIFIL was more vulnerable to armed incidents during periods when battalions had large personnel rotations every year. The implication was clear. Not only were bad actors taking advantage of inexperienced UNIFIL replacements arriving in southern Lebanon to replace experienced ones, but UNIFIL was working against its own best interests by failing to provide sufficient information to OGL's mobile teams to effectively resolve flare-ups. Additionally, UNIFIL's poor vetting of local points of contact selected to perform liaison functions with OGL's problem-solving teams made it difficult to resolve issues. It was uncomfortable to hear these deficiencies in a room filled with UNIFIL authorities, but they were important shortcomings to address.

Team Romeo was led by MAJ Allen S. "Al" Ingalls (USA), who had only recently arrived in UNTSO in July 1981. His team performed a key liaison function working with the local leaders and UNIFIL. Ingalls wasted no time establishing his credibility and demonstrated situational awareness by pointing out that a shortage of gasoline, the arrival of the tobacco harvesting season, and the occurrence of the Ramadan festival, which had ended on 3 August, all had likely contributed to the recent lull in fighting following "the storm." This sort of cultural awareness and prescient analysis was the sort of leadership that enhanced the US reputation in both UNTSO and UNIFIL. Likewise, he noted that the DFF was clearly taking steps to strengthen its positions and gain strongholds in the UNIFIL sector, yet another reason to question the SMIO's optimistic view of a potential IDF withdrawal. In the very short time Ingalls had been on the ground, he was already making a positive, professional impression.

During this conference, Team Tyre, led that day by CPT Dan Holstein (USMC), noted that the PLO had garnered a fair amount of goodwill during the previous months of heightened combat with the IDF but had managed to squander it quickly when they took emergency control of the gas stations that served the public. Following that move, Lebanese civilians were soon complaining that the PLO "gets everything," including the gasoline. These observations, while seemingly petty, were not insignificant. Team Tyre was often involved in negotiations with the PLO to resolve various issues, primarily between it and UNIFIL. And frequently, those conflicts were between the armed elements and civilians. I found that to be the case later when I twice served on Team Tyre. The more knowledge the team possessed about small things—like gas hoarding by the PLO and the dissension it was causing among the locals—the more information and leverage the team would have at its disposal to shape discussions and achieve peaceful outcomes. For example, gently pointing out PLO unpopularity with the locals could be just the trick to encourage them to be mindful of more accommodating behavior, like a willingness to work for the release of civilian hostages held by armed elements of one stripe or another.

In sum, the SMIO conference revealed that OGL's teams were indisputably valuable. What was also clear was that those teams seemed more aware of the facts on the ground than did UNIFIL's military intelligence staff. Unfortunately, UNIFIL lacked a certain precision in interoperability and coordination with OGL teams that would have helped both, a reality highlighted during the SMIO conference. Irishman COMDT Des Travers, on duty with OGL from 1979 to 1981, and later serving two tours with

UNIFIL, noted this lack of cooperation, occasioned by a degree of arrogance from some UNIFIL authorities:

> There was no agreed military modus between both UN entities;
> OGL teams crisscrossed contingent area of operations appar-
> ently gathering information, seemingly for the benefit of others.
> This untidy arrangement gave rise to mutual distrust and suspi-
> cion. The issue for me became so severe that on one occasion I
> was stopped at an Irish checkpoint and asked to state my busi-
> ness. This was relayed back to IRISHBATT operations who then
> cleared my way through the battalion's AO. Similarly, I was
> invited to meet a French staff officer at FRENCHBATT HQ.
> While there, I encountered the Battalion Commander who—via
> an interpreter which I feel sure he did not need—questioned me
> for entering his domain without prior clearance. The staff officer
> who invited me remained mute. It was, on reflection, a magnifi-
> cent display of French hauteur by the Battalion Commander.[26]

According to Travers, the issues between UNIFIL, UNTSO, and OGL
teams persisted over the years he worked with all of them. The central
problem was a failure to produce an integration mechanism to facilitate
mutual operations similar to cooperative arrangements normally found
in military units where areas of operations and reporting chains over-
lapped to accommodate actions like special operations, investigations,
and information gathering.[27] In reality, the mobile teams in OGL could
certainly benefit UNIFIL under the right circumstances, even that of an
Irish UNMO from OGL entering the Irish Battalion's area without being
challenged as if he had just arrived from Mars. But when the result was
suspicion and distrust, it was harder to work together as a team. Despite
these problems, I looked forward to the day when I could participate on
a team and involve myself in the nitty-gritty of peacekeeping. That time
arrived the second week of September 1981, when I was assigned to
Team Tyre, my first opportunity to test my negotiating skills in the field
and demonstrate how US officers could contribute to the effort.

Team Work in the "Wild West"

I reported to Team Tyre on Labor Day, Monday, 7 September 1981. Initially our labors were quiet. But that was interrupted by PLO antiaircraft

fire directed at IAF aircraft operating over the Tyre Pocket. That and the artillery shelling in the area were frequent occurrences, but fortunately our operations were unaffected. On Wednesday, however, our team had the opportunity to resolve the kidnapping of a Lebanese Army officer taken captive by armed elements. I deployed with another member of our team, MAJ Steve Strom (USA), to meet with the PLO liaison to Team Tyre, a CPT Barakat. When we arrived, we were warmly greeted by Barakat, who offered us *chai* in customary Arab fashion. We knew that launching directly into the matter would have been entirely rude, something I learned visiting the souk in Damascus. Hospitality was preferred over fast-paced business exchanges, whether negotiating with a rug vendor or a kidnapper. I also knew that Barakat thought it significant that two Americans were there to discuss matters directly with him. The PLO was very sensitive to the presence of US officers on the mobile teams. After all, they very much wanted to be embraced as the legitimate representative of the Palestinian people by the US, a recognition that had eluded the PLO to that point. In fact, in any other setting, it would have been unthinkable for a US Army officer to be negotiating directly with the PLO at all. But that was precisely what Strom and I were doing under the auspices and diplomatic covering of the UN. That rarity was not lost on me. It wasn't lost on Barakat either. After sharing our backgrounds, family stories, and our hope that everyone could live in peace in the place called the Middle East, Barakat flatly denied he knew anything about the kidnapping of the Lebanese officer. We then parted ways as amicably as we had met. Later, clearly after either giving the issue more thought or upon uncovering more information, Barakat contacted us and acknowledged "that the soldier has been kidnapped, was under interrogation, and was unharmed."[28]

We quickly notified the Lebanese Army, who naturally wanted the officer released immediately. For the next two days our team continued to meet with the PLO, consuming copious amounts of chai and sharing personal stories until Barakat, in a rather nonchalant manner—as if it were an afterthought—informed us that the officer had been released to his parents. It was then that we learned that when armed elements initially approached the Lebanese officer, he was not in uniform and was not forthcoming about his status as a Lebanese Army officer, no doubt fearful he would be detained as a spy. Captured spies have poor prospects in southern Lebanon, so his hesitancy and lack of candor was probably warranted. But his furtiveness raised suspicions, thus he was held against his will. On 10 September, when the armed elements who kidnapped him determined that he was not a threat to the PLO or their allies in the

LNM, he was released. The Lebanese Army liaison officer to Team Tyre—who worked with us on the release—was happy that his abducted comrade was unharmed. But he was nonetheless quite angry at the PLO for the kidnapping in the first place. This was the downside to kidnappings, even those that ultimately had a happy ending. The resentment that often resulted from incidents like this generated a mistrust that could fuel dangerous miscalculations on the part of aggrieved parties. This was precisely what teams like ours dealt with continuously. A downward spiral of eroding trust followed every incident.

This was also true between the armed elements and UNIFIL. On the upside, however that very week our team met with the PLO and DUTCH-BATT leaders to sort out differences. The discussion proceeded well. Those were the sort of exchanges that gave us hope that we could make things better. Yet a few months later Bozeman, back from Beirut, had quite a different experience. While on duty with Team Tyre, they received a call that a shooting was occurring at a UNIFIL checkpoint after Fijian soldiers searched a vehicle and confiscated arms from its trunk. Bozeman and a fellow UNMO headed to the scene right away. When they arrived, they quickly found themselves in the target zone with gunfire impacting near and all around them. Apparently the detained vehicle also had as a passenger the mother of one of the armed men involved in the shooting. When the mother was ordered to exit the vehicle by a Fijian soldier, she immediately began striking the soldier with her hands. In the process of restraining her, the Fijian soldier manhandled her roughly, causing her male family members to erupt in fury. The armed men hastily withdrew to nearby high ground, where they began firing at the Fijian soldiers. At that point, a Fijian captain in command of the UNIFIL team decided to charge the hill, an act that would have resulted in far more bloodshed. Bozeman, who outranked the officer, immediately countermanded that order. The infantry captain complied with the assertive naval officer in front of him, something the Fijian could have ignored since Bozeman was neither in his chain of command nor authorized to issue orders to UNIFIL forces. Nevertheless, the captain wisely complied, and Bozeman and his partner dutifully proceeded up the hill to negotiate a cease-fire. After some Turkish coffee and persuasive discourse, everyone agreed to stop shooting at one another. As Bozeman recalls, after that tense moment passed "We drove back to Tyre Barracks, had a great meal, and then got very drunk."[29] But Bozeman's wits and decisiveness had paid big dividends.

There were occasions when mobile teams like Team Tyre were not just in danger from the combatants. Sometimes they were terrorized by them.

On 30 December 1980, Team Zulu, Supko and Travers—who was standing in for Supko's regular partner, Frenchman Phillippe Jarty—were stopped at a roadblock north of Tyre by armed elements. The two UNMOs were returning from a mission to locate a downed IAF pilot who had ejected near a PLO position in the area. The armed men thought Supko and Travers were trying to help the downed Israeli officer, whom they regarded as an enemy. The angry hijackers stripped both men to their underwear, marched them away from their vehicle, and staged a mock execution, placing their rifles to Supko's and Travers's foreheads and pulling the triggers to cause an ominous click. Laughing, they then abruptly abandoned their terrified victims and stole their UN vehicle, along with their uniforms, equipment, and identification cards. Having survived a horrifying moment, both men proceeded southward and barefooted in the cold Lebanese winter. Eventually they were intercepted at a Fijian-manned outpost, where they were provided blankets and warm refreshments. Once they were retrieved by OGL, Supko would complain to the PLO liaison officer, but they never learned who had committed this obscene and despicable atrocity.[30] This is what UNMOs faced while trying to keep the peace, particularly in the Tyre Pocket.

Not every challenge Team Tyre faced was dangerous. MAJ Joe Serviss (USA) on one mission with the team was dispatched to return a French nun to her convent and orphanage, located in Sidon on the coastal road 40 kilometers north of Tyre. The previous day, the IAF had attacked a bridge along the coast between Tyre and Sidon. When Serviss arrived with the nun and a French UNMO accompanying them, they found the bridge largely intact but ringed with bomb craters. Negotiating the rough terrain in his UN vehicle, Serviss passed over the bridge and delivered the nun safely to her home. She was so grateful she gave him her small gold cross, which he has faithfully kept ever since. It wasn't a particularly stressful mission, but it went to the core of what we did in trying to bring people some peace. That was no small thing, and all of us in UNTSO knew it. Yet these were the sorts of situations—some dangerous, others terrifying, and some routine—that we faced working in the territory controlled by violent men fighting one another.

Some extraordinary situations required actions that conflicted UNTSO's standing rules. Take for example when Supko's Team Zulu was alerted to investigate an Israeli aircraft attack near Abbasiyah, 10 kilometers northeast of Tyre. When they arrived, Supko was told by the Lebanese Army that a young boy's arm was severed in the attack. Supko determined that the cause wasn't an attack, but a horrible accident. A

Lebanese Army soldier, startled at the sound of an Israeli jet flying over-head, grabbed his rocket-propelled grenade launcher and accidentally fired it. The rocket then hit the overhang of the building, ricocheted downward, and severed the boy's arm above the elbow. The youngster was then transported to UNIFIL's Swedish medical company hospital for treatment. To that point, Team Zulu was working within the rules. How-ever, afterward Supko visited the boy and learned that the child's mother was quite anxious to visit her son. Supko leapt into action. He located the mother and decided to find a way to transport her to the hospital himself. However, using a UN vehicle to transport a Shi'a Muslim woman through Christian DFF checkpoints along the dangerous coastal road was com-pletely unauthorized and risked accusations of favoritism to one side over the other. When Supko searched for off-duty volunteers willing to accompany him on this mission, the only person to step forward was a fellow US marine, Clay Grubb. Grubb knew that this was not a mission for the fainthearted. Together they found the boy's mother, put her in the back of their UN jeep, covered her with a pallet and tarp, and transported her to the hospital to see her son. In one single act, they broke all the rules, including using two UNMOs of the same nationality to go on a mobile patrol together, and then smuggling a local civilian through hos-tile DFF forces, who would have strenuously objected had the woman been discovered.[31] While it was an unauthorized act, it was also one of pure compassion that typified what American officers like Supko and Grubb were willing to do to bring a bit of humanity to a land consumed by conflict. No doubt, the people of Abbasiyah would not soon forget this gesture of kindness by two American UNMOs. Marines used to say in their recruiting ads that they were "looking for a few good men." Two of them showed up that day to perform a mission of mercy in southern Lebanon.

On my final day with Team Tyre, three artillery rounds exploded in the town. We tried but failed to locate where they impacted—there was so much preexisting debris in the town. Interestingly, SENBATT was responsible for reporting such firing incidents occurring in Tyre, but they reported absolutely nothing in this case. Team Tyre ultimately made the report, which caused me to make this observation in my after-action memorandum to UNTSO when I returned to Jerusalem: "The SENBATT contingency at Tyre guard is largely ineffective and generally unmilitary in appearance. Furthermore, during the period 1–14 September, Tyre guard failed to report any of the firing noted [in the author's report] above. This situation should be remedied before it gets worse."[32]

My concluding comment, I would eventually recognize, expressed an unrealistic expectation for some of the UNIFIL forces whose national policies were favorable toward particular parties to the conflict. There was no possibility of improvement. Senegal supported the PLO, and therefore SENBATT did also. Consequently, SENBATT was largely ineffective. They did not even seem to care when their friends, the PLO and its allies, were fired upon by other combatants. SENBATT simply occupied space in UNIFIL's area of operations. They were disengaged and largely ineffective in peacekeeping, reflecting the worst of UNIFIL. As Supko observed of UNIFIL battalions, "the battalion followed its home country's guidance regardless of its effect on adjacent battalions or UNIFIL as a whole."[33]

In fact, our teams observed that UNIFIL battalions were not all considered to be the "cream of the crop." After much interaction with UNIFIL as a team leader, Supko personally assessed the battalions from best to worst. The Fijian Battalion was good, and willing to get "into everyone's face" to accomplish their mission. The Norwegians and Dutch were also good and would put up a fight when it was warranted. The Irish, however, were hesitant about firing at all and therefore left themselves open to be tested and abused by combatants. In 1980, their battalion commander reportedly said as much to Grubb, who spent much time on OPs supporting UNIFIL.[34] However, Irishman Travers, who served in separate tours with both UNTSO and UNIFIL, firmly disputes this. The use of deadly force was "drilled into our soldiers almost like a mantra, learned by rote like our prayers."[35] That included self-defense, defense of a manned position, or when hostile forces attempted to disarm Irish soldiers. Yet, given all that happened to the Irish in 1980, events Grubb personally witnessed, it was hard to blame them for being cautious. And a cautious approach to using deadly force by the IRISHBATT was probably nearer the truth than any hesitancy to defend themselves from armed attack or in other critical situations, as they surely did at At Tiri.

Supko's harshest criticism fell on the Nepalese, Ghanaians, and Nigerians. He considered them nonchalant at best and in large measure posing no threat or deterrence to armed violence. They were there to "go along and get along." Worst of all—as I witnessed—were the Senegalese, who were all but PLO allies, a direct reflection of their nation's policy. The sad truth was that they and the other battalions from African nations, as Supko observed, were "simply not durable enough for peacekeeping operations."[36] Belgian COMDT Jean Lichtenberger—a hardened veteran of the war in the Congo—put it bluntly. UNIFIL "had no teeth."[37] Most

UNTSO officers—certainly US ones—agreed with Lichtenberger's assessment. In fact, even those among UNIFIL that did have sharp teeth were sometimes reluctant to bite. That deficiency served to dull UNIFIL's effectiveness and contributed to its image as a paper tiger.

When I returned to Jerusalem after my tour with Team Tyre, I had an increased appreciation for the role of the US in UNTSO, particularly in interacting with the PLO, which coveted US recognition. Little that we did with the PLO in southern Lebanon through our good offices had much to do with the eventual US recognition of the organization. But it was clear that the PLO was eager and willing to sit down with US officials at any level, including US military officers in their capacity as mobile team members or while serving as liaison officers. They understood that any pathway to peace necessitated the imprimatur of the US. Dealing with US officers provided opportunities for the PLO to assert that they were the legitimate representatives of the Palestinian people and the US should acknowledge them officially. Every contact, therefore, had the potential for the US and the PLO to improve their stature vis-à-vis one another. In that regard, Bozeman, while working for the UNLOB team in Beirut, had a rather interesting encounter, not only with the PLO, but with its top man.

French LTC Mayeur, who led UNLOB, routinely met with Arafat every two weeks. Arafat used UNLOB and Mayeur as his conduit to the UN secretary-general, Kurt Waldheim. The PLO chairman possessed very limited ability to speak English. Therefore, the challenge was to get any discussion between him and Mayeur transcribed to intelligible English, the official language of UNTSO. To do that, Mayeur tasked Bozeman to sit behind a temporary screen in the same room where the Frenchman and Arafat conferred. As they exchanged views, Mayeur would attempt to characterize in English what Arafat was saying and get his concurrence. As he did, Bozeman sat behind the screen transcribing the exchange into acceptable English, including clarifying garbled aspects of the discussion. Bozeman was sure that Arafat knew he was there but never actually laid eyes on him. Nevertheless, it was a remarkable convergence; a prominent Arab leader speaking with a Frenchman in broken English while an American naval officer—sitting behind a screen like a priest hearing a solemn confession—formulated the dialogue into English that would eventually be translated into German for the secretary-general. After these sessions, Bozeman dutifully shared the discussions with the US military attaché in the embassy in Beirut. "Colonel John Tolnay, USMC, the Naval Attaché at the Embassy in Beirut, was fully briefed by me every time Arafat showed up at our office. I even passed the idea through him that we let Arafat and one of the U.S. UNMOs in Beirut be 'inadvertently' photographed together so that Arafat could claim U.S. acceptance and we could deny it and say that the U.S. officer was on detached UN duty. It never panned out."[38]

It was just as well that Bozeman's intriguing—albeit creative—idea was not acted upon. If discovered, it could have resulted in an uproar inside Prime Minister Menachem Begin's Israeli government, which would have promptly accused UNTSO of serving as Arafat's foreign ministry.

Clearly, US officers were not authorized, outside of the auspices of UNTSO, to have any contact with the PLO. Nevertheless, it was just as clear that the PLO sought opportunities to sit with US officials at any level. Sometimes those opportunities were quite unexpected. CPT Mike Fallon (USMC), while serving on a then ILMAC OP positioned at Beaufort Castle before the PLO took complete charge of it, was held against his will there by the PLO for 18 days. During his captivity, Fallon contracted a horrible case of dysentery. So bad was his condition that his captor, a MAJ Saïd, evacuated him by ground to a hospital in the PLO stronghold of Nabatieh, 12 kilometers northwest of the castle. There he was treated by a Palestinian doctor who was none other than Yasser Arafat's brother. After he was well enough to travel, Dr. Fathi Arafat facilitated his release and return to OGL.[39] Ironically, Fallon's "rescue" was necessitated by the PLO's malevolence in originally holding him hostage. No doubt, they were certain to take credit for their eventual magnanimity to a US officer whom they had imperiled in the first place.

MAJ Denny Lindeman (USMC) also had a firsthand experience with the PLO. In April of 1981, while Lindeman was still assigned as the UN security coordinator in Syria, he was asked to fill in for a few officers away on leave who worked in the UNDOF operations center in Damascus. Unexpectedly, Lindeman was invited to lunch with a Syrian general, only to discover that the primary attendees were representatives of the PLO. Lindeman recalls what happened next:

> I was invited by the Syrian Liaison Office to have lunch with General Tiarya at 1400 hours on 29 April. There in attendance was the general, two professors from the International Peace Academy, New York, a PLO Information Officer, the Senior UN Field Service Personnel Chief, an Austrian lieutenant colonel, and a Canadian colonel. All of the conversation was directed to me. The subject was the honor and integrity of the PLO cause. At first, I suspected that the Austrian and Canadian were collaborators in the agenda. But as the conversation progressed, the Austrian and

Canadian did not address me, but the others. Their questions and comments were ignored and only the American remained the focus.[40]

During what turned out to be nearly a four-hour meeting, Lindeman was treated to what he describes as "a 3.5-to-4-hour diatribe on the just cause of the PLO and why America should support it."[41] That was to be expected from the PLO. Lindeman's meeting was more a lecture than a conversation, but it did highlight the significance the PLO placed on having access to US officers at the time. Through it all Lindeman was diplomatic and polite, a posture that was sure not to offend. However, a key aspect of this encounter was the extraordinary effort the PLO exerted to have an American official at the table, even if that required initiating the meeting with a degree of subterfuge to gain Lindeman's attendance.

All of these encounters between the US and the PLO, the routine ones primarily with the mobile teams, Bozeman's UNTSO translator duty, and the Lindeman ambush meeting, were indicative of the importance the PLO assigned to the US presence in UNTSO. Whether or not the US fully endorsed these encounters, that they occurred was an indication that the PLO understood that it was in their interest to groom a relationship with America whenever and wherever they could. Ultimately the US, Israel, and the PLO would connect through the 1993 and 1995 Oslo Accords that marked the start of a potential peace process.[42] Israel recognized the PLO as the legitimate representative of the Palestinian people, and the PLO recognized Israel as a state. It was a major step forward. However, to state the obvious, the American UNMOs were not responsible for the Oslo agreements. But we had been an honorable and respectful audience that hopefully showed the PLO that the US was trustworthy and wanted justice for all. So, in a small way, the US presence in UNTSO—particularly on the mobile teams—may well have had a larger impact than we thought at the time when we were engaged in conflict disputes, or surreptitious engagements behind screens transcribing notes, or sitting across the table from self-righteous representatives of the PLO. It all mattered.

The "Wild West" in Retrospect

Looking back on UNTSO and the two observer groups that worked in southern Lebanon, there is much to admire. First, UNTSO was fortunate to have high-quality officers, both US and international. In almost every case they contributed to the successful work of peace observation, and the US had a prominent role. In that regard, Clay Grubb was quite proud of his US comrades. "Especially in OGL in the 78–80-time frame, special team UNMOs held south Lebanon together and 'regular' UNMOs, especially [the] US, held OGL together by their initiative and dedication to the understood mission."[43]

The Yanks in UNTSO, as Grubb recalls, "often voluntarily undertook potentially dangerous missions," such as medical evacuations, or actions "simply for the benefit of the locals."[44] They were there to serve, recognized the danger, and were willing to take risks to achieve peace and goodwill. Moreover, their insight, initiative, and calmness under fire and in life-threatening moments were often demonstrated. There were also challenges. The behavior of hostile forces toward UNTSO and its observers— US and international alike—in southern Lebanon was annoying at best, and atrocious at worse. The DFF under Haddad—with the approval of the IDF—routinely harassed observers on our OPs as well as purloined or destroyed our equipment. The DFF also made determined efforts to restrict the movement of observers and in some cases threatened us with kidnappings and random firing incidents to deter us from doing our job. But the most egregious acts occurred when the IDF, DFF, PLO, and armed elements actually shot at or threatened to kill UNMOs.

One harrowing example of this occurred in Beirut on 2 August 1981. While on duty at UNLOB in Beirut, Jean Lichtenberger, who was a seasoned Belgian combat veteran, sustained life-threatening wounds when he was driving his UN vehicle through the city near the seaside promenade known as the Corniche. Departing from the US embassy in a UN vehicle Bozeman had just handed off to him, Lichtenberger was immediately stopped by a lone Lebanese militiaman who jumped into the car, ordering the Belgian to "keep driving." As Lichtenberger and his unwanted passenger drove off, other armed elements fired on them from a nearby hillside, filling the vehicle with 66 rounds from a .50-caliber machine gun. The hijacker, who may have been trying to avoid his attackers, was instantly killed. Lichtenberger acted quickly, opening his door and rolling out onto the pavement, but still sustained significant gunfire wounds to his legs. So bad was his bleeding that his attending surgeon at the American Hospital donated his own blood to Lichtenberger. Meanwhile, the US naval attaché assigned to the American embassy, COL Tolnay—with Bozeman's assistance—coordinated additional blood donations for the wounded UNMO.[45] Later Tolnay and Bozeman would visit the auto body shop holding the damaged vehicle. Bozeman was stunned. "When we went to look at the car in a nearby body shop, all I could think of was the last scene from *Bonnie and Clyde*. There had to be fifty or sixty bullet holes all over the car and the passenger's brain matter was splattered all over the roof of the passenger compartment."[46]

Lichtenberger was very fortunate to have survived. It was an example of what UNMOs could encounter at any moment, as well as an example of the decisiveness of American officers to step in to save another's life. But it was also a close call for Bozeman, who may have just missed by minutes being kidnapped himself.

Despite the ruthless behaviors of the hostile forces that we contended with in southern Lebanon and Beirut, there were no consequences for these lawless acts. Almost no one was held accountable, rarely was anyone brought to justice, and certainly those who did these acts were infrequently punished for their barbaric behavior. Southern Lebanon was truly the "Wild West" without a good saloon and without any prospect that the sheriff in town would garner the slightest respect from the outlaws who ran it. That said, UNTSO made the best of a bad situation and never flagged from its mandate, no matter how dangerous things got for US observers and their international partners.

Those of us in UNTSO understood the importance of our mission and we took our duties quite seriously. We recognized that we were disadvantaged, given the lack of support from the IDF, DFF, and PLO. I concluded—as others did—that, despite deficiencies, it can be said that UNTSO was of consequence. Indeed, UNTSO was mostly able to execute its mandate to observe and report violations of peace accords and truces despite constant interference from those who fomented violence. UNIFIL was less able to do that because it was never properly established to accomplish its mandate, one undermined by its very founders. Nonetheless, both organizations did the best they could with the cards they were dealt to maintain peace in that chaotic saloon. Unfortunately, any peace was not to be sustained. Both UNTSO and UNIFIL had ample evidence at hand through their own observations that more trouble was ahead for this land of perpetual conflict. Throughout 1980 and 1981, it was clear that the parties to the conflict, Israel and its DFF ally on the one hand, and the PLO and armed elements on the other, were not genuinely seeking a peaceful solution. They were seeking an advantage—a politico-military one—as they jockeyed about southern Lebanon preparing for the next phase of seemingly interminable violence.

Southern Lebanon had become the launch pad for the PLO's continued war against Israel. But southern Lebanon was also the forward battle area for potential Israeli assaults on its enemies to the north. Only three years after the 1978 Israeli invasion, it was clear to many of us that another war was on the horizon. "The storm" of July 1981 was all the evidence one needed to see that Israel—contrary to the stated opinion of UNIFIL's senior intelligence officer—was not about to give up the DFF enclave and quietly withdraw from southern Lebanon. They were actively planning for another war to deal a crippling blow to their enemies there. The Israelis saw no hope—not in the least—for a lasting peace coming from UN efforts. They knew war was inevitable. So did most of us watching from our vantage point on the ground in 1981 serving on OPs and mobile teams alike. It was as plain as the nose on your face.

10

The Gathering Storm Erupts

Throughout 1981, ominous signs pointed to a renewal of major hostilities in southern Lebanon. Indeed, 500 kilometers to the southwest of UNIFIL's Naqoura headquarters, an event was taking shape in Cairo that would elevate tensions in the region dramatically. On 6 October 1981, during a military parade commemorating Operation Badr, the Egyptian Army's counteroffensive across the Suez Canal to retake territory lost to Israel at the beginning of the 1973 Yom Kippur War, President Anwar Sadat was assassinated as spectators watched in stunned horror. When Sadat stood to salute those he thought were soldiers approaching the reviewing stands in an impromptu moment to honor him, in an instant they turned into deadly assassins. Members of the Egyptian Islamic Jihad pulled out hand grenades and threw them at Sadat. Then, using AK-47 assault rifles and submachine guns, the assassins fired hundreds of bullets into the reviewing stands, killing and wounding many spectators who were there to see Egyptian soldiers march past their nation's political and military leadership. Sadat, who was mortally wounded in the attack, died two hours later in the hospital.

I recall hearing about the incident on that awful Tuesday as I prepared to depart for southern Lebanon for another tour of duty with Team Tyre. We were all shocked. It was difficult to avoid the thought that we were now facing a huge threat to peace in the Middle East. Would there be a corresponding attempt in Israel? If there were, would it unleash more violence across the region? Was this the first of a number of attacks that might take place against those who supported the Camp David Accords signed 36 months earlier? To be sure, the treaty was regarded by Arab militants as a betrayal of them generally and of the Palestinians specifically. All of these thoughts ran through my mind as we busily set about assessing the situation. Before I departed Government House, I learned from LTC Bob Sholly that our colleague MAJ George Casey (USA), who was assigned to OGE, had attended the ceremonies. Casey was about 200 yards from the reviewing stands when the hail of fire broke out. At that distance he was not fully aware of the assault. However, all doubt was removed when open-top limos started passing in front of him with passengers bleeding and panic-stricken. He knew something was horribly wrong. Mercifully, he was unharmed. But that was the only good news surrounding the incident. For those in the stands with Sadat, it was pure chaos, death, and suffering. It was precisely the danger that could ignite the tinderbox called the Middle East.

Sadat's assassination was a poignant moment for UNTSO. It was an assault on peace itself. If Sadat—one willing to risk power, prestige, and indeed his life in the pursuit of peace—could be struck down mercilessly by radicals who opposed coexistence with Israel, could anyone in the Middle East survive peacemaking? The fatalism surrounding Sadat's murder left many people wondering if peace could ever be attained by anybody for anyone in the Levant, particularly in southern Lebanon, where tension was rising. More broadly, the assassination sent shockwaves around the globe.

Closer to home, MG Erskine was stunned.[1] His military assistant, Australian CPT Geoff Bell, said his boss was planning to attend the parade in Cairo as an invited guest.[2] He was to depart Jerusalem on the afternoon of 5 October to travel overland to Egypt. However, at the last minute Bell learned Erskine had inexplicably decided not to attend. It is doubtful that the UNTSO chief had credible intelligence that would have suggested an increased threat. However, it was no secret then that many Arabs were openly hostile to Sadat over Camp David.

My colleague MAJ Joe Serviss (USA), who worked in the UNTSO operations center with me, was on the waiting list to attend the ceremony. But he was never activated. Likewise, Serviss did not recall any unusual warnings at the time to avoid attendance. But he did acknowledge that the intelligence at the time was "pretty sketchy," meaning unclear.[3] Indeed, had there been serious concerns expressed by American intelligence services, Casey and other US military personnel in Cairo who attended the parade would have been warned. Yet, no warnings were indicated or forthcoming from anywhere.

Later that day, when Erskine was informed of the assassination of the Egyptian president, he was, according to Bell, "very shocked by the news."[4] Erskine immediately realized that he may have figuratively and literally dodged a bullet since he would have occupied a prominent position on the reviewing stand, with Bell likely not far away. In fact, four US personnel who attended the parade were wounded.[5] Doubtless also, Erskine must have been quite concerned about how the assassination would impact the Middle East, particular in the UNTSO area of operations.

Predictably, the news of Sadat's murder was joyously received among Arabs opposed to the Camp David Accords. PLO chairman Yasser Arafat was ecstatic. It was said he ordered the playing of celebratory music in the West Bank and the Gaza Strip upon hearing of Sadat's death. He was also seen "dancing, singing, and praising [the killers] as soon as he learned of the death," an act that many Egyptians found particularly insulting.[6] The evening of the assassination, MAJ Jack Hammell (USA), accompanied by his Damascus-based colleague MAJ Steve Cotter (USAF), was conducting a security assessment in northeastern Syria for UNDOF in his role as the UN security coordinator. From their hotel balcony in Al Qamishli, near the Turkish border, they observed an assembly of people dressed in black, carrying torches, and marching down the street to the sound of a single drum. Hammell ventured out to acquire a shortwave radio to learn what was going on. A local vendor provided one, but then curtly remarked, "That traitor Sadat was killed today."[7] The parade was celebratory, not one of mourning. But Hammell, sensing the volatility, departed early the next day with Cotter for Damascus.

In Lebanon, LTCDR Virg Bozeman (USN) maintained a flat located in Hamra, one of Beirut's major commercial districts. That night, his UN boss, French LTC Mayeur, warned him to remain in his apartment following a huge, growing celebration as news of Sadat's death spread across the region: "Colonel Mayeur called us and told us to stay inside for the rest of the night. Beirut erupted in celebration. There was celebratory gunfire going off all night long and, as I can recall, in the morning, there were four or five dead Beirutis killed by expended bullets falling from the sky and penetrating their skulls."[8]

However, in short order calm returned across the UNTSO area of operations with no unusual security measures taken, beyond generalized warnings to our observer groups. Thankfully, Egypt's leadership reasserted their support for the Camp David Accords. Peace between Israel and Egypt would continue. Within weeks Sadat would be succeeded by his vice president, Hosni Mubarak, who would hold that office for 30 years until he was forced to resign following the Egyptian Revolution of 2011. By April of 1982, the assassination leader, LT Khalid Islambouli, and his co-conspirators were tried, found guilty, and sentenced to death by firing squad or hanging.[9]

A shaky calm returned in the months following Sadat's death, even as tension across the region remained palpable. Nevertheless, the damage was done. Radical elements in the Arab world had sent a clear and unmistakable message: the Camp David Accords were a betrayal of the Arab people and anyone who agreed with them deserved to be gunned down in public. Conversely, Sadat's death played into the hands of Israel, which could point to a sad reality. Arabs who preferred conflict with Israel would not tolerate those who sought peace with the Jewish state. All of this did not portend well for peace in other quarters, certainly not in southern Lebanon, where there was every indication that all was not well as 1982 arrived.

Déjà Vu All Over Again

The tension was growing worse. The PLO was actively arming itself with Russian-made weapons. The IDF was determined to interdict that effort and destroy Arafat's positions in the Tyre Pocket and other Palestinian strongholds across southern Lebanon. While the summer of 1981 was distinctly more violent than what we previously observed, the indications for a potential Israeli invasion resembled what CPT Mike Fallon (USMC) witnessed in 1978. By late 1981, Erskine and the undersecretary-general for special political affairs, Sir Brian Urquhart, were both very concerned about the growing hostilities in southern Lebanon. Bell recalled the air of concern then: "UNTSO was well aware of the rising tensions and reported them regularly to UNHQ [United Nations Headquarters] during late 1981 and early 1982. This involved some UN shuttle diplomacy by Mr. Brian Urquhart, who was UN Under Secretary General for Special Political Affairs at the time. He visited at least some of the potential protagonists, including to my certain knowledge Israel and Jordan, possibly in late 1981, although he may have made other visits in early 1982 as well."[10]

So concerned were Erskine and Urquhart that they did not publicize their fear that a major conflict was in the offing, likely hoping to quietly forestall it. Bell, who was normally present for high-level discussions with Erskine was—for the first time in his service as military assistant—"kept out of the loop" by his UNTSO boss.[11]

Erskine and Urquhart were both busy men. In the early days of February 1982, Urquhart engaged in "shuttle diplomacy," moving among the parties to the conflict in southern Lebanon.[12] So urgent were Urquhart's shuttles that after meeting with the Israelis over the tension in the region, he decided to immediately fly via one of UNTSO's aircraft to Amman, Jordan, to meet with its leaders. As a testament to that urgency, it was the first time since 1968 that a UN flight had occurred over Israeli airspace into Jordan, requiring the UNTSO operations center to quickly coordinate the shutdown of both Israeli and Jordanian air defense units.[13]

Urquhart and Erskine certainly had reason to believe that a potential invasion was possible, given direct observation from the field. Bell recalls the reporting at the time from UNTSO's observers in southern Lebanon and in Tiberias, Israel. Tiberias had a front row seat to the IDF buildup in northern Galilee in preparation for an invasion. "My recollection is that OGL and OGG-T were both reporting instances of considerable troop movement and large areas of northern Israel being closed off, as well as significant concurrent increases in Israeli air activity. The scale of these manoeuvres [sic] was considered to be greater than if they were merely normal exercises. And I personally recall noting significant increases in military activity as I travelled through various parts of Israel, privately and with the General, indicating the increased military activity was not limited to the north."[14]

However, for those who recalled the run up to Operation Litani, there was a pattern of Israeli activity that was repeating itself. As baseball Hall of Famer and virtuoso of malapropisms Yogi Berra once said, it was "déjà vu all over again." Indeed, shortly after the 1978 invasion the situation in southern Lebanon looked more like unfinished business for Israel than a resolution of the PLO problem. Just months after Operation Litani concluded, tension was building anew. Indeed, the spring of 1980 saw the Battle of At Tiri, where UNIFIL's forces rebuffed MAJ Haddad's DFF as he attempted to expand his area of operations, and, days later, Haddad's retaliation when he rained down mortar fire on UNIFIL's headquarters at Naqoura. By June, the secretary-general noted that the situation then was "increasingly tense" despite the cease-fire that went into effect after that first invasion.[15]

Things were unstable as 1980 wore on. From 13 June to 11 December, the UN noted that the IDF was improving its ability to enter and conduct future combat in southern Lebanon: "There were an increased number of border encroachments along the Armistice Demarcation Line. Those encroachments took the form of new positions, the laying of minefields, the fencing-in of strips of land and the building of dirt tracks and asphalt roads. . . . The purpose of the border encroachment appears to be to create a new defensive line forward of the Armistice Demarcation Line."[16]

And in the same report to the UN Security Council, it was clear that the PLO also was determined to build its military strength in southern Lebanon, an action that would not be tolerated by Israel: "While the leadership of the PLO has renewed it assurances of co-operation with UNIFIL, the Force has continued to be faced by attempts by armed elements to infiltrate personnel and weapons into its area of operations.

There was a definite hardening of positions on the part of certain armed elements during recent months."[17]

Moreover, the Israelis were very aware of the PLO buildup in 1980, and they took action to attack Palestinian positions whenever they deemed it necessary. The UN was also aware of this as late as December of 1980. "[T]he Israeli forces have themselves stepped up their activities in and near the enclave. . . . They have established encroachments along the international border, increased their presence within the enclave, repeatedly violated Lebanese airspace and territorial waters and, on many occasions, have launched attacks against targets in Lebanon outside the UNIFIL area."[18]

There was little that UNIFIL could do about any of this, configured as it was. Nor was the UN very effective in ratcheting down efforts by the PLO and the IDF in undermining UNIFIL's ability to keep the peace. It was left to issue plaintive declarations by the end of 1980 that would be summarily ignored by the parties to the conflict: "It is essential that the parties desist from using the UNIFIL area for hostile acts against each other and take reciprocal steps to progressively reduce their presence in the area."[19]

In the period 13 December 1980 to 15 June 1981, all of the armed players were busy positioning themselves to enhance their tactical advantage. The UN secretariat was informed on 15 June, my fifth day occupying OP KHIAM, that the PLO and its allies were working hard to improve their tactical advantage in the UNIFIL area of operations for future combat (see map 10.1): "Armed elements have sought to relocate certain of their positions and to increase their presence with additional positions in the Fujian, Senegalese and Dutch sectors. In this connection, the PLO leadership has stated that it has had to relocate positions for defensive reasons."[20]

So too was the DFF busy patrolling, pressing against UNIFIL forces in the western sector near the village of Zibqin that overlooked a major defile. That terrain could serve as an infiltration route to and from the coastal road, where major combat would occur in a future invasion, just as it had in 1978 when Fallon observed the Israeli PLO clash in the Tyre Pocket. The DFF also was aggressively trying to occupy the high ground in the central sector near the village of Brashit—as it had at Hill 880 near At Tiri—to achieve better observation positions in support of current and future operations. As the storm clouds gathered, 1981 was increasingly a redux of 1978: "Attempts at incursions by the de facto forces into the UNIFIL area were mostly in the form of patrols sent out into areas contiguous to the enclave. The most serious of those was an attempt in February to move to the village of Zibqin in a combined patrol with IDF

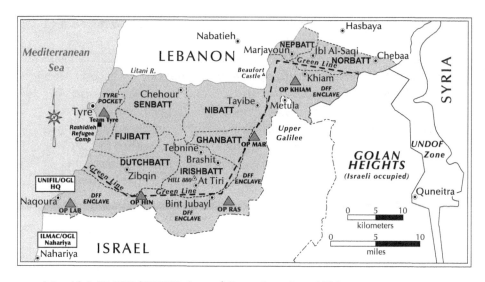

Map 10.1. UNIFIL/UNTSO Area of Operations, June 1981

personnel, which was blocked by the Dutch Battalion, and another to the village of Brashit, using an armoured [*sic*] personnel carrier and two civilian vehicles. In the latter case, the de facto forces fired at Irish personnel, who, in the end, were able to block the move."[21]

The UNIFIL forces successfully stymied both efforts in 1981, but there was a limit to what they could stop. They had no ability to deter IAF air attacks or IDF artillery strikes beyond simply reporting them to the UN: "On 2 March, following an Israeli air raid, armed elements fired into northern Israel. That was followed by another Israeli air strike. Shelling was initiated by the de facto forces [DFF] and the IDF in the northeastern sector and spread rapidly to the western sector and lasted until the next morning."[22]

From 27 March to 29 May 1981, a major flare-up in reciprocal artillery and rocket attacks took place between the PLO and its allies and the IDF with DFF supporters. In that period of time, the PLO alone fired no less than 2,472 rounds of artillery and rockets at the IDF and DFF forces, with many rockets landing in northern Israel. Between 27 March and 29 May, the IDF and DFF increased their response with nearly double that number, 4,678 rounds, some of which fell in several UNIFIL battalion areas.[23] If one thing was clear by the spring of 1981, it was this: there was no effective cease-fire in place and certainly none that was being enforced by anyone. Nevertheless, the UN Security Council was advised by the secretary-general that the UNIFIL commander at the time, MG William Callaghan (Irish Army), was doing his level best to bring the situation under control and "achieve a ceasefire."[24] The seriousness of the attacks was indisputable: "On 27 April, there were intense hostilities. . . . Throughout the period, I, and my senior advisors, as well as the Commander of UNIFIL, were in touch with both sides, with the view to bring those very heavy exchanges of fire to an end."[25]

After an exchange of at least 7,150 rounds in just two months in the spring of 1981, the idea of a cease-fire was a UN pipedream. For all intents and purposes, Israel and the PLO were at war that spring, a war that would escalate that summer.

The situation on the ground between the IDF and UNIFIL was also deteriorating. The IDF had been very active in the winter and spring of 1981. But UNIFIL's protests fell on deaf ears in Israel. The IDF was determined to ready itself for future combat in southern Lebanon and ignored UNIFIL's objections, shooing them away as one would a pesky gnat buzzing in one's ear: "The activities of the IDF in and near the UNIFIL area of operations further increased during the period under review. UNIFIL and UNTSO raised the matter of IDF activities repeatedly with the Israeli authorities. The presence of IDF personnel inside the enclave remained at a high level during the reporting period. IDF gun and tank positions were developed, and observation positions established. IDF personnel were regularly sighted in various localities in the enclave."[26]

Moreover, Israeli forces increasingly violated Lebanese airspace and territorial waters and had "on many occasions, launched attacks against targets in Lebanon outside the UNIFIL area."[27] There was no peace in 1981. At the least, it was the opening salvo of yet another invasion just a year away.

There was a brief respite between 29 May and 10 July. I witnessed that on OP KHIAM. Then, on 10 July, the floodgates were flung wide open and southern Lebanon was awash in violence during "the storm." The UN's reporting quite accurately described the situation:

> On that day, Israeli aircraft resumed strikes against targets in southern Lebanon north of the UNIFIL area. This led to heavy fighting between armed elements, on the one hand, and IDF and the *de facto* [DFF] force, on the other. On 13 and 14 July, widespread Israeli air strikes continued. Armed elements fired into the enclave and northern Israel. On 15 July, there was a particularly heavy exchange, with a total of about 1000 rounds of artillery, mortar and rockets fired by the two sides. On 16 and 17 July,

Israeli naval vessels joined in the firing, which was intense in all sectors. On 16 July, Israeli aircraft attacked and destroyed bridges on the Zahrani and Litani rivers. On 17 July, they attacked Beirut, causing heavy losses of life and damage to property. Exchanges of fire in all sectors, air strikes, and naval bombardments continued on 18 and 19 July and, on a gradual declining scale, until 24 July. During the period of intense violence in July, UNIFIL recorded the firing of some 7,500 rounds of artillery, mortar, tank, and naval cannons by the IDF and de facto forces, in addition to the air strikes by Israeli aircraft. UNIFIL also recorded the firing of about 2,500 rounds of artillery, mortar, and rockets by armed elements.[28]

From 12 to 25 July 1981, almost as many artillery and rocket rounds were exchanged as during the tense months of March, April, and May that year. On 12 July, the Security Council unanimously adopted resolution 490 (1981) calling for "an immediate cessation of all armed attacks."[29] The US announced it would delay a planned shipment of F-16 fighter aircraft to Israel in response to the bombing of Beirut and the death of almost 300 Palestinians in a strike intended to eliminate Yasser Arafat, a bombing Bozeman witnessed.[30] When "the storm" passed, there was little indication that peace would take hold. Indeed, not another storm but a hurricane was beginning to form.

Israel Prepares for War

For the remainder of 1981, the IDF's presence in the enclave was accompanied by further emplacements of howitzers and tanks along with observation posts.[31] And the DFF was equally busy lending a hand to Israel in planning for future operations. On 13 November, Haddad renewed his efforts to seize Hill 880 at At Tiri, where he had failed 19 months earlier in a very violent clash. This time he succeeded. The UN detailed its response to this latest Haddad effort to establish a foothold on the strategic position (see map 10.1).

The position was immediately surrounded by a unit of the Irish battalion. On 14 November, negotiations were initiated, in which the de facto forces made the claim, which was rejected by UNIFIL, that the hill was part of the enclave. . . . On 15 November, the de facto forces attempted to resupply their personnel on Hill 880. UNIFIL prevented this but agreed instead to provide food and water on a temporary basis, on humanitarian grounds and in order to prevent a clash. As of this time of reporting, the situation on Hill 880 remains unchanged, with UNIFIL surrounding the personnel of the de facto forces. . . . [I]t has been pointed out that the presence of the de facto forces on Hill 880 is provocative and risks jeopardizing the cease-fire, and that attempts to resupply this position could lead to a serious confrontation with UNIFIL.[32]

In response to UNIFIL's action to block DFF forces from being resupplied once they infiltrated and occupied Hill 880, Haddad, as he did in April of 1980, retaliated against UNIFIL's headquarters at Naqoura, stranding no less than 250 personnel "without water supply or suitable accommodations."[33] However, he didn't shell it this time, but rather opted to block UN personnel from traveling either in or out of the location as well as preventing resupply to it. Despite UNIFIL's willingness to provide essentials to the Haddad forces on Hill 880, he did not reciprocate. UNIFIL then decided, based on the last episode at Hill 880, that it was better to encapsulate Haddad than to remove him by force.[34] Unfortunately, the decision not to forcefully remove Haddad served to further undermine UNIFIL's authority. By leaving Haddad atop Hill 880, an objective he had relentlessly pursued, UNIFIL sealed his victory to seize better observation points, benefitting both the DFF and the IDF. This event culminated UNIFIL's efforts to keep the peace in southern Lebanon in 1981, a year filled with danger and ominous signs of war ahead.

US observers in UNTSO saw war coming for two years. It was clear as early as the summer of 1980 when MAJ Denny Lindeman (USMC) conducted a thorough reconnaissance of the Valley of Springs while on duty at OP KHIAM. The IDF was busy improving artillery positions on the northern side of their border with Lebanon, actively surveying and plotting firing positions, stocking 155 mm artillery ammunition, and improving their communication facilities to support future operations. Both UNTSO and UNIFIL were fully aware of the constant improvements that the IDF had undertaken. I would also observe the same level of preparatory activity a year later even as IDF soldiers emplaced survey points within yards of OP KHIAM. Moreover, the IDF unashamedly conducted routine fire missions from their prepared positions inside Lebanon, knowing full well that UNTSO and UNIFIL were essentially powerless to stop them from violating Lebanese sovereignty whenever and wherever they chose to do so. And the DFF continued to faithfully serve as the IDF's eyes and ears throughout southern Lebanon, particularly in the Valley of Springs, where Haddad maintained his headquarters in the village of Marjayoun.

By the spring of 1982, Joe Serviss also took note of the increased frequency of preparedness drills in the greater Jerusalem environs, noting, "Things were getting tense" and "Israel was exercising their sirens and searchlights in anticipation of an invasion."[35] Our international comrades also detected the increase in preparedness. Like Serviss, Erskine's military assistant, Bell, was aware of increased air raid drills that occurred "very regularly in Jerusalem" throughout May of 1982, just a month before the invasion.[36] "There were plenty of other indicators too, e.g., increased levels of cross-border attacks by both sides and increases in other cease-fire violations etc., all of which were faithfully reported to New York. I guess this was another advantage of having UNTSO in place in pre-satellite days, i.e., it could provide a non-partisan source of information regarding who did what to whom and when they did it."[37]

There were many indications observed by UNTSO in the months prior to June 1982 that the next time Israel invaded, it intended to finish the job. It was, as we used to say, a "BFO"—that is, a "blinding flash of the obvious." There was a big showdown ahead in the "Wild West" of southern Lebanon. Israel was waiting for the right moment to launch it.

The PLO Prepares for War

Nor had the PLO been idle. Since 1978 they had been busy rebuilding their strength. Indeed, by 1982 they numbered 15,000 fighters.[38] Though Israeli forces worked to attrit the PLO's strength with routine airstrikes and artillery bombardments, neither effort was sufficient to dampen the PLO's desire to attack Israeli forces, towns, and villages. Despite the fact that much of their equipment was aging and less formidable than the IDF's, they were seasoned fighters who had shown in 1978 that they could blunt the Israeli armored forces attempting to take the town of Tyre. Moreover, they were innovative, using techniques to mass their antitank direct fire systems on individual Israeli tanks to stop them dead in their tracks. They also had become quite expert in launching indirect fire from both rocket and artillery systems with deadly effect.

Following the 1978 Operation Litani, the PLO was working hard to acquire even better artillery systems to reach deeper into Israel. In 1981, they inked arms agreements with North Korea and Hungary for T-34 tanks and more BM-21 Katyusha rocket launchers.[39] Moreover, the PLO's army (PLA) had perfected its communications ability while moving toward operations that resembled those of a "coordinated military force," as opposed to the "syncretic tribal approach" of a gaggle of PLA-allied armed elements.[40]

COMDT Des Travers (Irish Army) recalls that the warning signs were clear, particularly among the armed elements in southern Lebanon, that the PLO was building its combat power for a renewed Israeli invasion. Specifically, Lebanese Army Intelligence was aware of a major rearming of the PLO in the Tyre Pocket and shared that information directly with Travers as early as November of 1980: "The growing belligerence and bravado of some of the 'actors' in the South were some of the indications. But for me the warning given me by the Lebanese G2 [Army intelligence] via Major Ali al-Khansa was the clincher when he reported to me that a large gun, a Soviet arty piece, 130mm caliber, had been hauled down south of the Litani and was in place in a site east of Tyre. When I reported this to UNIFIL operations they too saw it for what it was."[41]

While a report of one gun may appear minor, a Soviet 130 mm field gun that could achieve a range of 27.5 kilometers (17 miles) posed a significant threat to Israel. But the PLO had 48 130 mm and 155 mm long-range cannons by then. With those, plus 80 Katyusha rocket launchers, the PLO was able to range targets inside Israel, threatening towns and villages with significant firepower.[42] And if Travers was now aware of this from a Lebanese intelligence officer who had confided in him—who likely was not a friend of the PLO—it was certain that the Israelis would also be aware through their superior intelligence infrastructure and collection capability. UNIFIL was also cognizant of this rearming in late 1980. It could be of no surprise to them that soon the Israelis would strike at any PLO buildup this powerful. The heightened violence in July 1981 presaged Israel's willingness to target and destroy PLO capabilities in southern Lebanon in the months ahead.

Facing the Inevitable

Beyond the potential for renewed violence in southern Lebanon, the UN did seem to understand in its 11 December 1981 report that fulfilling the UNIFIL mandate was impossible as long as the parties to the conflict were not cooperative:

However, this situation in southern Lebanon remains precarious and fundamentally unstable. As stated in my annual report on the work of the Organization, "No cease-fire, peacekeeping operations, or other expedient for containing the conflict can, in the end, prevent new outbursts and violence as long as the basic elements of the problem are not tackled in negotiations involving all the parties concerned." As regards the mandate of UNIFIL, the difficulties which the Force has experienced since its inception have continued to obstruct the full implementation of the task allotted to it by the Security Council. The full co-operation of all parties which such implementation would require is, regrettably, still not forthcoming, although the value of the actual duties performed by UNIFIL is not in question.[43]

That same report correctly concluded with this rather obvious fact, one not only recognized by the UN but also clearly appreciated by the parties to the conflict, who were busy brushing UNIFIL aside as they made plans for yet another confrontation: "The inescapable fact remains, however, that the mandate of UNIFIL in relation to the remainder of its area of operations now controlled by the de facto forces still remains to be filled."[44]

No truer account could have been rendered. Put another way, certainly less diplomatically, UNIFIL simply could not fulfill its mandate in the face of noncooperative parties to the conflict. This was in stark contrast to UNDOF on the Golan Heights, which had the support of both Israel and Syria. In truth "the value of the actual duties performed by UNIFIL" may have been just as CPT Lenny Supko (USMC) noted in 1980. UNIFIL was "somewhat more [than] an impediment to the separated parties."[45] MAJ Jay Sollis (USMC) was less charitable. "We were a speed bump at best, a petty annoyance at worst. The Israelis were not the least bit concerned about the presence of UNTSO or UNIFIL."[46] To be sure, that "speed bump," as in 1978, would be quickly overcome or bypassed by determined Israeli forces the next time they decided to conduct an invasion.

As 1982 approached, the UN's Sir Brian Urquhart seemed aware that war could break out at any time, which is why he sped to the Middle East in February of 1982 to conduct another round of shuttle diplomacy. He reported his findings concerning the attitudes of both Israel and the PLO: "While all concerned indicated their wish that the present cease-fire be maintained, it is apparent that serious impediments remain in the way of UNIFIL fulfilling the objectives set out for it by the Council. This applies, in particular, to the further deployment of UNIFIL in its entire area of operations up to the international border."[47]

The expressions of hoped-for peace notwithstanding, UNIFIL was at a distinct disadvantage to deter further combat because it simply did not control all of southern Lebanon—specifically the Tyre Pocket and the IDF/DFF enclave—where war preparations were being actively made by the contending sides. The UN's leadership at the time began to awaken to the reality that UNIFIL's force structure was less than what was needed to keep the peace. However, it would take much more than additional forces to fix UNIFIL's fundamental problem, namely its ambiguous mandate and lack of territorial authority.

The UN's efforts in the winter of 1982 should have focused on clear public warnings that war was imminent. Many UNMOs knew it was coming. In sounding the alarm loudly, the UN might have ramped up international concern and pressure by the US and others to openly insist that both Israel and the PLO deescalate. Instead, the UN seemed more interested in bolstering UNIFIL's force structure. But without insisting that the hostile forces hand over the territory they held to UNIFIL, adding more UN troops would have been pointless. It would have made a slightly larger speed bump. Indeed, writing about force structure in the winter of 1981 as Israel and the PLO were busy preparing for war amounted to rearranging the deck chairs on a foundering ship. Yet, the UN secretary-general did so.

> In regard to the latter consideration, it is the strong recommendation of the Force Commander, and also the wish of the Lebanese Government that the ceiling for UNIFIL troops should be increased by no less than 1,000 to reinforce present operations as well as to make further deployment possible in a manner that conforms with resolution 425 (1978). As was indicated in my predecessor's report to the Security Council (S/14789), there is no question that UNIFIL, in its present strength, is stretched to the limit and, indeed, seriously over-strained. In these circumstances and for the reasons that the Force Commander has given, I fully support the recommendation for an increase by 1,000 of the troops [sic] strength of UNIFIL and hope that the Council will concur in that measure.[48]

Remarkably, while the secretary-general proceeded to seek more soldiers, nothing was specified concerning how those forces would be used to supplant the areas occupied by the PLO and the DFF, nor was there any intent to use them that way. To be sure, this report contained a feeble reference to the original resolution stating the UNIFIL mandate. But more troops would do nothing to address the underlying need to expel combatant forces from southern Lebanon unless the UN demanded such from both Israel and the Palestinians. More troops—to use a biblical illustration of the ancient Levant—amounted to putting new wine in an old wineskin with the hope it would not burst. Whether or not that parable would have made sense to the UN's leadership at the time, it should have been clear to them that adding more troops to a defective structure would not work. If the DFF and the PLO could not be dislodged from areas they held before UNIFIL arrived, no troop strength increases to support UNIFIL's flawed tactical stratagem would succeed. Unless the UN Security Council was willing to forcibly push the IDF, DFF, PLO, and armed elements out of southern Lebanon—something they had no stomach to do—then nothing would change. Israel knew it. And that is why the IDF was very busy in 1981 and early 1982 preparing to do that which the UN had no willingness to do, push the PLO out.

War

With the arrival of April 1982, I had returned to Washington, D.C., to assume new duties in the Defense Intelligence Agency's Directorate for Current Intelligence for the Middle East as an intelligence analyst focused on the Iran-Iraq War. That conflict was 6,200 miles from where I sat in the Pentagon. But the second war I was sure would break out, based on the intelligence I was reading, was 600 miles to the west of Iraq, in southern Lebanon. I left behind Yanks I had served with to deal with the deteriorating situation. I had little hope that they could keep the lid on violence there. UNIFIL surely was unable to do so with their limited forces and tactical misposition. And UNTSO had only the ability to report what was occurring on the ground. MAJ Kevin Kennedy (USMC) had for some months served as the OGL operations officer. He was very familiar with how violence could quickly materialize in southern Lebanon. Indeed, on 9 July 1981, the day he arrived, "the storm" erupted in southern Lebanon. After several months orchestrating OGL operations, he took over Team X-Ray from MAJ Herman Kafura (USA) and could see with his own eyes the preparations for war. In fact, the day Kennedy arrived in Nahariya, the town was being shelled by the PLO.

Kennedy could tell that "Things were heating up" in early 1982. In fact, there was some speculation that as early as April 1982 the Israelis were planning to invade southern Lebanon, but according to Kennedy that plan was "called off" in part because of US pressure.[49] In point of fact, on 25 April 1982 the UN Security Council was informed that the situation remained "extremely volatile" and that "the basic underlying tensions" were persistent.[50] "While the arrangements for the cease-fire in southern Lebanon, which came into effect in July 1981, have generally held, unresolved tensions have led to the very real danger of widespread hostilities being sparked in the area. It is for this reason, in particular, that I learnt with deep concern of the Israeli airstrikes into Lebanon on 21 April 1982."[51]

The cease-fire was an illusion. In fact, on 21 April 1982 an Israeli officer was killed by a land mine in southern Lebanon near the town of Tayibe south of Beaufort Castle while visiting a DFF gun emplacement in the central sector of UNIFIL. The Israelis retaliated by attacking the Palestinian-controlled coastal town of Damour south of Beirut, killing 23 people. On 22 April, the UN secretary-general issued a statement that "urgently demanded an end to all armed attacks and violations which jeopardized the cease-fire," noting again that the situation remained "extremely volatile."[52]

By late April and into May, tensions were escalating quickly and the leadership of both UNTSO and UNIFIL were very concerned:

IDF activities in the UNIFIL area of operations continue unabated. UNIFIL and UNTSO raised the matter repeatedly with the Israeli authorities. . . . The presence of IDF personnel and equipment inside the enclave remained at a high level. Further work was undertaken by [the] IDF to strengthen observation posts and gun positions. Increased training activity was observed in the vicinity of Khiam and, recently, also in the area around Yarin. [The] IDF increased its presence and activities in the eastern sector of the enclave, particularly in the Kafer Choube and Chebaa areas, and IDF patrols were frequently sighted along the perimeters of the Dutch and Ghanaian battalion areas of deployment.[53]

In every sector of UNIFIL, the IDF was very busy making final preparations to invade Lebanon and strike at the heart of their adversary, the PLO. Their projected avenues of approach would be similar to the ones the IDF took in 1978. It would be a repeat of Operation Litani, except this time it would bear a more sweeping appellation, Operation Peace for Galilee, with bolder combat objectives. While the invasion was a forgone conclusion, all it needed was the right provocation.

On 3 June 1982, assassins dispatched from Iraq attempted to take the life of the Israeli ambassador to the UK, Shlomo Argov. He was shot and gravely wounded. The assailants were thought to be from the Abu Nidal militant organization, a Palestinian splinter group harbored by Iraq but estranged from the PLO. To be sure, the PLO was engaged in the same sort of terror. Previously, on 4 April 1981, the PLO orchestrated the assassination of a 43-year-old Israeli diplomat, Yacov Barsimantov, who was serving as the second secretary in charge of political affairs in Paris. Nevertheless, the London attack on Argov was more likely committed by Iraqi-ally Abu Nidal in retaliation for Israel's air attack of Iraq's Osirak nuclear reactor on 7 June 1981. The likelihood that Iraqi dictator Saddam Hussein was seeking revenge was readily panned by Israel's leadership, who placed blame squarely on the PLO, using the Abu Nidal assassination attempt against Argov as a *casus belli* to undertake a war with Arafat.[54] In fact, Israeli defense minister Ariel Sharon admitted as much, noting in his memoirs that the Argov assassination attempt was "merely the spark that lit the fuse."[55] In truth, Arafat appeared—despite his own participation in the flare-up of artillery exchanges in the spring of 1982—to support the American-brokered cease-fire that followed "the storm" the previous summer. But in Israel's estimation, Arafat was simply using that cease-fire to forestall an IDF invasion so he could build up his military strength for a later confrontation. Moreover, Israel—and Sharon in particular—chafed under the notion that the US-brokered cease-fire that followed "the storm" did *not* address acts taken by PLO sympathizers against Israeli interests *outside* of southern Lebanon.[56] That condition was clearly established on 24 July 1981 when Israel accepted the cease-fire proposal negotiated by US ambassador Philip Habib. In fact, when Sharon visited US secretary of state Al Haig in Washington on 25 May 1982 to brief him on a prospective invasion plan should one occur, Habib reiterated that "Terrorist attacks against Israel and Jews in Europe are not included in the ceasefire agreement."[57] Even Israeli officials at the time appeared to acknowledge that the cease-fire was related to the PLO in Lebanon, not throughout the world: "If they shoot even one bullet at an Israeli settlement in the north or make preparations to do that," an Israeli official said, "Israel will always do what she has to do to defend herself."[58]

Yet despite the Habib limitation—restated to Sharon in Haig's office—Haig himself seemed to introduce a wider retaliation framework. In the course of the briefing, Haig may have—unwittingly and awkwardly—offered Israel tacit approval for future actions against the PLO in southern Lebanon, even if such a retaliation was based on an incident beyond Lebanese borders. Haig stated that any Israeli attack of terrorist strongholds in southern Lebanon must (1) have a nexus to "a perceivable and recognized international provocation," (2) be "proportional to that provocation," and (3) be "perceived to be" so.[59] Haig's "proportional" comment notwithstanding, Sharon must have been delighted with the phrase "recognized international provocation," which the 3 June attempted assassination would satisfy. For those of us—particularly US military observers in UNTSO—who were very familiar with how parties to the conflict in southern Lebanon could twist and manipulate *any* statement in *any* fashion to justify their actions, the Haig proviso would have provided sufficient leeway to Israel to justify the invasion.[60] As Supko dryly remarked of the parties to the conflict, "You have to understand one important truth. Everybody lies."[61] And Haig's imprecise statement made prevarication a bit easier for Sharon, who was eager to invade southern Lebanon in June 1982, even if the specified *casus belli* was suspect in nature, and indeed an exaggeration of the facts related to the provocation. As the inevitability of the invasion grew, Israel decided to ignore that Habib-specified limitation for the broader context offered by Haig, as well as the fact that Abu Nidal—now a pariah within the PLO—was acting apart from the PLO's operations in southern Lebanon.

Despite the PLO's denial that they were behind the assassination attempt in London, the die was cast, and Israel was determined to rid southern Lebanon of its enemies. Kennedy knew what was coming. "When Ambassador Argov was shot on 3 June in London, one knew immediately there would be war."[62]

Early on 6 June, that war commenced, having been preceded by Israeli air strikes on PLO targets in Beirut and artillery barrages in southern Lebanon on 4 and 5 June. MAJ Jay Sollis (USMC) recalls that "as soon as the Katyusha rockets started bracketing Nahariya," many people and some UMNOs elected to evacuate the town.[63] Yet on Monday, 7 June, several remaining UNMOs headed to the border to enter southern Lebanon, only to discover that there was a very long line of IDF military vehicles stacked up to head north. The IDF soldiers manning the gates in and out of Lebanon would not let anyone cross except LTC Al Baker (USA), who was the chief of OGL. Others wanted to cross, but the

Israelis were unrelenting. In time most UNMOs drifted back to Naha-riya, except Kennedy and Sollis, who were determined to enter Lebanon. Predictably, when they attempted to cross though the northbound gate, the IDF rebuffed them, saying, "no one can enter southern Lebanon." They were undeterred and took advantage of the mass pandemonium. Like the fictitious Indiana Jones slyly slipping through a hostile crowd, Kennedy and Sollis began walking toward the border gate, paralleling and closely hugging an IDF cargo truck to mask their presence from the gate guards. After surreptitiously entering Lebanon, they immediately doubled back to the southbound gate, where vehicles were returning to Israel, and asked to cross back. There, to their scheming delight, they were again refused entry by IDF guards, who pronounced that "no one can enter into Israel now." Successfully validated to remain in Lebanon by the same IDF who moments earlier had refused their passage north-ward, the marines thanked the guard and headed north on foot to OGL's headquarters in Naqoura to observe a war neither Yank intended to miss. And when they eventually arrived outside of Tyre that day, they found themselves situated near an IDF 155 mm field artillery battery com-manded by an expatriate from Brooklyn, New York. There, the two US marines observed an American artilleryman shell the town from the heights above, just as Fallon and his Finnish comrade had watched a sim-ilar battle four years earlier.

Meanwhile, the UN's reports detailed in a pithy fashion what all of us knew would be the case if the IDF threw its full might at the PLO, including the impotence of UNIFIL in forestalling such an invasion: "In accordance with instructions, UNIFIL troops attempted to prevent the entry and advance of the Israeli forces. . . . Despite the efforts of UNIFIL, from the start of the invasion, the overwhelming strength and weight of the Israeli forces precluded the possibility of stopping them, and UNIFIL positions in the line of the invasion were thus overrun or by-passed. . . . By 7 June, Israeli forces, comprising more than two mechanized divisions, with full air and naval support, had reached positions north of the UNI-FIL area of deployment."[64]

Israel had decided enough was enough. The solution was not only to push the PLO out of Lebanon but to change the character of the entire Lebanese government, to include assisting the rise of the Christian-led Lebanese party of Bachir Pierre Gemayel.[65] Doing so, they reasoned, would also drive Syria out of the beleaguered country's Beqaa Valley since Christian Lebanese wanted them gone. It would not prove to be an easy task.

When the UN Security Council voted for a resolution on 8 June that would have focused responsibility on Israel, the US vetoed it, not wanting to put their ally in an impossible political situation with language that US ambassador to the UN Jeane Kirkpatrick called "not sufficiently balanced to accomplish the objectives of ending the cycle of violence and establishing the conditions for a just and lasting peace in Lebanon."[66] Even if the resolution had passed, as two previous ones had that called for an end to the conflict, the IDF was well on its way to doing what it believed had to be done to push the PLO out of Lebanon for good. The IDF's six-and-a-half division force of 75,000 to 78,000 soldiers, 1,240 tanks, and 1,520 armored personnel carriers advanced on three main avenues of approach to isolate Beirut and present a *fait accompli* to the PLO.[67] Whereas the IDF's route of march into southern Lebanon in 1978 had been along the same general avenues of approach, four years later this new effort was three times larger and had no intent to stop at the Litani River. This invasion was designed to end the problem of the PLO in Lebanon and finish the job. As far as the IDF was concerned, half measures were untenable.

Many US UNMOs saw this invasion as a tragic inevitability, the result of an intractable conflict that resisted peace at every turn, despite a well-intended peace process that was so fecklessly designed and implemented by the UN that it could not succeed. We Yanks in blue berets tried our best to make that peace work in our service to UNTSO and its role in supporting UNIFIL. But we all knew that, despite our best efforts, it was a Sisyphean task. In this case, there was no Greek mythology at work, just the reality of the UNTSO and UNIFIL pushing a peacekeeping boulder uphill in southern Lebanon. It was a boulder that would eventually roll backward and over both peacekeeping organizations just as the IDF rolled north on 6 June 1982.

Only eight months after Anwar Sadat was assassinated by anti-peace terrorists, Lebanon was subjected to the worst violence it had witnessed since its civil war began in 1975. Unlike the celebration of Sadat's murder enjoyed by Arabs across the Levant who opposed the Camp David Accords, the death and destruction in southern Lebanon that exploded in June 1982 was not greeted with joyous songs and parades. Just death and agony, a sad constant in the Middle East. There was no peace, despite the best efforts of my colleagues in UNTSO and UNIFIL. And the consequences were significant.

11

Peace for No One

In summary, the 1982 war in southern Lebanon was not a discrete event, but rather like untreated heart disease, a series of predictably worsening events. Those of us in UNTSO saw it coming like a slow-moving train wreck. Nonetheless, we fulfilled our mandate to observe and report in the hope that the UN and the international community would encourage Israel and the PLO to cease their preparations for war in a land that had seen far too much of it. It was an empty hope. Yet the UN was there to encourage peace: UNTSO to observe and report violations, and UNIFIL ostensibly to enforce cease-fires. UNTSO observed. UNIFIL tried to enforce without teeth, a shortcoming that lies at the feet of the UN itself. The Security Council failed to formulate an effective mandate that would have empowered UNIFIL to successfully pacify southern Lebanon. To make matters worse, the UN undercut UNIFIL's mandate by ceding to the parties of the conflict huge swaths of territory central to implementing its peacekeeping mission. In essence, the UN surrendered to violence and threats from combatants in 1978, and in doing so set the conditions for mission failure in 1982.

Underlying that significant deficiency was the UN's foundational failure to understand that the parties to the conflict had no genuine interest in submitting to peace. The UN seemed more preoccupied with lofty UN resolutions calling for peace, rather than assembling a workable peacekeeping regimen. Meanwhile the US—a powerful influence in the region—was distracted with how the 1978 invasion might threaten the Camp David negotiation, doing little to effectively press all sides to fully cooperate with the UNIFIL mission.[1] For the intransigent combatants, peace was not the goal. National liberation on one side and national preservation on the other were the existential motivations of the PLO and the Israelis, respectively. The conflict between these mortal enemies was not ripe for reconciliation because the parties believed there was much remaining to fight over. Until the parties of any conflict see it in their best

208

interest to make peace, none is possible. The pursuit of peace cannot be compelled unless the agents—in this case the UN and primarily the US—are able to insist on a workable solution, including risking blood and treasure in the process. The UN in 1978—when UNIFIL was conceived—had no such will or intention. Nor was a post-Vietnam America eager to do so. Inevitably the UN's capacity, articulated or not, was moral suasion, not peace enforcement. Besides, peace between bitter rivals is rarely achieved solely through moralistic browbeating. There must be something in the mix that compels compliance. A more forceful posture and capability would have required genuine participation and cooperation by the parties to the conflict, including the real possibility that the international community—and the US in particular—would impose significant costs and sanctions against noncompliance. Neither costs nor sanctions for violations was present in 1978 or afterward.

 · Moreover, the conditions for peace in southern Lebanon were undermined by the weakened state of Lebanese governmental infrastructure and civil disorder, which had become a casualty of a civil war that began in 1975. One of the three key objectives of the UNIFIL mandate was to "assist the Government of Lebanon in ensuring the return of its effective authority in the area."[2] Indeed, even if sanctions were present to deal with recalcitrant combatants, there was no police or judiciary in southern Lebanon to punish bad actors—either military or civilian—among the civilian population. Anarchy ruled there. The Israeli invasion only made matters worse, tearing Lebanon asunder. As the war progressed through 1982 and into 1983, more pain and violence, some indescribably excruciating, even reached into the living rooms of Americans as the situation in Lebanon sank to new lows.

For those of us in UNTSO, including Americans, watching peace fail was hard to swallow, particularly as we recalled the war-weary faces of Lebanese men, women, and children etched into our memories. We had put our lives on the line every day in southern Lebanon to bring about peace. American officers had made our best effort to professionalize UNTSO with the military discipline we knew was necessary, which many of our like-minded international comrades in the organization already possessed. As we all went about our duties supporting UNIFIL, we had hoped that our efforts would succeed. But in our hearts and minds we knew it would not be sufficient to stop an invasion like that of 1982. We were unarmed and UNIFIL was simply not equipped to do the task it had been given. As the war played out, it was obvious that the UN effort in peacekeeping in southern Lebanon had fallen short. So too would Operation Peace for Galilee fall short. In fact, that operation could have been alternatively titled Operation Peace for No One.

The Consequences for Israel, the PLO, Lebanon, and Others

Wars have profoundly far-reaching consequences. This one had many for Israel, the PLO, Lebanon, and others. Israel's sweeping invasion in 1982 set in motion events that would reach far beyond its tactical, operational, and strategic objectives. Likewise, the PLO—which used the sovereign state of Lebanon as its primary launch point for attacking Israel—would pay a steep price for its unrelenting violence toward the Jewish state. While significantly less powerful than Israel, the PLO was equally culpable for death and destruction in southern Lebanon. Indeed, its proclivity to violence was the very behavior that caused its expulsion from both Jordan and Syria following the 1970 Black September conflict, when the PLO fled to Lebanon.

Sadly, there were profound consequences for the Lebanese people also, not only in the south, but in Beirut and across the footprint of Operation Peace for Galilee. The International Red Cross and Lebanese police estimated that the invasion led to 14,000 civilian deaths and 20,000 injuries.[3] Indeed, a major casualty was the very idea of peacekeeping as a strategy for places like Lebanon that had become so banefully violent over the years. Once a thriving, free-enterprise society that had embraced a confessional-style ruling arrangement among Christians, Sunni Muslims, and Shi'a Muslims, Lebanon had descended into a sanguinary quagmire that made life a living hell for its people. As the violence expanded across Lebanon, there also would be consequences for America, Great Britain, France, Italy, and others who were drawn into a multinational peacekeeping arrangement in the greater Beirut area. There the Multinational Force (MNF) would attempt to impose a peace that the UN was never able to effect prior to the 1982 Israeli invasion. Unfortunately, no peace resulted from the MNF either. More death and destruction for Western personnel and interests ensued in what amounted to an expansion of the Lebanese Civil War. Nor was the UN itself left unscathed from the war, one that would both claim UN lives and eventually contribute to a reduced role for the US as peacekeepers in the Levant in the years that followed. As the war played out, the consequences, unintended and otherwise, became evident as Lebanon was set ablaze by the unrelenting hostilities between Israel and the PLO. Consider how events unfolded and their consequences for peace.

Israel, Syria, and the PLO

Israel launched its 1982 offensive with a primary goal in mind: to drive the PLO out of Lebanon for good. Pursuant to that, Israel also wanted to install the Christian-led Lebanese government of Bachir Pierre Gemayel. The Israelis believed such a regime would be inclined to make peace with Israel. If that worked, not only would Israel have another neighbor seeking peace, but one that would be willing to press Syria to end its occupation of Lebanon at the earliest possible opportunity.[4] It was a perfect plan. It failed miserably. Israel soon found itself involved in a pitched conflict—indeed, a civil war. To be sure, Israel had early tactical and operational successes on the battlefield. In the initial phases of the invasion, the IDF and IAF were crushing the PLO while containing the forces of Syrian dictator Hafez al-Assad in the Beqaa Valley and blunting his army's ability to offer significant military support to PLO forces.

The IDF quickly advanced north on three major axes of approach (see map 11.1). Israel's plan was quite well-conceived and focused on (1) rapidly pushing the PLO out of southern Lebanon, (2) clearing PLO strongholds and camps out of the south, (3) isolating and cutting off retreating PLO fighters as they fled north to Beirut, and (4) blocking and deterring the Syrians from engaging IDF forces as they conducted their operation. In the east, the IDF pushed northward to blunt the Syrian Army, which had occupied Lebanon's Beqaa Valley since 1976 as part of the so-called Arab Defense Force that intervened after Lebanon's civil war began. The IDF plan was to stop the Syrians from reinforcing their troops in the Beqaa Valley or intervening in the IDF's assault northward on the coastal road. Further west, in the central sector, the IDF sent two divisions oriented on the PLO's Beaufort Castle stronghold. They were to seize it and prevent Arafat's forces from interfering with the IDF's advance in that sector. Once the castle was secured, those divisions would split, one advancing toward Jezzine to block the Syrians in the Beqaa Valley and obstruct their potential move westward, and the other to seize the important crossroads at Nabatieh and then continue onward to link up with advancing forces on the coastal road. In the west, the IDF advance up the coastal road to Tyre was designed to destroy PLO camps in the region and then continue northward to Sidon and Damour to link up

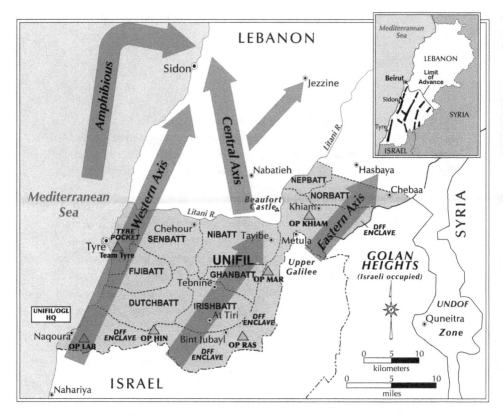

Map 11.1. Israeli Operation Peace for Galilee Invasion: Initial Axes of Approach and Ultimate Limits of Advance (Insert Box), 6 June–23 August 1982

with an amphibious assault to cut off PLO fighters fleeing toward Beirut.

By 9 June, the IAF had scored major air-to-air victories and neutralized the Syrian Air Force's ability to support Assad's ground troops. Simultaneously, the IDF was just six miles south of Beirut and in reach of isolating the PLO fighters who were attempting to flee to the city. By 22 June, the IDF and the IAF were effectively battling Syrian forces, who were trying to reach Beirut along the east-west Damascus–Beirut highway spanning the Beqaa Valley. The Syrians were rebuffed, and the next day they were in full retreat eastward. And by 25 June, the IDF had pushed Assad's beaten army back into the Beqaa, where the Syrians were unable to stop Israel's encirclement of Beirut.[5]

An IDF siege of Beirut would continue throughout July and into August. Finally, the situation for the PLO became so bad that US special envoy Ambassador Philip Habib, who was busily negotiating a cease-fire between Israel and the PLO, personally gave Chairman Yasser Arafat an ultimatum that he and his forces had 48 hours to leave Beirut.[6] Arafat acquiesced on 12 August. Between 21 and 31 August, he and 8,144 of his PLO fighters evacuated Lebanon by sea, with others departing by ground to Syria.[7] His troops would be disbursed across the Middle East, to Iraq, Jordan, Sudan, Syria, and North and South Yemen, while Arafat would set sail via Greece to establish an exile regime in Tunisia.[8] That evacuation would be overseen by an international peacekeeping force established on 25 August 1982 and composed of soldiers from the US, Great Britain, France, and Italy. That Multinational Force I in Lebanon (MNF-I) was the inspiration of the administration of US president Ronald Reagan and negotiated by Ambassador Habib. After landing in Beirut, MNF-I took up positions to effect the safe departure of the PLO and its troops from Lebanon. That evacuation occurred smoothly, and by 10 September MNF-I withdrew, having secured and supervised the PLO's successful withdrawal. Unfortunately, within a week following MNF-I's departure, mayhem erupted.

Despite the PLO's departure from Lebanon, the civil war there raged on between Muslim and Christian factions and their respective armies and militias. Moreover, Syria—while having suffered major losses on the ground and in the air by the IDF and IAF—was still rooted in Lebanon and able to influence activities in the greater Beirut area, where battles continued unabated among the Lebanese. To be sure, Israeli tactical and operational successes early in the conflict achieved a key objective in defeating the PLO. But Syria retained a major stake in the outcome of the war, a war that appeared to be headed toward an unambiguous victory for Israel. Consequently, in September 1982 Syria attempted to swing the politico-military pendulum in its direction by disrupting Israeli plans to firmly establish Maronite Christian rule in Lebanon. Assad was intent on maintaining his presence in Lebanon and—unlike the PLO—had no plans to evacuate the country. A hostile Christian-run Lebanon to his west was untenable for him. Assad had a major interest in the Trans-Arabian Oil Pipeline crossing Syria that terminated on the Lebanese coast near Zahrani, where he had stationed an intelligence unit to closely monitor events there.[9] Additionally, Assad's dominance in the Beqaa Valley served to guard the interests of Shi'a Muslims in Lebanon, who regarded his Alawite regime—a branch of Shi'ism—as a check on Lebanese Christians. Indeed, Syria's presence in Lebanon enabled Assad to keep a watchful eye on Sunni Muslims who might be sympathetic to their Muslim Brother-hood cousins whom the Syrian dictator was battling at home. Assad had many reasons to stay put in Lebanon and was not about to walk away and leave the country under the significant and newfound influence of Israel. Soon Assad would take deadly action to secure his interests in Leb-anon, a neighbor he intended to retain as a client state.

By 1982, the confessional political arrangement of the Lebanese gov-ernment was in a state of near failure, which Israel was happy to exploit by supporting the fortunes of a Christian-led government there. Indeed, Maronite Christian and Phalangist Bachir Pierre Gemayel was elected president on 23 August, even as the PLO was taking heavy losses and was largely surrounded by the IDF in Beirut.[10] Gemayel's election was warmly greeted by Israel, who believed he would quickly sign a peace treaty with Prime Minister Menachem Begin's government and immediately press the Syrians to leave the country, just as the PLO had recently been forced out. Syria would have none of that, and as a result orchestrated Gemayel's murder.[11] On 14 September, Gemayel and 26 other Christian Phalangist leaders were killed in a bomb attack by Habib Tanios Shartouni, a mem-ber of the anti-Phalangist Syrian Social Nationalist Party. Ironically, Shartouni was also a Maronite Christian, but he was profoundly opposed to any peace with Israel.[12] Israeli plans to install Gemayel's regime col-lapsed. And with that, their advance on Beirut dragged them deeper into a quagmire that became very unpopular in Israel, damaging Begin's ruling coalition while heightening the prominence of his left-wing opponents, particularly the Peace Now movement that at the time had assembled 400,000 antiwar protesters in Tel Aviv.[13]

Within 48 hours of Gemayel's assassination the situation in Lebanon worsened profoundly. Maronite Christians immediately—and wrongly—blamed Gemayel's assassination on Palestinian militants. The Maronite response was brutal. From 16 to 18 September, their militiamen—while Israel's Defense Minister Ariel Sharon and Israeli forces tacitly looked on—orchestrated massacres in the Sabra and Shatila Palestinian refugee camps in southwest Beirut.[14] The numbers of the slaughtered were in the hundreds, possibly 800 or more, most of whom were Palestinians and Lebanese Shi'ites.[15] The international outcry was deafening. Israel quickly disavowed any connection with the bloody atrocities. But those denials were not credible given Israel's close association with not only Christian militias angry over the assassination of Gemayel but also their prominent partnership with Saad Haddad's Christian militia DFF in the south, who despised the Palestinian presence in his country. The stench of rotting bodies in the Lebanese summer heat of 1982 was politically malodorous for Israel, whether or not blaming them for the massacres was completely justified. Certainly, there was enough antipathy between Christian Lebanese and Palestinians to provoke such a massacre. After all, the Palestinians had become a "state within a state," and that was deeply resented by the Christian Lebanese. Guilt by association was an easy conclusion, given Israel's ties with the Christian militia and their well-known goal to see a Christian government in Lebanon. The consequences of this war for Lebanon were awful. But in the end, the consequences for the Palestinians were also devastating. The Israeli invasion was a complete disaster for them. Their forces were defeated, their losses excessive—by some estimates 2,400 killed—and their leader Arafat was "on the lam," having to evacuate his "government" to Tunisia and disperse his troops across the Middle East.[16] Only MNF-I saved him, their sole mission at the time.

The Unintended Consequences for the US

With the assassination of Gemayel, the situation in Lebanon rapidly spiraled downward to the nadir of bloodshed at Sabra and Shatila. Feeling some responsibility following the hasty evacuation of MNF-I, the US, France, Italy, and later a contingent from the UK returned to Beirut in the form of MNF-II to assist the Lebanese government in restoring its authority in the country. Unfortunately, by then the government in Lebanon was in disarray and largely led by Christian factions, a situation unacceptable to the Muslim population.[17] As such, MNF-II from its reconstitution was viewed as taking sides in the Lebanese Civil War since Muslim factions were still contending with their Christian opponents over who would rule Lebanon. Sadly, the MNF-II mission was hauntingly similar to that of UNIFIL's in 1978. The MNF-II mission statement was very general and depended on the cooperation of the Lebanese government and other parties to the conflict. President Ronald Reagan's administration articulated it on 23 September 1982, a week before the US contingent to MNF-II arrived in Beirut: "The MNF (multinational force) is to provide an interposition force at agreed locations and thereby provide the MNF presence requested by the Government of Lebanon to assist it and Lebanon's armed forces in the Beirut area. This presence will facilitate the restoration of Lebanese Government sovereignty and authority over the Beirut area and thereby further its efforts to assure the safety of persons in the area and to bring to an end the violence which has tragically recurred."[18]

Unfortunately, the Lebanese government was less capable than it had been in March of 1978 when UNIFIL was arriving to take up its duties. By 1982, its new president had been killed, violence was rampant, contenting militias were engaged in battle, and Syria was biding its time to fill an eventual power vacuum that they knew would occur once the West waxed weary of its new—and, as it turned out, deadly—intervention in the "Wild West" known as Lebanon. Indeed, despite the lofty goals of the MNF-II as announced by the Reagan administration, there was no effectual Lebanese government to restore that would actually govern, much less provide security or end the violence over the long term.

Nonetheless, for a short duration after MNF-II returned in September 1982—with US marines as the dominant force—a semblance of calm emerged in Beirut. Streets were cleaned up, utilities returned to operation, and the government began to function as one would expect, even taking control of imports and exports from militia groups who had managed the port of Beirut with the malevolent skill of a mafia crime syndicate.[19] Moreover, the IDF had withdrawn to the southeastern portion of Beirut and occupied positions in and around the Shouf Mountains overlooking the city to impose a calm of sorts on warring Christian and Muslim factions in the hill country. That calm would not last.

On 18 April 1983, the US embassy in Beirut was bombed by Lebanese Shi'a militia supported by Iran, likely involving radical Hezbollah terrorists. Among the 63 people killed were Robert Ames, a senior Central Intelligence Agency analyst, and six others assigned to the CIA office in Lebanon, including Corporal Robert McMaugh (USMC), who was standing guard in front of the embassy.[20] Negotiations, largely facilitated by the US, picked up pace following that bombing. They resulted in the May 17 Agreement between Israel and Lebanon. It called for terminating the state of war between Israel and Lebanon that had persisted since 1948.[21] It provided for a staged withdrawal of Israeli forces conditioned on the imposition of a Christian-manned Lebanese Army "security zone" in southern Lebanon along the border with Israel. In other words, Israel would withdraw but continue to have a presence in southern Lebanon, just as it had with the DFF's occupation of territory intended for UNIFIL to control in accordance with the UN mandate. Syria and the PLO were excluded from the May 17 Agreement negotiations and consequently openly opposed the effort. In short order, Syria began rearming its Shi'a militia allies in the Shouf Mountains near Beirut. As a result, the violence escalated, even as Israel looked to the day it could leave Beirut behind to other warring armed elements.[22]

Throughout the summer of 1983, the civil war between Christian and Muslim factions raged on. Yet, consistent with the terms of the May 17 Agreement, the IDF began its withdrawal on 28 August from positions in the Shouf region to locations along the Alawi River south of Beirut and north of Sidon. Unfortunately, the IDF did so on its own schedule without coordination with either the Lebanese Army or MNF-II.[23] This left both Lebanese warring factions rushing to fill the void in the high ground overlooking Beirut and the MNF-II deployed below. More battles occurred, and in due time the MNF, including the US marines occupying positions in and near the Beirut International Airport (BIA) terminal, came under attack from Shi'a militia who regarded them as helping the Christian factions. To be sure, the Christian factions at the time were largely composed of what had been the Lebanese government and its army. And problematically, MNF-II's mandate stated specifically that it would "assist it [the Lebanese government] and Lebanon's armed forces."[24] Likewise, the US Marine Corps reflected that aspiration in its own mission statement: "to establish an environment which will permit the Lebanese Armed Forces to carry out their responsibilities in the Beirut area."[25] Muslims quickly interpreted that mandate and the US Marine Corps mission as being opposed to their interests.

Soon the MNF-II and the US would be drawn deeper into the conflict by America's open provision of arms to the Christian-dominated Lebanese military. In July 1983, pro-Syrian Druze units shelled BIA with a dozen 122 mm Katyusha rockets, wounding both Lebanese Army soldiers and US marines. The next month, 27 Katyusha rockets impacted BIA on 10 August. There were additional marine casualties. Shelling continued through the month, with US Marine Corps artillery finally joining in the fight. The fighting continued to escalate in September as hostilities between Christian and Muslim forces raged, with US forces aiding the largely Christian army units in the Shouf Mountains. In time, the marines' commanding officer, COL Timothy Geraghty (USMC), was very worried that, as exchanges of fire from both sides escalated, the threat to his forces would increase. His units were isolated and vulnerable at BIA. Moreover, he was concerned that his "involvement in the Lebanese internal struggle has exceeded our original mandate."[26] He was correct. Then, in mid-September, US naval gunfire was called on and fell on Shi'a targets. In late September, the USS *New Jersey,* with its 16-inch gun turrets, arrived on station with imposing firepower. Unsurprisingly, a cease-fire resulted. Nonetheless, by October it was clear that US forces were unambiguously part of the conflict, shelling targets in the Shouf Mountains from both land and sea to silence Shi'a militias who were engaged in hostilities with the Lebanese Army and, by extension, US marines precariously situated at BIA. If there was any question among Muslim factions concerning the US posture in the conflict, all doubt was removed.[27] The US, whether intentionally or not, had taken sides in this war. They were now the latest incarnation of the Crusader narrative. On 23 October 1983, radical Shi'a terrorists would give a cowardly and brazen response.

Early that morning, a suicide truck bomb exploded at the US Marine Corps barracks at BIA, killing 220 marines, 18 sailors, and 3 soldiers and wounding 130 more of the force. Minutes later, another explosion at the French barracks nearby claimed the lives of 58 French paratroopers. The Shi'a Islamic Jihad claimed responsibility for the bombing of the marines. Hezbollah's fingerprints were on the attack. No one took responsibility for the French terror attack, a strategy by the perpetrators to avoid further inciting angry Lebanese, who had been historically friendly with the French. But in the US there was shock and outrage over both bombings. Throughout the remainder of 1983 and into 1984, the situation for both Lebanon and the MNF-II worsened. Eventually the Lebanese Army's efforts to impose control in the Shouf Mountains region would fail, and its ability to protect Beirut would soon collapse. Shortly thereafter, an unsigned letter from the Lebanese foreign minister was circulated to the ambassadors of MNF-II countries recommending that they "deploy to safer locations."[28] On 24 February 1984, the Maronite Christian president of Lebanon, Amin Gemayel (Bachir Gemayel's brother), was compelled to travel to Damascus and consult with Syria's Assad on Lebanon's future. The price exacted would be Gemayel's renunciation of the US-sponsored May 17 Agreement with Israel.[29] Beyond Lebanon's inglorious submission to Syria as a de facto client, there was more humiliation for others. Involvement in the Lebanese Civil War would damage the prestige of Western nations—and the US in particular—as failed peacekeepers who had sacrificed much blood and treasure. Tragically, Israel's Operation Peace for Galilee had also paradoxically produced unintended victors, namely a patient and persistent Syria and its new ally, Hezbollah, the Iranian-sponsored terror organization that would fill the vacuum in southern Lebanon created by the PLO's defeat.[30] Israel may have beaten the PLO, but in the process it had unleashed more foes determined to vex the Jewish state.

This is what Israel had to show for its loss of 368 dead soldiers and 2,383 wounded from 6 June until 10 October 1982.[31] The cost of war is never confined to the defeated. With the rise of Hezbollah in southern

Lebanon, Israel seemed to ignore the Latin proverb *nota res mala, opima*, or "an evil thing known is best." Or as we say today, "Better the devil you know than the devil you don't." Israel's pursuit of war in 1982 resulted in banshee-like wailing from Jewish mothers. That would not change in the years that followed the folly of Israel's invasion, as violence continued in southern Lebanon.

The Impact on UNTSO

Sadly, UNTSO would not be unscathed by the violence in Lebanon following the 1982 invasion. On 25 September 1982, just eleven days after the assassination of the newly elected president of Lebanon, Bachir Gemayel, four UNTSO observers were tragically killed while serving with the newly constituted Observer Group Beirut (OGB). MAJ Randal Carlson (USA), CPT Karl Lasonen (Finland), COMDT Michael Nester (Ireland), and MAJ Harley Warren (USAF) were killed by a land mine about 10 kilometers east of Beirut, near Zandouqa (Zanduqah), while conducting a patrol.[32] OGB had only recently been formed from observers assigned to ILMAC in Beirut and augmented with 25 UNMOs redeploying there from OGL in Naqoura. As such, some of the families of these deceased observers resided in Nahariya with many other UNMOs and their families.[33] For OGL, this was a huge tragedy. If not for the invasion into Lebanon and the ensuing danger, the deaths of these UNMOs would have been averted as it is unlikely they would have been assigned to Beirut in the first place. While the UN had attempted to inject both UNTSO and UNIFIL into the Beirut situation, there was no support for an expanded UNIFIL role, particularly by the US, which was "unconvinced of the UN's ability to make an impact on the situation."[34] Additionally, Israel was firmly against bringing in UNIFIL. However, UNTSO's presence in Beirut was entirely another matter because its subordinate ILMAC was already on the ground there. Augmenting it with observers from OGL made sense. OGL was nearby, and its UNMOs were available since their usefulness in southern Lebanon had been marginalized following the invasion. At that point, having UNMOs report border violations in the southern region by the IDF was pointless. Besides, most of the UNMOs then, as MAJ Jay Sollis (USMC) recalls, were assigned to administrative duties for the time being.[35] The thinking then was that OGL's personnel could be used more effectively in Beirut. Regardless of the utility of dispatching its observers to OGB, Operation Peace for Galilee now had produced four more casualties, including two American officers, in September of 1982.

The 1982 invasion highlighted how UNTSO and UNIFIL were powerless to stop an invasion of the type Israel launched and the carnage that followed. Sadly, the MNF-II record was no more successful, with the exception of MNF-I's orderly evacuation of the PLO in August of 1982. However, there was another figurative casualty of the invasion: US support for UNTSO in the years to come. The legacy of Operation Peace for Galilee would set in motion a chain of events that would impact the future willingness of the US to put its soldiers at risk, either as UN military observers or as armed forces working with international peacekeeping coalitions. That risk was poignantly punctuated in February 1988 when the US chief of OGL, LTC William R. "Rich" Higgins (USMC), was kidnapped by armed radicals, likely from Hezbollah, and brutally murdered after a 17-month captivity.[36] With all that had occurred, including (1) the death of two American UNMOs in September 1982 referenced above, (2) the bombing of the US embassy in April 1983,[37] (3) the attack on the American and French barracks in October 1983, and (4) the targeting of American citizens for kidnapping between 1983 and 1986,[38] US policy makers had much to think about. As a result, the US began to reevaluate the efficacy of putting our forces in places like southern Lebanon and exposing them to heightened danger from radical Islamic threats.

However, the fulcrum shifted dramatically in 1993. While not occurring in the Middle East, in Somalia the Battle of Mogadishu that occurred on 3–4 October 1993 was a seminal and defining moment. There, American forces were supporting the United Nations Operation in Somalia (UNOSOM-II). During that battle, two US Black Hawk helicopters were shot down by Somali militiamen and a subsequent rescue operation was undertaken by US forces to rescue the downed personnel. In the process of that operation things went badly, resulting in the deaths of 18 US Army soldiers and the wounding of 73 others. The American public was horrified by the pictures of Somali militiamen desecrating the bodies of deceased American soldiers. What followed was a pullback by America from operations of this nature.[39]

All of these events resulted in a reluctance by US policymakers to expose our military to such operations, particularly those associated with the UN. In that environment, US participation in UNTSO was curtailed significantly. Today, the US role in UNTSO has all but disappeared, falling from 36 officers in 1981 to just 2 in 1997, where it currently remains.[40] The legacy of Operation Peace for Galilee paved the way for an eventual withdrawal of US participation in UNTSO. The Israelis had no such explicit intention and should not be directly blamed for it. But it was a terrible unintended consequence of war. Nevertheless, after 1982, the vacuum left by the forced departure of the PLO was filled by Hezbollah, which was not only anti-Israeli but profoundly anti-American. That also had implications for the threat posed to American officers in UNTSO by radical elements. Such was the case with Rich Higgins. Consequently, UNTSO would eventually see the departure of American officers who had done so much to leaven UNTSO's professionalism and manner of performance. That was a loss to UNTSO. It was also a loss for the US. To be sure, there was increased danger to American interests after the 1982 invasion. The Higgins murder revealed that. The threat to Americans in the Middle East was further exacerbated following the war on terror that began on September 11, 2001. It persists still.

Those of us who served with UNTSO—particularly in the "Wild West" of southern Lebanon—benefited from that service, even as we risked our lives. We learned about others, both friend and foe. More importantly, we learned about ourselves as warriors-cum-peacekeepers. And it strikes me to this day that, with our departure from UNTSO, our military services sacrificed the opportunity to gain important institutional knowledge about peacekeeping operations, including that which either makes them potentially successful or hinders them badly. Fundamentally, with the American departure from UNTSO, we and our services lost a unique opportunity to learn and grow institutionally, professionally, and personally. That growth opportunity was not what motivated the US when it first arrived in UNTSO in 1948. But growth in every respect was surely the case in 1981. And I was glad to be part of it.

Peace Lost

Much has been written on peace operations that would improve organizations like UNTSO and UNIFIL. The UN itself has for years struggled to craft a doctrine to define peacekeeping, peacemaking, and peace enforcement as a result of its own experience in the field, particularly in the Middle East. Indeed, the US military has spent much time attempting to sort out how American forces can support peacekeeping operations, even as it was backing away from such obligations following the post-1982 tumults in Lebanon and elsewhere. That discussion continues to this day in military circles, command and staff colleges, senior officer war colleges and universities, and among academics interested in peacekeeping, even as we emerge from years of counterinsurgencies after the terrorist attacks on the US homeland in 2001.

However, for those of us in UNTSO in 1981, no high-minded debating or doctrinal machinations were required. Just hard work, resourcefulness, patience, decisiveness, wits, and steely-eyed determination to exemplify the kind of leadership and good judgement we knew would be required for peacekeeping, despite our warrior instincts. Moreover, we understood our mandate. It was clear to us and others. Our challenge was to fulfil it in an environment where we were not wanted by the combatants, who cynically were more interested in fighting than in resolving their differences.

Yet we were realistic. We could no more stop an invasion by a determined Israel than we could alter the tidal flow of the Mediterranean Sea. Nor could UNIFIL stop it in 1982. UNIFIL was abstractly conceived and configured to enforce a peace in a place where peace was just a five-letter word. But we also understood that while we were unarmed observers in UNTSO, we were also the face of hope for those who so desperately needed it. The men, women, and children of the Levant had no desire for forever wars. In that regard, our motivations, as LTCDR Virg Bozeman (USN) so aptly put it, were both "noble" and "honorable" as we took up our role supporting UNIFIL.[41] That motivation has a place today. Nevertheless, the outcome in 1982 was a peace lost. Indeed, the Greek scholar Plato could have been speaking about Lebanon in 1982 when he said over two millennia earlier, "Only the dead have seen the end of war."

Operation Peace for Galilee was peace for no one. UNTSO couldn't stop that war. But in the end, our service in southern Lebanon was a tribute to nations and soldiers who were willing to work for peace in the face of unrelenting hostility. That is no small thing. And it is something for American policymakers to think about as they consider whether or not to participate in future peacekeeping efforts, whether as unarmed or armed sentinels of peace. What should guide their thinking as a result of our experience in UNTSO? Let's take a look.

12

Sentinels of Peace

In 1948, America was wise to step forward and be part of the UN peace-keeping effort following the tumultuous birth of Israel into modern statehood and the resulting conflict with its Arab neighbors. Having had a significant role in Israel's beginning, the US would find itself committed to calming the turbulent waters between Jews and Arabs in a land where both ethnicities claimed ownership—claims they indefatigably assert to this day. Over time, the American role in UNTSO proved valuable as a tangible commitment to peace in the region. Yet that role is now all but gone. The question for American policymakers today is important. Was abandoning UNTSO a wise policy, and what are the implications that accompanied that decision?

In 1981, the military services in the Pentagon were supportive of the US contribution to UNTSO. The Army's Foreign Area Officer (FAO) program, designed to train officers in regional studies, was one of the best among the services. The Army was quite eager to send military observers like myself and others who had been trained in Middle East studies to UNTSO. That assignment was, in their view, an excellent learning laboratory for those of us who would alternate between combat assignments and FAO tours. Indeed, specialists trained in Middle Eastern studies were well-equipped to offer analysis and advice concerning US relations and operations in a region where that insight was vital to national security decision-making. The other services also saw the UNTSO assignment as valuable for professional development and, like the Army, offered up top-notch officers to serve in the organization. In particular, the US Marine Corps regarded UNTSO duty as a "plum assignment," not only because it expanded understanding of the Middle East, but also for the rigors encountered in a hostile environment.[1] Similarly, the US Air Force considered it a valuable opportunity for their officers.[2] The US Navy likewise saw the benefits.

In 1981, the senior officer overseeing Army officer assignments to UNTSO was COL John Malchase David Shalikashvili. He was quite

committed to the work we were doing in UNTSO. That was not a surprise. Shalikashvili, who earned a master's degree in international relations from George Washington University, understood the need for Army
officers to have a keen appreciation for service with other nations, given
America's role in the world. His perspective, no doubt, was also influenced by his childhood. Born in Warsaw, Poland, in 1936 just prior to
World War II, he immigrated to the US in 1952, later rising to be the first
foreign-born chairman of the Joint Chiefs (CJCS) in US history.[3] But in
1981, while serving on the Army Staff in the Pentagon, he was focused on
foreign area assignments, and UNTSO in particular, to better hone the
skills of American officers, professionally and personally.

He was not a passive observer of things in UNTSO. He personally
debriefed me when I returned to the Pentagon in 1982, wanting to better
understand the US experience in UNTSO. Later in 1982, Shalikashvili
sought to see for himself and traveled to the Middle East.[4] When he
arrived in Nahariya, LTC Al Baker (USA) asked MAJ Kevin Kennedy
(USMC), then the team leader for Team X-Ray, to escort Shalikashvili
throughout OGL's area of operations and subsequent tour of the West
Bank. After getting clearance for Shalikashvili to enter southern Lebanon,
Kennedy escorted him to Team Tyre and all of the OPs from OP LAB in
the west to OP KHIAM 70 kilometers to the east.[5] Afterward, Kennedy
drove Shalikashvili through the Jordan Valley to Jerusalem, noting that
his guest was "a very nice guy."[6]

Shalikashvili was much more than that. He was very interested in the
UNTSO mission in 1982, and after he rose to CJCS the 1995 National
Military Strategy (NMS) reflected his support for peacekeeping. The
NMS process was established pursuant to the 1986 Goldwater-Nichols
Department of Defense Reorganization Act.[7] It requires the chairman of
the Joint Chiefs of Staff, the president, and the secretary of defense to
provide initial strategic direction to the armed forces in the overarching
National Security Strategy (NSS) prepared by the executive branch to
formulate national security goals and plans. In turn, the NMS outlines a
supporting strategic military framework for how the armed forces will
execute NSS goals. In 1995, there was plain language in the NMS concerning America's preparedness to engage in peacekeeping operations
during the administration of President Bill Clinton.

We remain prepared to support traditional peacekeeping operations on a case-by-case basis. When warranted by circumstances
and national interests, this support may include participation of

US combat units. When appropriate, we prefer to share the burden of peacekeeping with allies and friends. When the United States does participate, we will follow the guidelines of Presidential Decision Directive [PDD] 25, to include seeking a clear delineation of the objectives of each operation, ensuring an unbroken chain of command to the President, and ensuring rules of engagement to protect our forces and permit the proper execution of assigned tasks. The capabilities we provide will be carefully tailored, usually to reinforce and supplement the resources of our international partners. We recognize that peace operations are often different from traditional military operations in the tasks and capabilities they require of our Armed Forces. We are continuing to develop appropriate doctrine and training for these operations. Reserve component elements will take on increased responsibility for participating in and supporting peacekeeping missions.[8]

It was apparent from this wording that the Battle of Mogadishu[9]—when 18 American soldiers were killed while participating in UNOSOM II, the second phase of the UN's 1993 intervention in Somalia during that country's civil war—lingered over the construct of the 1995 NMS. The referenced PDD-25 was in response to the negative publicity following Mogadishu and set forth very restrictive requirements concerning whether the US would even vote for a new UN peacekeeping operation, contribute US troops to it, or commit troops to missions that might involve combat.[10] It also established conditions for US participation in future peacekeeping endeavors, including requirements that (1) American military officers would be in control of US troops; (2) the mission was in the best interests of the US government; and (3) there was popular domestic support for the operation.[11] The reference in the NMS to "ensuring an unbroken chain of command to the President and ensuring rules of engagement to protect our forces and permit the proper execution of assigned tasks" acknowledged the need to keep a tight rein on operations like Mogadishu, even though the UN did not control the use of US forces in that battle.[12]

Nevertheless, in the opening words, the NMS stated that the US would "remain prepared to support traditional peacekeeping operations on a case-by-case basis." The UNTSO mission would certainly have fit that description, indeed it was both traditional and an unarmed mission. We were not a combat force. To the contrary, we lacked any semblance of being combatants. But the US wanted to avoid another Mogadishu. As noted in the previous chapter, with all that had happened since Operation Peace for Galilee after 1982—the loss of American UNMOs, the US embassy bombing, the American and French barracks attacks, widespread American kidnappings, and Mogadishu—participation in UN peace operations would be deemphasized even as the ink was drying on the 1995 NMS. Despite Shalikashvili's interest and support for UNTSO in 1982, the above NMS language contained a de facto contradiction. On the one hand, "traditional" peacekeeping was acceptable. On the other, it would be so restricted as to make it improbable. Indeed, just two years later the NMS further diminished peacekeeping, mentioning it only in passing: "To execute this strategy the United States requires forces of sufficient size, depth, flexibility, and combat power to defend the US homeland; maintain effective overseas presence; conduct a wide range of concurrent engagement activities and smaller-scale contingencies, including peace operations. . . ."[13]

Peacekeeping completely fell by the wayside in every single NMS afterward. By 2004, under President George W. Bush, there was no mention of peacekeeping.[14] In 2011, under President Barack Obama there was one reference to peacekeeping.[15] Four years later, there were but two brief references to peacekeeping couched among other issues.[16] In the subsequent NMS of President Donald J. Trump, peace operations did not command a second's attention.[17] Consequently, the wanning support for US participation in peacekeeping led to a slow but certain withdrawal of Americans serving in UNTSO. Our numbers dropped from 33 in 1990, to 17 in 1994, and sank to just 2 in 1997, where it came to rest.[18] Despite Shalikashvili's understanding and seeming support for US participation in UNTSO in 1982, it was not enough to sustain the mission in southern Lebanon after 1995. It had simply become too dangerous in the eyes of national security decision-makers and not worth the risk.

For Better or Worse: The Case for American Participation in UNTSO

In 1981, it was clear to all of us assigned to UNTSO that there was value in having Americans pull their weight as part of an international effort in the Levant, particularly in southern Lebanon. We had done so since 1948 and continued in that effort up to 1982. We were making a difference, not only in fulfilling the UNTSO mandate, but in helping to make that organization better. When Kennedy escorted Shalikashvili through the region in early 1982, the future general, too, could see the value of Yanks on duty in southern Lebanon. And at least for a brief period after he rose to CJCS, Shalikashvili supported such missions. This advocacy would not last long. We have left UNTSO in large measure. But should we have remained there?

Reflecting on the four decades since my duties in southern Lebanon concluded, I have given much thought to peacekeeping. Occasionally I will come across an old picture or look at a handmade rug or engraving that Shelley and I brought back from the Middle East and recall our experience. More frequently, however, I will see something about Lebanon in the news after a violent incident and ask myself, "Did the peacekeeping effort even matter?" I continue to wonder.

In 1981, I had no earthly idea what to expect when I arrived in Jerusalem, moved to Damascus, and then—along with my fellow UNMOs—traversed southern Lebanon. My vantage point was that of a soldier trained for combat, not for peacekeeping. Certainly, I had learned much about the Middle East from my academic work. But there is no substitute for experiencing the Middle East in person—its people, landscapes, smells and sounds, the daily hustle and bustle of life, and the inevitability of conflict erupting without warning. Nothing that I had learned in my graduate studies prepared me for the challenges of being in the Middle East as a peacekeeper. Nor had I been taught how to calmly and diplomatically talk my way out of dangerous situations when a gun was thrust in my face. And that is the point. Peacekeeping is, as the saying goes, "a different breed of cat." My UNTSO colleagues and I were unarmed. We relied on presence of mind, a keen focus on the peacekeeping mission at hand, and our wits. We did not have the benefit of weapons of war strapped to our waist or slung over our shoulder. Creativity, focus, and the determination to deescalate and resolve conflicts were all we had in our peacekeeping holster. Our UNIFIL comrades were the ones with the weapons. They had options we did not have in UNTSO. If threatened, they could threaten to reciprocate with a potential use of force. But armed or not, all of us wondered at times—to ourselves and aloud—whether our efforts were "for better or worse." And like a coin, that is a two-sided question with a two-sided answer.

I believe that for those of us in UNTSO the answer to that question is "yes." It was for both better *and* worse. The better could be found in the US role and influence in UNTSO and the positive impression we had on our UNMO colleagues as well as the officers and troops in UNIFIL, whom we supported. That was something I am sure Shalikashvili understood in 1982, based on his debriefing of me when I returned to the Pentagon—indeed, something he would confirm for himself in later months. In the process of performing our duty in UNTSO, we were also the face of the US in southern Lebanon for the Israelis, the Lebanese Christian militia, the PLO, and other armed elements who were the latter's allies and cohorts. We were able to show all of them that, despite America's staunch support for Israel, US officers assigned to UNTSO were seriously committed to professionally doing our part to keep the peace. Our unarmed presence was a testimony to that end and therefore for the better.

We were also US representatives to the Lebanese people, who were in so many ways beleaguered and tormented with a conflict they did not seek, did not want, and longed to see resolved. Our faces were ones of commitment to them. We were determined to accomplish our mission, whether standing watch, conducting patrols, dodging bullets and artillery shells, talking and bluffing our way out of trouble, or on occasion flaunting the rules, like two roguish US marines did when they commandeered a UN vehicle to transport a distraught Lebanese mother under the cover of darkness through hostile territory to visit her critically injured son in the hospital. At times we knowingly broke the rules. Yet despite what we did officially and unofficially, we sometimes wondered if it amounted to anything resembling genuine peace. And while the Lebanese people also must have wondered whether our presence would actually yield peace, the fact that we were there among them was an eloquent statement to them, their families, and their children. That was for the better.

So too, our presence in Damascus and in the Sinai Desert with our Russian counterparts was an opportunity to experience the bipolar competition of that age in a unique light. The Russians in some ways shared our aspirations: seeking a better life, loving their families, and doing their duty as soldiers, albeit peacekeepers after a fashion. Likewise, the many nations who served in UNTSO and UNIFIL were cognizant of our presence and commitment to stand shoulder-to-shoulder with them as we did our part to keep the peace in the conflict-ridden Levant. If it is true that the better part of life is "showing up," then our presence in UN peacekeeping then and there was for the better.

In many ways we Yanks were ambassadors of goodwill, both to belligerents who threatened us and to international comrades who stood with us. In that regard, we represented our nation's commitment to peace even as the US stumbled in advancing peace in the wake of Israel's 1982 invasion. We were there wearing a brassard with both our UN shoulder patch and the American flag stitched on it. The imprimatur of the US was literally on us by virtue of our official assignment to UNTSO. Our lives were demonstrably on the line in a place where life could be snuffed out in a second. America had "skin in the game." Except it was not a game at all. It was deadly serious. We were not a showpiece, but America's embodied commitment to put its military forces in harm's way for peace. Nor were we there to receive a gratuitous participation trophy like a child running haplessly around a ball field. We were there to keep the peace in a place where peace would otherwise be absent. For everyone in southern Lebanon—whether they resented or respected our presence—it was an inescapable fact that we were on the ground with and between them and committed physically to peace. That too was for the better.

What is more difficult to reconcile is the other side of the coin, the worse. The UN was founded with good intentions. However, at the top level it was bedeviled by multidimensional politics, woeful wastefulness, inefficiency, circumambient bureaucrats, careerists, and a predisposition for ill-resolve. For years, the UN has struggled with how to conduct peacekeeping. The UN had no formal doctrine until 2008.[19] That lack of doctrine was evident when UNIFIL was formed. Moreover, UNIFIL was never properly empowered. While UNTSO's observation, reporting, and negotiating mandate was well-grounded over time, UNIFIL's mandate was weak and unenforceable. Nor were the belligerents compelled to observe it. Indeed, hostile forces flaunted UNIFIL's mandate by flagrantly occupying territory that was clearly assigned to UNIFIL. It remains a sad footnote that it was the UN, not the combatants, who was primarily responsible for undermining UNIFIL's mandate when the UN secretariat acquiesced to the PLO's retention of the Tyre Pocket and the DFF's occupation of the enclave. That was clearly for the worse.

Moreover, the UN's recruitment of armed forces for UNIFIL in 1978 lacked the discernment to ensure those military units—particularly those from non-Western nations—were competent and sufficiently trained for peace operations. Additionally, the UN's skittishness regarding the use of force in peace operations, as we observed in southern Lebanon, produced a hesitation to employ it. That made peacekeepers more susceptible to abuse and death by combatants who routinely resorted to force. It could have been mitigated had the UN unambiguously declared that UNIFIL would use force when necessary for self-defense, refusing to play the role of a paper tiger or to be manipulated and abused by recalcitrant and hostile parties. An assertive posture in the face of aggression, however, would have required a firm and uncompromising mandate. That the UN accepted a compromised UNIFIL as a fait accompli was a betrayal of the officers, noncommissioned officers, and soldiers who deployed to southern Lebanon and risked their lives to do a credible job. It was also a betrayal of the Lebanese people, who would have benefited from an effective UN peace operation. That was truly for the worse.

It did not have to be this way. There is a right way and a wrong way to go about configuring and conducting peace operations. The US military has actually invested much doctrinal thinking in this area, particularly in the wake of the counterinsurgencies we have fought since 9/11.[20] We could assist in and contribute to training and equipping UN forces to be successful inside properly constructed peace operations. However, we have flagged in recent years in even mentioning peace operations in our national and military strategy documents. Isolationism has overtaken internationalism, and with it a mistrust and wariness toward peacekeeping operations. We no longer see peacekeeping as a viable mission that we should undertake. Yet, if the US believes that the maintenance of peace should be an element of our national security, then we should be prepared to partake in peacekeeping that is consistent with our national strategy goals and properly vetted to ensure our participation will comport with our interests and benefit those in need of peace. Indeed, the Russian invasion of Ukraine on 24 February 2022 may well present a peacekeeping opportunity for the US and others in the future.[21]

Some Thoughts on America's Potential Peacekeeping Role

The decision to participate in peacekeeping operations, whether or not they fall under the auspices of the UN, is no small matter. Having been an eyewitness to peacekeeping on the ground in southern Lebanon and knowing how organizations like UNTSO and UNIFIL came into being, it occurs to me that there are key lessons that US authorities should contemplate concerning participation in peacekeeping. In addition to being a soldier on the ground in southern Lebanon, I acquired an understanding of national strategy decision-making throughout my career that informs my recommendations concerning peacekeeping missions. Below is a suggested framework that might be useful to decision-makers in guiding deliberations concerning the efficacy of participating in or initiating a peacekeeping mission like UNTSO or UNIFIL, including a potential one that may emerge in Ukraine. Undoubtedly, some of these suggestions are already part of the routine decision-making process today's leaders employ. However, given the special nature of peacekeeping operations and the potential danger inherent in them, these ideas, posed as questions, are worthy of consideration.

First, does the envisioned peace operations mission fit within the scope of America's national interests? To be sure, the term "national interest" can be vague and ambiguous depending on the usage and context. Nonetheless, our law requires both an NSS and an NMS that outline our national interests—however defined—and how they will be addressed militarily. If those documents state that peacekeeping is in our national interests, then as those opportunities emerge, our leadership must determine how we might participate. More specifically, how will we support and enable that peace mission so that it can succeed? That may take the form of a limited—albeit meaningful—configuration in a peace operation. We certainly did that within UNTSO. It might also entail contributing to the training, planning, deployment, and sustainment of peacekeeping operations. As far as giving expression to our potential participation, the US need look no further than the Shalikashvili mission statement of 1995 to update the current NMS.

Second, does our involvement justify the potential loss of American blood and treasure? The loss of American lives in Lebanon and Somalia has tempered our zeal to participate in UN peace operations. However, that alone should not prohibit consideration when a case can be made for US participation in peacekeeping. To be certain, that case would also depend on the perceived urgency in pressing for peace in any given circumstance. But our leaders should ask themselves if the case is truly compelling—that is to say: Does it clearly fit within our national interests as expressed in the NSS and NMS to justify risking American lives?

Third, are the eight elemental questions posited by the Weinberger-Powell doctrinal framework satisfied? That doctrine—derived from the post–Vietnam War experience as well as that of MNF-I and MNF-II in Beirut—was developed by Secretary of Defense Casper W. Weinberger[22] and expounded on later by General Colin Powell when he served as the CJCS before Shalikashvili.[23] The questions include: (1) Is a vital national security interest in the balance? (2) Are there clear and attainable objectives (pursuant to a mission or mandate)? (3) Have the risks and costs been fully and objectively weighed and analyzed? (4) Have all other nonviolent policy means been fully exhausted? (5) Is there a plausible exit strategy to avoid endless entanglement? (6) Have the consequences of the action been fully considered? (7) Is the action supported by the American people? (8) Is there genuine and broad international support for the mission? This doctrinal approach offers a framework for orderly thinking that may have some benefit to peacekeeping. But like all doctrine, it is not absolute in every situation. In any case, its parameters could be applicable in ensuring that we do not inadvertently entangle ourselves in situations that would harm rather than advance our national interests. The lessons of UNIFIL come to mind here.

Fourth, is the peacekeeping effort clearly defined, including (1) the desired ends, (2) the ways to pursue the mission, (3) the means or resources by which the mission is to be executed and accomplished, and (4) a clear understanding of the risks associated with the strategy? This ends-ways-means test is a familiar one among military strategists.[24] It should also be present in peace operations. It was lacking in the development, planning, deployment, and sustainment of UNIFIL. What is the end to a peace operation? How will that be achieved? What means will be employed to do so? And have the risks to soldiers we wedge between combatants been fully weighed? The UN secretariat in 1978 rushed to implement UNIFIL. That irresponsible haste materialized as ill-preparedness, deficient performance, and the loss of soldiers conducting operations in southern Lebanon.

Fifth, is the peacekeeping organization sufficiently manned, trained, and equipped to accomplish the mission, with clear rules of engagement for the use of deadly force when it is authorized to protect peacekeepers and ensure success? UNTSO had skilled officers who quickly adapted to the peacekeeping challenge. UNIFIL, however, had young and inexperienced soldiers who were not properly prepared. While American forces are ready for war, peace operations require tailored training and orientation. As we found in southern Lebanon as unarmed observers—a configuration that US planners may elect to employ in the future—one's wits must frequently suffice for the lack of a firearm or other physical means of protection and persuasion. So too with armed peacekeepers. Whether armed or unarmed, training in deescalation techniques, cultural awareness concerning parties to the conflict, composure under pressure, and steely-eyed objectivity that rejects favoritism are all necessary components to successful peacekeeper preparation. Furthermore, peace enforcement requires a clear and unambiguous set of rules of engagement for the use of deadly force. The UN has struggled for years over the definition of peace enforcement.[25] The US should not repeat that mistake. Clear rules of engagement governing when force is essential and how self-defense is employed are a vital consideration.

Sixth, is the envisioned force properly prepared to deploy to its area of responsibility? That includes an awareness of the environment, the challenges of terrain, the capabilities of potential hostile forces, and an appreciation for the culture of the parties to the conflict? UNIFIL was unprepared to occupy southern Lebanon as an effective force. While the efforts of men like CPT Mike Fallon (USMC) were critical in helping UNIFIL initially occupy tactical positions on short notice, we can and must do better. Peace operations cannot be a "y'all come" affair. Proper and professional planning for the use, deployment, occupation, employment, and sustainment of forces is not debatable, and time must be devoted to getting this right. It requires thoughtful preparation and knowledgeable leadership with full situational awareness going into the operation.

Finally, if a situation emerges that might threaten our commitment to the mission, is there sufficient resolve by American leadership to finish the job? Misfortune occurs in peacekeeping as it does in combat. If our national leadership is not committed to staying the course, particularly in peace operations, then we should not participate at all. We must retain the backbone to execute the mission once it is undertaken, particularly when things go badly, as they frequently did in UNIFIL.

These suggestions could serve as a sound basis for US leadership in deciding whether or not to participate in peace operations. Some may find them to be obvious, trite, or naive. But for many others, like the citizens of our nation who will be called on to serve in or support peace operations—particularly those deploying to do so—these considerations could be helpful in vetting our participation in peacekeeping while building public support *ab ovo*.

Conclusion

Harry Truman was a combat veteran long before he was the president of the US. In his former life as an artillery officer, he personally saw the destructiveness of war. He willingly fought when his nation dispatched him to combat. To this day, he is the only man in history who has given an order to deploy nuclear weapons in war. It is little wonder that he was fond of saying, "Our goal must be—not peace in our time—but peace for all time." I recall in 2017 seeing these exact words prominently displayed on a wall in the Truman Presidential Library in Independence, Missouri. As I pondered them and considered Truman's wartime decisions, it struck me that—in the solitude of his quiet daily walks in Independence, far from the cry of battle—he must have asked himself, "Was it worth it to kill so many to avert the deaths of so many more?" There is every evidence historically that he believed it was necessary to give that order. That momentous decision has had lasting implications until today. He was correct to do so. But his point concerning peace today might better be expressed another way. The objective must be—not peace in our time—but the *possibility* of peace for *all* time.

Peace is not something that can be assured, not as long as the specter of violence remains unchecked in this world. And peacekeeping is not a passive activity. It takes work. It takes commitment. And it takes an awareness that lives will be lost by peacekeepers in the process. Peacekeeping is not a garden party. Ask any of the families of the 36 military observers and 14 civilians who died in UNTSO from 1948 to 2015, or the 314 UNIFIL soldiers who lost their lives attempting to keep peace from 1978 to 2019, or the four UNMOs killed by an Israeli air attack that completely destroyed OP KHIAM in 2006, my temporary home 25 years earlier.[26]

Despite the good intentions in establishing the UN and the proliferation of democratic systems around the world, tyranny, suffering, and war are persistent. Dictators continue to deprive freedom from those under their oppressive boots. Terrorism—the scourge of our time—is afoot in every region of the world. Violence is a certainty. Peace is not guaranteed. It is hoped for, a good thing to pursue and within the art of the possible, but never a foregone conclusion. If peace is to be attained, people of good will and determination—with cool and courageous resolve—must be present and willing to take the risks to secure it. And with the attainment of peace comes the prospect for freedom, prosperity, and justice, the very attributes that are the aspirations of many people.

That is America's challenge when it comes to peace operations in the future. Will we overcome our hesitation to participate in peacekeeping? To be sure, we have been rightly cautious after our experiences in Lebanon and Somalia. Moreover, our engagement in fighting terrorism has created increased threats to Americans around the world. But if we believe that promoting peace in regions of the world that are vexed by war is not only in our national interests, but the right thing to do, then participation in peace operations is worth considering. The options for us range from diplomatic moral suasion to peace observation, as we did in UNTSO, to the possibility of participating in well-configured peace enforcement arrangements. Within this spectrum, however, are opportunities to train and to assist peacekeeping organizations, and indeed to occupy dangerous ground with friends and allies as an unambiguous presence for peace. Do we have the will?

In the spring of 1985, then-MAJ Tommy Cates (USAF)—who was my Virginia Military Institute classmate and who also served in UNTSO in 1982—briefed the Joint Chiefs of Staff on whether the US should continue to participate in UNTSO. He convinced them then that our role was vital. Cates recalls their reaction. "Their final question to me was would I go back . . . and I said that I could be packed in less than 24 hours."[27] We Yanks, like Cates, were ready to do what needed to be done, including many who served before, during, and after me.

In the years since Cates gave his briefing, peace operations have taken on backwater dimensions for America. No longer are there 36 young and eager officers representing their nation striving for peace with UNTSO. That US role has evaporated in recent years. The question before us is whether the US will once again embrace that possibility of positively influencing peace operations as it once did with UNTSO? Or will we be satisfied with the current state of peace operations in a world where those missions need much improvement. We have the doctrine, we have the ability to make wise decisions, we have the influence to press the case for peace where it deserves to be pursued, and we have the capability to make things better. Indeed, a new generation of Yanks today would readily do so, as we did in our time as peacekeepers. I am certain that if he were alive today, COL Bob Sholly (USA) would say to a new crop of UNMOs what he said in his farewell to UNTSO in 1983. He was optimistic then, yet pragmatic about peacekeeping: "Don't expect single handedly to bring about peace. Don't allow your frustrations to overload what your commonsense expectations should be. I would recommend to each observer to maintain personal objectivity and dedicate himself to United Nations principles and objectives. Do your job."[28]

Sholly expected that of us in UNTSO and led us accordingly. He knew the mission was important. Yet the cynics might say, there is not much the US can accomplish with peacekeeping operations in this fallen world, where human nature is so readily given to violence. That may be sadly true. But the Yanks who donned a blue beret before and after 1981 would have none of that. We were American fighting men who, for a season, were willing sentinels of peace. And as we ventured out every day and night to help a war-weary people, we dared believe the cynics wrong. And that was for the better.

Epilogue
The Yanks Reflect

When I returned to the US in February of 1982, I had much to consider after my tour in the Middle East. I knew that I was professionally better for the experience. Because I was a Middle East specialist, exposure to life in that region was vitally important for my professional development. No amount of well-intended academia could equal what real life offered, the sights, smells, and sounds of human interactions between Semitic groups whose lives were ordinary yet fractured amid profound conflict. For years to come, when I encountered people expressing their version of the "intolerance of ambiguity"—reducing the complexity of Middle East issues to simplistic explanations—I would remind them that nothing was simple there. Many failed to grasp the point. Conflicts in the Levant defy easy solutions, and living there removed all doubt to the contrary.

I had the privilege of serving with superb officers—Army, Navy, Marine Corps, and Air Force—whose example helped me be a better soldier. I was young and inexperienced, but my American colleagues modeled leadership and thoughtfulness that I would embrace for the rest of my career. The Army did not send me to UNTSO for that primary purpose. Nonetheless, it was a huge fringe benefit.

I was also personally better for the people I had met, Arabs and Israelis alike. Sadly, many IDF soldiers and their DFF satraps showed me how not to pursue peace. Likewise, the PLO and their armed elements were abhorrent. Nonetheless, there were good examples. Everyday Israelis, a Syrian butcher who loved Americans, and Yosef Adawin, my Palestinian landlord, whose heartfelt hopes for peace were genuine and sincere. I would have discovered none of this in ivy-covered university halls or the massive corridors of the Pentagon, and certainly I would not have learned about this complex culture in the field training artillery units. Without my time in UNTSO, I would have missed serving with international officers—professionals just like me—with whom I developed friendships and broader perspectives. I grew to admire and appreciate them, and through them to learn a bit more about America, our merits, and our demerits. That was an invaluable lesson about the importance of alliances, partnerships, and common humanity. My fondness for them continues.

But chiefly, I was most honored to serve with brave and devoted fellow countrymen who took their job as military observers so very seriously. They were some of the best people I had encountered to that point in my brief career. And since then, I have reflected admiringly on both their accomplishments and misadventures, some quite dangerous and others potentially deadly. However, setting nostalgia aside, did our efforts matter?

They did. Accordingly, I have concluded that our service in UNTSO was—as then LTCDR Virg Bozeman (USN) noted when he arrived in OGL—both "noble and honorable service." And given our mandate to observe and report violations of cease-fires and agreements while encouraging peace among combatants, we largely succeeded. Moreover, our American influence was beneficial not only to UNTSO but to those we supported, like UNIFIL. Even so, the UNTSO and UNIFIL partnership, despite our efforts, was not entirely successful. In a sense, it was a failed symbiosis, not by intent but rather in design. UNTSO had a clear mandate that was attainable, even in the worst situations when combatants deliberately obstructed our mission. Whether the combatants painted our OP windows black, damaged our equipment, pilfered our provisions, crashed our gates, shelled our positions, or fired at us, we were able to observe and report those violations and did so dutifully. Despite the abuse, we were often able to summon the professionalism to sit down over a cup of chai or Turkish coffee and reason things out with the combatants. As Bozeman did, we were all ready to climb that hill to sit and talk to those who only moments earlier were raining fire down on us. The IDF, DFF, PLO, and the latter's armed elements may have made our mandate difficult to fulfill, but they never dampened our desire to fulfill it.

That was particularly true with the Yanks I served with. We all knew that we had a prominent profile in UNTSO. We represented America and—in a sense—had an obligation, a *noblesse oblige*, to act gallantly and honorably. We were a powerful nation, and accompanying that prestige was a responsibility to do our duty, and not leave it undone. Not only were our international comrades observing our performance, but so too were the combatants. Would we be impartial, just, and fair-minded? Or would we acquiesce to become advocates for one side or the other? It was not an easy task. Nor was it easy for us to exchange our combat field uniforms for diplomat pinstripes. We were trained to be fighters, not peacemakers. But we were also trained and committed to executing the missions we were given. Now we would be peacekeepers. Our mission was to use our wits and leadership skills to encourage people, as the Scriptures say, to "beat their swords into plowshares and their spears into pruning hooks."[1] However, we would have been simply satisfied if they had chosen a new path, one away from violence and misery, toward peace and prosperity. We did not go to the Middle East in an effort to change it into something it wasn't and would not become, a much smaller version of America. Nonetheless, we held out hope that people living amid conflict could have the possibility of the peace we enjoyed in America. As I sat at my desk in the Pentagon watching southern Lebanon disintegrate in the summer of 1982, I could not erase from my memory the faces of the men, women, and children I left behind. The images just kept replaying—innocents forced to endure a living hell while the PLO and Israel appropriated their towns, villages, and fields as a battleground to continue a blood feud that began in earnest in 1948. That was wrong. It will always be wrong.

Just as I have pondered my UNTSO experience over time, so too have the Americans I served with contemplated how they were professionally and personally impacted by our lives as sentinels for peace. They have generously shared their written thoughts with me in correspondence. I have encapsulated them here for others to consider, especially those in our government who wonder about the efficacy of peacekeeping.

COL Mike Fallon (USMC, Retired) has done much reflection on his UNTSO tour. While earning a master's degree in comparative governments of the Middle East at American University, his thesis advisor was the noted Jewish-American scholar Dr. Amos Perlmutter.[2] Fallon, like many of us, was predisposed to a favorable image of Israel. However, he quickly realized after arriving in UNTSO that his "scholarly learning in the proverbial ivory tower in Washington D.C. did not exactly map [correspond] to my practical application as a UN Military Observer who served in Egypt, Israel, Gaza, Lebanon, and visited Syria." In other words, his experience revealed another side of the story: "Observing how each of those governments operated, programs for their people and constituents, and how they managed their five militaries was the real education that broadened my horizons and opened up how I would interact with populations and governments, both local and national going forward."

That was no small insight. And from his experience, he derived three more lessons:

Lesson 1: I never took a country's national policy at face value, rather always sought local opinions. Lesson 2: Based on observation as a neutral observer to combat in Lebanon between the PLA and the IDF, I confirmed my own personal experience from Vietnam, that the force who shoots first normally carries the day at the tactical level of war. Lesson 3: After observing the PLA stop and defeat the IDF tank columns with Sagger missiles . . . I became a believer in missile warfare versus armor warfare. I personally used the experience to teach my Battalion Landing Team, 1st Battalion, 1st Marines how we would fight tanks and kill tanks with TOW [antitank] missiles. Training with TOW's paid off in Desert Storm [1991], where along with the 1st Tank Battalion on my right flank, we participated in the single largest tank battle in Marine Corps history.

Fallon's lessons showed how his UNTSO experience impacted him as both a man and a marine during war and peace. That experience benefitted the Marine Corps as well.[3]

COL Lenny Supko (USMC, Retired) also recalled how his UNTSO assignment impacted him personally:

I came away from that tour with a much clearer picture of the Arab-Israeli conflict. . . . I came in as an avid supporter of Israel and left as still a supporter of Israel because of the Holocaust, and that they were the only democracy friendly to the West surrounded by hostile Arab regimes. My eyes were opened by the fact that they (all concerned) LIE, to themselves, the world, and to their benefactors. Maybe I became a better liar also . . . when dealing with the armed elements, the Lebanese Army, or the IDF, I never told them the complete truth because that would destroy whatever credibility I had with either player. I also came away with the realization that we [US] ain't as bad as we sometimes make ourselves out to be. Whenever there was a situation that required real "professional" problem-solving or the application of military prowess, an American was called upon to weigh in.

Likewise, Supko was unimpressed with UNIFIL: "I was shocked by the absolute ineptitude of UNIFIL as a whole and the genuine irrelevance of the UN on the world stage in that sort of military venture."

He was right. He was also correct about his practice of being guarded with what he revealed to warring parties. Being careful with information each group shared with him enhanced his credibility as a trusted agent. Supko knew sometimes groups would lie to him to see if that same lie showed up elsewhere. It was a game of breadcrumbs. They were always testing him, and if he compromised what they shared with him, that could threaten his credibility, indeed his very life. No master's degree taught him that lesson. The Marine Corps gained a very wise officer from his UNTSO experience.[4]

COL Clay Grubb (USMC, Retired) also appreciated the value of his assignment to southern Lebanon, particularly in understanding conflict: "UNTSO was considered a 'primo assignment' for Marine officers because it's a chance to learn about war when we don't have one ongoing. At the captain level, the distinction is even greater, since company grade officers learn about 'combat' in war, but rarely about 'war' itself."

There were also personal lessons Grubb would take from the remarkable UNTSO learning laboratory. Exposed to many sides of the conflict, he observed this: "People are people, while societal standards may vary, we are all still 97 percent alike. Every culture has fanatics, but the overall culture should not be judged by them."

He also learned much about tribalism in warring countries, a lesson no military officer should miss. "In our society, if one of our cousins commits a crime, we are supposed to cooperate with the police. In most of the rest of the world, it would be considered immoral to submit a family member to the jurisdiction of a government dominated by a different clan." In that regard, shame and honor were in competition with guilt and innocence.

But his observations about applying what he learned from the UNTSO venture should make all of our military services sit up and take note. Later Grubb would find himself designing operational principles to deal with "opposing force tactics for evaluations of future operational concepts or hardware systems." In the process he would push for capabilities that "would also be viable in the more confusing conflicts" like those we encountered in UNTSO. Indeed, that UNTSO experience would pay dividends in future conflicts when he was a war-gamer for Marine Corps forces focused on the Persian Gulf. "We war-gamed and trained staffs for Iran and then in early 1990 shifted to Iraq. With all the focus on armored maneuver, those of us with UNTSO backgrounds did all we could to educate leaders on the national and tribal alliances and objectives of the area and the way local politics would play."

Grubb's UNTSO lessons were well-learned and applied in later conflicts also: "In European Command we were tasked with sending 'Truce Observers' into Kosovo before that war. There was significant senior discussion on how to surreptitiously arm the observers. I was able to get that idea vetoed, based on UNTSO. Our protection in OGL was that we were not armed."

Grubb knew what a huge asset it was in UNSTO's observer mission to not rely on weapons, but rather to depend on calm responses, focused actions, and quick wittedness. That was a lesson he learned on the ground in southern Lebanon, even when he had a Galil rifle shoved into his chest on OP HIN in April of 1980.[5]

COL Kevin Kennedy (USMC, Retired) highlighted his lessons as well. First, he regarded UNTSO as a unique opportunity. As Kennedy put it, "if there is a war going on, I wanted to be there or as close to it as possible." Indeed, when he slipped past Israeli guards to surreptitiously cross the border with then-MAJ Jay Sollis, both were determined to personally observe the 1982 invasion. Second, Kennedy saw UNTSO as an opportunity to work and live with officers from other countries, which he assessed was "probably the best part" of the experience: "I met some really great guys and very much enjoyed serving with them. My UNTSO tour also exposed me to the challenges and difficulties of UN peacekeeping [involving] an international response to difficult situations where major powers don't want to be directly involved but do need some sort of arrangement to at least help keep the lid on crises. . . . Peacekeeping is not the solution to conflicts but does contribute to maintaining stability."

Kennedy would learn that peacekeeping is hard work, and it takes more than a peace arrangement to bring about lasting peace. It absolutely requires the willingness of the combatants. Moreover, Kennedy's UNTSO experience would lead him to continue to serve the UN after his retirement from the US Marine Corps. He would go on to serve as a senior UN official in Somalia, Haiti, Iraq, the Sudan, Timor-Leste, the Balkans, Pakistan, and the occupied Palestinian territories as well as leading numerous UN missions to Africa, Asia, and the South Pacific. To this day, Kennedy believes his UNTSO experience, "while maybe not decisive, opened my eyes to the UN's work which I found very interesting." Clearly his UNTSO assignment was decisive in his public service that followed.[6]

COL Jay Sollis (USMC, Retired) was pragmatic in his assessment. He also saw the UN for what it was, despite his commitment to do his part implementing UNTSO's mandate: "I credit the UN with being perhaps the last best hope of mankind, but I came away with the distinct impression that it amounts to a forum for parliamentary shadow boxing—full of high-minded sound and fury."

Yet Sollis possessed an enduring sense of duty while in UNTSO, noting that he and his American colleagues "felt as though we were supposed to accomplish something—who knows what—not merely enjoy a pleasant, relatively carefree vacation." He could not have been more correct. In his estimate UNTSO "was an enormously beneficial experience—certainly among the highlights of my career."[7]

LTC Denny Lindeman (USMC, Retired) also garnered important lessons. In dealing with friends and foes alike, Lindeman learned "to respond in humility and economy to questions about my culture, outlook, beliefs and opinions." That had a diplomatic component as well: "Later in my position in Damascus, I encountered Syrian government staff and administrators in other UN agencies. That forced me to refine and deepen my skills in diplomatic discourse. When you discipline yourself to question more than declare, you listen more than speak and your response is primarily based on what you thought you heard rather than what you personally believe, your capability to understand others increases exponentially."

The UNTSO experience was one of personal and professional growth for Lindeman, but it also led to this profound insight: "My perspective on society and the nature of man widened considerably. In comparison with my previous experience growing up in the US, on the ground with the ARVN [Vietnamese Army] infantry in Vietnam, and working in Israel, Lebanon, and Syria, I came to understand how critical the Judeo-Christian ethic is to the peaceful function of communities. Readily apparent is that the Judeo-Christian ethic is the only true foundation for civil law and equal justice. Without Judeo-Christian ethics, laws become only a tool of those in power and corruption and chaos become the result."

On that depressing morning when Lindeman and I surveyed the tragic results of a Syrian mass murder in Hama in April of 1981, we both knew that there was no substitute for a world view founded on "civil law and equal justice" to avoid "corruption and chaos."[8]

My Army colleague LTC Joe Serviss (USA, Retired) found his time in UNTSO interacting with Middle Eastern people to be educational, noting that exposure to a new culture "had been very beneficial both while on active duty and with my second career in academia." Likewise, he gained important insights in dealing with military officers from foreign lands and providing the right example that fosters cooperation and trust. He also learned firsthand that peacekeeping is a dangerous business, particularly when your OP takes incoming artillery fire. In that regard, all of us benefitted in one way or another from exposure to perilous combat situations, even those we did not seek or instigate.[9]

So too, LTC Jack Hammell (USA, Retired) found his UNTSO service beneficial personally and professionally from both his time traveling across Syria to his assignment as an operational planner in Government House. It raised in him an awareness that his service had implications beyond what he accomplished on the job. His service was profoundly personal and made him more aware of what it meant to place the welfare of others above self: "I was definitely a better officer because I finally understood that, as an officer, the higher that I rose in the ranks, the more selfless service I owed to others. That, to me, is what being an officer came to mean: serve first and accept whatever 'bennies' follow."

That is a lesson we all learned.[10]

CDR Virg Bozeman (USN, Retired) credits his time in UNTSO as an important component of his life. Surviving many close calls in southern Lebanon provided him with a well-framed perspective. That included the realization that he was quite able to "function in the midst of uncertainty, fear, and danger," all of which redounded to an "inner strength and self-confidence." His experience certainly extended to his performance of duty as a naval officer. "I think my tour at UNTSO made me an asset to my follow-on commands who would see me as a unique source of understanding about the Middle Eastern puzzle." And beyond his military service, Bozeman found—as a political aide to a prominent Maine legislator—that his experience in the Middle East was well-received by his civilian colleagues when dealing with the "puzzles" of both politics and policy. Bozeman sensed that they appreciated some of the wisdom he acquired about complex issues in the Middle East, like those he confronted—even at gunpoint—in southern Lebanon. As Bozeman's temples grayed, he realized his adventures in the Levant were enormously beneficial in life afterward.[11]

COL Steve Cotter (USAF, Retired), who followed me to Syria in 1981, was "pleasantly surprised" that—despite the Syrian government's anti-Americanism—"the people of Syria were reasonably friendly to Americans." He also—as I did—worked closely with the Soviet officers both in Damascus and later in Cairo. He considered both tours to be a "unique opportunity" that gave him great insight into a nationality that at the time was our foremost adversary. In the years that passed, Cotter would reflect on his time of service with the Russians and others, noting, "how lucky I am to be an American." Later, as a senior officer, Cotter also found his UNTSO experience a great asset in working with Arab allies, who were impressed with his background living in Egypt and Syria. "My experience in UNTSO was a valuable asset that paid huge dividends with my Arab counterparts." So it was with all of us.

Finally, my VMI classmate LTC Tommy Cates (USAF, Retired) was sent to UNTSO to replace MAJ Harley "Chopper" Warren (USAF) when he was killed in 1982 by a land mine near Beirut. Cates recalls that the Air Force was very selective in who they dispatched to the Middle East, only six officers yearly. He felt "personally blessed" to be among them despite the sorrowful reason for his assignment. Cates befriended the Lebanese Army liaison officer to OGL while serving on Team Zulu. That officer would ask him to be the godfather to his daughter. Nevertheless, like many of us Cates arrived in the Middle East predisposed to support Israel. But in time his perception would change. "My assignment helped me be a better person by simply serving with other people from different countries. Also, it helped me to see Arabs and especially Palestinians in a different light. Throughout my military career, Israel was always shown as the 'white knight' and my time in Southern Lebanon showed me another side. I left with much more empathy for the Palestinians. The refugee camps were always hard for me to go into."

He also derived a professional benefit from his UNTSO service later as an intelligence officer working with liaison officers from Egypt, Israel, and Lebanon. However, he recalled it was always humorous whenever he "attempted to speak Arabic, Hebrew, or French." Sadly, he would learn later that his Lebanese Army friend had been killed. For many of us, our associations there mattered long after we left. For Cates it was intensely personal.[12]

The reflections of my colleagues create a mosaic of my own feelings about how UNTSO impacted me personally and professionally as a soldier spanning a 28-year career. Likewise, the lessons of UNTSO helped me as a legislator in the Virginia General Assembly for a decade and a half following my Army service. Sometimes even legislators needed to make peace. Frankly, it was impossible for any American military observer in UNTSO to come away unchanged in attitude about those fighting one another, unchanged in understanding the complexity of Middle Eastern conflict, unchanged in empathizing with those subjected to the baleful conditions of war, unchanged in relating to your fellow officers, and unchanged about seeing personally how blessed we were to be Americans living in a nation where freedom and peace are taken for granted. You could not be unchanged after seeing what we saw, doing what we did, and learning what we learned. Not sharing those things here would be a disservice to those who served so well there.

In 1988, the Nobel Committee awarded the Nobel Peace Prize to military observers who had served in UN peacekeeping operations since 1948. Of those 500,000 persons from 53 nations, 733 of them lost their lives.[13] Remarkably, many of my American colleagues were unaware of the Nobel honor. I am not surprised. They did not serve to receive distinctions of that nature. They had no expectation of that. Nonetheless, they served with the same genuine intent that Abraham Lincoln expressed in his timeless Second Inaugural Address: "With malice toward none with charity for all, with firmness in the right as God gives us to see the right, let us strive on to finish the work we are in to bind up the nation's wounds. . . ."[14]

These brave Yanks—anonymous but deserving Nobel Peace Prize winners—embodied these words, seeking in their own time to bind the wounds of a war-weary people. They simply wanted to do what was right because it was right to do it.

I have reflected on these experiences, and so too should America as we think about peacekeeping and our role in it. UNTSO is now in our past. But our military services should capture the lessons from our participation in it. We Yanks in blue berets gained invaluable insights that not only touched us personally but made us better officers, stronger people, and enlightened professionals. Devoted and well-meaning professors at lecterns did not deliver that harvest. They could not. But the rugged realities we encountered in the "Wild West" of southern Lebanon and other places serving as sentinels of peace changed and taught us more than we could have ever imagined or hoped for. Now let us hope again, hope for peace, and hope for an abundant role for America to achieve it when and where it is needed. Peace not just in our time, but the *possibility* of peace for *all* time.

Notes

Introduction

1. The patriarchal age is the era of the three Israelite biblical patriarchs, Abraham, Isaac, and Jacob, according to the narratives of Genesis 12–50, NKJV.

2. "Research Starters: Worldwide Deaths in World War II," The National World War II Museum, www.nationalww2museum.org/students-teachers/student-resources/research-starters/research-starters-worldwide-deaths-world-war.

3. "Peace, Dignity and Equality on a Healthy Planet," United Nations, www.un.org/en/about-us/history-of-the-un.

4. United States Holocaust Memorial Museum, "Postwar Refugee Crisis and the Establishment of the State of Israel," encyclopedia.ushmm.org/content/en/article/postwar-refugee-crisis-and-the-establishment-of-the-state-of-israel.

5. United Nations Truce Supervision Organization (UNTSO), *General Information for UNMOS*, vol. 2, *UNTSO SOP* (UNTSO, June 1981), 1–4.

6. "Legends, William R. Higgins," Marine Corps Coordinating Council of Kentucky, kentuckymarines.org/legend/legends/william-r-higgins/.

1. Up to Jerusalem

1. CDR Virgil Bozeman III, US Navy (Retired), memorandum to the author, 11 December 2020.

2. Then MAJ George Casey would one day rise to be a four-star general and the chief of staff of the US Army. His accomplishments would surely have made his father—MG George W. Casey Sr.—very proud. Casey Sr. gave his life commanding the 1st Cavalry Division in Vietnam the same year George was commissioned as a second lieutenant in the Army.

3. "Timeline: Israel's Attacks on Al-Aqsa Mosque," *Middle East Monitor*, 1 August 2017, https://www.middleeastmonitor.com/20170801-israeli-attacks-on-al-aqsa-mosque/.

4. Bozeman, memorandum, 11 December 2020.

5. Patrick Seale, *Asad: The Struggle for the Middle East* (Berkeley: Univ. of California Press, 1989), 328–329.

6. LTC Barry Gwyther (Retired), Australian Army, memorandum to the author, 10 January 2021.

7. United Nations Truce Supervision Organization (UNTSO), *General Information for UNMOS*, vol. 2, *UNTSO SOP* (UNTSO, June 1981), 11.

2. A Legacy of Conflict

1. Paul L. Maier, *In the Fullness of Time: A Historian Looks at Christmas, Easter, and the Early Church* (Grand Rapids, Mich.: Kregel, 1991), 11.

2. The Levant takes its name from the French word for "rising," as in the rising of the sun in the east that ships would view from the Mediterranean Sea as they approached the coastline.

3. Yvette Talhamy, "The Syrian Muslim Brothers and the Syrian-Iranian Relationship," *Middle East Journal* 63, no. 4 (2009): 561–580.

4. "Camp David Accords and the Arab-Israeli Peace Process," *U.S. Department of State, Milestones: 1977–1980 Office of the Historian*, https://history.state.gov /milestones/1977-1980/camp-david.

5. "Origins and Evolution of the Palestine Problem: 1917–1947 (Part I)," *United Nations, The Question of Palestine*, https://www.un.org/unispal/history2 /origins-and-evolution-of-the-palestine-problem/part-i-1917-1947/.

6. David McCullough, *Truman* (New York: Simon and Schuster, 1992), 617.

7. McCullough, *Truman*, 620.

8. United Nations Truce Supervision Organization (UNTSO), *General Information for UNMOS*, vol. 2, *UNTSO SOP* (UNTSO, June 1981), 2

9. "Resolution 181 (II). Future government of Palestine," United Nations, 29 November 1947, https://www.un.org/unispal/document/auto-insert-185393/.

10. The total numbers of combat soldiers from Israel and Arab states are in question. This may be due to the hasty assembly of combat forces on both sides. Yoav Gelber appears to have the best estimates in his book *Palestine, 1948: War, Escape and the Emergence of the Palestinian Refugee Problem* (Brighton, Oreg.: Sussex Academic Press, 2006). However, I have elected to use a range estimate. In any condition, the Israelis appear to have mustered significantly more fighters, thereby accounting for their performance in 1948.

11. "Origins and Evolution of the Palestine Problem: 1917–1947 (Part II)," *United Nations, The Question of Palestine*, https://www.un.org/unispal/history2 /origins-and-evolution-of-the-palestine-problem/part-ii-1947-1977/; Andrew Theobald, "The United Nations Truce Supervision Organization (UNTSO)," in *The Oxford Handbook of United Nations Peacekeeping Operations*, ed. Joachim A. Koops, Norrie MacQueen, Thierry Tardy, and Paul D. Williams (London, UK: Oxford Univ. Press, 2015), 122.

12. UNTSO, *General Information for UNMOS*, 2.

13. UNTSO, *General Information for UNMOS*, 2.

14. Laurie Milner, "The Suez Crisis," BBC British History in Depth, 3 March 2011, https://www.bbc.co.uk/history/british/modern/suez_01.shtml#: ~: text=Britain

% 20was% 20therefore% 20committed% 20to% 20protect% 20the% 20canal., Indian% 20forces% 20were% 20sent% 20to% 20protect% 20the% 20canal.

15. *The Original Amateur Hour* was an American radio and television program. The show was a continuation of *Major Bowes Amateur Hour,* which had been a radio staple from 1934 to 1945. MAJ Edward Bowes, the originator of the program and its master of ceremonies, was ultimately succeeded by Ted Mack when the show was brought into television in 1948. Popular in the US in the 1950s, contestants competed in a talent show. Viewers were invited to call in and vote for their favorite act. Not all of the performers were that gifted. No doubt President Eisenhower did not rate the 1956 war as a talent winner.

16. United Nations, United Nations Charter, Chapter VI: "Pacific Settlement of Disputes" (Articles 33–38), https://www.un.org/en/about-us/un-charter/chapter-6; Chapter VII: "Action with Respect to Threats to the Peace, Breaches of the Peace, and Acts of Aggression" (Articles 39–51), https://www.un.org/en/about-us/un-charter/chapter-7.

17. UNTSO, *General Information for UNMOS, 2.*

18. First United Nations Emergency Force (UNEF I), *Facts and Figures,* https://peacekeeping.un.org/mission/past/unef1facts.html.

19. UNTSO, *General Information for UNMOS, 2.*

20. First United Nations Emergency Force (UNEF I), *Background,* https://peacekeeping.un.org/mission/past/unef1backgr2.html.

21. UNTSO, *General Information for UNMOS, 2.*

22. First United Nations Emergency Force (UNEF I), *Background.*

23. "Events Leading to the Six Day War (1967)," Israeli Ministry of Foreign Affairs, 7 November 2021, https://www.gov.il/en/Departments/General/events-leading-to-the-six-day-war.

24. LTG Odd Bull (28 June 1907–8 September 1991) was a career officer in the Royal Norwegian Air Force who rose to the position of chief of Air Staff. He is probably best known outside Norway for his role as chief of staff of the United Nations Truce Supervision Organization (UNTSO) between 1963 and 1970, a period that coincided with the Six-Day War between Israel and its Arab neighbors. He wrote a memoir of his experiences during this time, which was published as *War and Peace in the Middle East: The Experiences and Views of a UN Observer,* https://en.wikipedia.org/wiki/Odd_Bull.

25. "United Nations Security Council Meeting, S/PV.1347/Rev.1," United Nations, 5 June 1967, https://documents-dds-ny.un.org/doc/undoc/gen/n70/083/53/pdf/n7008353.pdf?openelement.

26. "United Nations Security Council Meeting, S/PV.1347/Rev.1," https://documents-dds-ny.un.org/doc/undoc/gen/n70/083/53/pdf/n7008353.pdf?openelement.

27. Mohamed Abdel Ghani El-Gamasy, *The October War* (Cairo, Egypt: American University in Cairo Press, 1993), 79; George W. Gawrych, *The Albatross*

of Decisive Victory: War and Policy Between Egypt and Israel in the 1967 and 1973 Arab-Israeli Wars (Westport, Conn: Greenwood, 2000), 3.

28. UNTSO, *General Information for UNMOS,* 3.

29. UNTSO, *General Information for UNMOS,* 3.

30. UNTSO, *General Information for UNMOS,* 3.

31. UNTSO, *General Information for UNMOS,* 3.

32. UNTSO, *General Information for UNMOS,* 3.

33. White House Memorandum of Conversation with President Gerald Ford, Secretary of State Henry Kissinger, and Israeli Prime Minister Yitzhak Rabin, 11 June 1975, 5, www.fordlibrarymuseum.gov/library/document/0314/1553116.pdf.

34. Michael Omer-Man, "This Week in History: Israel's Deadliest Terror Attack," *Jerusalem Post,* 11 March 2011, https://www.jpost.com/Features/In-Thespotlight/This-Week-in-History-Israels-deadliest-terror-attack.

35. Tom Cooper and Sergio Santana, *Lebanese Civil War,* vol. 1, *Palestinian Diaspora, Syrian and Israeli Interventions 1970–1978* (Warwick, England: Helion, 2019), 79.

36. Cooper and Santana, *Lebanese Civil War,* 79.

37. UNTSO, *General Information for UNMOS,* 4.

38. For politico-military reasons, the United Nations did not prefer to give the South Lebanese Army (SLA) formal recognition in southern Lebanon and therefore referred to them as the De Facto Forces (DFF).

3. The UNTSO-US Culture

1. Andrew Theobald, "The United Nations Truce Supervision Organization (UNTSO)," in *The Oxford Handbook of United Nations Peacekeeping Operations,* ed. Joachim A. Koops, Norrie MacQueen, Thierry Tardy, and Paul D. Williams (London, UK: Oxford Univ. Press, 2015), 121.

2. United Nations Truce Supervision Organization Chiefs of Staff, https://en.wikipedia.org/wiki/United_Nations_Truce_Supervision_Organization#cite_note-58; United Nations Archives and Records Management Section, "Summary of AG-404 United Nations Truce Supervision Organization (UNTSO) (1948–Present),"https://search.archives.un.org/downloads/united-nations-truce-supervision-organization-untso-1947-present.pdf.

3. James H. Allan, *Peacekeeping: Outspoken Observations by a Field Officer* (Westport, Conn.: Praeger, 1996), 42.

4. Allan, *Peacekeeping,* 42.

5. Theobald, "The United Nations Truce Supervision Organization (UNTSO)," 125.

6. "Assassination Account of UN Mediator Count Folke Bernadotte," https://en.wikipedia.org/wiki/Folke_Bernadotte.

7. "Israel Charges Bernadotte," *Palestine Post,* 12 July 1948; "Bernadotte Assailed, Associated Press, San Francisco Chronicle, July 12, 1948," http://cojs.org /bernadotte_assailed-_associated_press-_san_francisco_chronicle-_july_12-_1948/

8. "Assassination Account of U.S. Counsel Thomas C. Wasson," https:// en.wikipedia.org/wiki/Thomas_C._Wasson.

9. "The 1948 Assassination of US Navy CPO Herbert Walker," https:// historyhub.history.gov/message/32932.

10. United Nations Truce Supervision Organization (UNTSO), "Mandate," https://untso.unmissions.org/mandate.

11. COL Leonard M. "Lenny" Supko, US Marine Corps (Retired), personal journal, 9 November 1979.

12. Andrew I. Killgore, "In Memoriam Col. Robert W. Rickert (1912–1995)," *Washington Report on Middle East Affairs,* September 1995, 39–94, https:// www.wrmea.org/1995-september/ol.-robert-w.-rickert-1912-1995.html.

13. Killgore, "In Memoriam."

14. Killgore, "In Memoriam."

15. Killgore, "In Memoriam."

16. White House Memorandum of Conversation with President Gerald Ford, Secretary of State Henry Kissinger, and Israeli Prime Minister Yitzhak Rabin, 11 June 1975, 5, www.fordlibrarymuseum.gov/library/document/0314/1553116.pdf.

17. United Nations Truce Supervision Organization (UNTSO), *General Information for UNMOS,* vol. 2, *UNTSO SOP* (UNTSO, June 1981), 3.

18. LTC Joseph A. Serviss, US Army (Retired), memorandum to the author, 9 December 2020.

19. CDR Virgil Bozeman III, US Navy (Retired), memorandum to the author, 11 December 2020.

4. The Road to Damascus

1. United Nations Truce Supervision Organization (UNTSO), *General Information for UNMOS,* vol. 2, *UNTSO SOP* (UNTSO, June 1981), 9; "United Nations Media Photo," United Nations, 26 November 1973.

2. President Ronald W. Reagan, "Remarks at the Annual Convention of the National Association of Evangelicals in Orlando, Florida, March 8, 1983," Reagan Foundation, https://www.reaganfoundation.org/media/50919/remarks_ annual_convention_national_association_evangelicals_030883.pdf.

3. "Report of the Secretary-General concerning the Agreement on Disengagement between Israeli and Syrian Forces," United Nations, 30 May 1974, https://documents-dds-ny.un.org/doc/undoc/gen/nl7/401/61/pdf/nl740161.pdf?openelement.

4. "United Nations Resolution 481 (1980) / adopted by the Security Council at its 2256th meeting, on 26 November 1980," United Nations, 3, https:// digitallibrary.un.org/record/17834? ln=en#record-files-collapse-header.

5. John Mackinlay, *The Peacekeepers: An Assessment of Peacekeeping Operations at the Arab-Israeli Interface* (London, UK: Unwin Hyman, 1989), 149

6. Mackinlay, *The Peacekeepers,* 149.

7. Mackinlay, *The Peacekeepers,* 150.

8. Mackinlay, *The Peacekeepers,* 150.

9. James H. Allan, *Peacekeeping: Outspoken Observations by a Field Officer* (Westport Conn.: Praeger, 1996), 63.

10. Allan, *Peacekeeping,* 63.

11. "United Nations Report of the Secretary-General on the United Nations Disengagement Observer Force (for the period 24 May 1980 to 20 November 1980)," United Nations, 3, https://digitallibrary.un.org/record/18618? ln=en# record-files-collapse-header.

12. United Nations Report on UNDOF, 24 May to 20 November 1980, 4.

13. United Nations Report on UNDOF, 24 May to 20 November 1980, 6.

14. Allan, *Peacekeeping,* 46.

15. Milos Strugar, "The UNTSO Story," *UN Chronicle* 35, no. 3 (fall 1998), https://www.questia.com/magazine/1G1-54259332/the-untso-story.

16. LTC Barry Gwyther, Australian Army (Retired), memorandum to the author, 10 January 2021.

17. United Nations Report on UNDOF, 24 May to 20 November 1980, 5.

18. "United Nations Report of the Secretary-General on the United Nations Disengagement Observer Force (for the period 21 November 1980 to 20 May 1981)," United Nations, 3, https://digitallibrary.un.org/record/18618? ln=en#record-files-collapse-header.

19. "United Nations Report of the Secretary-General on the United Nations Disengagement Observer Force (for the period 21 May 1981 to 20 November 1981)," United Nations, 4, https://digitallibrary.un.org/record/18618.

20. United Nations Report on UNDOF, 24 May to 20 November 1980, 5; United Nations Report on UNDOF, 21 November to 20 May 1981, 5; United Nations Report on UNDOF, 21 May to 20 November 1981, 5.

21. "U.S. Imports of Crude Oil," US Energy Information Administration, www.eia.gov/dnav/pet/hist/LeafHandler.ashx?n=PET&s=MCRIMUS1&f=M; "U.S. Imports from Saudi Arabia of Crude Oil," US Energy Information Administration, www.eia.gov/dnav/pet/hist/LeafHandler.ashx?n=PET&s=MCRIMUSSA2&f=M.

22. Adam B. Ulam, *Expansion and Coexistence: Soviet Foreign Policy 1917–73,* 2nd ed. (New York: Holt, Rinehart, and Winston, 1974), 414.

23. Karl Marx, *Capital,* vol. 1, trans. Ben Fowkes (London: Penguin, 1990).

5. The Bright and Dark Sides of Syria

1. Acts 9:11, www.biblegateway.com/passage/? search=Acts+9&=NKJV.

2. LTC John M. "Jack" Hammell, US Army (Retired), memorandum to the author, 15 June 2020.

3. Patrick Seale, *Asad: The Struggle for the Middle East* (Berkeley: Univ. of California Press, 1989), 336–337.

4. Seale, *Asad,* 328–329.

5. Seale, *Asad,* 316, 325.

6. R. Shareah Taleghani, "Breaking the Silence of Tadmor Military Prison," *Middle East Report* (summer 2015), 21.

7. Liz Sly, "Syria's Muslim Brotherhood Is Gaining Influence over Anti-Assad Revolt," *Washington Post,* 12 May 2012, https://www.washingtonpost.com /world/syrias-muslim-brotherhood-is-gaining-influence-over-anti-assad-revolt /2012/05/12/gIQAtIoJLU_story.html.

8. "Syrian Troops Massacre Scores of Assad's Foes," *Washington Post,* 25 June 1981, https://www.washingtonpost.com/archive/politics/1981/06/25 /syrian-troops-massacre-scores-of-assads-foes/1b60763a-e7d9-4cc0-b354-dbaea5edca77/.

9. "Syrian Troops Massacre Scores of Assad's Foes," *Washington Post.*

10. "Syrian Troops Massacre Scores of Assad's Foes," *Washington Post.*

11. "Syrian Troops Massacre Scores of Assad's Foes," Washington Post.

12. Associated Press, "Bomb Explosion in Syria Kills 64 And Hurts 135 in Crowded Area," *New York Times,* 30 November 1981, A1, https://nytimes.com /1981/11/30/world/bomb-explosion-in-syria-kills-64-and-hurts-135-in-crowded-area.html.

13. James H. Allan, *Peacekeeping: Outspoken Observations by a Field Officer* (Westport Conn.: Praeger, 1996), 58.

14. Allan, *Peacekeeping,* 58.

6. UNTSO in the Central Levant

1. COL David Betson, Irish Army (Retired), memorandum to the author, 28 December 2020.

2. Betson, memorandum, 28 December 2020.

3. COL David Betson, Irish Army (Retired), memorandum to the author, 4 December 2021.

4. Betson, memorandum, 28 December 2020.

5. École biblique et archéologique française de Jérusalem, commonly known as École Biblique, is a French academic establishment in Jerusalem specializing in archaeology and biblical exegesis.

6. The term "dispensing wisdom" was a favorite one of MAJ Denny Lindeman (USMC). It was his formulaic expression for providing necessary advice. But "dispensing wisdom" better expresses the marine's notion of passing on important lessons, as he did with me concerning the Russians and other matters.

7. LTC Joseph A. Serviss, US Army (Retired), memorandum to the author, 9 December 2020.

8. Serviss, memorandum, 9 December 2020.

9. COL Kevin M. Kennedy, US Marine Corps (Retired), personal papers, "United Nations Truce Supervision Organization, Observer Group Lebanon Duty Roster: 1–15 October 1981," 23 September 1981, 1–4.

10. United Nations Security Council, "Report of the Secretary-General on the United Nations Interim Force in Lebanon, (11 December 1979 to 12 June 1980), S/13994," United Nations, 12 June 1980, 9.

11. United Nations Security Council Resolution 128, [S/4023], 11 June 1958, http://unscr.com/en/resolutions/doc/128.

12. LTC Michael Fallon, US Marine Corps, Navy War College paper, "United Nations Peacekeeping Forces in Palestine: An Overview, 1948 to Present," ILMAC Organization Chart, February 1978 (Newport, R.I., December 1988).

13. United Nations Truce Supervision Organization (UNTSO), *General Information for UNMOS,* vol. 2, *UNTSO SOP* (UNTSO, June 1981), 3–4; United Nations Truce Supervision Organization, Observer Group Lebanon (OGL) Historical Background Paper Sub-Paragraph I(4), "Organization," circa 1981, 3.

14. United Nations Security Council, "Report of the Secretary-General on the United Nations Interim Force in Lebanon, (11 December 1979 to 12 June 1980), S/13994," United Nations, 12 June 1980, 4.

15. COL Clay Grubb, US Marine Corps (Retired), memorandum to the author, 21 March 2021.

16. Kennedy, personal papers, "United Nations Truce Supervision Organization, Observer Group Lebanon Duty Roster: 1–15 October 1981" (23 September 1981), 1–4.

17. CDR Virgil Bozeman III, US Navy (Retired), memorandum to the author, 11 December 2020.

18. Bozeman, memorandum, 11 December 2020.

19. MG E. A. Erskine, MSG, DSO Force Commander UNIFIL, *International Peace Keeping Operations Preparation Command and Control,* circa 1981, 145–146.

20. COL John B. "Jay" Sollis, US Marine Corps (Retired), memorandum to the author, 13 January 2022.

21. Serviss, memorandum, 9 December 2020.

22. Serviss, memorandum, 9 December 2020.

23. LTC Barry Gwyther, Australian Army (Retired), memorandum to the author, 10 January 2021.

24. Gwyther, memorandum, 10 January 2021.

25. Betson, memorandum, 28 December 2020.

26. Betson, memorandum, 28 December 2020.

27. Bozeman, memorandum, 11 December 2020.

28. Erskine, *International Peace Keeping Operations,* 13.

29. The term "DFF" was used by UNTSO to refer to the unofficial South Lebanese Army (SLA) formed by MAJ Saad Haddad, a Christian Lebanese Army offi-

cer, when the breakup of the official Lebanese Army began during that country's civil war in 1976. He declared a zone of about 650–700 square kilometers as "Free Lebanon" in 1980. UN authorities did not officially recognize them or the area they occupied as legitimate, naming it "the enclave."

30. Erskine, *International Peace Keeping Operations*, 13.

31. Serviss, memorandum, 9 December 2020.

7. The Woes of UNIFIL

1. "Israelis at Funerals for Gail Rubin," *New York Times*, 18 March 1978, 26, https://www.nytimes.com/1978/03/18/archives/israelis-at-funeral-for-gail-rubin.html.

2. Michael Omer-Man, "This Week in History: Israel's Deadliest Terror Attack," *Jerusalem Post*, 11 March 2011, https://www.jpost.com/Features/In-Thespotlight/This-Week-in-History-Israels-deadliest-terror-attack.

3. COL Michael O. Fallon, US Marine Corps (Retired), memorandum to the author, 16 April 2021.

4. Brigadier General Richard F. Vercauteren, US Marine Corps (Retired), memorandum to the author, 20 March 2021.

5. "Further Report on the Status of the Cease-Fire in the Israeli-Lebanese Sector, (S/11663/Add.52), 1 March 1978," United Nations, 1, https://digitallibrary.un.org/record/1467597.

6. As noted in the previous chapter, the term "armed elements" encompassed the Palestine Liberation Organization (PLO), its Army (PLA), the secular-Marxist Popular Front for the Liberation of Palestine (PFLP), the Democratic Front for the Liberation of Palestine (DFLP), the leftist pan-Arabist Lebanese National Movement (LNM), and the Shi'a Muslim group AMAL, an Iranian-leaning religious and political group.

7. "Further Report on the Status of the Cease-fire in the Israeli-Lebanese Sector, (S/11663/Add.52), 1 March 1978."

8. COL Michael O. Fallon, US Marine Corps (Retired), memorandum to the author, 10 March 2021.

9. Fallon, memorandum, 16 April 2021.

10. Fallon, memorandum, 10 March 2021.

11. Fallon, memorandum, 16 April 2021.

12. Fallon, memorandum, 10 March 2021.

13. "Mideast Situation—UNTSO—Report on the Status of the Cease-Fire, Further Report on the Status of the Cease-Fire in the Israel-Lebanon Sector, (S/11663/Add.53), 15 March 1978," United Nations, https://www.un.org/unispal/document/auto-insert-182073/.

14. Fallon, memorandum, 10 March 2021.

15. Fallon, memorandum, 10 March 2021 and 23 March 2021.

16. Tom Cooper and Sergio Santana, *Lebanese Civil War,* vol. 1, *Palestinian Diaspora, Syrian and Israeli Interventions, 1970–1978* (Warwick, UK: Helion, 2019), 78.

17. United Nations, "Mideast Situation—UNTSO—Report on the Status of the Cease-Fire, Further Report on the Status of the Cease-Fire in the Israel-Lebanon Sector, (S/11663/Add.53), 15 March 1978," United Nations, https://www.un.org/unispal/document/auto-insert-182073/.

18. "United Nations, Report (S/11663/Add.53), 15 March 1978," United Nations, https://www.un.org/unispal/document/auto-insert-182073/.

19. Fallon, memorandum, 10 March 2021 and 23 March 2021.

20. Fallon, memorandum, 10 March 2021 and 23 March 2021.

21. MG E. A. Erskine, MSG, DSO Force Commander UNIFIL, *International Peace Keeping Operations Preparation Command and Control,* circa 1981, 25; Cooper and Santana, *Lebanese Civil War,* 78.

22. "Israeli Invasion of Southern Lebanon, March 1978—Deployment of UN Peace-keeping Force-Israeli Withdrawal," *Keesing's Record of World Events* (formerly *Keesing's Contemporary Archives*), vol. 25 (June 1979), Israeli, Lebanon, page 29648.

23. Cooper and Santana, *Lebanese Civil War,* 79.

24. Jimmy Carter, *The Blood of Abraham: Insights into the Middle East* (Fayetteville: Univ. of Arkansas Press, 1993), 92–93.

25. Erskine, *International Peace Keeping Operations,* 37.

26. United Nations Charter, Chapter VII: "Action with Respect to Threats to the Peace, Breaches of the Peace, and Acts of Aggression (Articles 39–51)," https://www.un.org/en/about-us/un-charter/chapter-7.

27. United Nations Charter, Chapter VI: "Pacific Settlement of Disputes (Articles 33–38)," https://www.un.org/en/about-us/un-charter/chapter-6.

28. United Nations Security Council Resolution 425, 19 March 1978, http://unscr.com/en/resolutions/doc/425.

29. Erskine, *International Peace Keeping Operations,* 3–4; United Nations Security Council Resolution 425, 19 March 1978.

30. United Nations Security Council Resolution 426, 19 March 1978, http://unscr.com/en/resolutions/doc/426.

31. "Report of the Secretary-General on the United Nations Interim Force in Lebanon for the Period 19 March to 13 September 1978," United Nations, https://digitallibrary.un.org/record/224442.

32. Fallon, memorandum, 10 March 2021 and 23 March 2021; United Nations Interim Force in Lebanon, "UNIFIL, UNMAS Recommit to End Threats Posed by Landmines in South Lebanon," 4 April 2019, https://unifil.unmissions.org/unifil-unmas-recommit-end-threats-posed-landmines-south-lebanon.

33. United Nations Interim Force in Lebanon, "UNIFIL, UNMAS Recommit to End Threats Posed by Landmines in South Lebanon."

34. LTG Emmanuel A. Erskine, Ghanaian Army (Retired), *Mission with UNIFIL: An African Soldier's Reflections* (London, UK: Hurst, 1989), 18–19.

35. Erskine, *International Peace Keeping Operations*, 6.

36. Erskine, *International Peace Keeping Operations*, 31.

37. Erskine, *International Peace Keeping Operations*, 4; Erskine, *Mission with UNIFIL*, 36–37.

38. Erskine, *Mission with UNIFIL*, 36–37.

39. Erskine, *Mission with UNIFIL*, 36–37.

40. Cairo Agreement (1969), https://en.wikipedia.org/wiki/Cairo_Agreement_ (1969). The Cairo Agreement or Cairo Accord was an agreement reached on 2 November 1969 between Yasser Arafat and the Lebanese army commander General Emile Bustani. Egyptian president Nasser helped to broker the deal. Although the text has never been officially published, the Lebanese daily newspaper *An-Nahar* purportedly published it on 20 April 1970. The agreement established principles under which the presence and activities of Palestinian guerrillas in southeast Lebanon would be tolerated and regulated by the Lebanese authorities.

41. Erskine, *International Peace Keeping Operations*, 5; Erskine, *Mission with UNIFIL*, 36–37.

42. Erskine, *International Peace Keeping Operations*, 14.

43. Erskine, *International Peace Keeping Operations*, 31.

44. Erskine, *Mission with UNIFIL*, 37.

45. Erskine, *International Peace Keeping Operations*, 5.

46. Erskine, *International Peace Keeping Operations*, 61.

47. Vercauteren, memorandum, 20 March 2021.

48. Fallon, memorandum, 10 March 2021.

49. John Mackinlay, *The Peacekeepers: An Assessment of Peacekeeping Operations at the Arab-Israeli Interface* (London, UK: Unwin Hyman, 1989), 47.

50. *Keesing's Record of World Events*, vol. 25 (June 1979), 29648.

51. Erskine, *International Peace Keeping Operations*, 8.

52. Erskine, *International Peace Keeping Operations*, 8.

53. Mackinlay, *The Peacekeepers*, 49.

54. Fallon, memorandum, 18 April 2021.

55. Erskine, *International Peace Keeping Operations*, 18.

56. "United Nations Charter, Chapter VI: Pacific Settlement of Disputes," United Nations, https://www.un.org/en/about-us/un-charter/chapter-6.

57. Fallon, memorandum, 10 March 2021.

58. United Nations Security Council, "Report of the Secretary-General on the United Nations Interim Force in Lebanon, (19 March 1978 to 13 September 1978), S/12845," United Nations, 13 September 1979, 4–5, https://digitallibrary.un.org/record/224442?in=EN.

59. "Report of the Secretary-General on the United Nations Interim Force in Lebanon, (19 March 1978 to 13 September 1978), S/12845," 3.

60. Joachim A. Koops, Norrie MacQueen, Thierry Tardy, and Paul D. Williams, eds., *The Oxford Handbook of United Nations Peacekeeping Operations* (London, UK: Oxford Univ. Press, 2015), 249.

61. Erskine, *International Peace Keeping Operations,* 8.

62. Mackinlay, *The Peacekeepers,* 57.

63. "Report of the Secretary-General on the United Nations Interim Force in Lebanon, (19 March 1978 to 13 September 1978), S/12845," 3.

8. UNMO Duty in the "Wild West"

1. CDR Virgil Bozeman III, US Navy (Retired), memorandum to the author, 11 December 2020.

2. LTC Dennis C. "Denny" Lindeman, US Marine Corps (Retired), memorandum to the author, 18 January 2021.

3. "Nigerian Officer in UNIFIL Sentenced to 15 Years in Jail and Deported," *JTA Daily News Bulletin,* December 26, 1979, 3, http://pdfs.jta.org/1979/1979-12-26_244.pdf?_ga=2.190971114.1575810936.1620649555-1313427079.1620649555.

4. COL Clay Grubb, US Marine Corps (Retired), memorandum to the author, 21 March 2021.

5. LTG Emmanuel A. Erskine, Ghanaian Army (Retired), *Mission with UNIFIL: An African Soldier's Reflections* (London, UK: Hurst, 1989), 74.

6. Erskine, *Mission with UNIFIL,* 71–85.

7. MAJ Gordie Breault, US Air Force, "A Night to Remember," *UNTSO News* 1, no. 2 (March–April 1980), 14.

8. Breault, "A Night to Remember," 14.

9. COL Clay Grubb, US Marine Corps (Retired), memorandum to the author, 10 May 2021

10. Grubb, memorandum, 26 April 2021.

11. Erskine, *Mission with UNIFIL,* 44.

12. Erskine, *Mission with UNIFIL,* 83–84.

13. Grubb, memorandum, 28 April 2021.

14. Erskine, *Mission with UNIFIL,* 176–177.

15. COL Leonard M. "Lenny" Supko, US Marine Corps (Retired), personal journal, 28 January 1980.

16. COL Michael O. Fallon, US Marine Corps (Retired), memorandum to the author, 10 March 2021; and Supko, personal journal, 28 January 1980.

17. CDR Virgil Bozeman III, US Navy (Retired), memorandum to the author, 1 January 2021.

18. Bozeman, memorandum, 11 December 2020.

19. LTC Joseph A. Serviss, US Army (Retired), memorandum to the author, 9 December 2020.

20. Serviss, memorandum, 9 December 2020.

21. James H. Allan, *Peacekeeping: Outspoken Observations by a Field Officer* (Westport Conn.: Praeger, 1996), 66.

22. Grubb, memorandum, 21 March 2021.

23. Grubb, memorandum, 21 March 2021.

24. Grubb, memorandum, 21 March 2021.

25. Steve Hindy, "Between Beirut and a Hard Place," *Vice Magazine* (23 January 2014), https://www.vice.com/en/article/nnqnyz/between-beirut-and-a-hard-place-0000205-v21n1.

26. Grubb, memorandum, 28 January 2021. I made efforts to obtain an official report of the 16 April 1980 murder of the two Irish soldiers by a Haddad militiaman. The UN archives indicated they had no such report, and the Defense Intelligence Agency (DIA) did not find one after I submitted a Freedom of Information Act (FOIA) request on the matter.

27. LTC Barry Gwyther, Australian Army (Retired), memorandum to the author, 10 January 2021.

28. Bozeman, memorandum, 11 December 2020.

29. COL Des Travers, Irish Army (Retired), memorandum to the author, 19 February 2021.

30. COL Leonard M. "Lenny" Supko, US Marine Corps (Retired), memorandum to the author, 17 February 2021.

31. Supko, personal journal, 30 May 1980.

32. COL L. Scott Lingamfelter, US Army (Retired), *Desert Redleg: Artillery Warfare in the First Gulf War* (Lexington: Univ. Press of Kentucky, 2020), 43–44, 45, 63, 277.

33. LTC Dennis C. "Denny" Lindeman, US Marine Corps, (Retired), memorandum to the author, 21 January 2021.

34. Associated Press, "Haddad Accuses UN of 'Spying' in S. Lebanon," *Jerusalem Post*, 31 August 1980, 2.

35. "Haddad Accuses UN of 'Spying' in S. Lebanon," *Jerusalem Post*.

36. COL Kevin M. Kennedy, US Marine Corps (Retired), personal papers, "United Nations Truce Supervision Organization (UNTSO) Observer Group Lebanon (OGL) Mission Briefing, July–August 1981," 7.

37. COL Leonard M. "Lenny" Supko, US Marine Corps (Retired), memorandum to the author, 12 February 2021.

38. COL John B. "Jay" Sollis, US Marine Corps (Retired), memorandum to the author, 13 January 2022.

39. Supko, memorandum, 12 February 2021.

40. Allan, *Peacekeeping,* 66.

41. Allan, *Peacekeeping,* 66.

42. Two postscripts to this story: First, the reporting of Healy as a "Royal Australian Air Force" member would have been odd, as they are not known to use the "royal" prefix. Therefore, the story likely was rushed, unsubstantiated, and not fact-checked, which would have been a normal procedure. Second, there

was a tin and concrete structure that housed the "Golden Chicken" across from the OGL headquarters, where two civilians reported that "a Digger is dead." The press often met there and maybe picked up on the story and assumed the "digger" referenced was an Australian who was shot.

43. Supko, personal journal, 9 November 1979.

9. UNMO Teams in the "Wild West"

1. Steve Hindy, "Between Beirut and a Hard Place," *Vice Magazine* (23 January 2014), https://www.vice.com/en/article/nnqnyz/between-beirut-and-a-hard-place-0000205-v21n1.

2. Interestingly, later that day the DFF and the IDF attempted to seize OP HIN (see previous chapter), where Grubb was monitoring the mission that resulted in the wounding and killing of Irish soldiers on 18 April of 1980, even as MAJ Harry Klein was trying to deescalate the situation. To this day, Grubb believes that the DFF and the IDF immediately began an effort to cover up the incident.

3. COL Clay Grubb, US Marine Corps (Retired), memorandum to the author, 21 March 2021.

4. Robert Snell, "Deported Dearborn Man Arrested in Lebanon," *Detroit News,* 30 January 2015, www.detroitnews.com/story/news/local/wayne-county /2015/01/30/feds-deport-dearborn-ice-cream-man-tied-killings/22599779/.

5. In late 2015, Mahmoud Bazzi was tried before a Beirut military court. The Irish solider who was wounded, John O'Mahony, testified and identified Bazzi as the man who shot him and led the two other Irishmen to their deaths. Initially in 2015, Bazzi was found guilty of "collaboration with Israel" and sentenced to five years of hard labor. On 21 December 2020, a Lebanese military court found Bazzi guilty of the 18 April 1980 murders of PVT Thomas Barrett and PVT Derek Smallhorne. The court sentenced Bazzi to life in prison, but immediately reduced this sentence to 15 years due to his age (he was 76 at the time of his conviction), https://db0nus869y26v.cloudfront.net/en/At_Tiri_incident.

6. COL David Betson, Irish Army (Retired), memorandum to the author, 18 January 2021.

7. COL Desmond Travers, Irish Army (Retired), memorandum to the author, 19 February 2021.

8. United Nations Security Council, Official Records, Thirty-Sixth Year, 2292nd Meeting, 17 July 1981, New York, 4–5. https://digitallibrary.un.org /record/551441.

9. William Claiborne, "Rocket Barrage Kills 3 in Northern Israel," *Washington Post,* 16 July 1981, A20.

10. Claiborne, "Rocket Barrage Kills 3 in Northern Israel."

11. "Special Report of the Secretary-General on the United Nations Interim Force in Lebanon, S/14789," United Nations Security Council, 11 December 1981, 12.

12. United Nations Security Council, Official Records, Thirty-Sixth Year, 2292nd Meeting, 17 July 1981, New York, 4–5.

13. CDR Virgil Bozeman III, US Navy (Retired), memorandum to the author, 16 February 2021.

14. COL Kevin M. Kennedy, US Marine Corps (Retired), personal papers, "United Nations Truce Supervision Organization (UNTSO) Observer Group Lebanon (OGL) Mission Briefing, July–August 1981," 10–15.

15. UNTSO/OGL Mission Briefing, July–August 1981, 10–15.

16. "Minutes of Military Intelligence Officers (MIOs) Conference in Tibnin IRISHBATT on 14 August 1981," United Nations Interim Force in Lebanon (UNIFIL), 26 August 1981, 2–3.

17. "Minutes of Military Intelligence Officers (MIOs) Conference," United Nations Interim Force in Lebanon (UNIFIL), 3.

18. CPT Lee. S. Lingamfelter, US Army, "Liaison Officer After Action Report," United Nations Truce Supervision Organization (UNTSO) Memorandum, 20 August 1981, 1.

19. "Minutes of Military Intelligence Officers (MIOs) Conference," 4.

20. LTC Barry Gwyther, Australian Army (Retired), memorandum to the author, 10 January 2021.

21. "Report of the Secretary-General on the United Nations Interim Force in Lebanon," United Nations Security Council, 12 December 1980 to 12 June 1981, 13.

22. Grubb, memorandum, 15 April 2021.

23. COL John B. "Jay" Sollis, US Marine Corps (Retired), memorandum to the author, 13 January 2022. (CPT Jay Sollis was given this advice by MAJ Lenny Supko before Sollis deployed to UNTSO.)

24. The decision to create a new Team X-Ray to liaise with the DFF and the PLO in the enclave was no doubt a political one. Team Zulu's reputation had become sullied after the At Tiri incident, when Irish soldiers were killed and wounded. The "new" Team X-Ray would mark, hopefully, a new page in cooperation.

25. COL Kevin M. Kennedy, US Marine Corps (Retired), personal papers, "United Nations Truce Supervision (UNTSO) an Observer Group Lebanon Command Briefing," circa 1981, 3–6.

26. Travers, memorandum, 19 February 2021.

27. Travers, memorandum, 19 February 2021.

28. CPT Lee S. Lingamfelter (USA), "Team Tyre After Action Report," United Nations Truce Supervision Organization (UNTSO) Memorandum, 28 January 1981, 1–2.

29. CDR Virgil Bozeman III, US Navy (Retired), memorandum to the author, 11 December 2020.

30. Supko, memorandum, 12 February 2021.

31. As a practical matter, the rule prohibiting two UNMOs of the same nationality from accompanying one another on a mobile patrol made sense. If the two UNMOs were of different nationalities and were hijacked or in some way

threatened, the UN could call on the good offices of two nationalities—not just one—to put diplomatic pressure on the captors to release the UNMOs.

32. Lingamfelter, "Team Tyre After Action Report," 2.

33. Supko, memorandum, 17 February 2021.

34. COL Clay Grubb, US Marine Corps (Retired), memorandum to the author, 12 February 2021.

35. Travers, memorandum, 19 February 2021.

36. Supko, memorandum, 17 February 2021.

37. Supko, memorandum, 12 February 2021.

38. Bozeman, memorandum, 11 December 2020.

39. COL Michael O. Fallon, US Marine Corps (Retired), memorandum to the author, 10 March 2021.

40. LTC Dennis C. "Denny" Lindeman, US Marine Corps (Retired), memorandum to the author, 23 January 2021.

41. Lindeman memorandum, 23 January 2021.

42. US Department of State, Office of the Historian, "Milestones 1993 to 2000: The Oslo Accords and the Arab-Israeli Peace Process," https://history.state.gov/milestones/1993-2000/oslo.

43. COL Clay Grubb, US Marine Corps (Retired), memorandum to the author, 11 May 2021.

44. Grubb, memorandum, 11 May 2021.

45. "Observer Group Lebanon: The Dangers of Driving in Beirut," *UNTSO News* 2, no. 4 (July–August 1981), 16.

46. Bozeman, memorandum, 16 February 2021.

10. The Gathering Storm Erupts

1. COL Geoff Bell, Australian Army (Retired), memorandum to the author, 18 March 2021.

2. CPT Geoff Bell was a thoroughly professional Australian Army officer. He, his wife, Maria, and Shelley and I served together in Observer Group Jerusalem. Bell was in an ideal place to observe and note Erskine's reaction to the Sadat assassination and is an unimpeachable source.

3. LTC Joseph A. Serviss, US Army (Retired), memorandum to the author, 19 March 2021.

4. Bell, memorandum, 18 March 2021.

5. UPI, "Three Americans Wounded in the Assassination of Egyptian President," 8 October 1981, https://www.upi.com/Archives/1981/10/08/Three-Americans-wounded-in-the-assassination-of-Egyptian-President/7189371361600/.

6. "Egyptian Columnists: We Do Not Regret the Death of Arafat, Who Expressed His Joy at Sadat's Assassination," *MEMRI*, https://www.memri.org/reports/egyptian-columnists-we-do-not-regret-death-arafat-who-expressed-his-joy-sadats-assassination.

7. LTC John M. "Jack" Hammell, US Army (Retired), memorandum to the author, 25 January 2021; COL Stephen D. Cotter, US Air Force (Retired), memorandum to the author, 27 September 2021.

8. CDR Virgil Bozeman III, US Navy (Retired), memorandum to the author, 18 March 2021.

9. William E. Farrell, "5 Sadat Assassins Executed in Egypt," *New York Times,* 16 April 1982, A-1, https://www.nytimes.com/1982/04/16/world/5-sadat-assassins-executed-in-egypt.html.

10. Bell, memorandum, 18 March 2021.

11. Bell, memorandum, 18 March 2021.

12. "Special Report of the Secretary-General on the United Nations Interim Force in Lebanon, S/14869," United Nations Security Council, 16 February 1982, 2.

13. Bell, memorandum, 18 March 2021.

14. Bell, memorandum, 18 March 2021.

15. "Special Report of the Secretary-General on the United Nations Interim Force in Lebanon, S/13994," United Nations Security Council, 12 June 1980, 10.

16. "Special Report of the Secretary-General on the United Nations Interim Force in Lebanon, S/14295," United Nations Security Council, 12 December 1980, 17.

17. "Special Report of the Secretary-General on the United Nations Interim Force in Lebanon, S/14295," United Nations Security Council, 12 December 1980, 20.

18. "Special Report of the Secretary-General on the United Nations Interim Force in Lebanon, S/14295," United Nations Security Council, 12 December 1980, 20.

19. "Special Report of the Secretary-General on the United Nations Interim Force in Lebanon, S/14295," United Nations Security Council, 12 December 1980, 21.

20. "Special Report of the Secretary-General on the United Nations Interim Force in Lebanon, S/14537," United Nations Security Council, 15 June 1981, 11–12.

21. "Special Report of the Secretary-General on the United Nations Interim Force in Lebanon, S/14537," United Nations Security Council, 15 June 1981, 15.

22. "Special Report of the Secretary-General on the United Nations Interim Force in Lebanon, S/14537," United Nations Security Council, 15 June 1981, 15–16.

23. During the following dates in 1981, these exchanges of artillery occurred:

DATE	ARMED ELEMENTS	DFF/IDF
27 March	unknown	unknown
28 March	200 rounds	200 rounds
29 March	30 rounds	100 rounds
30 March	205 rounds	340 rounds

DATE	ARMED ELEMENTS	DFF/IDF
3 April	319 rounds (from Tyre 90 rounds)	400 rounds (on Tyre only 50)
8 April	11 rounds	30 rounds
9 April	440 rounds	650 rounds
10 April	19 rounds	31 rounds
17 April	15 rounds	
18 April	60 rounds	60 rounds
19 April	limited	27 rounds (at Fijians)
20 April	313 rounds	450 rounds
21 April	10 rounds	230 rounds
24 April	210 rounds	140 rounds
25 April	62 rounds	185 rounds
26 April	0 rounds	125 rounds
27 April	340 rounds (41 additional rockets in Western Galilee)	800 rounds (jets against Tyre Pocket)
29 April	52 rounds	150 rounds
4 May	limited	300 rounds
6 May	limited	
13 May		150 rounds
17 May	limited	
18 May	limited	64 rounds
19 May	4 rounds	72 rounds
20 May		21 rounds
21 May	6 rounds	
24–28 May	limited, 18 rounds	66 rounds (24 May)
29 May	27 rounds	37 rounds

Source: "Special Report of the Secretary-General on the United Nations Interim Force in Lebanon, S/14537," United Nations Security Council, 15 June 1981, 15–18.

24. "Special Report of the Secretary-General on the United Nations Interim Force in Lebanon, S/14537," United Nations Security Council, 15 June 1981, 18.

25. "Special Report of the Secretary-General on the United Nations Interim Force in Lebanon, S/14537," United Nations Security Council, 15 June 1981, 17–18.

26. "Special Report of the Secretary-General on the United Nations Interim Force in Lebanon, S/14537," United Nations Security Council, 15 June 1981, 18–19.

27. "Special Report of the Secretary-General on the United Nations Interim Force in Lebanon, S/14537," United Nations Security Council, 15 June 1981, 19.

28. "Special Report of the Secretary-General on the United Nations Interim Force in Lebanon, S/14789," United Nations Security Council, 11 December 1981, 12.

29. "Special Report of the Secretary-General on the United Nations Interim Force in Lebanon, S/14789," United Nations Security Council, 11 December 1981, 12.

30. Charles Mohr, "U.S., Reacting to Raids, Puts off Announcement of Israeli F-16's," *New York Times,* 18 July 1981, section 1, 1, https://www.nytimes.com /1981/07/18/world/us-reacting-to-raids-puts-off-announcement-on-israeli-f-16-s .html.

31. "Special Report of the Secretary-General on the United Nations Interim Force in Lebanon, S/14789," United Nations Security Council, 11 December 1981, 13.

32. "Special Report of the Secretary-General on the United Nations Interim Force in Lebanon, S/14789," United Nations Security Council, 11 December 1981, 13.

33. "Special Report of the Secretary-General on the United Nations Interim Force in Lebanon, S/14789," United Nations Security Council, 11 December 1981, 13.

34. "Special Report of the Secretary-General on the United Nations Interim Force in Lebanon, S/14789," United Nations Security Council, 11 December 1981, 12.

35. Serviss, memorandum, 9 December 2020.

36. Bell, memorandum, 18 March 2021.

37. Bell, memorandum, 18 March 2021.

38. Richard A. Gabriel, *Operation Peace for Galilee: The Israeli-PLO War in Lebanon* (New York: Hill and Wang, 1984), 47, 81.

39. John Mackinlay, *The Peacekeepers: An Assessment of Peacekeeping Operations at the Arab-Israeli Interface* (London, UK: Unwin Hyman, 1989), 71.

40. Mackinlay, *The Peacekeepers,* 71.

41. COL Desmond Travers, Irish Army (Retired), memorandum to the author, 19 February 2021.

42. Gabriel, *Operation Peace for Galilee,* 50–51.

43. "Special Report of the Secretary-General on the United Nations Interim Force in Lebanon, S/14789," United Nations Security Council, 11 December 1981, 14.

44. "Special Report of the Secretary-General on the United Nations Interim Force in Lebanon, S/14789," United Nations Security Council, 11 December 1981, 15.

45. COL Leonard M. "Lenny" Supko, US Marine Corps (Retired), memorandum to the author, 17 February 2021.

46. COL John B. "Jay" Sollis, US Marine Corps (Retired), memorandum to the author, 13 January 2022.

47. "Special Report of the Secretary-General on the United Nations Interim Force in Lebanon, S/14869," United Nations Security Council, 16 February 1982, 1.

48. "Special Report of the Secretary-General on the United Nations Interim Force in Lebanon, S/14869," United Nations Security Council, 16 February 1982, 2.

49. COL Kevin M. Kennedy, US Marine Corps (Retired), memorandum to the author, 15 November 2021.

50. "Special Report of the Secretary-General on the United Nations Interim Force in Lebanon, S/14996," United Nations Security Council, 25 April 1982, 1.

51. "Special Report of the Secretary-General on the United Nations Interim Force in Lebanon, S/14996," United Nations Security Council, 25 April 1982, 1.

52. "Special Report of the Secretary-General on the United Nations Interim Force in Lebanon, S/15194," United Nations Security Council, 10 June 1982, 11–12.

53. "Special Report of the Secretary-General on the United Nations Interim Force in Lebanon, S/15194," United Nations Security Council, 10 June 1982, 10–11.

54. Ze'ev Schiff and Ehud Ya'ari, *Israel's Lebanon War* (New York: Simon and Schuster, 1984), 97–101.

55. Lawrence Joffe, "Obituary of Shlomo Argov," *Guardian*, 24 February 2003, https://www.theguardian.com/world/2003/feb/25/israelandthepalestinians.lebanon.

56. Gilad Sharon, *Sharon: The Life of a Leader* (New York: Harper Collins, 2011), 257.

57. Sharon, *Sharon*, 258.

58. David K. Shipler, "Cease-Fire in Border Fighting Declared by Israel and the PLO; U.S. Sees Hope for Wider Peace," *New York Times*, 25 July 1981, section 1, 1, https://www.nytimes.com/1981/07/25/world/cease-fire-border-fighting-declared-israel-plo-us-sees-hope-for-wider-peace.html.

59. James Chace, "The Turbulent Tenure of Alexander Haig," *New York Times*, 22 April 1984, https://www.nytimes.com/1984/04/22/books/the-turbulent-tenure-of-alexander-haig.html.

60. Brian R. Parkinson, "Israel's Lebanon War: Ariel Sharon and Operation Peace for Galilee," *Journal of Third World Studies* 24, no. 2, *Historical and Contemporary Political, Economic, and Social Developments in the Third World* (fall 2007): 68.

61. Supko, memorandum, 12 February 2021.

62. Kennedy, memorandum, 15 November 2021.

63. Sollis, memorandum, 13 January 2022.

64. United Nations Security Council, "Special Report of the Secretary-General on the United Nations Interim Force in Lebanon, S/15194/Add.1," United Nations Security Council, 11 June 1982, 3.

65. Mackinlay, *The Peacekeepers*, 77.

66. United Nations Security Council, "2377th Meeting Held in New York on Tuesday, 8 June 1982, at 10 p.m."; https://documents-dds-ny.un.org/doc/undoc /gen/nl8/200/57/pdf/nl820057-pdf?openelement.

67. Mackinlay, *The Peacekeepers, 77–75*; Gabriel, *Operation Peace for Galilee, 80–81.*

11. Peace for No One

1. Alexandra Novosseloff, "The United Nations Interim Force in Lebanon (UNIFIL I)," in *The Oxford Handbook of United Nations Peacekeeping Operations,* ed. Joachim A. Koops, Norrie MacQueen, Thierry Tardy, and Paul D. Williams (London, UK: Oxford Univ. Press, 2015), 249.

2. United Nations, "United Nations Interim Force in Lebanon (UNIFIL) Mandate," https://unifil.unmissions.org/unifil-mandate.

3. Robert Fisk, *Pity the Nation: Lebanon at War,* 3rd ed. (New York: Oxford Univ. Press, 2001), 255.

4. Christopher Paul, Colin P. Clarke, Beth Grill, and Molly Dunigan, "Lebanese Civil War, 1975–1990 Case Outcome: COIN Loss (Mixed, Favoring Insurgents)," in *Paths to Victory: Detailed Insurgency Case Studies* (Santa Monica, Calif.: RAND Corporation, 2013), 388–389; Brian R. Parkinson, "Israel's Lebanon War: Ariel Sharon and Operation Peace for Galilee," *Journal of Third World Studies* 24, no. 2, *Historical and Contemporary Political, Economic, and Social Developments in the Third World* (fall 2007): 63–84.

5. Richard A. Gabriel, *Operation Peace for Galilee: The Israeli-PLO War in Lebanon* (New York: Hill and Wang, 1984), 104–105.

6. Parkinson, "Israel's Lebanon War," 76.

7. Ze'ev Schiff and Ehud Ya'ari, *Israel's Lebanon War* (New York: Simon and Schuster, 1984), 224–228.

8. BBC, "1982: PLO Leader Forced from Beirut," http://news.bbc.co.uk /onthisday/hi/dates/stories/august/30/newsid_2536000/2536441.stm.

9. LTG Emmanuel A. Erskine, Ghanaian Army (Retired), *Mission with UNIFIL: An African Soldier's Reflections* (London, UK: Hurst, 1989), 18.

10. Parkinson, "Israel's Lebanon War," 73.

11. Parkinson, "Israel's Lebanon War," 77.

12. Parkinson, "Israel's Lebanon War," 77.

13. Peace Now, https://peacenow.org.il/about/odot.

14. Parkinson, "Israel's Lebanon War," 77.

15. BBC, "Flashback: Sabra and Shatila Massacres," http://news.bbc.co.uk/2 /hi/middle_east/1779713.stm.

16. Gabriel, *Operation Peace for Galilee,* 164–165.

17. John Mackinlay, *The Peacekeepers: An Assessment of Peacekeeping Operations at the Arab-Israeli Interface* (London, UK: Unwin Hyman, 1989), 69.

18. "Deputy Press Secretary Speaks on the Situation in Lebanon (September 1982)," Public Papers of the President Ronald Reagan Administration, https://www.reaganlibrary.gov/archives/speech/statement-deputy-press-secretary-speakes-situation-lebanon-2.

19. Mackinlay, The Peacekeepers, 81.

20. Eric Weiner, Bureau of Diplomatic Security, US Department of State, "Remembering the 1983 Suicide Bombings in Beirut: The Tragic Events That Created the Diplomatic Security Service," https://2017-2021.state.gov/remembering-the-1983-suicide-bombings-in-beirut-the-tragic-events-that-created-the-diplomatic-security-service/index.html.

21. Associated Press, "Text of the Agreement Between Israel and Lebanon on Troop Withdrawal," New York Times, 17 May 1983, A12, https://www.nytimes.com/1983/05/17/world/text-of-the-agreement-between-israel-and-lebanon-on-troop-withdrawal.html.

22. Mackinlay, The Peacekeepers, 82–83.

23. COL Timothy J. Geraghty, Peacekeepers at War (Dulles, Va: Potomac Books, 2009), 52.

24. "Deputy Press Secretary Speaks on the Situation in Lebanon (September 1982)."

25. Geraghty, Peacekeepers at War, 7.

26. Geraghty, Peacekeepers at War, 7.

27. Mackinlay, The Peacekeepers, 86.

28. Mackinlay, The Peacekeepers, 87.

29. Thomas L. Friedman, "Gemayel Decision on Pact Reported," New York Times, 29 February 1984, https://www.nytimes.com/1984/02/29/world/gemayel-decision-on-pact-reported.html.

30. Parkinson, "Israel's Lebanon War," 70.

31. JTA Daily News Bulletin, "Israel's Army Reports 368 Soldiers Were Killed and 2,383 Were Wounded in Lebanon War," 13 October 1982, http://pdfs.jta.org/1982/1982-10-13_193.pdf? _ga=2.66119403.430022409.1641669957-1542143741.1641574295; Richard A. Gabriel, Operation Peace for Galilee: The Israeli-PLO War in Lebanon (New York: Hill and Wang, 1984), 236.

32. UPI, "2 Americans Killed in Lebanon," New York Times, September 26, 1982, section 1, page 22, https://www.nytimes.com/1982/09/26/world/2-americans-killed-in-lebanon.html; United Nations Security Council, "Report of the Secretary-General in Pursuance of Security Council Resolution 521 (1982)," S/15408/Add.1, 27 September 1982, 2.

33. Erskine, Mission with UNIFIL, 96–97.

34. Mackinlay, The Peacekeepers, 77–78.

35. COL John B. "Jay" Sollis, US Marine Corps (Retired), interview by the author, 8 January 2022.

36. "Legends, William R. Higgins," Marine Corps Coordinating Council of Kentucky, https://kentuckymarines.org/legend/legends/william-r-higgins/.

37. Fisk, *Pity the Nation,* 255.

38. Fisk, *Pity the Nation,* 83, 170–2, 300, 486–487, 565, 584–593.

39. Paul D. Williams, "The United Nations Operation in Somalia II (UNOSOM II) (UNIFIL I)," in *The Oxford Handbook of United Nations Peacekeeping Operations,* ed. Joachim A. Koops, Norrie MacQueen, Thierry Tardy, and Paul D. Williams (London, UK: Oxford Univ. Press, 2015), 427–440.

40. United Nations, "Monthly Summary of Troop Contributions to Peacekeeping Operations as of 31 December 1977," https://peacekeeping.un.org/sites/default /files/dec-1997.pdf; United Nation Truce Supervision Organization (UNTSO), "Facts and Figures," https://untso.unmissions.org/facts-and-figures.

41. CDR Virgil Bozeman III, US Navy (Retired), memorandum to the author, 11 December 2020.

12. Sentinels of Peace

1. COL John B. "Jay" Sollis, US Marine Corps (Retired), memorandum to the author, 4 January 2022.

2. LTC Tommy G. Cates, US Air Force (Retired), memorandum to the author, 29 January 2022.

3. Joint Chiefs of Staff, "13th Chairman of the Joint Chiefs of Staff," https:// www.jcs.mil/About/The-Joint-Staff/Chairman/General-John-Malchase-David-Shalikashvili/.

4. COL Kevin M. Kennedy, US Marine Corps (Retired), memorandum to the author, 15 November 2021.

5. Interestingly, Shalikashvili was not a sanctioned member of UNTSO simply because he was the US staff director for UNTSO personnel. He was certainly not under the diplomatic covering of the United Nations at the time. Therefore, he was not permitted to enter Lebanon via the United Nations. However, Baker and Kennedy gained permission for him to do so. Given his status as a senior American officer, the IDF permitted him to cross—interestingly, a permission that was not theirs to grant. Nonetheless, his presence in southern Lebanon was probably not officially approved.

6. Kennedy, memorandum to the author, 15 November 2021.

7. Congress.gov, "H.R.3622-Goldwater-Nichols Department of Defense Reorganization Act of 1986," 99th Congress (1985–1986), https://www.congress .gov/bill/99th-congress/house-bill/3622.

8. Joint Chiefs of Staff, "National Military Strategy of the United States of America 1995: A Strategy of Flexible and Selective Engagement" (Washington D.C.: GPO, 1995), 9, https://nssarchive.us/wp-content/uploads/library/nms/nms1995.

9. Paul D. Williams, "The United Nations Operation in Somalia II (UNOSOM II) (UNIFIL I)," in *The Oxford Handbook of United Nations Peacekeeping Operations,* ed. Joachim A. Koops, Norrie MacQueen, Thierry Tardy, and Paul D. Williams (London, UK: Oxford Univ. Press, 2015), 427–440.

10. The Institute for Policy Studies, "Peacekeeping and the United Nations," https://ips-dc.org/peacekeeping_and_the_united_nations/.

11. Quynh-Nhu Vuong, "U. S. Peacekeeping and Nation-Building: The Evolution of Self-Interested Multilateralism," *Berkeley Journal of International Law* 21, no. 3 (2003): 804, 812–814.

12. The Institute for Policy Studies, "Peacekeeping and the United Nations," https://ips-dc.org/peacekeeping_and_the_united_nations/.

13. Joint Chiefs of Staff, "National Military Strategy of the United States of America 1995: A Strategy of Flexible and Selective Engagement," 21.

14. National Security Strategy Archives, "The National Military Strategy of the United States of America: A Strategy for Today; A Vision for Tomorrow" (2004), https://nssarchive.us/wp-content/uploads/library/nms/nms2004.

15. Department of Defense, "The National Military Strategy of the United States of America, Redefining America's Military Leadership" (Washington, D.C., 2011), https://dod.defense.gov/Portals/1/Documents/pubs/2011-National-Military-Strategy.pdf.

16. Joint Chiefs of Staff, "The Military Strategy of the United States of America, The United States Military's Contribution to National Security" (Washington, D.C., June 2015), https://www.jcs.mil/Portals/36/Documents/Publications/2015_National_Military_Strategy.pdf.

17. Joint Chiefs of Staff, "Description of the National Military Strategy" (2018), https://nssarchive.us/wp-content/uploads/2020/04/UNCLASS_2018_National_Military_Strategy_Description-1.pdf.

18. United Nations Peacekeeping, "Troop and Police Contributions" (1990–2021), https://peacekeeping.un.org/en/troop-and-police-contributors; United Nations Truce Supervision Organization (UNTSO), "Facts and Figures," https://untso.unmissions.org/facts-and-figures.

19. Cedric de Coning, Julian Detzel, and Petter Hojem, *UN Peacekeeping Operations Capstone Doctrine* (Oslo, Norway: Norsk Utenrikspolitisk Institutt, 2008), 1, https://www.unocha.org/sites/dms/Documents/DPKO%20Capstone%20doctrine%20(2008).pdf

20. Army Doctrine Publication ADP 3-07, *Stability,* 31 July 2019, iii, https://armypubs.army.mil/epubs/DR_pubs/DR_a/pdf/web/ARN18011_ADP%203-07%20FINAL%20WEB.pdf; US Army FM 100-23, *Peace Operations,* 1994, 15–18, https://www.bits.de/NRANEU/others/amd-us-archive/fm100-23%2894%29.pdf; US Army FM 100-5, *Operations,* (1993), 13-0–13-8, https://www.bits.de/NRANEU/others/amd-us-archive/fm100-5%202893%29.pdf.

21. Institute for the Study of War, "Ukraine Conflict Updates," 24 February 2022, https://www.understandingwar.org/backgrounder/ukraine-conflict-updates.

22. Casper W. Weinberger, speech before the National Press Club, "The Uses of Military Power," 28 November 1984, http://insidethecoldwar.org/sites/default/files/documents/Statement%20by%20Secretary%200f%20Defense%20

Weinberger%20at%20National%20Press%20Club%2C%20November%
2028%2C%201984.pdf.

23. Jeffery Record, "Back to the Weinberger-Powell Doctrine?" Air University, *Strategic Studies Quarterly* (fall 2007), 79–95, https://www.airuniversity.af.edu /Portals/10/SSQ/documents/Volume-01_Issue-1/Record.pdf.

24. COL Dale C. Eikmeier (USA), "Ends, Ways, Means: A Logical Method for Center-of-Gravity Analysis," *Military Review* (September–October 2007), https://www.armyupress.army.mil/Portals/7/military-review/Archives/English /MilitaryReview_20071031_art009.pdf.

25. Trevor Findlay, *The Use of Force in UN Peace Operations* (New York: Oxford Univ. Press, 2002), 2.

26. Andrew Theobald, "The United Nations Truce Supervision Organization (UNTSO)," in *The Oxford Handbook of United Nations Peacekeeping Operations,* ed. Joachim A. Koops, Norrie MacQueen, Thierry Tardy, and Paul D. Williams (London, UK: Oxford Univ. Press, 2015), 129; United Nations Interim Force in Lebanon, "FAQs," https://unifil.unmissions.org/faqs; "UN Military Observers Killed by Air Strike in Lebanon," United Nations News and Media Photo, 23 July 2006, https://www.unmultimedia.org/s/photo/detail/122/0122753.html; Albert J. Vinke, "The Bombing of UN Post Khiam (2006)," *Historiek,* 12 October 2021, https:// historiek.net/het-bombardement-op-vn-post-khiam-in-libanon-2006/142915/.

27. LTC Thomas G. Cates, US Air Force (Retired), memorandum to the author, 18 September 2021.

28. "Colonel Sholly Ends His Mission in Jerusalem," *UNTSO News* 4, no. 2 (July–August 1983), 5.

Epilogue

1. Isaiah 2:4, NKJV, "He shall judge between the nations, And rebuke many people; They shall beat their swords into plowshares, And their spears into pruning hooks; Nation shall not lift up sword against nation, Neither shall they learn war anymore," https://www.biblegateway.com/passage/?search=Isaiah+2&version =NKJV.

2. Wolfgang Saxon, "Amos Perlmutter, 69, Expert on Middle Eastern Affairs," *New York Times,* 16 June 2001, https://www.nytimes.com/2001/06/16/world /amos-perlmutter-69-expert-on-middle-eastern-affairs.html.

3. COL Michael O. Fallon, US Marine Corps (Retired), memorandum to the author, 26 December 2021.

4. COL Leonard M. "Lenny" Supko, US Marine Corps (Retired), memorandum to the author, 27 December 2021.

5. COL Clay Grubb, US Marine Corps (Retired), memorandum to the author, 28 December 2021.

6. COL Kevin M. Kennedy, US Marine Corps (Retired), memorandum to the author, 3 January 2022 and 8 June 2022.

7. COL John B. "Jay" Sollis, US Marine Corps (Retired), memorandum to the author, 3 January 2022.

8. LTC Dennis C. "Denny" Lindeman, US Marine Corps (Retired), memorandum to the author, 28 December 2021.

9. LTC Joseph A. Serviss, US Army (Retired), memorandum to the author, 30 December 2021.

10. LTC John M. "Jack" Hammell, US Army (Retired), memorandum to the author, 1–2 June 2022.

11. CDR Virgil Bozeman III, US Navy (Retired), memorandum to the author, 2 June 2022.

12. LTC Tommy G. Cates, US Air Force (Retired), memorandum to the author, 29 January 2022.

13. The Nobel Prize, "The Nobel Peace Prize, 1988," https://www.nobelprize.org/prizes/peace/1988/summary/.

14. Lincoln Memorial, "Lincoln's Second Inaugural Address," https://www.nps.gov/linc/learn/historyculture/lincoln-second-inaugural.htm.

Bibliography

Books

Allan, James H. *Peacekeeping: Outspoken Observations by a Field Officer.* Westport Conn.: Praeger, 1996.

Blue Helmets: A Review of United Nations Peace-Keeping, 3rd ed. New York: United Nations Publications, 1996.

Carter, Jimmy. *The Blood of Abraham: Insights into the Middle East.* Fayetteville: Univ. of Arkansas Press, 1993.

Charter of the United Nations and Statute of the International Court of Justice. New York: United Nations Publications, 1945.

Coning, Cedric de, Julian Detzel, and Petter Hojem. *UN Peacekeeping Operations Capstone Doctrine.* Oslo, Norway: Norsk Utenrikspolitisk Institutt, 2008.

Cooper, Tom, and Sergio Santana. *Lebanese Civil War.* Vol. 1, *Palestinian Diaspora, Syrian and Israeli Interventions, 1970–1978.* Warwick, UK: Helion, 2019.

Davis, M. Thomas. *40 Km into Lebanon: Israel's 1982 Invasion.* Washington, D.C.: National Defense Univ. Press, 1987.

El-Gamasy, Mohamed Abdel Ghani. *The October War.* Cairo, Egypt: American University in Cairo Press, 1993.

Erskine, LTG Emmanuel A. (Retired). *Mission with UNIFIL: An African Soldier's Reflections.* London, UK: Hurst, 1989.

Findlay Trevor. *The Use of Force in UN Peace Operations.* New York: Oxford Univ. Press, 2002.

Fisk, Robert. *Pity the Nation: Lebanon at War,* 3rd ed. New York: Oxford Univ. Press, 2001.

Gabriel, Richard A. *Operation Peace for Galilee: The Israeli-Palestinian War in Lebanon.* New York. Hill and Wang, 1984.

Gawrych, George W. *The Albatross of Decisive Victory: War and Policy Between Egypt and Israel in the 1967 and 1973 Arab-Israeli Wars.* Westport, Conn.: Greenwood, 2000.

Geraghty, COL Timothy J. *Peacekeepers at War.* Dulles, Va.: Potomac Books, 2009.

The Institute for Policy Studies. "Peacekeeping and the United Nations." https://ips-dc.org/peacekeeping_and_the_united_nations/#:~:text=A%20Presidential

%20Decision%20Directive%20%28PDD%2025%29%2C%20signed% 20by,to%20fight%20and%20win%20wars%2C%20unilaterally%20 whenever%20necessary.%E2%80%9D.

International Peace Academy. *Peacekeepers Handbook*. New York: Pergamon, 1984.

Joint Chiefs of Staff. "National Military Strategy of the United States of America 1995: A Strategy of Flexible and Selective Engagement." Washington D.C.: GPO, 1995. https://nssarchive.us/wp-content/uploads/library/nms/nms1995.

Keesing's Record of World Events, vol. 25. London: Longman, June 1979.

Koops, Joachim A., Norrie MacQueen, Thierry Tardy, and Paul D. Williams, eds. *The Oxford Handbook of United Nations Peacekeeping Operations*. London, UK: Oxford Univ. Press, 2015.

Lingamfelter, COL L. Scott, US Army (Retired). *Desert Redleg: Artillery Warfare in the First Gulf War*. Lexington: Univ. Press of Kentucky, 2020.

Mackinlay, John. *The Peacekeepers: An Assessment of Peacekeeping Operations at the Arab-Israeli Interface*. London, UK: Unwin Hyman, 1989.

Maier, Paul L. *In the Fullness of Time: A Historian Looks at Christmas, Easter, and the Early Church*. Grand Rapids, Mich.: Kregel, 1991.

McCullough, David. *Truman*. New York: Simon and Schuster, 1992.

National Military Strategy of the United States of America: "A Strategy of Flexible and Selective Engagement." Washington D.C.: Joint Chiefs of Staff, 1997.

Paul, Christopher, Colin P. Clarke, Beth Grill, and Molly Dunigan. "Lebanese Civil War, 1975–1990 Case Outcome: COIN Loss (Mixed, Favoring Insurgents)." In *Paths to Victory: Detailed Insurgency Case Studies* Santa Monica, Calif.: RAND Corporation, 2013.

Schiff, Ze'ev, and Ehud Ya'ari. *Israel's Lebanon War*. New York: Simon and Schuster, 1984.

Seale, Patrick. *Asad: The Struggle for the Middle East*. Berkeley: Univ. of California Press, 1989.

Sharon, Gilad. *Sharon: The Life of a Leader*. New York, Harper Collins, 2011.

Ulam, Adam B. *Expansion and Coexistence: Soviet Foreign Policy 1917–73*, 2nd ed. New York: Holt, Rinehart, and Winston, 1974.

US Army Doctrine Publication ADP 3-07. *Stability*. Washington, D.C.: GPO, 2019.

US Army FM 100-23. *Peace Operations*. Washington, D.C.: GPO, 1994.

US Army FM 100-5. *Operations*. Washington, D.C.: GPO, 1992.

United Nations Truce Supervision Organization (UNTSO). *General Information for UNMOS*. Vol. 2, *UNTSO SOP*. Jerusalem, Israel: UNTSO, June 1981.

Journals

Breault, MAJ Gordie, US Air Force. "A Night to Remember." *UNTSO News* 1. no 2. (March–April 1980): 14.

Hindy, Steve. "Between Beirut and a Hard Place." *Vice Magazine*, 23 January 2014, https://www.vice.com/en/article/nnqnyz/between-beirut-and-a-hard-place-0000205-v21n1.

Killgore, Andrew I. "In Memoriam Col. Robert W. Rickert (1912–1995)." *Washington Report on Middle East Affairs* (September 1995): 39–94. https://www.wrmea.org/1995-september/ol.-robert-w.-rickert-1912-1995.html.

Parkinson, Brian R. "Israel's Lebanon War: Ariel Sharon and Operation Peace for Galilee." *Journal of Third World Studies* 24, no. 2, *Historical and Contemporary Political, Economic, and Social Developments in the Third World* (fall 2007): 68.

Vuong Quynh-Nhu. "U.S. Peacekeeping and Nation-Building: The Evolution of Self-Interested Multilateralism." *Berkeley Journal of International Law* (2003): 804, 812–14.

Strugar, Milos. "The UNTSO Story." *UN Chronicle* 35, no. 3 (fall 1998), https://www.questia.com/magazine/1G1-54259332/the-untso-story.

Talhamy, Yvette, "The Syrian Muslim Brothers and the Syrian-Iranian Relationship." *Middle East Journal* 63, no. 4 (2009): 561–80.

UNTSO Staff Writer. "Observer Group Lebanon: The Dangers of Driving in Beirut." *UNTSO News* 2, no. 4 (July–August 1981): 16.

UNTSO Staff Writer. "Colonel Sholly Ends His Mission in Jerusalem" *UNTSO News* 4, no. 2 (July–August 1983): 5.

Newspapers

Associated Press. "Bomb Explosion in Syria Kills 64 and Hurts 135 in Crowded Area." *New York Times*, 30 November 1981.

Associated Press. "Haddad Accuses UN of 'Spying' in S. Lebanon." *Jerusalem Post*, 31 August 1980.

Associated Press. "Text of the Agreement Between Israel and Lebanon on Troop Withdrawal." *New York Times,* 17 May 1983, A12. https://www.nytimes.com/1983/05/17/world/text-of-the-agreement-between-israel-and-lebanon-on-troop-withdrawal.html.

Chace, James. "The Turbulent Tenure of Alexander Haig." *New York Times*, 22 April 1984. https://www.nytimes.com/1984/04/22/books/the-turbulent-tenure-of-alexander-haig.html.

Claiborne, William. "Rocket Barrage Kills 3 in Northern Israel." *Washington Post*, 16 July 1981, A20.

"Egyptian Columnists: We Do Not Regret the Death of Arafat, Who Expressed His Joy at Sadat's Assassination." *MEMRI*, Special Dispatch, no. 814. https://www.memri.org/reports/egyptian-columnists-we-do-not-regret-death-arafat-who-expressed-his-joy-sadats-assassination.

"Israel Charges Bernadotte." *Palestine Post*, 12 July 1948, 1.

"Israel's Army Reports 368 Soldiers Were Killed and 2,383 Were Wounded in Lebanon War." *JTA Daily News Bulletin,* October 13, 1982. http://pdfs.jta .org/1982/1982-10-13_193.pdf?_ga=2.66119403.430022409.1641669957 -1542143741.1641574295.

"Israelis at Funerals for Gail Rubin." *New York Times,* 18 March 1978. https:// www.nytimes.com/1978/03/18/archives/israelis-at-funeral-for-gail-rubin .html.

Joffe, Lawrence. "Obituary of Shlomo Argov." *Guardian,* 24 February 2003. https://www.theguardian.com/world/2003/feb/25/israelandthepalestinians .lebanon.

Mohr, Charles. "U.S., Reacting to Raids, Puts off Announcement of Israeli F-16's." *New York Times,* 18 July 1981, section 1, 1. https://www.nytimes.com/1981/07 /18/world/us-reacting-to-raids-puts-off-announcement-on-israeli-f-16-s.html.

"Nigerian Officer in UNIFIL Sentenced to 15 Years in Jail and Deported." *JTA, Daily News Bulletin,* 26 December 1979. http://pdfs.jta.org/1979/1979- 12-26_244.pdf?_ga=2.190971114.1575810936.1620649555-1313427079. 1620649555.

Omer-Man, Michael. "This Week in History: Israel's Deadliest Terror Attack." *Jerusalem Post,* 11 March 2011.

Saxon, Wolfgang. "Amos Perlmutter, 69, Expert on Middle Eastern Affairs." *New York Times,* 16 June 2001. https://www.nytimes.com/2001/06/16/world /amos-perlmutter-69-expert-on-middle-eastern-affairs.html.

Shipler, David K. "Cease-Fire in Border Fighting Declared by Israel and the PLO; U.S. Sees Hope for Wider Peace." *New York Times,* 25 July 1981, section 1, 1. https://www.nytimes.com/1981/07/25/world/cease-fire-border-fighting- declared-israel-plo-us-sees-hope-for-wider-peace.html.

Sly, Liz. "Syria's Muslim Brotherhood Is Gaining Influence over Anti-Assad Revolt." *Washington Post,* 12 May 2012. https://www.washingtonpost.com /world/syrias-muslim-brotherhood-is-gaining-influence-over-anti-assad- revolt/2012/05/12/gIQAtIoJLU_story.html.

Snell, Robert. "Deported Dearborn Man Arrested in Lebanon." *Detroit News,* 30 January 2015. https://www.detroitnews.com/story/news/local/wayne- county/2015/01/30/feds-deport-dearborn-ice-cream-man-tied-killings /22599779/.

"Syrian Troops Massacre Scores of Assad's Foes." *Washington Post,* 25 June 1981. https://www.washingtonpost.com/archive/politics/1981/06/25/syrian-troops- massacre-scores-of-assads-foes/1b60763a-e7d9-4cc0-b354-dbaea5edca77/.

UPI. "2 Americans Killed in Lebanon." *New York Times,* 26 September 1982. https://www.nytimes.com/1982/09/26/world/2-americans-killed-in-lebanon .html.

———. "Three Americans Wounded in the Assassination of Egyptian President." 8 October 1981. https://www.upi.com/Archives/1981/10/08/Three-Americans- wounded-in-the-assassination-of-Egyptian-President/7189371361600/.

Memorandums, After Action Reports, Draft Papers

"Minutes of Military Intelligence Officers (MIOs) Conference in Tibnin IRISH-BATT on 14 August 1981." *United Nations Interim Force in Lebanon (UNIFIL)*, 26 August 1981.

Erskine, MG E. A., MSG, DSO Force Commander UNIFIL. "International Peace Keeping Operations Preparation Command and Control." 1981. (Unpublished papers of the author).

Lingamfelter, CPT Lee S., US Army. "Liaison Officer After Action Report." *United Nations Truce Supervision Organization (UNTSO) Memorandum,* 20 August 1981.

———. "Team Tyre After Action Report." *United Nations Truce Supervision Organization (UNTSO) Memorandum,* 28 January 1981.

"Understanding the Interrelationship of Peace-Keeping and Peace-Making." Prepared by the Operations Staff United Nations Truce Supervision Organization Under the Direction and Guidance of Major General E. A. Erskine, MSG, DSO, Chief of Staff. *United Nations Truce Supervision Organization (UNTSO) Draft Paper(s),* 1982.

Official Transcripts

"Deputy Press Secretary Speakes on the Situation in Lebanon (September 1982)." Public Papers of the President Ronald Reagan Administration. https://www.reaganlibrary.gov/archives/speech/statement-deputy-press-secretary-speakes-situation-lebanon-2.

Reagan, President Ronald W. "Remarks at the Annual Convention of the National Association of Evangelicals in Orlando, Florida, March 8, 1983." Reagan Foundation.

"Statement to the Knesset by Prime Minister Begin on the Terrorist Raid and the Knesset Resolution, 13 March 1978." Israel Ministry of Foreign Affairs.

Weiner, Eric, Bureau of Diplomatic Security, United States Department of State, "Remembering the 1983 Suicide Bombings in Beirut: The Tragic Events That Created the Diplomatic Security Service." https://2017-2021.state.gov/remembering-the-1983-suicide-bombings-in-beirut-the-tragic-events-that-created-the-diplomatic-security-service/index.html.

"White House Memorandum of Conversation with President Gerald Ford, Secretary of State Henry Kissinger, and Israeli Prime Minister Yitzhak Rabin." 11 June 1975, 5. https://www.fordlibrarymuseum.gov/library/document/0314/1553116.pdf.

Index

Page numbers in italics refer to illustrations.

Abu Jihad (Khalil Ibrahim al-Wazir), 108
Abu Nidal, 204, 205
Adawin, Bassam, 93
Adawin, Yosef, 92–93
Agreement on Disengagement, 64
Akiya Bridge, 111, 114, 128
Alawite sect, 23, 84 85, 87, 89, 213
alcohol, availability of, 24, 56, 68, 81, 82
Aleppo, Syria, 84–85
Allan, Jim, 41, 42, 51, 64–65, 66, 89, 148, 159
AMAL (Shi'a-affiliated political party), 106, 172
Americans: culinary skills of, 76–77, 133–34; image of, 43–44, 50–53, 77, 79, 83, 105; Israeli/Arab attitudes toward, 47–48, 50–51, 56–58, 88–89, 135; reputation of, 46–47, 51–53, 56–58, 71. *See also* United States
Anderson, Ed, 132
Arab Defense Force, 211
Arab League, 26
Arafat, Fathi, 183
Arafat, Yasser: assassination attempt on, 168–69, 196; and Black September, 23; exile regime of, 213, 215; IDF attacks on PLO strongholds, 204, 211; and Lebanon evacuation, 213; and PLO's occupation rights in Lebanon, 121, 127; and Sadat's

murder, 190; seeking US approval, 152, 182–83
Area of Separation (AOS), 62, 64, 69
Argov, Shlomo, 204, 205
Armistice Demarcation Line, 28, 192
Army of Free Lebanon, 39–40
Assad, Hafez al-: brutality of, 84–88; and entrenchment in Lebanon, 211, 212, 213–14; political repression by, 16, 22, 23; Russian support for, 90; and Syrian Civil War, 84–85, 87–89
Assad, Rifaat al-, 84, 85
At Tiri, Lebanon, 136–37, 164, 166, 192, 193, 196

Baalbek, Lebanon, 82
Ba'ath Party, 23, 84, 85
Babylonian captivity, 60
Badolato, Ed, 114
Badyoukov, Youri, 73–74
Baker, Al, 104, 132, 166, 205, 224
Baldwin IV, king of Jerusalem, 145
Balfour Declaration (1917), 24–25
Barakat (PLO captain), 177
Barsimantov, Yacov, 204
bartering, 77–79, 83
Battle of Mogadishu, 220, 225–26
Bauman, Charlie, 132, 137
Bazzi, Mahmoud, 165, 166
Beaufort Castle, 142, 144, 145, 150, 183, 203, 211
Begin, Menachem: and Camp David Accords, 24, 38; and Operation

279

Litani, 109, 115; and Operation Peace for Galilee, 214; US pressure on, 130, 149

Beirut International Airport (BIA) attack, 217–18

Beirut, Lebanon: dangers to peacekeepers in, 185–86, 190; French influence in, 24; IAF air strikes in, 167–68, 196, 205; IDF siege of, 207, 211–13; ILMAC in, 34, 101–2, 109, 127; MNF forces in, 215–16, 218, 231; PLO evacuation, 213; refugee camp massacres in, 214

Beit Yahoun, Lebanon, 164

Bell, Geoff, 7, 189, 191, 192, 198

Beqaa Valley, 211, 212, 213

Berkheiser, Steve, 132, 137–38

Bernadotte, Folke, 42

Berra, Yogi, 192

Betson, Dave, 7, 94, 99, 105, 132, 165–66

Bint Jubayl, Lebanon, 110, 113

Black September (1970), 23, 210

Blice, Anthony "Drew," 132

Blum, Yehuda Z., 167

Bockman, Timo, 126–29

Bosra, Syria, 81

Bozeman, Virgil, 7, 10, 132; and Arafat assassination attempt, 196; culinary skills of, 133–34; and Israeli air strikes, 168; and OGL assignment, 105, 146–48, 151–52, 178, 185–86; and Sadat assassination, 190; spontaneous wit of, 15, 151–52, 178; and UNTSO training, 54–56; and Yasser Arafat, 182–83, 184

Brady, Terry, 132

Brashit, Lebanon, 193–94

Breault, Gordy, 132, 137

Brezhnev, Leonid, 74

Brill, Bruce, 10, 11–17, 59–62, 96, 97

British Broadcasting Corporation (BBC), 98

British Mandate of Palestine, 25

Bull, Odd, 33

Bush, George W., 226

Byrnes, James "Digger," 104, 107, 132

Cairo Accord (1969), 121

Callaghan, William, 195

Calnan, Gary, 16, 62–63, 95

Calnan, Kathy, 16, 62

Camp David Accords, 24, 36, 38, 188, 189, 190, 207, 208

Carlson, Jim, 132

Carlson, Randal, 219

Carswell, Hal, 132

Carter, Jimmy, 38, 115

Casey, George, 10, 18, 55, 56, 188, 189

Cates, Tommy, 7, 235

Chaim (Israeli major), 149

Chapter VI, UN Charter (conflict resolution process), 30, 117, 128

Chapter VII, UN Charter, 30, 116

Chaqra, Lebanon, 146

Chtaura, Lebanon, 82

Church of the Holy Sepulchre, 14, 15, 22

Clinton, Bill, 224

Coastal Road Massacre (1978), 38. See also Lebanese invasion

context, importance of, 97

"cooking and looking," 56, 68, 105–6, 133–34, 161–62

Cote (Canadian major), 147

Cotter, Steve, 190

course of action assessment (COA), 118

cultural values, and conflict, 24

Damascus, Syria: culture in, 24, 56, 76–83; terrorists in, 84–85, 88–89

Damascus Road Experience, 60

Damour, Lebanon, 167, 203, 211

Davidenko, Misha, 73

Dead Sea, 91, 92, 96

De Facto Forces (DFF), 39; and At Tiri, 136–37, 196, 197; and Beaufort Castle, 203; checkpoints of, 180; dislike of UN peacekeepers, 40; enclave of, 120–22, 129, 135, 144, 146, 170, 175; Khiam destruction by,

139–40, 154–56; and local residents, 159–61; and murder of Irish soldiers, 149, 165; and Operation Litani, 109–15; and Operation Peace for Galilee, 210–15; and UNIFIL mortar attack, 192; UN peacekeeper harassment by, 129, 139, 143, 147–50, 151, 156–57, 162

Defense Intelligence Agency, 202

Deir Mimas, Lebanon, 142, 143

de la Forge, A., 138

Democratic Front for the Liberation of Palestine (DFLP), 106, 172

Deutsch, John, 132

Digger (stray dog), 162–63

Dijkstra, Leo G., 170

Directorate for Current Intelligence for the Middle East, 202

Dome of the Rock, 12

Druze Islamic sect, 22, 217

Dung Gate, 13

DUTCHBATT (Dutch Battalion), 136, 149, 153, 168, 178

Egyptian Islamic Jihad, 188

Egyptian-Israel Mixed Armistice Commission (EIMAC), 28, 30

Egyptian Revolution (2011), 190

Eisenhower, Dwight D., 29–30

Emil, Abu, 149

Erskine, Emmanuel, 18, 94, 98; and arms limitations, 116; and combatant resistance, 121–23; and concept of peacekeeping, 107; praise for UNMOs, 104; preparedness planning and, 118–20, 123–24, 130; and Sadat assassination, 189; and shuttle diplomacy, 191–92; soldier support by, 138

Eshkol, Levi, 31

Espinassy, Jean, 114

Fagerstrøm, Olle, 170

Fallon, Mike, 7–8, 238–39; culinary skills of, 134; Operation Litani

observation and, 109–15; PLO interactions with, 183; UNIFIL deployment reconnaissance, 116, 126–29, 233

Fatah, 38, 108

FIJIBATT (Fiji Battalion), 136, 153, 168, 178, 181

First Gulf War, 156

food and water, local, 69, 82–83

Force Mobile Reserve (FMR), 136

force structure, 201

Ford, Gerald R., 36, 50

Foreign Area Officer (FAO) program, 223

Forssberg, Carl, 94

Framework for Peace in the Middle East. See Camp David Accords

France: influence in Syria, 24, 80, 81; Syria rule by, 60. See also FRENCHBATT (French Battalion)

Franey, Pierre, 133

Free Lebanon Army, 39

FRENCHBATT (French Battalion), 176; competence of, 46, 104, 107, 125, 127–28, 138; and French barracks bombing, 218; and Suez Crisis, 28–31. See also France

Galilee, 59, 109, 137, 158, 192. See also Operation Peace for Galilee

Garden Tomb, 16

Gaza Strip, 26, 29, 31, 52, 98, 190

Gemayel, Amin, 218

Gemayel, Bachir Pierre, 206

General Armistice Agreements (1949), 26

Geraghty, Timothy, 217

GHANBATT (Ghanaian Battalion), 146, 147, 153, 172

Göksel, Timur, 164, 165

Golan Heights, 31, 33, 35, 36; description of, 59–60; and OGG-D, 67–70, 67; UNDOF operations in, 61, 65–66

Goldwater-Nichols Department of Defense Reorganization Act, 224

Gom, Alfred, 134
Government House, 16, 17, 33, 40,
    94–95, 98, 120
Government of Free Lebanon, 40
Great Temple, 12, 14
Green Line, 136, 143
Gregson, Wallace "Chip," 132
Grubb, Clay, 7, 132; and Americans'
    dedication, 140, 185; and DFF
    harassment, 148–50, 164–65; and
    local residents, 135, 180–81; and
    mobile teams, 171; and respect for
    French forces, 138
Gulf of Aqaba, 30
Gwyther, Barry, 7, 69, 132; observer
    experiences of, 105, 150, 171; SL's
    friendship with, 81, 103, 167; and
    UN bureaucracy, 17
Gwyther, Jo, 103, 167

Habib, Philip, 204–5
Haddad, Saad: and Battle of At Tiri,
    136–37; and Beaufort Castle, 142,
    150; Israeli alliance with, 40, 106,
    115; OP harassment by, 157–58,
    164–65, 185; southern Lebanon
    operations area of, 136–37; and
    UNIFIL's Naqoura headquarters
    assault by, 138–39, 196–97; and
    Valley of Springs, 196–98
Haganah, 26
Haig, Al, 204–5
Hama, Syria, massacre in, 85–88
Hammell, Jack, 7, 83, 94, 190
Hamra, Beirut, Lebanon, 190
Hasbaya, Lebanon, 167
Hashemite Kingdom of Jordan-Israel
    Mixed Armistice Commission
    (HKJ-I-MAC), 94
Healy, Damien, 162–63
Herod Antipas (Roman tetrarch of
    Galilee), 59
Herzog, Isaac Halevi, 25
Hezbollah, 40, 216, 218, 220, 221
Higgins, William Richard "Rich," 6,
    43
Hill 705, 143

Hill 880, 136, 193, 196–97
Hindy, Steve, 164, 165
Hitler, Adolph, 1
Holstein, Dan, 132, 175
Homs, Syria, 81
house hunting, Damascus, 78–79
Hoyer, Paul, 55
Huet, Jacques, 146–48
Hula Valley, 60
Husnian, Azad "Al," 17, 18, 95,
    98–99, 100
Hussein, Saddam, 156, 204
Hussein bin Talal, 23, 24

Ibl al-Saqi, Lebanon, 141, 160
Imhoff, Mike, 132
Ingalls, Allen S. "Al," 132, 175
intelligence preparation of the
    battlefield (IPB), 119, 125, 126
international combat units, 107
International Red Cross, 16, 172, 210
"intolerance of ambiguity," 20, 23, 40,
    97
Iran-Iraq War, 202
IRISHBATT (Irish Battalion), 153,
    164–66, 176, 181; murder of Irish
    soldiers by DFF, 136, 149, 165
Iskandar, Abu, 164
Islambouli, Khalid, 190
Israel: creation of, 3–4; and
    "economic miracle," 10–11; and
    UNTSO relations, 41, 43–45,
    48–50
Israel Defense Forces (IDF): Arafat
    assassination attempt by, 168;
    artillery bombardment by, 144–45,
    150, 167–69, 196–97; checkpoints
    manned by, 91, 93, 134; dislike of
    UN/US peacekeepers by, 49,
    134–35, 148–53, 158–59, 193;
    and Khiam devastation, 139–40,
    154–56; and Lebanese invasion
    (1978), 39; and occupation of
    Southern Lebanon, 121–22, 128,
    167, 169, 195–96, 202–3; and
    Operation Litani, 109–15; and
    Operation Peace for Galilee, 204,

210–15; and Six-Day War, 31–35; transmission interception by, 153; and Valley of Springs, 173; and Yom Kippur War, 35–38
Israeli Air Force (IAF), 31, 115, 167, 168, 177, 179, 194, 211, 212, 213
Israel-Lebanon Mixed Armistice Commission (ILMAC), 101
Israel-Syria Mixed Armistice Commission (ISMAC), 28

Jarty, Phillippe, 179
Jericho, Israel, 91–92
Jerusalem, 10–13, 88, 92–93, 163
Jesus, biblical sites and, 11, 14, 15, 16, 22, 59–60, 76, 96
Jewish Temple Mount Faithful, 15
Jezzine, Lebanon, 211
Johansson, Karl Oskar, 118
Joint Chiefs of Staff (CJCS), 224, 227, 231
Jordan River, 11, 26, 33, 40, 52, 91, 98
Jordan Valley, 50, 91, 224
Judkins, Jim, 132
Justice, Steve, 132

Kafr Dunin, Lebanon, 172
Kafura, Herman, 132, 202
Kaira, Erkki R., 64
Kasmiya Bridge, 111, 114, 121
Kennedy, Kevin, 7, 132, 202–3, 205–6, 224, 226
Khadala Bridge, 111, 114
Khansa, Ali al-, 199
Khiam, Lebanon, destruction of, 139–40, 144, 153–55
Killgore, Andrew I., 49, 50
Kirkpatrick, Jeane, 207
Kiryat Shmona, Israel, 167
Kissinger, Henry, 35–36, 64, 65
Klein, Harry, 132, 136, 164–65

Labbuna, Lebanon, 101
Laciar, Edwardo, 132, 134, 140–41
land mines, 65, 69–70
Lasonen, Karl, 219

League of Nations, 1–2
Leary, Byron V., 47
Lebanese Civil War, 39, 82, 117, 128, 210, 215, 218
Lebanese invasion (1978), 38–40
Lebanese National Movement (LNM), 106, 159, 172, 178
Lefebvre, Jean, 132, 134, 141–42, 143, 146, 151, 153–55
Lehi (Zionist group, aka Stern Gang), 42
Levant, 1, 20–22, 21, 23, 24
Leverette, Thomas E., 119
Lewis, Sam, 137
Lichtenberger, Jean, 132, 181–82, 185–86
Lindeman, Brenda, 62
Lindeman, Denny, 7, 132; and American cuisine, 76–77, 133; and drinking water, 83; and Hama massacre, 85–88; and Israeli anti-UN bias, 156–57; and PLO seeking American support, 183–84; and Russians, 63, 68, 71, 72
Lingamfelter, Marguerite, 133
Lingamfelter, Shelley Glick: and Damascus, 67, 72, 76, 78–81, 84; and Jerusalem, 88, 92, 163; and Nahariya, 167; touring, 8, 9–10, 13, 14, 16, 18
Litani River, 38–39, 120, 121, 122, 168. See also Operation Litani
Lloyd, Jill, 79, 81
Lloyd, Trevor, 79, 81, 132
Lynn, Stuart, 132

MacDonald, Charles G., 20
MAC House, 94
Mackinlay, John, 64–65, 124, 125–26, 130
Maier, Paul L., 20
Marjayoun, Lebanon, 139, 140, 142, 150, 160, 198
Markaba, Lebanon, 101, 148
Maronite Christians, 22, 128, 213–14, 218

Maroun al-Ras, Lebanon, 101, 110, 113
Marshall, George C., 25
Marshall-Cormack, Pat, 132, 134, 140, 141, 144, 151, 161–62, 163
Marshall Plan, 25
Marwahin, Lebanon, 101, 159
Marxist-Leninist economic theory, 74–75
Mayeur, LTC, 182, 190
May 17 Agreement, 216–17, 218
McMaugh, Robert, 216
Meir, Golda, 49–50
METT-T (Mission, Enemy, Terrain, Troops, and Time Available), 57, 124
Metula, Israel, 139, 144
Military Decision-Making Process (MDMP), 118
Misgav Am, Israel, 137
Mixed Armistice Commissions (MACs), 28, 42, 43, 52
mobile teams, 5, 106, 171–76, 173, 174
Mohammed, 14, 22
Morizet, Jean Paul, 151
Moses, 11, 22
Mount Dov, 144
Mount Hermon, 61, 62, 66, 69
Mount Moriah, 12
Mount of Olives, 12, 17
Mount Tabor, 59
Moynihan, Joe, 104, 132
Mubarak, Hosni, 190
Multinational Force in Lebanon (MNF), 210, 213, 215–17, 218, 220, 231
Murphy-O'Connor, Jerome "Father Jerry," 96–97
Muslim Brotherhood, 16, 22, 23, 84–85, 89, 214; and "long campaign of terror," 84

Nabatieh, Lebanon, 167, 183, 211
Nahariya, Israel, 102, 103, 167–68, 171, 205

Naqoura, Lebanon: French defense attachment at, 138; IDF attacks and, 37, 112, 192, 197; OGL headquarters in, 100, 102, 103; UNIFIL staff headquarters at, 119–20, 129
Nasser, Gamal Abdel, 28–30, 31, 44
National Military Strategy (NMS), 224–25, 226, 231
National Security Strategy (NSS), 224, 231
Nazareth, Israel, 59
NEPBATT (Nepalese Battalion), 153, 168
Nester, Michael, 219
NIBATT (Nigerian Battalion), 153, 172
Nielsen, Ole, 136
1948 war, 25–28, 27
NORBATT (Norwegian Battalion), 141, 144, 153, 159, 160, 167, 168, 172
North Atlantic Treaty Organization (NATO), 62

Obama, Barack, 226
Oberndorfer, Gerald J., 119, 126
observation posts (OPs), 4, 55, 56, 68–69
Observer Detachment Damascus (ODD), 66, 67–75, 67
Observer Group Beirut (OGB), 219
Observer Group Egypt (OGE), 52, 119, 188
Observer Group Golan-Damascus (OGG-D), 67–70, 67
Observer Group Golan-Tiberias (OGG-T), 59, 70, 192
Observer Group Jerusalem (OGJ), 93–95, 95
Observer Group Lebanon (OGL), 39, 101–7; area of operations, 102, 103, 173, 174; in Beirut, 219–20; international battalion comparisons in, 180–82; leadership of, 165–66; and local residents, 178–80; mobile teams, 5, 106, 171–76, 173, 174

Odd Bull, 33
Old City, Jerusalem, 12
OP baskets, 77
Operation Badr, 188
Operation Litani, 39, *39*, 109–15, *112*, 117, 120–21
Operation Peace for Galilee, 204, 210–15, *212*, 218, 219–20, 222, 226
OP HIN, 101, 139, 149, 159, 164, 167
OP KHIAM: DFF harassment near, 161; Israeli activity near, 156–57, *158*, 159, 170, 195, 197; location of, 101, 145; PLO activity near, 151–52. *See also* Khiam, Lebanon
OP LAB, 101, 139, 224
OP MAR, 101, 133, 139, 146, 147–48
OP RAS, 101, 109–15, 128, 150, 164
Osirak nuclear reactor, 204
Oslo Accords (1993 and 1995), 184
Ostayan, Garo, 77–78

Palestine, division of, 3–4, 20, 24–26
Palestine Liberation Army (PLA), 106, 172, 199, 239
Palestine Liberation Organization (PLO): arms buildup by, 191, 198–99; and battle for Khiam, 139; and Beaufort Castle, 142, 145, 150; and Coastal Road Massacre, 38; and evacuation of Lebanon, 213; harassment of peacekeepers by, 146–47, 151–52; Israeli diplomat assassination by, 204–5; and Israel's Operation Litani, 39, 109–15; and Israel's Operation Peace for Galilee, 210–15, *212*; Lebanon presence of, 23; local residents and, 175–76; and seeking US recognition, 176–78, 182–84; Shabbat attack by, 108–9; and "the storm," 167–71; Tyre Pocket occupation by, 120–23, 131, 170, 198–202; and undermining UN peacekeepers, 186, 193
Palmyra, Syria, 81, 85

Partition Plan (1947), 25, 43
Paul (Apostle, Saul of Tarsus), 59–60, 76
peacekeeping: decision-making process and, 230–33; objective of, 233–35; participant's role in, 223–26; value of, 226–30
Peace Now movement, 214
Perlmutter, Amos, 238
Perrin, Noel, 68, 78, 154
Phalangist Christians, 214
Popular Front for the Liberation of Palestine (PFLP), 106, 172
Potter, J., 119
Powell, Colin, 231
Presidential Decision Directive (PDD) 25, 225

Qalaat Doubiye (ruin), Lebanon, 146
Qana, Lebanon, 172
Qillaya, Lebanon, 112, 114
Quneitra, Syria, 62

Rabin, Yitzhak, 36–37, 50
Reagan, Ronald, 63, 151–52
Reardon, John, 132
religion, and conflict, 22
Ribicoff, Abraham A., 108
Rickert, Robert W., 47, 49–50
Riley, William Edward, 47
Rollins, Paul, 132
Rubin, Gail, 108
Russians: characteristics of, 66, 70–75; combatants' dislike of, 46, 66, 68–69, 88; Sunni terrorist bombing and, 88–90
Russians, The (Hedrick Smith), 70

Sabbagh, Bassam al-, 78, 79, 81
Sabbagh, Jamal al- "Baba," 78–79, 80–81
Sabra Palestinian refugee camp, 168, 214, 215
Sadat, Anwar: assassination of, 188–91; and Camp David Accords, 24, 38; and Yom Kippur War, 35

Saïd (PLO major), 183
Saladin (Salah al-Din Yusuf ibn Ayyub), 145
Salvan, Jean, 127
Samuel the Prophet, tomb of, 12, 13
Sea of Galilee, 59, 60, 91, 96
SENBATT (Senegalese Battalion), 136, 153, 168, 172, 180–81
senior military intelligence officer (SMIO), 170, 172, 173, 175
September 11, 2001 (9/11), 221, 230
Serot, André, 42
Serviss, Carolyn, 99
Serviss, Joseph A., 7, 132; initial international hostility and, 99–100, 104, 105; peacekeeper experience and, 48, 107, 142, 179, 198, 242–43; and Sadat assassination, 189
Shabbat attack, 108–9
Shaida, Vladimir, 72
Shalikashvili, John Malchase David, 223–24, 226–28, 231
Sharon, Ariel, 204–5
Shartouni, Habib Tanios, 214
Shatila Palestinian refugee camp, 214, 215
Shi'a Muslims, 22, 40, 84, 106, 172, 214, 216–18
Sholly, Robert H., 100, 166, 188, 235
Shouf Mountains, Lebanon, 216–17, 218
Shu'afat community, Jerusalem, Israel, 92, 93
shuttle diplomacy, 36, 191, 200
Sidon, Lebanon, 115, 167, 179, 211, 217
Simon of Cyrene, 14
Sinai Desert, 4, 18, 29, 40, 98, 228
Sinai Peninsula, 29–30, 31, 35, 38, 44, 128
Sinai Separation of Forces Agreement, 36
Sinai II Agreement, 36
Six-Day War (1967), 31–35, 34, 44
60-Minute Gourmet (Franey), 133
Smith, Hedrick, 70

socioeconomics, and conflict, 23
Sollis, Jay, 7, 104, 132, 159, 200, 205–6
Somalia, fighting in, 220, 225, 231, 234
souks, 76–77
South Lebanese Army (SLA). See De Facto Forces (DFF)
Stepanenko, Yuri, 71–72
Stern Gang (Lehi), 42
St. Mema Monastery (Lebanon), 142
Stockbridge, Harriet, 97
Stockbridge, Ralph B., 97, 99
"storm, the," 167–71, 173, 175, 187, 195, 196, 202, 204
Straits of Tiran, 29, 30, 31
Strom, Steve, 132, 177
Suez Canal, 28, 31, 33, 35, 36, 98, 188
Suez Crisis (1956), 28–31, 32
Sunni Muslims, 22–23, 84–85, 89, 213–14
Supko, Lenny, 7, 132; depiction of combatants by, 163, 205; and IDF/DFF Khiam occupation, 140, 154; and interaction with local residents, 172, 179–80; international battalions rated by, 181; on Israeli and Arab attitudes, 48; and maintaining neutrality, 159; and UNIFIL's ineffectiveness, 153, 200
Syria: bureaucracy in, 79–81; civil war in, 22, 23, 83–88, 89; culture of, 76–83; French influence in, 24, 60, 81; French rule in, 60; hatred of Russia in, 88–89; peacekeepers in, 67–70, 67; presence in Lebanon, 213–14, 216–18; and Yom Kippur War, 35–38
Syrian Air Force, 212
Syrian Arab Republic, 60, 65
Syrian Social Nationalist Party, 214

Tadmor prison (Palmyra, Syria), 85
Tali'a Muqatila (Fighting Vanguard), 85

Tayibe, Lebanon, 203
Team Metula, 172
Team Romeo, 172, 175
Team Sierra, 159, 172, 173
Team Tyre, 106, 171–72, 175–76,
    178–80
Team X-Ray, 162, 163, 172, 202, 224
Team Zulu, 164, 172, 173, 174, 179,
    180
Tel Aviv, Israel, 10, 12, 55, 59, 96–97,
    108, 113, 214
Temple Mount, 12
Thant, U, 33
Thomas, Bob, 132
Tiarya (Syrian general), 183
Tiberias, Israel, 59, 67, 70, 91, 128,
    192
Tolnay, John, 182, 185
Trans-Arabian Oil Pipeline, 213
Travers, Des, 7, 132, 166, 175–76,
    179, 181, 199
Truman, Harry, 2, 24–25, 233–34
Trump, Donald J., 226
Tyre, Lebanon: battle for, 112,
    114–15; clashes in, 167–68,
    191–93; PLO's occupation in,
    120–21, 131, 170, 179, 199, 229
Tyre Barracks, 172, 178

Ukraine, Russian invasion of, 230
Umar ibn al-Khattāb, 60
UN General Assembly, 3, 6, 30
United Kingdom (UK), Palestine
    administration and, 4
United Nations (UN): Charter, 30,
    116, 117, 128; formation of, 2;
    profile of, 43–46; resolutions of,
    117, 118, 121, 124, 196, 201
United Nations Disengagement
    Observer Force (UNDOF), 36, 44,
    52, 61, 63–66, 69
United Nations Emergency Force
    (UNEF) I and II, 30, 44
United Nations Interim Force in
    Lebanon (UNIFIL), 3, 108–31;
    area of operations, 120, 124,
    125–29, 139, 194; arms control

and, 118–19, 122–23; birth of,
    116–20; combatants' resistance
    and, 120–22; headquarters
    location and, 119–20; planning
    deficiencies and, 117–18, 119–20,
    123–24, 129–31; and troop
    deployment, 123–29; UN support
    of, 124, 130–31
United Nations Military Observers
    (UNMO), 4; area of operations
    (June, 1981), 47, 138–39; danger
    and, 150–52, 162–63, 185–86;
    duties of, 132–33
United Nations Observation Group in
    Lebanon (UNOGIL), 101
United Nations Operation in Somalia
    (UNOSOM-II), 220, 225–26
United Nations Relief and Works
    Agency (UNRWA), 121
United Nations Special Committee on
    Palestine, 25
United Nations Truce Supervision
    Organization (UNTSO): area of
    operations, 139, 194; bureaucratic
    nature of, 41–43; combatant
    sympathies and, 44, 47–51;
    international composition of,
    46–48, 47; mission of, 1–3;
    Operations Center, 93–101; and
    position of neutrality, 43–46,
    57–58; reactive approach of, 51;
    structure of, 51–54, 53; training
    program in, 54–55; US
    participation in, 46, 54, 56, 57–58
United States: peacekeeping role of, 6,
    223, 226, 230–35; and
    peacekeeping value, 226–30; and
    UNTSO, 46, 54, 56, 57–58. See
    also Americans
UN Liaison Office in Beirut (UNLOB),
    147, 168, 182, 185
UN Middle East Peacekeeping
    Organization (1981), 53
UN Military Observer Personnel
    (1981), 47
UN Palestine Commission, 3
UN Resolution 50, 43

UN Resolution 128, 101
UN Resolution 350, 54
UN Resolution 425, 117, 121, 124, 201
UN Resolution 426, 118
UN Resolution 490, 196
UN Truce Commission, 42
UNTSO Operations Center, 93–101
Urquhart, Brian, 52, 191–92, 200
USS *New Jersey*, 217

Valley of Armageddon, 59
Valley of Springs (Meadow of Springs), 140–63, 197, 198
Vartan, Zaven, 164
verbal orders of the commander (VOCO), 123
Vercauteren, Dick, 109, 123, 132
Vincent, Patrick, 164
Voshchinski, Yuri, 74–75

Wadi Raqqad, 61
Wailing Wall, 13
Waldheim, Kurt, 182
Waldron, Jim, 156–57
Walker, Herbert M., 42
Warren, Harley "Chopper," 219, 244

Washington Post, 86, 87
Wasson, Thomas C., 42, 47
Wazir, Khalil Ibrahim al- (Abu Jihad), 108
Weinberger, Caspar, 231
Weinberger-Powell doctrinal framework, 231
Weizmann, Chaim, 10
West Bank, 11, 26, 33, 92
Western Wall Plaza, 13
Wilson, John, 103–4, 107, 132, 133, 166
Wilson, Todd, 132
Wilson, Woodrow, 25
Woolshlager, Johnny, 132, 166
written fragmentary orders (FRAGO), 123, 129

Yarmouk River, 60
Yishuv, 25
Yom Kippur War (1973), 35–38, *37*, 44
Yousef, Yousef, 135

Zahrani, Lebanon, 127, 213
Zandouqa (Zanduqah), Lebanon, 219
Zibqin, Lebanon, 193